TEXT, CHURCH AND WORLD

TEXT, CHURCH AND WORLD

Biblical Interpretation in Theological Perspective

FRANCIS WATSON

T&T CLARK INTERNATIONAL
A Continuum imprint
LONDON • NEW YORK

Published by T&T Clark International
A Continuum imprint
The Tower Building, 11 York Road, London SE1 7NX
15 East 26th Street, Suite 1703, New York, NY 10010

www.tandtclark.com

British Library Cataloguing-in-Publication Data
A catalogue record for this book is available from the British Library

ISBN 0567080587 (paperback)

Typeset by Trinity Typesetting, Edinburgh
Printed on acid-free paper in Great Britain by Antony Rowe Ltd, Chippenham

Contents

Preface

The position developed in this book is, in one sense, a familiar one: that biblical interpretation should concern itself primarily with the theological issues raised by the biblical texts within our contemporary ecclesial, cultural and socio-political contexts. At a time when many former hermeneutical certainties are encountering sustained and effective challenge, the familiar but still controversial claim that biblical interpretation should no longer neglect its theological responsibilities is due for reformulation and restatement.

In offering such a restatement, I am heavily dependent on recent hermeneutically-oriented work within both biblical studies and systematic theology. Several of the chapters that follow simply present critical appreciations of recent work within literary, canonical or feminist perspectives, and even where I have taken a more independent line I have often developed this by way of dialogue with other hermeneutical proposals. At the same time, I have been acutely aware that to argue for the primacy of theology within biblical interpretation is to adopt a minority position, with all the vulnerability that this entails. Despite the recent vogue for interdisciplinary work of various kinds, it remains unusual for biblical scholars to advocate a renewed dialogue with systematic theology as the way forward for their own discipline. In exploring the possibilities of such a dialogue, I have often had to go my own way, in relative isolation from current debate.

If the results of this interdisciplinary engagement are judged to be merely idiosyncratic, then I shall have failed; for what is needed above all is not individual performances but communal agreement as to how a theologically-oriented exegesis could be established, developed and practised. Clearly, such a consensus will not in the foreseeable future comprehend more than a minority of biblical scholars. Indeed, I am not at all sure that the position outlined here constitutes the basis for a consensus even in this limited sense. It is not difficult to foresee some of the points at which it will be challenged, perhaps with good reason. Is my decision to work with the final form of the text too dismissive of the real concerns and achievements of the historical–critical paradigm? Should I have presented a theological perspective as one legitimate approach among many, rather than ascribing some form of normativity to it? Is it really possible to welcome the postmodern/poststructuralist emphasis on textuality while rejecting its anti-realism on theological grounds? Can one accept the force of the feminist critique of the biblical texts and still reaffirm their status as holy scripture, or is this an impossible balancing-act? And, granted that particular theological choices will at some point have to be made, why is the goal presented as a specifically *trinitarian* hermeneutic? Insofar as such critical questions accept that the goal of a theologically-oriented interpretative practice is worth striving for (while disagreeing about the form that this should take), then something, at least, may have been achieved. Criticisms that implicitly or explicitly deny that a real and fundamental problem exists in this area can, I think, be discounted.

A number of people kindly read parts of this book in typescript: Martin de Boer, Mark Brett, Sarah Coakley, Colin Gunton, Grace Jantzen, Werner Jeanrond, Gerard Loughlin, Alistair McFadyen, Stephen Moore, Iain Provan, Christopher Rowland and Nicholas Watson. I am grateful to them for their perceptive comments and criticisms and for their encouragement and support. Nicholas Watson and Stephen Moore deserve special thanks in that they also read and commented on an earlier draft which was subsequently discarded. The weekly postgraduate seminar in systematic theology at King's College London has proved an invaluable setting within which to explore the relation between exegesis, hermeneutics and theology, and I am grateful to my colleagues Colin Gunton, Christoph Schwöbel and Brian Horne for allowing me to participate in it and for their friendly criticisms of my first tentative efforts in this area. Colleagues in biblical studies – and especially Graham Stanton, Leslie Houlden and Judith Lieu – have raised a rather different set of critical questions which have helped me to sharpen and clarify my hermeneutical thinking at many points.

Francis Watson
King's College London
Advent 1992

Introduction

Text, church and world: the terms are amorphous and opaque prior to an explanation of the senses in which they are to be employed. The first task is therefore to offer some preliminary definitions. Why have precisely these terms been selected to bear the weight of the argument that follows?

Text

The text in question is the biblical text; for the goal is a theological hermeneutic for biblical interpretation – that is, a theoretical framework within which an exegesis oriented primarily towards theological issues can come into being. This is therefore not an exercise in general hermeneutics. The problems that arise here are specific to biblical studies, although there may well be analogies elsewhere.

Reflection on the significance for biblical studies of general hermeneutics or literary theory is indeed a necessary task, and any attempt to rethink the aims and strategies of biblical interpretation can only benefit from exposure to recent work in these fields.[1] At certain points, this body of work raises issues that are important both for biblical interpretation and for theology – for example, in the case of the poststructuralist emphasis on the inescapability of textuality and the inaccessibility of non-textual 'truth'. In general, however, I have preferred to engage in dialogue with recent work within biblical studies and theology. Much of this work announces its 'literary' affiliations, and an awareness of its background within literary studies is indispensable. Yet the hermeneutic or interpretative paradigm towards which the following chapters move is a theological rather than a literary one, and the idea that a literary perspective is, as such, already 'theological' seems to me to be without foundation. There may well be common concerns; but, at least in my usage, the terms 'theology' and 'theological' relate to a distinct discipline – that of 'systematic theology', or 'Christian doctrine'. It is widely felt that the relationship between biblical studies and theology (in this narrow sense) is problematic: biblical studies is routinely criticized for its lack of theological awareness, and theology is

1

equally routinely criticized for misuse of the biblical texts in seeking their support for theological decisions reached on other grounds. This is, however, a local or regional issue that cannot adequately be treated within the sphere of a general hermeneutics or literary theory. What is true of the biblical texts is not necessarily true of other kinds of text; the idea that the Bible should be read 'just like any other book' is misleading, not just as a statement about the Bible but also in its suggestion that all texts indiscriminately must be subjected to the control of a single reading-perspective. All hermeneutical reflection is influenced by particular traditions of interpretation, and there is nothing arbitrary about the decision to work within a specifically theological context.

Nevertheless, current usage of the general term 'text' remains important in its emphasis on the relative autonomy or self-sufficiency of the written artefact. 'Text' is not synonymous with 'work', a term referring to productions which remain perpetually within their author's sphere of influence. To think of a 'work' is to imagine an author with a particular range of intentions and meanings to be communicated; it is to focus on the process and the circumstances which brought the work to birth.[2] To think of a 'text', on the other hand, is to focus on the finished product, abstracted from its relation to a progenitor and considered in terms of its *use*. The application of the term 'text' to the biblical writings accords with their general reticence about their relation to an author, and their evident orientation towards communal use. It also implies the inadequacy of a hermeneutic which sees them as addressed only to a specific group with sharply-defined, purely local needs.

It follows that a 'text' is not to be regarded primarily as a 'historical source' which enables us to add to the store of our knowledge of the past. In the case of the 'historical source', and in the interpretative practice that corresponds to it, the written artefact effaces itself and becomes transparent to a reality distinct from itself. It is this extra-textual reality which is the real object of investigation, and the written artefact is valuable only in so far as it permits access to that which is other than itself. The intention may indeed be to allow the reconstructed historical circumstances to reflect back upon the interpretation of the written work, but here too a primacy is ascribed to the historical circumstances, which control the subsequent interpretation. On the other hand, the term 'text' implies in current usage that no such easy distinction is possible between reality and the means by which it is mediated. That is not to say that a text is a self-contained world, unrelated to reality outside itself. The point is rather that in its textual embodiment reality is inevitably *shaped and reconstructed* out of a heterogeneous mass of raw material; it is not simply transcribed or repeated. The access to extra-textual reality offered by the text will therefore be indirect, for it proves impossible to separate the extra-textual content from its textual form, the referent from its verbal representation. A certain opacity and resistance to penetration attend the phenomenon of the text.

These considerations have an obvious bearing on the historical-critical paradigm which remains dominant in biblical studies. Thus, a 'quest of the historical Jesus' which strives to penetrate and break open the text, in search of fragments of extra-textual reality possibly preserved there, has perhaps failed to recognize that the reality of Jesus is only accessible to us through the mediation of an irreducible textuality. Yet the idea that the historical-critical method is based upon a simple mistake meets with a resistance that is, in part, justified. The contemporary concept of the 'text' is not without its own blindnesses and contradictions. Theologically, it can take us no further unless we counterbalance its claim to autonomy by asserting the fundamental hermeneutical significance of the reading community as the location from which the text derives its being and its rationale.

Church

The primary reading community within which the biblical text is located is the Christian church. 'Biblical text' here comprises the collections conventionally designated as the Old and the New Testaments. On the basis of a different understanding of the biblical text, it is also possible to assert that its primary reading community is the synagogue. In an attempt to overcome a history of hermeneutical conflict over this issue, it has been suggested that synagogue and church may be envisaged as a single reading community in so far as they hold the 'Hebrew scriptures' in common. Yet the supplementation of this body of writing with a new scripture entails such a drastic rereading and (at some points) relativizing of the old that it becomes in effect a different collection of writings to the holy scripture of the Jewish community. Either the Hebrew scriptures are the sole property of the Jewish community, in which case the Christian church should renounce all claim on them; or they can also be read as the Christian Old Testament, distinct from the New Testament but insepa- rable from it and shaping the way that it is read, as well as being reciprocally shaped by it. In preferring the latter option, one enters into potential tension not so much with the Jewish community as with the historical-critical approach to the 'Old Testament', where the status of these writings as Christian holy scripture has long been problematic. Despite the complications that it entails, however, the claim that the

Christian church is the primary reading community for the texts of the Old and the New Testaments is not self-evidently wrong, and may at least serve as a working hypothesis. A phenomenological account of the role of the biblical texts within the church will help to bring to light the implications of this hypothesis.

The Bible embraces writings in a variety of literary genres, but these genres are transformed by the fact of canonization. The canon converts poetry and prose, narrative, law, prophecy and epistles alike into 'holy scripture'. Genre is determined not only by a text's intrinsic characteristics but also by its communal usage, and it is arbitrary to claim that a text is 'really' a mere letter or poem and that its role as holy scripture was imposed on it later – as it were, against the grain. That view supposes that texts are wholly limited and confined by their immediate circumstances of origin, and that as soon as they stray from their appointed time and place they will be 'misread'. Yet it is of the nature of writing – unlike speech – to stray from its appointed time and place, and the possibility that writing will transcend the time and place envisaged by its author is therefore part of its structure from the very beginning.[3] 'Holy scripture' as a generic category is not an alien imposition upon texts whose essential being and meaning is to be found elsewhere, for texts do not give their essential being and meaning to be known apart from the process of their reception. The reception of some texts but not others as holy scripture assigns to them a complex function within the life of the community.

The primary function of holy scripture is to be read publicly in the context of communal worship. The church is most literally a 'reading community' when, week by week, passages from the Old Testament, the epistles and the gospels are read aloud in the hearing of the congregation. Within the canonical writings, the selection of some passages and not others is a matter of practical expediency and not of principle, and will in any case vary. On the other hand, to substitute a non-canonical writing (an excerpt, say, from Augustine's *Confessions* or Julian's *Revelations of Divine Love*) would be not just another liturgical innovation but a challenge to the canonical principle, according to which only certain books are to be publicly read. This challenge might take a stronger or a weaker form, according to context, and might or might not be justified; it is mentioned here only in order to point to the clarity with which the canonical principle normally operates. While, within the context of private reading, many other texts can be valued and reread as sacred writings, the distinction between canonical and non-canonical texts is acknowledged here too (at least if the reader is a member of the Christian community). To claim that the primary function of the canon is to determine which books may be read in communal Christian worship is therefore not to understand it as a super-ficial, quasi-legal entity with only a limited sphere of influence. The priority of the Christian community over the individual means that communal decisions of this kind may be internalized by the individual in a manner that is far from superficial.[4]

It is possible to envisage a liturgy in which the reading of holy scripture was regarded as self-sufficient, its meaning being so clear and straightfor-ward that it required only to be read in order to make the desired impact on the hearers. Yet the link between preaching and the reading of holy scripture seems to be firmly enough established for it to be possible to regard preaching as essentially scriptural interpretation, and this link therefore indicates that a belief in the self-sufficiency of the text as read is not in practice accepted.[5] In most imaginable non-ecclesial contexts in which stories might be read aloud, the need for interpretation is not felt. In an ecclesial context, however, stories and other literary forms are (at least in principle) accompanied by an interpretation whose primary aim is to make the necessary connections between the world of the text and the world of the congregation in both its gathered and its dispersed state. Explanation of particular difficulties encountered in the world of the text may be necessary, but this is subordinate to the main interpretative task. The perceived need for formalized interpretation of this kind stems not so much from the obscurity of holy scripture as from its unique value. Non-canonical stories read in most non-ecclesial settings are, broadly speaking, interchangeable. It matters little whether one story is read rather than another, for there is an inexhaustible, infinite fund of stories (and of course non-narrative texts) upon which to draw. Connections between the worlds of the text and of the reader may be discovered or created and may contribute to the reader's enjoyment, but the supplementation of reading by an interpretative practice whose role is to specify and to formalize these connections remains unusual. In so far as the biblical texts in their ecclesial, canonical role are accompanied by this supplement, there is ascribed to them a 'surplus of meaning', a depth of signification that is not immediately apparent from the surface of the text as simply read. But the fact that the true meaning is regarded as non-manifest is also, paradoxically, an indication of a lack or deficiency in the texts, which must be supplemented or mediated by interpretation. The concept of 'holy scripture' indeed implies an authoritative, normative status, and yet this authority is encountered not in unmediated exposure to a numinous text but through the mediation of preaching. Holy scripture is thus compatible with a degree of interpretative freedom.[6]

Interpretative freedom is, however, limited by another mode of scrip-tural interpretation, communal rather than individual, no longer flexible but resistant to change. In the creed (the Nicene Creed may serve as an example of the genre), ecclesial interpretation encounters the limits within which it must work and beyond which it must not stray.[7] Transgression is of course possible, just as it is possible to read non-canonical in place of canonical texts; but it remains, objectively, transgression, and is recognized as such. As interpretation of holy scripture, the creed fulfils a number of roles. First, it asserts that holy scripture is not a miscellany of texts with no ultimate unifying principle but that it constitutes a single narrative of creation, redemption and final salvation. The highly selective nature of the points in the story to which reference is made is intended not to exclude the history of Israel or of Jesus' ministry but to outline the overarching context within which they are to be set. Second, the Nicene creed discovers a trinitarian pattern in the scriptural narrative, which tells first of 'the Father, the almighty, maker of heaven and earth', then of 'the only Son of God' who 'became incarnate of the Virgin Mary and was made human', and then of 'the Holy Spirit, the Lord, the giver of life' – a life which is presumably both present and future. This chronological ordering of Father, Son and Spirit is, however, not absolutized; for, prior to his incarnation the Son was 'true God from true God', and 'through him all things were made'; and prior to Pentecost the Holy Spirit was already the Lord who 'spoke through the prophets'. The Nicene Creed posits the immanent as well as the economic trinity, and the order of disclosure therefore cannot represent the final truth. Third, it is asserted that this trinitarian story is a *true* story, in such a way that the worshipper is compelled to make this assertion his or her own: '*I believe...*' (*credo*). Narrative and truth are not played off against one another but held indissolubly together. Yet even this structure, which apparently leaves so little room for manoeuvre, is not at all as inflexible as it seems; for it is simply an outline which requires to be filled out by the far more varied content of holy scripture and by the interpretative reflection of preaching. The reading of scripture, preaching and the creed mutually determine, limit and reinforce one another.

The purpose of these reflections is not to offer a full account of the role of holy scripture within the church but to outline a complex existing function to which a theologically-oriented interpretative practice would have to relate. Of course, theological reflection can be a purely individual and individualistic activity, or it can be addressed to communities other than the ecclesial one. If theology is to be Christian, however, the ecclesial community must be seen as its primary point of reference. Yet the preceding discussion may have suggested a false view of the ecclesial community as an enclosed, perhaps idealized space, and it is therefore necessary to redress the balance by considering text and church in relation to 'the world'.

World

In its ecclesial sense, the term 'world' refers to the vast social space that surrounds and encompasses the church, within which it is to fulfil its mission. It is possible, however, to correlate text, church and world in such a way as to assert the world's right to determine the meaning of the biblical text over against its role within the church. We cannot take it for granted that the church is the primary location of the biblical texts, for this assumption is in fact challenged not simply by individuals but by institutional structures. Biblical interpretation is a university-based as well as a church-based activity, and this dual location creates the possibility both of co-operation and of conflict.

University-based biblical scholars can understand themselves as part of a 'secular' institution, representing the interest of the non-ecclesial 'world' in the biblical texts. It is held that the secular institution is interested in these texts partly by virtue of the disinterested pursuit of truth that is its mission, partly because of their pervasive influence on western history and culture, and partly in order to counter the influence of those who allegedly misuse the texts in ways that may be socially damaging. The standing of biblical scholarship within the academy is said to be dependent on its sharing the 'secularity' of the rest of the academy. In an essay entitled 'Hermeneutics', dating from 1974, C. F. Evans refers to the pressure that this commitment to academic secularity encounters when it suggests conclusions unwelcome or unacceptable to religious believers. In the context perhaps of a lecture or seminar, some conventional belief is negated, and a cry of protest ensues. 'Is this', Evans asks, 'the kind of cry which it is proper to be uttered in the context of study at a university? If so, the question may be asked whether there are any other subjects of a kind that a similar cry could legitimately arise in the study of them, or whether theology is peculiar here' (*Explorations in Theology 2* (1977), 83). A commitment to academic secularity will make one unwilling to accept that 'theology is peculiar here'. The church is represented as a threat to the quest for truth, and the idea that academic scholarship should aim to serve its proclamation is resisted – for 'the university, as it now understands itself, could hardly tolerate such an activity within it' (82). As conscientious employees of the academic institution, we should instead strive 'to ensure as far as possible that exegesis is studied in such a way that it does *not* issue in proclamation' (83; my italics).[8] In biblical scholarship, on this view, the secular world defends itself against the church and asserts itself as the primary location for biblical interpretation. A radically different understanding of the place of biblical scholarship within the university is a necessary consequence of the claim that the public liturgical reading of holy scripture is hermeneutically primary, together with its interpretation through preaching and creed.

Advocates of academic secularity presuppose that the various disciplines that comprise the modern university are all engaged in the same quest for a single truth, employing criteria and methods that are ultimately commensurable. In participating in this enterprise, it is said, theology must loosen or sever links with the community that has a vested interest in its labours.[9] For the sake of consistency, the same demand for total autonomy over against external vested interests would have to be imposed upon other academic disciplines. The social role of the university would then be the production of a truth pursued 'for its own sake' and therefore unrelated to any other social activity. But that would be to ignore the fact that the different academic disciplines are able to pursue their various truths precisely because each has its own social base outside the academy, in the form of a community interested in its labours. Theology is in no way unusual in this respect. Nor is it anything other than normal to experience certain tensions between the demands of the social base (for confirmations of existing opinion, or for quick, marketable results) and the independence of mind that suspects and resists easy solutions. Yet the academy itself has a certain tendency to encourage easy solutions that conform to its own internal norms and that ignore the interests of the social base. A true 'academic freedom' might therefore consist not in high-minded aloofness from such supposedly vulgar concerns but in challenging the self-sufficiency that disregards the reality of dependence on an interested community beyond the bounds of the academy. In the case of the academic secularity that is the theological version of this ideology, one would have to question whether academic freedom is really served by defining biblical exegesis in such a way as to exclude, 'as far as possible', the concerns of the Christian community. The interest of the Christian community in the theological disciplines pursued in the academy consists not only in the particular interests of empirical individuals but in a communal concern that current Christian discourse and praxis should be exposed to critical testing in order to determine whether it is a truthful and appropriate expression of the church's vocation within the world.[10]

There is therefore no need to correlate text, church and world in such a way that the academy, representing the world, offers an independent location for the text over against the church. The Enlightenment's belief that the world offers a kind of secular salvation from the Babylonian captivity perpetuated by the church puts severe strains on one's credulity, however popular it may still be as a justification for the academic study of theology and religion. Since the community of faith may exist within the academy just as in other spheres of worldly existence, there is no need to envisage a perspective on the biblical texts which is fundamentally different from an ecclesial one. It is true that non-believing perspectives on the text are a possibility and indeed a reality, for the academy does not normally impose doctrinal tests on those who teach and work within it. Such perspectives may have their own positive contribution to make to the self-critique of the Christian community, even if their readings of the text cannot be accepted as they stand.[11] But precisely because the academy does not impose doctrinal tests, there can equally be no obligation to accept the myth of salvation through secularity and to read the biblical texts in the light of it. The assumption that faith is incompatible with proper academic standards or with openness to alternative viewpoints is ultimately a mere prejudice, whatever the practical grounds for caution over this issue.

In correlating text, church and world, the term 'world' must instead be understood theologically. The world may be seen, first, as a possible source of truth for the church. Members of the community of faith are 'in the world' in the sense that they also participate fully in the life of the wider society. The community of faith does not withdraw its members from the world; rather, it alters the manner of their participation in the world. The church is not an enclosed, self-sufficient sphere, for its members can never leave behind the broader socio-linguistic formation that continues to permeate every aspect of their lives, but can only alter their stance within this formation. It follows that any correct apprehension of Christian truth or the praxis that must accompany it will occur only through the mediation of a discourse that is not in itself distinctively Christian. It is true that the church must preserve 'the faith which was once for all delivered to the saints', and it is true that this faith is grounded in the texts of holy scripture. Yet this scripturally-grounded faith should not be understood as a static entity which enables us to escape from the stream of historical becoming. Any reaffirmation of that faith will occur only within and through the medium of contemporary discourse – a situation that suggests that faithfulness to the truth does not lie within the church's control but is dependent on the promise that 'I am with you always, to the close of the age'. This promise would mean that the truth may be truly apprehended through the mediation of any given social discourse. As the miracle of Pentecost indicates, there is no language in which the mighty works of God may not be proclaimed; and, conversely, the mighty works of God can only be proclaimed through the mediation of a language normally employed by a broad socio-linguistic group for quite other purposes. Language is not a transparent medium but shapes and forms the reality of which it speaks; for linguistic agents, there can be no encounter with a reality that is not already shaped and formed by language. The church may therefore not perceive itself as an enclosed, sealed sphere in which truth is preserved in pure form, untouched by the passing fashions of the age. The church too is permeated by contemporary discourse and its passing fashions, and this is the indispensable, inescapable medium through which truth is to be apprehended.

The world is the context of the church just as the church is the context of the biblical text, and the term 'world' points secondly to the public nature of the claims made by the church on the basis of the biblical text. This does not mean that the world offers neutral criteria on the basis of which Christian proclamation can be demonstrated to be true. There are many truths in the world, and many criteria for determining them; what counts as valid truth in one social context may be quite incommensurable with the truth acknowledged in another. Most of these truths understand themselves as purely local, and have no pretensions to universality. It is tempting to say that this is also the case with Christian truth: that here we have one communally-authoritative story among others, true only within its communal context and to be judged purely by its capacity to generate fruitful, creative responses to the challenges of life within the world. Yet to renounce all claim to universality would be a drastic distortion of the Christian story itself, set as it is within the universal horizons of creation and eschaton. If one wished to strip this story of its universal pretensions, rereading it and the biblical narratives from which it is derived as simply one story among others, then it would be hard to differentiate this programme from the world's assumption that the Christian story is simply false. The world too is capable of a relatively positive assessment of the potential of the Christian story for generating fruitful perspectives and patterns of life. What it resists is the claim that this story is a (or *the*) true story. This resistance is manifold and absolutely serious: the true story, it is said, is that there is no finally true story – or, if there is, it is certainly not the Christian story. If, in speaking of the church's permeation by the world's language, it was necessary to relativize the boundary between church and world, at this point a sharply-delineated boundary is indispensable. The coincidence of these two points identifies a peculiar difficulty for faith and theology: that the community of faith is entirely dependent on a language or discourse which is constantly developing ways of resisting and concealing its claims. This situation must simply be endured in the hope and expectation that the miracle of Pentecost will again occur, as worldly discourse becomes the medium through which the mighty works of God are proclaimed.

The miracle of Pentecost is not an inner-ecclesial event but an event in which the church addresses the world. This points towards a third sense of the term 'world' in relation to the church, that it is the sphere and object of the church's mission: 'Go into all the world and preach the gospel to the whole creation' (Mk. 16.15). This mission is not to be understood as the striving of a totalitarian institution to subject every kind of otherness to its own peculiar ideology. Whenever and wherever it appears to take such a form, it is not the mission of the church that is being carried out. The church's mission is grounded in and limited by the Father's sending of the Son as the particular form of the divine love for the world. If God's love for the world is simply a state of affairs, then the world might be regarded as already redeemed, replete, in possession of all that it needs. If, however, the world is the object of God's loving *action*, then it must be understood as unredeemed, impoverished, lacking what it needs in order to be what it ought to be. In the incarnation or becoming-human of the Son of God, the inner-trinitarian divine love is definitively opened up so as to embrace and comprehend human beings within itself, and it therefore approaches and addresses them with a human form and a human face.[12] The gospel is the message and the praxis of the divine humanism and humanity. It is the message of the divine affirmation of humankind and human community, and of the divine negation of every negation of human community, including those that are religiously inspired and that the biblical texts may appear to sanction. This affirmation, with the corresponding proclamation and praxis, takes place against the background of an existing negation, a flaw that limits, distorts and destroys the community or *koinonia* for which human beings, created in the image of the triune God, are intended and destined. This reading of the biblical story of redemption will be elaborated and defended at various stages in later chapters. The point here is simply to assert that the biblical story itself refuses to permit its own enclosure and confinement within the walls of the church, but requires the community of faith to look outwards into the conflict-ridden sociopolitical sphere in which it is of course already located and implicated. It is crucially important to emphasize not only the hermeneutical significance of the Christian community as the primary location of the biblical texts, but also the world as the primary location of the Christian community.

Text, church and world are thus related to one another as three concentric circles. The text, the innermost circle, is located within the church, and the church is located within the world, the outermost circle. There seems to be no reason in principle why biblical interpretation should not be practised within this hermeneutical framework. Yet an argument to this effect, located within the academy, can only be developed in dependence on the existing state of academic debate in the relevant areas. It is therefore necessary to reflect on the specific context of the hermeneutic I am here proposing.

To engage in a quest for a theological hermeneutic for biblical studies entails an interdisciplinary approach which brings biblical studies and systematic theology into dialogue with one another. Interdisciplinary work has its risks and dangers. Since the starting-point is normally one discipline rather than the other, the first danger is that one may acquire only a superficial acquaintance with the 'foreign' discipline and thus fail to achieve any real dialogue. The second, opposite danger is that one may in effect transfer one's allegiance from the old discipline to the new. Desiring to bring biblical studies into dialogue with (say) theology or literary theory, one may become so enamoured of the new perspectives that one loses sight of the old ones. Once again, the dialogue that is essential for effective interdisciplinary work fails to materialize. These two dangers are in principle avoidable; but a third may prove more intractable. What if the two disciplinary perspectives prove to be incommensurable? What if, like oil and water, they refuse to mix? Despite the common ground they might be presumed to share, the relation between biblical studies and theology is widely held to be problematic. Although theologians often draw upon the work of biblical scholars and biblical scholars sometimes relate their work to particular theological trends, sustained interdisciplinary work between the two fields is surprisingly rare. It is now quite common for biblical scholars to acquire a degree of competence in literary studies, sociology or anthropology, and there is an established body of work upon which one can draw in relating such perspectives to the biblical texts. But this is not the case in relation to systematic theology, even though many biblical scholars have theological interests and commitments of one kind or another.

There are various reasons for this remarkable anomaly. One, already mentioned, is biblical scholarship's commitment to 'secularity', and a further function of this commitment is to ensure that all participants in the discipline operate according to the same rules. It is held that anything stemming too directly from 'faith' would prove a hindrance to dialogue. 'Faith' here is understood as a subjective, private orientation unfit to enter into public discourse, and, having been compelled by the structure of the discipline to internalize this view, it is difficult to enter into dialogue with a discipline such as systematic theology which decisively rejects it. A further problem is that the historical-critical paradigm seems to condition its practitioners to believe that the biblical texts are unable to bear very much theological weight. (They are, after all, simply fragile remnants of historical circumstances quite different from our own.) Even where those who engage in historical-critical practice are firmly committed to the abiding authority and truthfulness of the biblical texts, that does not necessarily mean that any significant dialogue with systematic theology will take place: for it is often held that the theological significance of a text may be derived directly from its literal, historical meaning without any need for an additional disciplinary framework. According to Karl Barth's exemplary formulation, systematic theology 'does not ask what the apostles and prophets said but what we must say on the basis of the apostles and prophets' (*Church Dogmatics*, I,1 [1932], 16). But if this distinction is rejected, so that what we must say is virtually identified with what the apostles and prophets said, then the need for systematic theology over and above biblical exegesis will not be properly appreciated. The role of systematic theology here would simply be to confirm and defend the content of the biblical revelation as already determined by exegesis.[13]

In biblical studies, theological issues come closest to the surface at those points where exegetical decisions cease to be neutral but locate one at a particular point in the spectrum that runs from 'conservative' to 'radical'. Disregarding the extremes (advocacy of the Mosaic authorship of the Pentateuch, for example, or – at the other end – denial of Jesus' historical existence), there remains a wide range of issues where opposing positions are readily understood in terms of this spectrum. For example, a critic may argue that the empty tomb story is a late apologetic legend. The more conservative exegete naturally wishes to refute this claim, and offers a variety of reasons why the 'radical' arguments are unpersuasive, why Paul may be presumed to have known this story, and why it should therefore be regarded as early. In this debate, lateness and earliness are very closely associated with presumption of empirical falsehood and truth respectively, and, since theological as well as historical issues are obviously involved here, it is easy to assume that in entering into the historical debate one is at the same time engaging with the theological issues. This assumption may be made on both sides of the debate. The conservative exegete will believe that he or she is defending a central element in the historic, apostolic faith against dangerous and misleading innovations. The radical exegete may believe that he or she is defending the principle of theological freedom over against those who can read the texts only in the light of ready-made dogmatic systems.[14]

Neither belief should be too hastily disparaged; there are indeed important theological issues at stake. The point is, however, that in such a discussion the real theological issues remain on the margin. A certain faith commitment, one way or the other, accompanies and motivates one's advocacy of the corresponding historical case; but the 'faith commitment' itself is construed as a deeply personal orientation which it would be improper to parade in public. Exegesis functions as a public surrogate for a private faith, and appears to constitute an existentially sufficient sphere for personal theological commitments. The result, however, is biblicism: a biblicism of the right, which, being already committed to 'scripture alone', is at least consistent, and a biblicism of the left in which supposedly radical historical-critical results create the illusion of being in the vanguard of theological progress. It is, indeed, the radical historical-critical scholar who has pushed the privatizing of faith to the furthest extreme. Here, and especially in a university setting, 'faith' is far more likely to take a non- or anti-ecclesial form than in the case of the more conservative colleague. How is this 'faith' to be characterized? As a certain sense of the mystery or wonder of existence, perhaps – a residue of a former religious commitment that has dwindled away under the impact of critical scholarship, also leaving behind a settled dislike of what is perceived as the dogmatism of ecclesial religion. Such an experience or self-understanding is of course not to be belittled. The point here is simply to identify it as the end-product of a biblicism of the left which has committed itself unreservedly to historical-critical negations, and as a barrier to serious dialogue with systematic theology.

From the side of biblical studies, the barriers are indeed formidable. In the chapters that follow, I may perhaps appear to have evaded or minimized real problems by the decision to work with the final form of the text and by the no doubt inadequate attempts to subject historical-critical practice to critical analysis. In asserting that Christian theology as an ecclesial discipline is both possible in itself and relevant for biblical interpretation, I will already have offended the sensibilities of those who believe that being a historian rather than a theologian is a positive advantage for a biblical scholar. Yet the theological question refuses to go away, as some biblical interpreters would apparently like it to. There are others, on both sides of the disciplinary divide, for whom the present situation is deeply unsatisfactory and who are themselves exploring the possibility of bringing the disciplines into fruitful contact with one another. This book, intended as ground-clearing pro-legomena to a future interpretative practice, offers a contribution to an exploratory process that is already under way.

PART ONE

THE AUTONOMOUS TEXT

At the heart of current debate and controversy within biblical studies is the issue of the final form of the biblical texts. This is not simply one debate among others, of a piece with the challenges to an existing consensus on, say, pre-monarchical Israel or the nature of Pauline theology. Challenges of this kind represent the normal workings of biblical scholarship. The claim that the object of study should be the texts in their final form is, however, a far more fundamental challenge to an existing consensus; for the consensus at this point is not just a limited agreement about the shape of a particular problem but the basic agreement which determines the nature of the field within which biblical scholarship operates. It has been agreed that the primary task of biblical scholarship is to reconstruct the diachronic historical processes underlying the text as it now stands. One searches the text for the clues it may (perhaps inadvertently) offer as to its own prehistory: its use of written sources and other traditional material, for example, or its relation to historical agents, purposes and events. While not everything that falls into the category of 'conventional scholarship' betrays this diachronic bias, it is pervasive enough to serve as the general framework within which particular findings must be set. To work with the final form of the texts, removed from this diachronic framework and envisaged now as relatively autonomous linguistic artefacts, is therefore to propose a major reorientation or paradigm-shift within the discipline.

It is true that, in one sense, there is no final 'final form', for diachronic processes of transmission continue to affect the shape of the text after the moment of relative stabilization beyond which it is protected from wholesale radical revision. Strictly speaking, the final form of a biblical text – the form in which we now encounter it on the printed page – is the product not only of the biblical authors and editors but also of later scribal activity and modern text-critical reconstruction and hypothesis. The fact that it varies from one edition to another – to say nothing of the problem of translation – indicates that a strict concept of finality in which every last letter is in place is untenable. A further difficulty arises from the shift from the concept of originality to that of finality. Modern textual criticism assumes the concept of an 'original' text which one attempts to recover from later corruptions. But where a text is the product not only of individual authorship but also of communal tradition, is the concept of originality still tenable? Does the final form of Daniel or Esther include or exclude the material found in the Greek but not in the Hebrew/Aramaic version of these books? Does the final form of the Gospel of Mark include or exclude the post-resurrection narrative of Mark 16.9–20? (The early church evidently felt that Mark 16.1–8 was too obscure and ambiguous to function adequately as the ending of the gospel: our existence is already obscure and ambiguous enough as it is, and the role of the gospel is to bring light to our darkness, not to perplex us with gratuitous new difficulties.) In the face of such considerations, the concept of the final form loses a little of its initial clarity; but it remains possible to speak of the relative stabilization of the text and therefore of a relative finality. The Gospel of John circulated in various textual traditions (with or without the story of the adulterous woman, for example (John 7.53–8.11)), but only by way of a poststructuralist *tour de force* could one deny that a single, relatively stable textual object is transmitted in all of these traditions.

Granted that, with these qualifications, the concept of the final form of the biblical text is coherent and viable, what grounds are there for the interpretative decision to work with it in relative independence of the modern interpretative tradition's diachronic bias? This decision proposes a paradigm-shift, and such a far-reaching proposal must rest upon something more substantial than boredom with the old ways and enthusiasm for every untested novelty. There appear to be three main possibilities here. Current work on the final form of the text is undertaken, first, under the influence of perspectives derived from literary studies. The historical-critical tradition here stands accused of an insensitivity to the complex unity that character-izes the literary work of art. It is also criticized for dissipating its energies on speculative reconstructions that serve only to distract attention from the texts themselves. Whatever the justice of this critique, a considerable body of exegetical work has established the capacity of this approach to function as a workable paradigm for interpretative practice. A second possible justification for working with the final form is communal usage. It is only in their final, canonical form that the biblical texts have functioned as communally authoritative within synagogue and church. Especially in the work of Brevard Childs, this canonical approach offers distinctive and sometimes illuminating perspectives. Yet the formalistic tendency in Childs' approach is a limitation as well as a strength, and it must be complemented by the third and most compelling reason for working with the final form: that this is the form of the text most suitable for theological use.[1] This suitability derives not only from the fact that theology is an ecclesial discipline and must therefore take seriously the ecclesial form of the text, but also from the theological judgement that the subject-matter or content of the biblical texts is inseparable from their form.

In the four chapters that follow, I shall offer a critical appreciation of the work of two recent advocates of the irreducible reality of the final form of the text – Hans Frei and Brevard Childs – followed by an exegetical response to some of the issues that such work raises. This will serve to relate my own proposals to existing discussion, and will also identify points at which, in my judgement, contemporary interpretative theory and practice is deficient.

Chapter 1

Narrative and Reality

The history of modern biblical scholarship is often represented as the gradual triumph of critical enlightenment over pre-critical darkness.[1] Partly as a consequence of the new status accorded to the biblical text by the Reformation, certain intractable problems gradually began to impose themselves. To what extent should the newly literalized biblical text be seen as a transcript of reality? How far might one extend the traditional claim that the biblical writers accommodated themselves to the often primitive intellectual and cultural climate in which they found themselves? What kind of knowledge may we legitimately expect the Bible to provide, and how is this to be correlated with knowledge derived from other sources? Out of questions such as these the tradition of critical biblical scholarship was born, a tradition increasingly prepared to defy the taboo against questioning the reliability and veracity of the biblical writings.[2] Questioning was undertaken (so the story goes) not with purely negative intent, but with the purpose of distinguishing much more sharply than ever before between that which lies at the centre of Christian faith and that which belongs only on its periphery.[3] It became clear that all of the biblical writings were conditioned at every point by their original historical and socio-cultural locations, although that did not prevent one from seeing the broader human and religious content beneath or behind the time-bound form.

This conventional representation of the history of modern biblical scholarship has the social function of assuring the present interpretative community that it is proceeding along the right lines, in continuity with the founding fathers of the discipline. Like Moses on Mount Pisgah, they glimpsed and testified to the promised land which it is our privilege and duty to occupy ever more conclusively. Conversely, a radical reassessment of the achievement of seventeenth, eighteenth or nineteenth century scholarship might constitute a challenge to the interpretative priorities and

19

assumptions of the present. This is what makes Hans Frei's *The Eclipse of Biblical Narrative* (1974) a far more important work than its subtitle ('A Study in Eighteenth and Nineteenth Century Hermeneutics') might suggest. Frei's claim is that something went wrong in biblical interpretation at that time which has remained uncorrected ever since.

According to Frei, biblical interpretation during this period committed the fundamental mistake of identifying meaning with reference. A narrative text's meaning is held to be dependent on establishing its relation to entities outside itself. On the one hand, there is 'ostensive reference', the assumption that the text's meaning must lie in its relation to real persons and events, which may be more or less adequate or distorted. On the other hand, when ostensive reference threatens to break down, there is also the possibility of 'ideal reference'. People were thus able to 'claim an ideal rather than an ostensive referent as the true explicative meaning of the stories. They would then plead that this, rather than a historical fact claim, is also their applicative, still meaningful significance' (*Eclipse*, 119). In both cases, however, a gap opens up between text and meaning. Meaning, identified with ostensive reference, is now found in more or less 'real' events or persons outside the texts, or, identified with ideal reference, with general religious or moral truths which can be known independently of the texts and which the texts serve merely to illustrate. The gap between text and meaning is wide open even when there is no desire to attack the credibility of the text in deist fashion; when, for example, the 'neologians' of the later eighteenth century understand the gospels' reference to the devil as a deliberate 'accommodation' to the cultural circumstances of the time, thereby presupposing that 'the genuine meaning of such passages, the authors' actual intention in them, is not identical with the words and descriptions of the text' (61). Even conservatives, arguing for a close correlation between texts and external, historical reality, did so by appealing to general criteria of credibility which make it possible to distinguish between event and text. Frei cites as a typical example of this the assertion of S. J. Baumgarten (1706–57), that 'so many agreed-upon, undeniable testimonies of antiquity serve to confirm the biblical history that one will have to reject all history if one will not accept that of the Bible'. This exemplifies an 'acknowledgment of responsibility to a court of general credibility for anything, sacred or secular, that claims to be a fact' (89). By contrast, 'for the older interpreters neither the human author (alone or together with his setting) nor the empirical–historical fact described by the statement had the logical distinctness or independence from the words of the statement that was necessary to make this kind of argument as well as the skeptical counter-argument cogent' (80).

What makes Frei's case so provocative and interesting is his belief that all this need not and should not have been the case, a belief based in the first instance on literary rather than theological considerations. The central thesis of his study is that 'a realistic or history-like (though not necessarily historical) element is a feature, as obvious as it is important, of many of the biblical narratives that went into the making of Christian belief' (10). Although biblical commentators recognized this, their preoccupation with history or allegory meant that 'the *meaning* of the stories was finally something different from the stories or depictions themselves, despite the fact that this is contrary to the character of a realistic story' (11). A realistic narrative resembles a historical account, and is thus 'history-like', above all in the sense that it does not point beyond itself to some quite different external reality. On this view, 'even the miraculous accounts are realistic or history-like (but not therefore historical and in that sense factually true) if they do not in effect symbolize something else instead of the action portrayed' (14). Realistic, history-like narrative is characterized, in other words, by its *irreducibility*. Here, 'there is neither need for nor use in looking for meaning in a more profound stratum underneath the structure (a separable "subject matter") or in a separable author's "intention", or in a combination of such behind-the-scenes projections' (281). According to Frei, this model was available to eighteenth century exegetes in the form of the novel; and yet 'the new tradition of *literary* realism was never applied to the technical task of biblical interpretation... On apologetic as well as historical grounds the question of the factuality of biblical reports, and the cognate debate over whether its putative factuality or the recognition of some central ideational themes was really the important thing about the Bible, prevented any serious attention to narrative shape in its own right' (150).

On the basis of such statements, Frei might be understood as calling for the kind of 'literary approach' to biblical narrative that has in fact been developed in the two decades since his book was published.[4] Yet he writes not as a literary critic but as a theologian, and much of the interest of his book lies in its intermingling of literary and theological categories. Thus, the story he tells begins with a 'fall' taking the form of a reversal. In the thought of the Reformers, 'the world truly rendered by combining biblical narratives into one was indeed the one and only real world, it must in principle embrace the experience of any present age and reader' (3). Biblical interpretation therefore aimed at 'incorporating extra-biblical thought, experience, and reality into the one real world detailed and made accessible by the biblical story – not the reverse' (3). In the seventeenth and eighteenth centuries, however, the point is not to incorporate the world into the text but the text into the world. 'Do the stories and whatever concepts may be drawn from them describe what we apprehend as the real world? Do they fit a more general framework of meaning than that of a single story?' (5). The relation between text and world has been reversed; a world comes into being apart from that which the biblical texts project, and those texts must accommodate themselves to the new world as best they can. This reversal is depicted as a transition from a desirable to an undesirable state of affairs: it is a good thing when the world is incorporated into the biblical texts, but a bad thing when the world asserts its independence. The literary judgement about the misunderstanding of realistic, history-like narrative is bound up with some kind of theological programme.

We cannot simply identify here a straightforward protestant neo-conservatism, for Frei justifies his preference for Reformation biblical interpretation on literary rather than theological grounds. The attempt to interpret the Bible as incorporating the world springs, he argues, from a correct apprehension of one of its predominant literary characteristics, identified by Erich Auerbach in his well-known comparison of biblical narrative with the *Odyssey*: 'Far from seeking, like Homer, merely to make us forget our own reality for a few hours, it seeks to overcome our reality: we are to fit our own life into its world, feel ourselves to be elements in its structure of universal history… Everything else that happens in the world can only be conceived as an element in this sequence; into it everything that is known about the world… must be fitted as an ingredient of the divine plan' (*Mimesis* [1946], 15; quoted, *Eclipse*, 3). A typological or figural exegesis, which seeks not only to unify the narratives into a single story but also to incorporate extra-textual reality into itself, is thus in accord with the fundamental nature of the text, which, unlike narratives which aim merely to please, is characterized by a claim to absolute authority: 'It insists that it is the only real world, that it is destined for autocracy. All other scenes, issues, and ordinances have no right to appear independently of it, and it is promised that all of them, the history of all humankind, will be given their due place within its frame, will be subordinated to it' (*Mimesis*, 15). Auerbach believes that it is very difficult to maintain any such claim today, and this makes his position all the more valuable for Frei as a purely literary judgement about the peculiarly imperious nature of these particular narratives, which demands that all extra-biblical 'experiences, events, concepts' be 'ranged figurally into the smaller as well as the overarching story' (*Eclipse*, 3). Thus, despite appearances, Frei is not really interested in assimilating study of biblical narrative to the study of the novel; for if that happened, the differentiating characteristic of biblical narrative – its imperious claim to rule the world, to contain potentially the whole of reality – would be hopelessly compromised.

What are the theological implications of all this? It is one of the peculiarities of *The Eclipse of Biblical Narrative* that, although Frei's motivation is clearly theological, the theological dimension is held in abeyance and literary–critical judgments determine the analysis. These literary–critical judgments – on 'realistic' narrative, on 'figuration' as a means of incorporation into the biblical world, and so on – serve as surrogates for theological concerns that never explicitly appear yet constantly make their influence felt. We may observe these concerns, in their native theological habitat, in Frei's briefer and less well-known work, *The Identity of Jesus Christ* (1975).

'In many ways Christians acknowledge Christ as a personal presence' (*Identity*, 12). What do they mean by this? Presence implies both the bodiliness of the object of presence and the knowledge of his or her identity, through memory and imagination, on the part of the subject (14–15). Thus the resurrection must in some sense be the basis of Christ's presence now (16). Does this imply a literal, physical resurrection (27)? But imagination breaks down when it tries to depict Jesus' being raised, suggesting that the resurrected Jesus may be inaccessible as such and making it difficult to move directly from resurrection to presence (28). Two ways out of this dilemma suggest themselves. The first would be to make Jesus present by reducing him to a purely symbolic figure. We might, for example, develop the idea that 'in Jesus the typical human situation finds its most concentrated symbolical expression'. We might represent him as the wandering stranger who, unlike the foxes and birds, has no resting-place: 'How symbolic of the real essence of our humanity from which we so often run away into the false hiding place of earthly security!' (30). There would be no need then for anything more than the most symbolic of resurrections (31). But that would be to turn Christian talk of the concrete presence of Jesus into a universalizing myth. The alternative is to relate presence more closely to identity, which should be understood not metaphysically but in terms of its manifestation in a series of intentions and actions which can be reported in a narrative sequence (45).[5] Here, then, is the fundamental theological reason for insisting on the irreducibility of the gospels: they are not myth, and their meaning must not be separated from their narrative form.[6]

For Frei, the misunderstanding of the gospel as myth is both new (existentialism, the new hermeneutic) and old (Gnosticism). When Gnostics behold the saviour, they behold themselves (60), whereas 'the Gospel story's indissoluble connection with an unsubstitutable identity in effect divests the savior story of its mythical quality' (59). A literary criticism which insists on finding 'Christ figures' in modern novels (Melville, Kazantzakis, Greene) must similarly be rejected (68–80), for their own sake as much as for his:

for 'the novel [which the gospels resemble in part] is the special vehicle for setting forth unsubstitutable identity in the interplay of character and action' (82). In Bultmann and Tillich 'the *question* rather than the story becomes the governing context with which the person is identified' (89), and a comparable substitution occurs when the new hermeneutic traces Jesus' actions back to his inner disposition; here, 'identity is given a status independent of, prior to, and only tenuously connected with the story' (90). By contrast, Frei's view 'illustrates a healthy regard for the intrinsic significance of the outward life' (98).[7]

There is, in fact, no innermost essence or hidden meaning that can be detached from the gospel narrative, and Frei applies this principle of the irreducibility of narrative to a number of christological themes. For example, although the resurrection is the climax of the story, the story would be violated if one found even here 'the "meaning" integrating the previous "events"' (123). The principle of irreducibility is also directed against conventional historical-critical practice. If we ask, for example, whether the historical Jesus applied the christological titles to himself, we are told that this is 'a speculative matter that takes us beyond the pattern and structure of the narrative' (135).

At this point, however, a previously-suppressed difficulty unexpectedly surfaces. It is acknowledged that, after all, everything really does hang on the question whether the history-like story of the gospels is – at least in some ultimate theological sense, not necessarily to be identified with the empirical level – a *true* story. 'If a novel-like account is about a person who is assumed to have lived, the question of factuality is virtually bound to arise, for psychological if no other reasons, either at specific points or over the whole stretch of the account' (140). Unfortunately, 'the force or urgency of the *question* does not make a positive *answer* to it any more credible'. It is especially in the final stage, where the narratives represent the risen Jesus, that story and history must coincide, if at all (141). One cannot deny that the question of fact is important for the accounts (146), but it is impossible to say how the transition from this literary observation to faith can occur (147). 'Belief in Jesus' resurrection is more nearly a belief in something like the inspired quality of the accounts than in the theory that they reflect what "actually took place."' Yet the believer 'would have to affirm that the New Testament authors were right in insisting that it is more nearly correct to think of Jesus as factually raised, bodily if you will, than not to think of him in this manner' (150). 'There appears to be no argument from factual evidence or rational possibility to smooth the transition from literary to faith judgment'. Without historical evidence to the contrary, 'there is a kind of logic in a Christian's faith that forces him to say that disbelief in the resurrection of Jesus is rationally impossible' (151). 'Why some believe and others do not is impossible for the Christian to explain. Like many a pilgrim, he may find himself strangely on both sides at the same time. All he can then do is to recall that the logic of his faith makes it rationally impossible for him not to believe' (152).[8]

The Identity of Jesus Christ encloses the literary–hermeneutical argument, developed at greater length in *The Eclipse of Biblical Narrative*, within a theological frame. Faith, seeking understanding, attains it by way of a literary detour. The starting-point is the theological question of the meaning of Christian assertions about the presence of Christ. It turns out that this question has to be reformulated as a question about Christ's identity; and, since identity is said to be narratively constituted, the argument turns at this point away from pure theology towards the more 'literary' formulations also characteristic of *The Eclipse* ('realistic' narrative understood in terms of irreducibility). The return from the literary context back to faith is a mysterious affair which either happens or fails to happen: the wind blows where it wills.

Frei is right to acknowledge that recognition of the irreducibility of narrative should not serve as a substitute for the question of truth. The problem is that he appears to have no means at his disposal whereby to reintegrate this question into the narrative framework. As the creeds indicate, narrative and truth are by no means incompatible. The question whether or not a story is a true story is posed by all kinds of readers, sophisticated and unsophisticated, adults and children, and cannot be dismissed as an illegitimate attempt to subject an autonomous narrative world to extrinsic reality. Yet for Frei the question can only be answered by appealing to a mysterious, uncontrollable event, and in practice he is happier to remain on the 'literary' level of his hermeneutical proposal – especially in *The Eclipse of Biblical Narrative*, where the question of a legitimate theological referentiality to replace illegitimate 'ostensive' and 'ideal' forms is never raised.[9] The irreducibility of narrative is Frei's sole normative dogma, and its defence against the threatened encroachments of historical-critical and especially existentialist approaches is his primary concern. It is an important point to make, and the pervasive influence of the illegitimate identification of meaning with ideal or ostensive reference justifies the tenacity with which he asserts it. But when the question is raised as to what we are now to do, theologically, with this irreducibly narrative text, Frei is far from certain. The dilemma posed by reality outside the self-contained world of the text is exacerbated by the claim of this particular text to be destined to contain the whole of that external reality. (We recall how in *The Eclipse of Biblical Narrative* Frei claimed, with the help of Auerbach, that the extension of typological and figural exegesis beyond the bounds of the text was necessitated by the peculiarly imperious nature of the biblical text.) Yet Frei's preference for a self-contained text makes him very cautious about developing this suggestion in interpretative practice. Once we allowed the real world into the world of the text, what guarantee would there be that it would not take over, forcing the text to conform to its own imperatives? Would we not be in constant danger of using the text to speak about reality, thus denying its integrity? 'Precisely because we must insist that the story has an integrity in its own right and yet want to affirm some important affinities between patterns of meaning in it and those we ourselves understand, we have to be *extremely wary* about supplying the Gospels too freely with our own profoundest convictions or our analyses of the structures of distinctive human being' (*Identity*, 48; my italics). Extreme wariness about allowing text and reality to touch one another means that in practice such contact will constantly be evaded in order to preserve the integrity of the story in its self-containment and isolation.[10]

The claim of the texts to incorporate reality within themselves means, however, that the possibility of contact cannot be finally ruled out. Events in history *may*, Frei thinks, dimly reflect something of the pattern of agony and hope definitively set forth in Jesus: the American civil war, for example, or attempts to end racial discrimination, or perhaps eventually even the sufferings of the Vietnamese (162–63; we recall the historical setting of Frei's main work in the America of the early 1970s). Yet the parabolic application of Christ's passion and resurrection is strictly limited (163), and we do better to look forward to that future mode of Christ's presence which 'will be a significant, incorporative summing up of history in a manner that we should be fools to try to imagine or forecast in literal fashion' (160–61). If the incorporation of reality into the text requires the parousia, who are we to anticipate that ultimate hermeneutical event? But this agnosticism permits and indeed requires us to turn away from troubling contemporary realities, glimpsed as if from a great distance, so as to return to the autonomous world of the text safe in the knowledge that only at the parousia will the barrier between text and reality be broken down. The self-contained text is a place of refuge, but it is also in danger of becoming a place of illusion, a wilful refusal of reality. The failure to speak adequately of the text's relation to the extratextual, historical–theological reality of Jesus is of a piece with the reluctance to allow any contact between the text and any other historical reality. The world must not be allowed to contaminate the text.[11]

A further indication of this problem may be found in comparing Frei's conception of 'realistic' narrative with Auerbach's. In *The Eclipse of Biblical*

Narrative, Frei can hardly speak too highly of Auerbach. Among 'authors who have been particularly influential on my thought', he is given priority over Karl Barth and Gilbert Ryle; the impact of *Mimesis* is said to be 'evident throughout this essay' (vii). Auerbach is invoked not only to analyse the biblical claim to authority and the tradition of typological or figural interpretation but also to underpin Frei's claims about 'realism' or 'realistic narrative'. 'Erich Auerbach suggests that the realistic tradition has persisted through the ebb and flow of its own fortunes in Western literature. But he also sees three historical high points in its development: the Bible, Dante's *Divine Comedy*, and the nineteenth-century novel, especially in France' (*Eclipse*, 15). Despite the use of the term 'development', implying differ- ence, Frei is chiefly interested in what the Bible, Dante, and the nineteenth century French novel are said to have in common – participation in a persisting 'realistic tradition'. Yet Frei's understanding of 'realism' is at variance with Auerbach's. Frei interprets 'realism' in formalistic fashion as denoting the containment of meaning within the text, irreducibility to non- narrative discourse. For Auerbach, however, realism is a potent socio- political concept standing for the serious representation of the problems and conflicts of ordinary people, over against classicism's ruling that tragic heroes or heroines must be drawn solely from the ruling class whereas lower class figures can emerge from the background only for comic purposes. The origins of this realism lie in the Bible: both in Old Testament narrative, where the treatment of the problematic nature of ordinary life is contrasted with the exclusive Homeric preoccupation with the heroic exploits of the ruling class (*Mimesis*, 22); and in the gospels, for example in the represen- tation of the rustic Peter as a tragic rather than a comic figure, in a manner 'incompatible with the sublime style of classical antique literature' (42). Frei's version of 'biblical realism' ignores all this, since its polar opposite is not classicism but symbolic narrative such as myth or allegory. As a literary concept, this realism is too broad and undifferentiated to be useful.[12] As a theological concept, it serves Frei's purpose (opposition to historical criticism and to demythologizing) but lacks the range and incisiveness of Auerbach's non-theological usage, which Frei does not attempt to exploit theologically.

For Auerbach although not for Frei, Christian realism is to be sharply differentiated from its counterpart in the modern novel, despite the common concern with ordinary life (*Mimesis*, 555). Christian realism is characterized by the use of figuration through which the biblical texts and extra-biblical reality are incorporated into a single divine plan. The realism which Auerbach looks for in the novel is quite differently constituted: 'The serious realism of modern times cannot represent man otherwise than as embedded in a total reality, political, social, and economic, which is concrete and constantly evolving' (463). Stendhal's influence on modern realism is evident especially in 'his politicizing of the idyllic concept of Nature' (466). Flaubert's realism gives him an insight into 'the problematic nature and the hollowness of nineteenth-century bourgeois culture' (490). By contrast, Auerbach castigates the advocates of *l'art pour l'art* who 'contemptuously avert their attention from the political and economic bustle, consistently value life only as literary subject matter, and remain arrogantly and bitterly aloof from its great practical problems, in order to achieve aesthetic isolation for their work' (506). On the other hand, what we find in Zola's *Germinal* 'is, beyond a shadow of a doubt, the core of the social problem of the age, the struggle between industrial capital and labor... Even today it has lost none of its significance and indeed none of its timeliness' (512).

It is this humanistic, highly politicized concern with the relation between literature and social reality that motivates Auerbach's entire account of 'the representation of reality in western literature'. A critical theological appropriation of this account might still be worthwhile, although Auerbach's book – self-consciously conservative in its anti-modernism even at the time of its publication – is now somewhat dated.[13] Yet Frei is interested solely in the formalist paradox or irony of a realism isolated from reality.

As mentioned above, Frei in *The Identity of Jesus Christ* offers an existentialist reading of the gospel story as a mythical representation of human lostness in the cosmos, only to reject it as un-Christian. Existentialist mythologizing employs the language of an abstract universality ('the real essence of our humanity'), and this is countered by an insistence on the ultimacy and irreducibility of the personal narrative (the biography) of the unsubstitutable individual, of which the novel serves as the icon. 'No specific man is another specific man, and if the unsubstitutable story that establishes a man's identity finds a substitute story, even under his name, we have another person instead' (82). Such a statement cannot avoid offering its own version of 'the real essence of humanity', located now in the irreducible individuality of the individual rather than an ontological homelessness.[14] The pendulum swings from one position to the other, from an ontology of abstract universality to one of concrete individuality, and the ease with which, within its two-dimensional plane, it makes this movement suggests the inner affinity of the two positions. Where they are at one is in conceiving of the individual, *qua* individual, as representative of humanity, and in their refusal of the third dimension necessary to reintegrate this movement into reality: the concept of the *structured, differentiated interrelatedness* of humankind, according to which individual human identity is constituted within and not in isolation from its communal or social matrix. Such a concept would rule out both an abstract universalism and Frei's privileging of the individualizing genres of novel and biography as hermeneutical aids to the understanding of the gospels.

Frei's self-contained text is a privileged space in which one unsubstitutable individual (the reader) encounters another (Jesus). In its largely justified emphasis on the important tautology that narrative is narrative, this hermeneutic of self-containment proves unable to achieve an adequate correlation of the text with the church and the world. Indeed, the perceived need to protect the text from the world may stem from the failure adequately to address the church's proper concern with the fundamental truth of the biblical story of salvation: for if, and only if, this story is true, then all worldly reality must be understood in the light of it. The claim that the text is fundamentally true liberates it from self-containment and enables it to shed its light on worldly realities – now, and not just at the parousia.

Chapter 2

Canon and Community

In a well-known article on 'Contemporary Biblical Theology' (1962), Krister Stendahl advocated a rigorous distinction between the descriptive task (discovering 'what it meant' – a historical enterprise) and the theological task of translation ('what it means'). His main emphasis lies on the importance of an autonomous descriptive method, which, he claims, has three main advantages. First, 'once we confine ourselves to the task of descriptive biblical theology as a field in its own right, the material itself gives us means to check whether our interpretation is correct or not'. A hermeneutic of description offers objective criteria; procedures are available for checking the correlation of text and interpretation.[1] (Where, on the other hand, the descriptive task is subordinated to the theological one, or even ignored altogether, arbitrariness reigns.) Second, 'this descriptive task can be carried out by believer and unbeliever alike' (422). This hermeneutic unites rather than dividing, for the term 'description' denotes precisely that relation to the object which is obtained when questions of truth and significance have been bracketed out. Third, the theological task itself will benefit from this distinction between description and translation. As the Reformation shows, 'all theological renewal and creativity has as one of its components a strong exposure to the "original" beyond the presuppositions and the inherited frame of thought of our immediate predecessors in the theological task' (430). The descriptive task makes theological freedom possible, it is intended not to oppose the translation of meaning past into meaning present but to further it. And yet an ambivalence and an uncertainty remain. 'With the original in hand, and after due clarification of the hermeneutic principles involved, we may *proceed toward tentative answers* to the question of the meaning here and now' (422, my italics). Whereas the descriptive task is comparatively straightforward (we can all join in and check each other's results against the original), the task of translation is

30

fraught with difficulties; an arduous road towards a goal that we glimpse only from afar.

Stendahl's argument is important not because it is original but as a clear statement of the self-understanding of most practitioners of historical-critical exegesis.[2] The basic position is constantly restated because it is still not accepted by the majority of those who care about the Bible and by the minority within the academy who represent and articulate their concerns. Thus, nearly three decades later, it is reiterated – in updated form, of course, but with its fundamental structure unaltered – by Heikki Räisänen, according to whom '"New Testament theology" ought to be replaced… with two different projects: first, the "history of early Christian thought" (or theology, if you like), evolving in the context of early Judaism; second, critical philosophical and/or theological "reflection on the New Testament", as well as on its influence on our history and its significance for contemporary life' (*Beyond New Testament Theology* [1990], xviii). Again, the emphasis is on the autonomy of the historical task and on the need for great circumspection in undertaking the theological one. The arguments of Stendahl and Räisänen are, in fact, not primarily individual points of view but actualizations of a schema which is constitutive of the historical-critical paradigm. To be initiated into this paradigm is to internalize this schema and to be ready to actualize it wherever the integrity and independence of historical work seems to be threatened by theological encroachments.[3] The schema functions, in other words, within the struggle of two interpretative paradigms – the first conforming more readily to academic–institutional criteria, the second deriving from a far broader social base – for control of a single textual object.

In many respects, the work of Brevard Childs – encompassing both the Old and the New Testaments – would seem to represent exactly the kind of thing that this schema is intended to oppose. Although, unlike Frei, Childs is a biblical scholar by training, his work could be seen as a systematic rejection of the primacy of 'description' in the interpretative task. Already in 1964 he writes: 'The genuine theological task can be carried on successfully only when it begins from within an explicit framework of faith. Only from this starting point can there be carried on the exegetical task which has as its goal the penetration of the theological dimension of the Old Testament. Approaches which start from a neutral ground never can do full justice to the theological substance because there is no way to build a bridge from the neutral, descriptive content to the theological reality' ('Interpretation in Faith', 438).[4] Childs freely employs the language of theological normativity, in defiance of the convention that prescribes a merely 'tentative' use of such language in a manner distinct from and marginal to the main body of the exegesis: 'It is a testimony of the Christian church as a community of faith that God has chosen the vehicle of sacred scripture through which to make himself known to the church and the world, both in the past, present, and future... To take the concept of canon seriously is to assign to scripture a normative role and to refuse to submit the truth of its testimony to criteria of human reason' (*Exodus* [1974], 300). This normative language necessitates a marginalizing of the historical approach which is the mirror-image of the latter's marginalizing of theological concerns in order to preserve its own autonomy: 'Of course it is legitimate and fully necessary for the historian of the ancient Near East to use his written evidence in a different manner, often reading his texts obliquely, but this enterprise is of a different order from the interpretation of sacred scripture which we are seeking to describe' (*Introduction to the Old Testament as Canon* [1979], 76). The language is familiar, and no more represents a distinctive and individual point of view than does the opposing programme as outlined by Stendahl and Räisänen. It is slightly unusual to find a biblical scholar employing the rhetoric of Reformed dogmatics, but the rhetoric itself seems to offer little more than another restatement of an old concern.

Thus far we seem to be doomed to repetition. Historical critics find that theology subjects the text to alien norms, and advocate a descriptive method which remains faithful to the meaning of the text conceived in terms of its circumstances of origin. The theologically-minded object that this is to detract from the nature of holy scripture as (in some sense) the vehicle for divine self-disclosure, and seek to develop a consonant mode of interpretation. One effect of this is merely to fuel historical-critical resistance, and the controversy thus circulates without any possibility of resolution. What is noticeable about this circular, circulating discourse is the deep dependence of each side on the other. Each derives from its opposite an image of an unsatisfactory interpretative practice over against which it can advertise its own virtues and present its findings in the oppositional form which ensures a sense of purpose and of progress.

It would be possible (although unjust) to allow Childs' work to be wholly absorbed into this circulating discourse, in which case he would lose any claim to significance in his own right and become a mere representative of one side of the constant to-and-fro movement. Yet there is one element in his position which breaks out of the debate as construed thus far, his discovery that the concept of 'description' is anything but straightforward. The conventional debate circles around the concept of description, with one side insisting on its autonomy while the other asserts its inadequacy as an approach to its object. Both sides tend to accept, however, that the term 'description' is a fair representation of historical-critical practice. In his 1964 article, and in explicit opposition to Stendahl, Childs already sees the limitations of this naïve empiricism: 'It is commonly assumed that the responsible exegete must start with the descriptive task and then establish a bridge to the theological problem. It is felt that th∴ real problem lies with the second task. Rather, the reverse is true. The basic issue revolves about the definition of the descriptive task. What is the content which is being described and what are the tools commensurate with this task? This is far from obvious' ('Interpretation', 437). To appeal for an autonomous 'description' is to ignore the fact that there is no such thing as a pure description of a neutral object; description always presupposes a prior construction of the object in terms of a given interpretative paradigm. The assertion that historical-critical practice undertakes the 'description' of the biblical texts is dependent on a prior interpretation of these texts as historical artefacts – chance remnants of a previous stage of human history – whose meaning is wholly determined by their historical circumstances of origin. The value of this working hypothesis certainly does not lie in its alleged naturalness or superior fidelity to the object, for the nature of the object is not a pure datum but is precisely what is under discussion. Childs disputes the appropriateness of this particular construal: 'Because this literature [the Old Testament] has had a special history as the religious literature of ancient Israel, its peculiar features must be handled in a way compatible to the material itself. A corpus of religious writings which has been transmitted within a community for over a thousand years cannot properly be compared to inert sherds which have lain in the ground for centuries' (*Old Testament*, 73). This claim is not some desperate fideistic gamble, it is a proper and necessary phenomenological distinction between cultural artefacts whose effects extend only a short way beyond their immediate, originating circumstances and those whose effects transcend their initial environment and determine, in some measure, the course and shape of a community significantly extended in space and time.[5] In the second case, 'canonicity' – an extended history of effects – may appropriately be conceived as a property of the object to be described, and it is *this* descriptive task that Childs undertakes in his emphasis on the text's final form.[6] The objects to be described are the canonical scriptures of enduring religious communities, and it is sheer reductionism to insist that canonicity is an extraneous distortion of a more fundamental essence which can be recovered only by historical methods.[7]

The significance of this change of orientation may best be grasped with the help of some examples.

The part and the whole

An orientation towards historical origins leads one to emphasize the prehistory of a given *part* of a text: its presence within some earlier text (perhaps with a quite different meaning), its original function in some extra-textual (e.g. cultic or didactic) context, its representation – more or less adequate or distorted – of historical persons and events. This privileging of often complex diachronic relationships at the expense of synchronic ones construes the existing text as an assemblage of originally discrete parts related to one another in an artful or artificial manner by a final redactor whose activity is always belated and secondary. On the other hand, an orientation towards historic function will reverse the value-system under-lying this terminology of 'original' and 'secondary', asserting the integrated wholeness and the full reality of the final product of the prehistory. The shift, in other words, is from the privileging of the discrete part to the privileging of the part as integrated into the whole.

In a work which helped to establish the dominance of the historical-critical paradigm in English-speaking Old Testament scholarship, S. R. Driver wrote: 'As soon as the book [of Genesis] is studied with sufficient attention, phenomena disclose themselves which show incontrovertibly that it is composed of distinct documents or sources, which have been welded together by a later compiler or redactor into a continuous whole' (*Introduction to the Literature of the Old Testament* (1891), 6). Childs' canonical perspective does not deny the facts here alluded to, but it does sensitize one to the value-system implicit in the metaphorical language in which they are here clothed. It is of the nature of 'documents' to be 'distinct': the mixed metaphor arising from the correlation of the solemn legal term with the technologically-oriented 'welding together' highlights the arbitrariness of this latter process. Still more revealing is the correlation of the technological metaphor with the evocative natural symbolism of the 'source'. The 'source' derives from a time when the world was younger and when writing was less distanced from its ultimate 'source' in nature herself: belated moderns must therefore strive to return *ad fontes*.[8] The technology which 'welded together' the sources serves both to preserve the possibility of the return (so that we remain indebted to it) and to mark the moment of transgression at which the sources were concealed (so that it is an obstacle to be overcome). The 'sources' are the site of primary, primal reality. The artifice of technology constructs from them a product whose secondary, subordinate reality is derived solely from that which it preserves and conceals. The outcome is the relative unreality of the final form of the text, whose veil of illusion one must penetrate in order to attain to reality itself.

The reality of the discrete parts contrasts with the unreality of the whole.

The reorientation proposed by Childs would lead one to abandon the metaphor of the source, connoting a primal reality derived from nature and superior to the half-reality of the products of technology, as a romantic illusion, and to give full value to the technological metaphor. The textual artefact is the product of the welding together of disparate raw materials, and the possibility that the marks of their various origins can sometimes still be faintly discerned in no way detracts from the final text as the primary site of their reality. It is the prehistoric forms of the text which possess only a shadowy reality, and not the final form. That earlier reality has been all but erased in the welding process, and its surviving traces are often ambiguous and subject to the most varied assessments. Even where one does encounter phenomena which, for Driver, pointed so irresistibly to distinct documents, it is their integrated function in the present form of the text rather than their discrete function in hypothetical pre-texts which must be given precedence.

The metaphor of the source is also prominent in the criticism of the gospels, where it can denote both a hypothetical text partially incorporated into existing texts (for example, the Q (*Quelle*) hypothesis) and an existing text (Mark). Any initial impression that source-criticism has affected the study of the gospels less deeply than the study of the pentateuch is refuted by its inescapable presence in most other types of historical-critical operation (the 'quest of the historical Jesus', form-criticism, redaction-criticism). One effect of the abolition of the metaphor of the source here would be to establish the integrity of Matthew and Luke alongside Mark; their genetic relationship with Mark would no longer constitute the hermeneutical key to their interpretation. While scholarship may have made out a good case for Matthew's use of Mark and Q, 'the crucial hermeneutical issue at stake is the role to which this literary insight is assigned in interpreting the present Gospel. The canonical approach contests the literary model which makes the interpretation of Matthew dependent on the exegete's ability to reconstruct the diachronistic relationship between the Gospel and the sources' (*The New Testament as Canon* (1984), 61). The fact that parts of the Gospel of Matthew are reworkings of earlier texts should not so dominate interpretation as to deny the reality of the present whole.

If such references to the unreality of the final form in the historical-critical paradigm seem exaggerated, one might ponder the implications of Barnabas Lindars' claim that 'the effort to get behind the Fourth Gospel is not simply a literary–critical game, but an *inescapable task* in the process of discovering the *real meaning*' (*Behind the Fourth Gospel* (1971), 22, quoted by Childs, *New Testament*, 122; my italics). If diachronic reconstruction is necessary for the recovery of the real meaning, then the final form of the text is steeped in unreality. In the only too probable event that diachronic reconstruction will never adequately represent the actual historical process, we will have to conclude that much of the real meaning of the Gospel of John is lost for ever. This will naturally apply to other biblical texts also, and it is indeed precisely this message of general uncertainty that prolonged exposure to historical–critical practice is likely to convey. One can try, up to a point, to make a virtue out of this necessity, but it is important to note that this uncertainty is the product of a hermeneutic which privileges the study of the discrete parts of the gospels in their diachronic relationships, and that the unreality of the final form is built into the hermeneutical model.

For Childs, however, the reality of the final form of the gospels is more complex than has been suggested so far. The canonical titles – the Gospel according to Matthew, Mark, Luke, John – emphasize both the integrity of the individual texts, in opposition to every attempt at a *Diatessaron*, and the unity of the story as preserved in these four versions. Thus an exegetical emphasis on the separateness of the four accounts, on the points at which difference is particularly noticeable, may meet the first criterion (the integrity of the individual texts) but not the second (their unity). Thus, 'on the one hand, the three Synoptic accounts of Peter's confession cannot be merely fused into a unity. Such a move fails to do justice to the different roles of the individual Gospels and the unique texture of each witness. On the other hand, the critical advice not to attempt to establish any larger canonical relationship beyond that of historical development... does not begin to come to grips with the theological problem of scripture's role for a community of faith' (179). The accounts should be seen as complementary: 'Matthew's famous addition of vv. 17–19 could lead to a distorted theology of the church triumphant unless it is constantly kept in relation to Mark's account of Peter's confession which has closely linked in the one oracle Peter's true confession with the immediate threat of its misunderstanding' (180). On the other hand, Mark's account is also problematic when read in isolation, and Matthew attempts to respond to the problems it raises: 'How can the witness of such fragile tradents who were so prone to the misunderstanding of Christ's message ever become the normative witness for successive generations of Christians?... A sharp distinction is made between Christ's church which is grounded upon an apostolic testimony revealed by God himself, and those fully human disciples who were inclined to error and misunderstanding. The church's acceptance of the authoritative role of the canonical witness rests on the belief that God has chosen to use the testimony of the apostles in such a way as to guide his church in spite of the frailty of the vehicle of revelation' (180). This passage also illustrates another of Childs' emphases: that the canon has not been arbitrarily and extraneously imposed upon the texts, as the historical-critical paradigm tends to assume, but recognizes the claim implied in the texts themselves (here, in Mt.16.17–19). The main point, however, is the concern to integrate the parts into a greater whole (here, the fourfold canonical gospel) in opposition to a hermeneutic which prefers to play them off against each other.

It would be easy to conclude that in such an analysis Childs has simply forgotten his claim to be engaged in a form of *description*; its theologically normative force lies close to the surface. Yet it should be possible to *describe* a complex textual object in which four texts are set alongside side one another without any attempt to integrate them into a single narrative, without any diachronic explanation, and with the expectation that it is a single story that is rendered in this polyphonic manner. Whether Childs has described this object well or badly, he is surely right to claim that, contrary to critical belief, it does exist and is therefore open to descriptive treatment. The fact his description is *motivated* does not disqualify it, since an unmotivated description independent of any interpretative frame or purpose is impossible to imagine.[9]

Concrete and generalized historicity

According to the historical-critical paradigm, a text is bound in perpetuity to its historical circumstances of origin. Any subsequent life that it enjoys will entangle it in misunderstanding and misuse as circumstances change and the manner of its origin is forgotten. There is, in fact, something contrary to the nature of the text in the act of belated reading, unless one acknowledges one's belatedness by reading it as a communicative act directed towards people other than oneself – the original, intended addressees. The fact that in the church (or synagogue) context such self-abnegating reading is structurally impossible is seen as a sign of the contradictoriness of communal usage. Over against this doctrine of the concrete historicity of the text, one might, with Childs, set the equally and necessarily doctrinaire claim that it is church usage that is primary and historical-critical practice that is contradictory. The peculiar historicity of these texts is constituted not genetically but by the fact that they have been uninterruptedly read and reread as authoritative within a particular community. It is by definition the final form of these texts which equips them for and launches them into this historical role, and this final form must therefore be the primary object of investigation, rather than the historical circumstances of origin.[10]

As one of the primary liturgical and devotional texts of the Christian and Jewish communities, the psalms offer an appropriate test-case. According to Childs, 'the crucial historical critical discovery came with the form-critical work of H. Gunkel who established conclusively that the historical settings of the psalms were not to be sought in particular historical events, but in the cultic life of the community' (*Old Testament*, 509). The result was that 'the more sharply the lines of the original sociological context emerged within ancient Israel, the sharper became the rupture with the traditional Jewish–Christian understanding of the Psalter' (510). The traditional messianic psalms now seemed to be directed not towards the future but towards a reigning monarch, and to be closely linked with similar Egyptian and Babylonian texts. The Davidic psalms of book I were anchored in circumstances which included prayers for rain and the exorcism of demons. A hitherto unknown enthronement festival was postulated as the origin of the hymns. 'In the light of this development, it is hardly surprising that the traditional use of the Psalter by the synagogue and church appeared highly arbitrary and far removed from the original function within ancient Israel' (510). Once again we detect the presence of the evaluative schema which identifies reality with the origin and dismisses subsequent usage as unreal.

This gulf between the generalized historicity postulated by liturgical or devotional usage and the concrete historicity postulated by form-criticism is mediated, according to Childs, by the final, canonical form of the text.[11] It is not the case that concrete historicity gives way to a generalized role only by way of a rupture with the text, for the text in its canonical form has already been structured in such a way as to prepare it for this generalized role. Thus, again proceeding descriptively, we note that the canonical collection is prefaced by a psalm in praise of meditation on the Torah, and that 'the present editing of this original Torah psalm has provided the psalm with a new function as the introduction to the whole Psalter... As a heading to the whole Psalter, the blessing now includes the faithful meditation on the sacred writings which follow. The introduction points to these prayers as the medium through which Israel now responds to the divine word. Because Israel continues to hear God's word through the voice of the psalmist's response, these prayers now function as the divine word itself. The original cultic role of the psalms has been subsumed under a larger category of the canon... The introduction is, therefore, the first hint that the original setting has been subordinated to a new theological function for the future generations of worshipping Israel' (513–14). The meaning of Ps. 1 is itself transformed as it is employed as the hermeneutical key to the texts that follow, now conceived not in terms of original function but as a response to God's word which is itself incorporated into that word.

At one point, however, the canonical form appears to introduce its own form of concrete (even if fictitious) historicity, in those psalm titles which associate the psalms with specific events in the life of David: for example, with the occasion 'when he feigned madness before Abimelech, so that he drove him out, and he went away' (Ps. 34), or 'when Nathan the prophet came to him, after he had gone in to Bathsheba' (Ps. 51), or 'when Doeg the Edomite came and told Saul, "David has come to the house of Ahimelech"' (Ps. 52). How are we to understand the redactors' activity here? Childs notes that 'the incidents chosen as evoking the psalms were not royal occasions or representative of the kingly office. Rather, David is pictured simply as a man, indeed chosen by God for the sake of Israel, but who displays all the strengths and weaknesses of all human beings... The effect of this new context has wide hermeneutical implications. The psalms are transmitted as the sacred psalms of David, yet they testify to all the common troubles and joys of ordinary human life in which all persons participate... The effect has been exactly the opposite from what one might have expected. Far from tying these hymns to the ancient past, they have been contemporized and individualized for every generation of suffering and persecuted Israel' (521). These psalm titles indicate that the generalized historicity for which they are preparing the texts is not without its own mode of concretion which anticipates that future readers will derive from their own experience analogies with David's experiences of danger, betrayal or guilt. This concretion operates *within* the generalized historicity of the canonical texts: other examples might be found in the historical note that prefaces most of the prophetic books and in the many contextual indications in the Pauline letters. The canonical function of these instances of concrete historicity is not, however, to legitimate a hermeneutical programme which uses them to render ineffectual the generalized historicity of communal usage. On the contrary, they operate within that broader category.[12]

Childs' opposition to an exaggerated emphasis on concrete historicity leads him to criticize R. E. Brown's approach to the study of the Johannine epistles. Childs notes that 'Brown's exegesis of I John is made to rest completely upon his theoretical reconstruction of the opponents of the author' (*New Testament*, 482); everything the author says is directed against the hypothetical contrary opinions of the 'secessionists'. There are indeed instances of concrete historicity within this text – for example, in the statement about the secession in 2.19 – and yet to make these one's central exegetical principle is, in typical historical-critical fashion, to ignore the fact that the text in its present form and location is part of the canon and therefore relatively independent of its circumstances of origin. One might instead choose to emphasize that this text, generically evidently a letter, nevertheless lacks the characteristic epistolary introduction and conclusion: 'Regardless of how one is to explain the omission, the effect of the present structure of I John is to move its interpretation in exactly the opposite direction from that proposed by Brown, and to universalize its message for the whole church' (487).

It is, in other words, inherent in the genre of (biblical) canonical text to be transmitted in a form which has erased, to a greater or lesser extent, most of the particularities of its circumstances of origin. From the historical-critical point of view, this erasure is both lamented as the loss of the only context which could make satisfactory sense of these texts, and exploited as an invitation to remedy the damage by historical hypothesis and reconstruction. In a canonical perspective, however, the erasure is to be seen as an intentional act rather than a regrettable accident, and welcomed as such, since it subordinates a merely historical curiosity about what was really happening in, say, the Johannine community to the ability of the text to function in quite different later circumstances. The pious hope that the quest for concrete historicity would ultimately serve the contemporary actualization of the text is belied both by the realities of historical-critical practice and – the crucial theoretical point – by the fact that this practice *begins* by ignoring or destroying precisely the vehicle which mediates between situation of origin and subsequent actualization, that is, the canonical form.

Individual and community

The rise of the historical-critical tradition during the nineteenth century coincided with the widespread availability of the idealist schema crystallized by Carlyle in the dictum that 'the history of the world is but the biography of great men'. This schema places over against its individual 'great man' the broad mass of lesser mortals who, even where they are illuminated by the radiance streaming forth from the hero, will not generally be capable of grasping the revelation in all its native originality but will circumscribe, codify, and domesticate it, assimilating it to their existing cultural forms. The essential individuality of genius is lost when it is converted into a common cultural possession; the fire which the hero originally stole from the gods is preserved only in the humdrum mediocrity of the domestic hearth. The community proves unworthy of its geniuses, but it nevertheless preserves their essential being in traditional forms which permit its rediscovery by the great man's invisible ally, the contemporary interpreter. It is possible to detect the enduring influence of this schema in the tendency of the historical-critical paradigm to privilege individuality (the 'authentic') at the expense of the communal (the 'inauthentic' or 'secondary').[13]

Historical-critical investigation showed how 'the authentic poetic tradition of Jeremiah was transformed by cloaking the prophet's message in the later, prose language of the Deuteronomic tradition' (Childs, *Old Testament*, 346). When, for example, we read the lament, 'Wilt thou be to me like a deceitful brook, like waters that fail?' (Jer. 15.18), we can be sure that 'here… we have the genuine words of Jeremiah and an intimate dialogue between him and his God. Here the soul of the prophet is laid bare' (John Paterson, 'Jeremiah' [1962], 548). When, on the other hand, the prophet pronounces in stereotypical language a curse upon 'the man who does not heed the words of this covenant which I commanded your fathers…' (Jer. 11.3–4), we seem to be at one remove from the authentic Jeremiah, in the presence of a circle of disciples influenced by Deuteronomic tradition who have assimilated the unique voice of their master to the traditional formulas. The necessary analysis of the various languages employed in Jeremiah becomes tendentious when the distinction between the 'authentic' and the 'inauthentic' is allowed to determine the exegesis of the entire book: 'Over against this hermeneutical reflex a canonical approach to the book strives to understand the full dimension of the interpreted testimony. Although it does not burden the canonical profile with claims of historicity, it acknowledges the normative theological shaping of the material by the canon. It does not seek to play off the various levels of tradition against each other, but rather follows the leads within the composite as to how the parts relate theologically' (Childs, *Old Testament*, 353). In particular, the canonical shaping sheds light on the relationship between law and prophecy. The book is silent about the much-discussed historical question of Jeremiah's attitude towards the Josianic reform, a matter which is therefore irrelevant to its canonical witness: 'Rather, it placed Jeremiah within the tradition of preachers of the law and provided the later community with a prophetic interpretation of how the law properly functioned within the divine economy. To take this interpretation seriously rules out both an alleged conflict between the law and the prophets, and also a legalistic subordination of the latter into a minor role' (353). An individuality which is left frozen in its own isolation is communally useless; it requires a communal appropriation encompassing both its (relatively) individual traits and a mediating discourse in which those traits are related to broader strata of tradition. The function of the canonical process is not to permit the bourgeois interpreter to construct out of the text an individuality conceived in his or her self-image, for the purpose of intimate communion; it is 'to mediate the prophetic word for every future generation' (354).

The underlying presence of the schema of the great man in the nineteenth-century quest of the historical Jesus – and, in modified form, in its twentieth-century continuation – is signalled at the outset of Schweitzer's celebrated survey. In the quest of the historical Jesus, we are 'dealing with the most vital thing in the world's history', since he still reigns as 'the alone Great and alone True', 'the prime example of that antithesis between spiritual and natural truth which underlies all life and all events, and in Him emerges into the field of history' (*Quest of the Historical Jesus* (ET 1910), 2). He is, however, not quite alone in his greatness, for the theology which strives to recover that greatness from the dead wood of tradition also participates in it: German theology is 'a great, a unique phenomenon in the mental and spiritual life of our time', and 'the greatest achievement of German theology is the critical investigation of the life of Jesus' (1). True greatness can be recognized only by the true greatness which it helps to call forth. This rhetoric of superlatives is valuable in disclosing, in its thematic of a decontextualized, dematerialized 'greatness' in which the personal incarnates the transcendent, one of the ideological roots of the scholarly obsession with salvaging precious 'authentic' material from the mass of inferior tradition in which it has been buried. Even the quite different and more sober rhetoric of the 'new quest' betrays the presence of the same idealist schema when, for example, an authority is vested in the authentic words and practice of Jesus which is denied to the productions of the early church.

Childs touches on these issues in an excursus on the interpretation of the parables near the end of his work on the New Testament. He criticizes Jeremias' claim that 'the authoritative form of the gospel for the Christian church is to be located in the reconstructed *ipsissima verba* of Jesus', and notes that many other scholars 'agree in placing the highest value on the actual words of Jesus and deprecating the subsequent history of the church's transmission as full of misunderstanding and distortion' (*New Testament*, 537). While it is true that 'one can at times easily discern stages in the growth of certain of the parables' (536), it is another thing altogether to evaluate the earliest material positively and the later negatively: 'The various elements of growth, embellishment, and alteration which Jeremias has so carefully described should not be dismissed as distorting accretion, but rather considered as an aid in understanding the special nature of the church's construal of Jesus' message' (540).

This account of Child's hermeneutical proposal has emphasized the sense in which his procedure remains *descriptive*, despite the normative theological claims that are never far away. His primary achievement is to establish the *reality* of the object of that description, the canonical text as preserved and used in the Jewish community and/or Christian church, in opposition to a hermeneutic which systematically denies that reality or renders it invisible in its quest for an allegedly 'deeper' reality somewhere in the present text's prehistory.[14] We must now address the issue of the relation of the hermeneutical argument to Childs' rather traditional protestant commitment to the sole sufficiency and normativity of holy scripture for the church. Is this theological commitment necessarily entailed in the hermeneutic? I shall suggest that this is not the case.[15]

In the final, canonical form of the text, the redactors prepared it for an authoritative role within a communal context. Phenomenological description of the sacred scriptures of the two religious communities can make this fact visible, and it can also encompass the fact that these texts continue to fulfil that communal role to this day. What Childs does not notice, however, is the fact that the canon fails to make the abstract notion of an 'authoritative role' concrete. Far from bringing interpretative conflict to an end by excluding aberrant texts, the canon merely establishes a new field for interpretative conflict. In the harmonious and orderly world constructed by Childs, the canonical texts are unfailingly helpful in mediating the many-sided will of God to the reader or hearer who is located within the community of faith. In reality, however, the act of reading or hearing will always be enmeshed in interpretative conflicts about how the 'authoritative role' is to be actualized. The canon, in other words, is a necessary but not a sufficient mediation between the 'original texts' and the present. It offers the texts for use in the present, it tells us that we ought to use them in our own theological tasks, but it does not tell us how we are to do so. It does not tell us, for example, that – as Childs seems to imply – the texts are all essentially on a level, and that the truth they offer lies not in the individual text but in the complementarity and balance established by the entire collection. It neither forbids nor prescribes a preference for Job over the Torah, John over the synoptics, Paul over the gospels. It does not tell us whether or not we should allow certain Jewish texts written in Greek rather than Hebrew to add their contributions to the debate. It gives no guidance as to how to cope with its apparent contradictions, improbabilities, and other difficulties. It offers no clear answer to the question whether its 'authority' is unique and absolute or whether it is to be co-ordinated with other kinds of authority. Its division into two parts is the clearest possible mark of the still more fundamental hermeneutical rift over the issue of the sufficiency of the first part or its need for supplementation by a second – a rift institutionalized by the two main conflicting forms of 'the canon', in the face of which the notion of a unitary canon seems an ahistorical abstraction. Hermeneutically significant though the canon may be, it does not tell us which community we should belong to in order to receive the full benefits of its witness, nor does it enable us to escape the interpretative dilemmas

with which actual communal membership has already burdened us. Participation in a community in which 'the canon' is operative is consistent both
with the belief that Jesus was a deceiver who sought to lead the people astray
and who has done untold harm in the world, and with the belief that the
entire canonical literature points to him as its centre and goal. The form of
the canon presupposed in this latter belief has served on occasion to
legitimate the ideological and material harrassment and oppression of
adherents of the other form. It is one thing to describe the formal outlines
of the canonical object, over against an interpretative tradition which has
rendered it invisible; it is quite another to assert, as Childs does, the *adequacy*
and the *sufficiency* of the canon for guidance of the community into the
truth.[16]

Childs' belief in the sufficiency of the canon appears to commit him to
the view that the history of conflict in which it is entangled was the result
of avoidable error, that it originates in a culpable decision to permit the
intrusion of extraneous elements into the discursive field. He is concerned
with the function of the canon within the (Jewish/Christian) community,
and the reason why its conflict-laden history within empirical communities
is never acknowledged is that he is operating with a concept of an *ideal*
community of faith to which real communities only occasionally and
imperfectly correspond. Thus we are told in a typical formulation that 'the
canonical shape of Genesis serves the community of faith and practice as a
truthful witness to God's activity on its behalf in creation and blessing,
judgment and forgiveness, redemption and promise' (*Old Testament*, 158).
This statement is not incorrect, but it is one-sided. Since 'the community
of faith and practice' refers only to the ideal dimension of existing
communities, the fact that Genesis in its canonical form has always been a
site of interpretative conflict is ignored. In the history of interpretation we
encounter readings which appeal to one or another aspect of this text in
support of the substitution of the Christian for the Jewish community as the
true people of God, the divine right of kings, the sanctity of patriarchal
marriage, fundamentalist pseudo-science, apartheid, and Zionism. Each of
these readings is located within specific social practices, and each of them
evokes counter-readings from those adversely affected by those practices.
Yet Childs' ideal 'community of faith and practice' is oblivious to the
function of the canonical text as a site of ideological conflict. It is alone with
the text, free from and untrammelled by historical realities. Naturally its
members, being human, must also participate in these realities, but their
essential life lies outside them in their communion with the perfect, all-
sufficient text which mediates the divine will and activity.[17]

Childs' important hermeneutical proposal locates the texts in their proper ecclesial context, but misconstrues that context as a self-contained, autonomous space isolated from the world. In fact, the world permeates that space, and the 'truthful witness' offered by the canonical text cannot simply be read off its surface but must be given and discovered in the midst and in the depths of the conflict-ridden situations in which it is inevitably entangled.

Chapter 3

Multiplicity and Coherence

The preceding discussions of Frei and Childs have pointed both to the importance of their hermeneutical proposals and to problems in the way that the text, newly independent from its historical circumstances of origin, is correlated with the church and the world. In neither case is there any significant recognition of the hermeneutical significance of the location of the church within the world; and in the case of Frei even the transition from the literary plane to the ecclesial–theological one is problematic, if the question of the truth of the texts is regarded as constitutive of the latter. The question of 'truth' – that is, an appropriate theological understanding of reference – will have to be deferred to later chapters. This chapter and the following one will respectively address two important issues that arise out of the discussion thus far, with the aim of further clarifying the decision in favour of the final form of the text and establishing this as the basis for the more explicitly theological perspective of the chapters that follow. If the text is to be properly correlated with the world, then it is necessary to incorporate a realistic socio-political orientation into the synchronic, 'literary' perspective (chapter 4); there is a danger otherwise that the text will be treated as a self-contained aesthetic object. First, however, the objection must be addressed that the marginalizing of conventional historical concerns simply evades the important questions they raise. I shall argue that, far from being an evasion, a synchronic, 'literary' perspective may be seen as a response to intractable problems within the historical-critical paradigm itself – problems that compel one to ask whether much of the work carried out within this paradigm is of any real scholarly value. As in later chapters, exploration of hermeneutical or theological problems will involve not only theoretical considerations but also exegetical practice, in order to *show* – and not just to assert – that a genuinely different exegetical practice is a real possibility.

There is no reason in principle why diachronic and synchronic perspectives should not complement rather than contradict each other, and in certain respects it is theologically important that they should do so. To exclude historical considerations entirely would result in a seriously deficient theology. But it may be important not to accept too readily the conciliatory view that historically-oriented interpretation *as currently practised* can co-exist harmoniously with the newer synchronic perspectives. In discussing a sample of scholarly views on a representative historical-critical issue (identification of variant traditions in Gen. 37), my intention is not to determine which of them offers the best explanation of the phenomena of the text but to analyse the means whereby a 'position' on such an issue is constructed.[1] I shall suggest that the plurality of scholarly opinions on a given topic may be in principle irreducible, and that the regulative goal of a future consensus may therefore be unattainable. Monographs, commentaries and articles accumulate, but the proliferation of positions and the constant deferment of the hoped-for consensus may be indicative not of progress but of circularity.

The disillusionment stemming from the perception that particular claims to progress conceal a fundamental circularity is perhaps the main pragmatic reason for the decision to adopt a radically different interpretative paradigm, in which the phenomena that the old approach failed to explain are reread from within a new perspective. There is, however, no logically compelling way from one paradigm to another. As Thomas Kuhn has argued, 'the competition between paradigms is not the sort of battle that can be resolved by proofs', and 'the transfer of allegiance from paradigm to paradigm is a conversion experience that cannot be forced' (*The Structure of Scientific Revolutions* (1970[2]), 148, 151). What is at stake is not simply 'relative problem-solving ability' but the question 'which paradigm should in future guide research' (157). Also at stake, therefore, is 'a choice between incompatible modes of community life' (94).

In Gen. 37.25, after his brothers have consigned Joseph to a pit, they see 'a caravan of Ishmaelites coming from Gilead'. This gives Judah the idea of selling Joseph rather than killing him, a suggestion that the brothers accept. The scene is set for the moment of sale, but at this point the reader encounters an unexpected difficulty: 'Then Midianite traders passed by; and they drew Joseph up and lifted him out of the pit, and sold him to the Ishmaelites for twenty shekels of silver; and they took Joseph to Egypt' (v. 28). Did the Midianite traders thwart the brothers' plan by reaching the pit first and selling Joseph to the Ishmaelites themselves?[2] In that case, why is there no mention of the brothers' frustration and anger? Alternatively, does 'they drew' refer to the brothers, and are the Midianite traders to be identified with the Ishmaelites? Presumably this identification is correct, for

v. 36 reports that the *Midianites* (and not the Ishmaelites) sold Joseph in Egypt, whereas 39.1 ascribes the sale to the Ishmaelites. But if these two terms are synonymous, what is the point of the gratuitously confusing difference in terminology?

The allegorical tradition of Philo and Origen saw such stumbling-blocks on the surface of the biblical text as a fissure through which the initiated elite might pass so as to behold the true, hidden meaning of the text behind the letter. Classical source criticism propagated a suitably modernized version of this hermeneutic, finding in Gen. 37.28 the point at which the whole chapter (and, by implication, the whole Joseph story) split into two relatively self-contained narratives. Summarizing the account of W. O. E. Oesterley and T. H. Robinson, written during the heyday of source-critical confidence, we start from the assumption that the problematic references to Ishmaelites and Midianites are incompatible (*An Introduction to the Old Testament* (1934, 29–31). In the second part of v. 28, the brothers sell Joseph to the Ishmaelites, as they had previously decided; in the first part, Midianites remove him from the pit, without any sale. Having established this starting-point for division, other doublets come into view. Two reasons are given for the brothers' hatred of Joseph: Jacob's favouritism, manifested in the special coat, and Joseph's dreams. Two brothers intervene to save Joseph's life: Reuben has him placed in a pit, and Judah recommends the sale to the Ishmaelites. Thus, assembling this information into separate narratives, in one story Joseph's dreams arouse his brothers' jealousy and they decide to kill him. Reuben saves him by having him placed in the pit, from which he is removed in the brothers' absence by Midianite traders. On returning to the now empty pit, Reuben despairs at the loss of his brother and, on the return home, Jacob mourns the loss of his son. In the other version, the special coat is the mark of Jacob's favouritism. His brothers plot to kill Joseph, but having removed his coat they accede to Judah's suggestion that he be sold to a passing caravan of Ishmaelites. The coat is dipped in goat's blood as a sign to Jacob of his son's death.

The Midianite version is interested in Reuben, and this suggests that its provenance was northern Israel; the Ishmaelite version's interest in Judah suggests a Judean origin. The criterion of the divine name cannot be used here to distinguish the narratives, but a link may be made with the doublets in Gen. 12.10–20 and Gen. 20 (Sarah's removal into a royal harem). Here the criterion of the divine name leads the earlier narrative to be allocated to J. The second narrative speaks of 'God' rather than of 'Yahweh', yet seems otherwise much closer stylistically to J than to P. In this narrative, the truth is revealed to Abimelech in a dream, and the corresponding interest in revelatory dreams in Gen. 37 suggests that the 'Midianite' story is to be linked with Gen. 20 in a special source generally designated as 'E' (Elohistic).

In Gerhard von Rad's commentary, the explanatory power of the documentary hypothesis has begun to ebb, at least as regards this chapter. Von Rad does not believe that the two causes of the brothers' hatred necessarily stem from two sources: 'One could prefer to consider this complex motivation, so true to life, as an indication of the successive, preliterary growth of the material in the Joseph story' (*Genesis* (ET 1972[9]), 350). Thus vv. 3–11 (the coat and the dreams) are seen essentially as a unity setting forth the problem out of which the whole narrative will grow – 'not so much the external circumstances within the framework of which the story will move as the inward tensions which must be seen if what follows is to be understood rightly' (352). In the second half of the chapter, however, the traditional source division remains intact: in the J version Joseph is sold to the Ishmaelites at Judah's suggestion, in the E version he is stolen by the Midianites from the pit where he has been placed following Reuben's intervention (353). A further difficulty is noted in vv. 21–22. When Reuben heard of his brothers' plot against Joseph, 'he delivered him out of their hands, saying, "Let us not take his life"' (v. 21). The following verse simply repeats this: 'And Reuben said to them, "Shed no blood…"' (v. 22). The new start signified by 'And Reuben said to them…' overlooks the fact that Reuben is already speaking, and it is just such difficulties that lead to source-division. Such a division would, however, be unwelcome here, for it would suggest that Reuben intervened to save Joseph's life in *two* versions of the story, leading to the complication either of a second Reuben source or to the presence of Reuben in J (the Judah/Ishmaelite source) as well as in E (the Midianite one).[3] Both theories would mar somewhat the attractive symmetry and tidiness of the consistent two-source hypothesis. Von Rad suggests emending 'Reuben' in v. 21 to 'Judah' to solve the problem (353).

Claus Westermann provides a final example of a conventional tradition–historical reading of this chapter. Westermann follows the current tendency to reject an analysis of the Joseph story in terms of the documentary hypothesis, but continues to argue for the presence of identifiable variants and additions.[4] There is in fact a basic similarity of approach between his observations and those of scholars who employ the documentary hypothesis here. Joseph's dreams (37.5–11) are seen as a later addition breaking the original link between v. 4 (where the coat is the cause of the brothers' hatred) and v. 12 (where the scene is set for Joseph's departure from the safety of the paternal home): 'Following the narrative law of the single strand (*Einlinigkeit*, H. Gunkel) it is to be assumed that this [i.e. the coat as the sign of favouritism] was the only cause of conflict in the underlying story' (*Genesis*

37–50 (ET 1986), 35). This reverts in part to the analysis of Oesterley and Robinson, although supported now not by a coherent source hypothesis but by a 'narrative law' which excludes repetition. (What is the status of this law? If the redactor of chapter 37 does not recognize it, why should anyone else have done so?) In v. 22, 'And Reuben said to them' is probably an addition (41), and the familiar distinction is again made between a Reuben/ Midianite variant and a Judah/Ishmaelite one: it is the latter which is the intruder into an otherwise coherent narrative (42). The resulting incoherence derives not only from the Ishmaelite/Midianite problem but also from Reuben's surprise at not finding Joseph in the pit (v. 29), although he is not excluded from participation in Judah's plot. 'The narrator of the Joseph story obviously intends to let his listeners know that he has at his disposal two versions of how Joseph came down to Egypt and will let both speak' (40).

These three approaches to the tradition–history of Gen. 37 are agreed in explaining the Ishmaelite/Midianite problem in terms of variants, but otherwise they go their separate ways. Each of them has a certain plausibility; they all respond to real phenomena of the text, they are not arbitrary, and yet they are incompatible with one another. This incompatibility does not stem only from the fact that the earlier scholars employed the documentary hypothesis here, for most of their observations can readily be restated independently of that comprehensive framework. Rather than immediately declaring a preference for the text in its final form, it is worth reflecting on the implications of this interpretative situation, exploring the possibility that in this case (and no doubt in others too) the hypothetical solutions to the problems the interpretative tradition sets itself are *irreducibly plural*; that is, that there are no adequate grounds for even a provisional decision in favour of one solution over the others. That does not exclude the possibility of a decision against a particular tradition–historical hypothesis. If, for example, Joseph's two dreams were assigned to different sources in accordance with the narrative law of *Einlinigkeit*, it would be possible to reject this suggestion on the basis of Pharaoh's two dreams in Gen. 41, together with the explanation that 'the doubling of Pharaoh's dream means that the thing is fixed by God and God will shortly bring it to pass' (v. 32). The irreducible plurality of solutions to a problem does not imply a complete relativism in which any solution is as good as any other. It implies that, even after less plausible solutions have been eliminated, adequate criteria for judging between the solutions that remain will be lacking.

Since none of the three solutions summarized here has access to new information denied to the others, we may say that they all share the same set of possibilities, just as the players in a game of chess start with the same set of pieces. Their differences arise out of decisions to deploy one piece rather than another, to make one possibility rather than another the key to the solution of a particular difficulty. One solution deploys the fact (recognized by all the players) that the Joseph narrative is different in character from the earlier patriarchal narratives; this fact is set in opposition to earlier attempts to incorporate this narrative into a comprehensive source-hypothesis. This is obviously the move of a competent rather than an incompetent player, but it is not clear that it is a move that all competent players are obliged to make. It remains open to the defenders of a traditional source-critical analysis to argue that many of the phenomena that are said to support the conventional analysis in Gen. 1–36 (anomalies, doubling, and so on) are also present here, and that this fact (again recognized by all) favours a comprehensive explanation.[5] The admitted difference between the Joseph story and the rest of Genesis is compatible with the view that both J and E included an earlier version of this connected narrative alongside their other material. In other words, one player deploys this particular piece while another refrains from doing so, and there are good but not compelling reasons for both decisions.

At one point plurality does seem to be reducible to unanimity, the differentiation between the Reuben/Midianite and the Judah/Ishmaelite strands. The interpreters disagree about how important a role to assign to this move, about whether or not it opens up further moves; but they agree that, in itself, it is a move that should be made. But has plurality really been excluded here? We recall that in Gen. 37.21–22 there is evidence of *two* Reuben sources. Twice in consecutive verses Reuben appeals to his brothers not to take Joseph's life, and the introduction to the second verse ('And Reuben said to them') is redundant. The repetition and the interjection of the superfluous introductory phrase would in another context count as clear criteria for source-division. V. 22 refers to the pit, an essential stage-prop in the Midianite version of the story; v. 21 does not refer to it, and is compatible with the version in which Judah proposes the sale of Joseph to the Ishmaelites. Thus (one might argue), in one version Reuben alone seeks to save Joseph's life, whereas in the other he and Judah both do so. The possibility of linking the sons of Jacob in pairs is confirmed by the depiction of the joint action of Simeon and Levi in 34.25, again undertaken in defence of the family. This view – again, possible but not compelling – actualizes a possibility that the other players are presumably aware of but tacitly agree to overlook. Oesterley and Robinson do not mention it; von Rad suggests that the redactor has in v. 21 substituted 'Reuben' for 'Judah'; and Westermann regards the superfluous introductory phrase in v. 22 as a later gloss. The consensus over the differentiation of a Reuben and a Judah version is, in fact, artificially constructed by suppressing a piece of evidence that might complicate an attractively simple picture. Even in this showcase example of successful source analysis, an adequately grounded unanimity is unattainable and we cannot escape the irreducible plurality of the possible solutions.

An interpretation that gave due weight to such considerations would have no alternative but to set out a representative range of possibilities and to resist the convention that plural possibilities must always be reduced to the singularity of a provisional preferred solution. On Joseph's dreams, for example, one would have to say that a source analysis ascribing this explanation of the brothers' hatred to E is indeed a possibility. But, having laid out a coherent analysis of the entire chapter on this basis, the interpreter would then have to retract it. It must not be allowed to solidify in the reader's mind, for it is only one possibility among others. This section (vv. 5–11), breaking the connection between v. 4 and v. 12, may have been added as a programmatic anticipation of the course of the entire narrative; analysis into J and E strands may be irrelevant here. Or vv. 5-11 may be an integral part of the original narrative, intended not only to anticipate the future course of the narrative but also to represent the brothers' escalating hatred. These three representative views are typical of the range of alternatives on offer, and the role of the interpreter would be not only to state them but also to ensure that, by sleight of hand, a possibility does not begin to harden into a probability.

It is very unlikely that the resolute, principled scepticism of such a mode of interpretation could ever become popular. The role of the interpreter, it is held, is not just to set out possibilities but to make decisions, whether firm or tentative; for much of the legitimacy of the historical-critical project rests on the claim that it is able to provide not merely speculative possibilities (as its opponents have always asserted) but *results*. The consumer of this product does not wish to be left floating aimlessly in a sea of proliferating possibilities. He or she soon tires of the discussion and demands the satisfaction of closure, even if awareness of the possibilities canvassed by other interpreters reveals that even a tentative closure is premature. In a postmodern era, a detective story in which possibilities endlessly proliferate without any final resolution is certainly thinkable, but the sensibility required to appreciate its subtleties is still rare. Many readers will find it tedious, and for the foreseeable future it will be outsold by the conventional product which offers its consumers the satisfaction of a final unmasking of the truth, even if that 'truth' bears unmistakeable traces of artifice. In the case of scholarly biblical interpretation, that artifice is tacitly acknowledged in the tendency to link a particular solution indissolubly with the name of the scholar who originated it. We do not find ourselves in an impersonal realm of accepted results, developed and tested by a united scholarly community. We have 'von Rad's view', 'Westermann's view', and so on, and these individualized 'views' fulfil the dual function of formally preserving the ever-receding possibility of a final consensus while challenging potential players to try their hand at outwitting the established masters of the game by skilful redeployment of the pieces. Thus the game is perpetuated. It will always seem that there is new work to be done even in the most traditional of areas, for a slightly different arrangement of the pieces will always be a possibility for a moderately skilful and inventive player.

If conventional critical techniques result in an irreducible plurality that cannot be seen as a slow, painstaking approach towards an adequate solution, can the chapter in question be read as a single, relatively coherent narrative? And how would such a reading perspective affect the phenomena noted by source analysis?

In traditional source criticism, the main problem of Gen. 37 is the separation of two principal narrative strands (J and E). But the Joseph story is said to open with an excerpt from P: 'This is the history of the family of Jacob [*ēlleh tôl'dôth ya'aqōb*]. Joseph, being seventeen years old, was shepherding the flock with his brothers; he was a lad with the sons of Bilhah and Zilpah, his father's wives; and Joseph brought their evil talk to their father' (37.2). Von Rad comments: 'Obviously P follows a different tradition about the origin of dissension between Joseph and his brothers... The note remains a torso' (*Genesis*, 350). But, if the redactor has indeed wrenched this note out of its original context in the hypothetical priestly document, there are a number of points at which it is remarkably appropriate to its new context. The reference to Joseph's age characterizes the dreamer of vv. 5–11 as relatively youthful: the dreams are precocious anticipations of an adult destiny. The reference to shepherding prepares for v. 12, where the brothers' pasturing the flock near Shechem sets the scene for the crime out of which the whole narrative will develop. The report on the 'evil talk' of just four of Jacob's sons cannot in itself explain 'the origin of the dissension between Joseph and his brothers' but nevertheless hints at the problem of fraternal dissension with which the story will be chiefly concerned. Finally, a special relationship between Jacob and Joseph is already implied. In one sense, this note does not lead anywhere; there is no mention of Jacob's reaction or any other sequel. In another sense, it serves as a prelude to the continuous narrative that will begin immediately afterwards, introducing in outline several of its most important themes.[6]

In the passage that follows, we learn that Joseph's brothers come to hate him because of the coat (a symbol of paternal favouritism) and because of his dreams. While it is possible to see here alternative explanations of the brothers' hatred, the only text we possess does not do so. 'When his brothers saw that their father loved him more than all his brothers, they hated him, and could not speak peaceably to him' (v. 4). Next, 'Joseph had a dream, and when he told it to his brothers they only hated him the more' (v. 5). Hatred is represented here not as a static attitude but as escalating, out of control, towards the outbreak of hostile action that will tear the family apart. The growth of hatred is again underlined after the account of the first dream when the narrator reports that 'they hated him *yet more* for his dream and his words' (v. 8b). Tension mounts still higher when an account of a second dream follows, and this time even the doting father feels bound to remonstrate while the brothers maintain an ominous silence.

The coat signifies the favouritism of the father, of which Joseph is the passive object. At first, the brothers hate Joseph only because of what he represents through paternal favouritism: their own exclusion from the father's love. It is the action of the father that evokes hatred of the object of that action; hatred arises 'when his brothers saw that their father loved him more...' (v. 4). In the dream narratives, however, Joseph indicates that he has internalized the exalted status bestowed on him by the father. His own self-image has become conformed to the paternal image of the favourite son. As the father exalts the son and humiliates his brothers through the gift of the coat, so the son now claims transcendent sanction for this situation of inequality. His sheaf stood upright while theirs gathered round it and bowed down to it. Even if this is dismissed as a fantasy born of a naïve will to power, the fact that it is externalized in the verbal form of a *claim* to power is reason enough for hatred; and in any case the possibility cannot be ruled out that the dream may actually be *true*. Angry incredulity is fuelled in part by the secret fear that the dream really did occur as a revelation from a transcendent source.

Thus the coat and the dreams complement one another. The dreams on their own would not evoke such hatred if they were not grounded in the objective fact of paternal favouritism as signified by the coat. The coat in itself prevents the brothers from speaking peaceably to Joseph but will hardly lead them to kill him. Hatred escalates as an external mark of an elect status is internalized and projected into the natural world and into the heavens. The coat and the dreams are also complementary in their functioning during the rest of the narrative. They can be set alongside one another as equal causes of offence. As the narrator's point of view shifts from the wandering Joseph to the brothers, they identify him not in terms of the coat but in terms of the dreams: 'Here comes this lord of the dreams [*baʿal haḥᵃlōmōth*]' (v. 19). Yet, as they reverse the content of the dreams by abasing him and exalting themselves over him, they must also strip him of his coat, 'the long robe with sleeves that he wore' (v. 23). The dreams and the coat together are the symbols of their humiliation which must both be confronted. From this point on, however, the symbolism of the two entities diverges. The coat, dipped in blood, comes to signify not the exaltation but the death of the beloved son; but it also signifies the unstable restoration of the unity of the family, threatened by the dreams, on the basis of the expulsion of one of its members and the deception of the father. (Here, oddly, history repeats itself, for Jacob had once deceived his own father by way of a garment.) The brothers have now seized control of this symbol, but it is not yet clear that the threat of the dreams has been averted by the reversal of their message of exaltation and humiliation achieved by placing Joseph in the pit. While Joseph is alive, the possibility remains that the divine purpose implied by the dreams will be fulfilled, and that this fulfilment will now occur, ironically, by way of the brothers' hostile act.

In the narrative that we possess, therefore, the coat and the dreams are intimately bound up with one another and any attempt to allocate them to different narratives is beside the point. The present form of the text has erased its own prehistory, and the occasional trace of that prehistory that still shows through is simply a sign of the reality and the comprehensiveness of that act of erasure.

The coat and the dreams constitute the primary symbolism of the Joseph narrative, representing the interplay between exaltation and deception which the narrative will continue to unfold. But a literary approach must also demonstrate its fruitfulness in dealing with the minor details of the text. One such, already noted, is the phrase, 'And Reuben said to them' (v. 22), included despite the fact that Reuben was the speaker in the previous verse. This minor anomaly is not susceptible only of a tradition–historical solution, for its effect on the final form of the narrative must also be examined. The brothers' hatred has been raised to its highest intensity by Joseph's dream reports, and his acceptance of his father's commission to visit them, far from the safety of the paternal home, creates in the reader a sense of apprehension. Thus it comes as no surprise when Joseph's imminent arrival leads to the plot to kill him. 'But when Reuben heard it, he delivered him out of their hands, saying, "Let us not take his life." And Reuben said to them, "Shed no blood; cast him into this pit here in the wilderness, but lay no hand upon him" – that he might rescue him out of their hand, to restore him to his father' (vv. 21–22). The effect of the apparently superfluous phrase ('And Reuben said to them') is to insert a pause between the two verses. In v. 21 Reuben simply urges the pure negation of his brothers' scheme: 'Let us not take his life.' The dramatic pause inserted by the additional introductory formula signifies the transition from the negation of one projected future to the affirmation of an alternative future. Pure negation is insufficient, for the tension must somehow be resolved; and Reuben therefore suggests the symbolic humiliation represented by the pit. Meanwhile, the reader's view of the brothers has had to be revised. Previously they have been united in their implacable hatred. Now one of them, the eldest, is detached from the consensus; he plays no part in the initial plot, his first intervention ensures that the plot is not fulfilled, and his second intervention suggests a compromise future in which family harmony is restored by means of an act of purely symbolic violence. The detachment of Reuben from the consensus takes place *retrospectively*, for there is nothing in the description of the plot in vv. 18–20 to suggest that the brothers are anything other than unanimous.[7]

The reference to the 'Midianite traders' (*'ᵃnāshîm midyanîm sōḥᵃrîm*) remains hard to read. The passage describing the sale of Joseph would make coherent sense if the phrase 'then Midianite traders passed by' were omitted, and the assumption that it stems from the prehistory of the narrative may be correct.[8] The final narrator suggests that the terms 'Ishmaelites' and 'Midianites' may be interchangeable: Joseph is sold in Egypt to Potiphar by 'Midianites' (37.36: *mᵉdanîm*) and/or by 'Ishmaelites' (39.1), and the possibility that the Midianites pre-empted the brothers' plan to sell Joseph to the Ishmaelites is thus falsified by the later course of the narrative. The third person plural ('and they drew Joseph out of the pit and sold him to the Ishmaelites' (37.28)) must therefore refer to the brothers, although the prior reference to the Midianites makes this awkward.[9] The verb 'passed by' does contribute to the progress of the narrative in the sense that it marks the moment of decision: the caravan is no longer moving towards the brothers, as in v. 25 ('And looking up they saw a caravan of Ishmaelites coming from Gilead'), and it will shortly be moving away from them. Are the Midianite traders conceived of as one distinct element in the Ishmaelite caravan? If so, the Midianites would be Ishmaelites, but not all Ishmaelites would be Midianites. According to Gen. 25.2, Midian was one of the sons of Abraham whom Keturah bore to him, after Sarah's death. He was only indirectly related to Ishmael, but was sent by Abraham 'eastward to the east country', along with his brothers (25.6). Since this vague geographical reference places Midian in the vicinity of Ishmael and his descendants (25.12–18), it is possible that the narrator understands the term 'Ishmaelite' to include all the descendants of Abraham whose line does not run through Isaac. (Midianites are said to be 'Ishmaelites' in Judg. 8.24.) Be that as it may, there is an ironic appropriateness about the presence of descendants of Ishmael and Midian at this particular juncture. Ishmael and Midian were both expelled from the family of Abraham in order to protect the chosen son (21.8–14, 25.6). Years later, in the person of their descendants, they return and exact their revenge. By their arrival at the critical moment, they secure the expulsion of the chosen son himself, whom they buy and sell as a slave. Indeed, it is possible that a third of the excluded sons of Abraham is also present here, in addition to Ishmael and Midian. The reference to *ᵃnashîm midyanîm* ('Midianite men') in v. 28 is slightly altered in v. 36, where Joseph is sold by *mᵉdanîm* ('Medanites'). The consonant *yod* has perhaps dropped out accidentally, but as it stands the text of v. 36 refers to the descendants of Medan, another of the sons of Abraham and Keturah (25.2). He too was expelled, and he too has now returned to exact his revenge. The collusion between these three sons of Abraham and the ten sons of Jacob may have as its underlying ground the fact that the chosen son constitutes a threat (of humiliation) to the latter just as his predecessor in this role had constituted a threat (of expulsion) to the former. Such an interpretation can perhaps hardly have been 'intended' by the narrator, since it may well arise out of fortuitous circumstances such as textual variants and discrepancies of spelling. But just as, in the world of the narrative, the presence of the Ishmaelites and Midianites is both a chance event and essential for the development of the plot, so chance events of textual transmission can create the possibility of new symmetries.

In distinguishing a Midianite from an Ishmaelite strand, source analysis also detaches Reuben and Judah, who both independently fulfil the role of rescuing Joseph from the plot to kill him. A reading of the final form of the text must, however, make sense of the presence of both brothers within the narrative. In v. 29, Reuben returns to the pit, seeking to rescue his brother and to restore him to his father, as v. 22 indicates; but to his surprise and horror he finds that Joseph is no longer there. In the hypothetical earlier form of the narrative, Joseph has disappeared because, unknown to all the brothers, he has been stolen by the Midianites. In the present form, Reuben's surprise distinguishes him from Judah and other brothers, who have sold Joseph to the Ishmaelites for twenty shekels of silver. When he returns to his brothers, saying, 'The lad is gone; and I, where shall I go?' (v. 30), the brothers know very well that the lad is gone since they are responsible for his disappearance. Nothing is said in the account of the sale about Reuben's absence, and this results in exactly the same literary device as we noted in vv. 18–22: the retrospective detachment of an individual from the group. It emerges after the event that Reuben had been absent when Judah and the others planned and carried out the sale, just as his absence from the initial plot to kill Joseph emerges only retrospectively. On the first occasion, Reuben's will prevails: Joseph is not killed. However, the second occasion marks the failure of his plan to restore Joseph to his father. Far from their fulfilling the same role, Judah outwits Reuben by means of the sale.[10]

This discussion has shown that, in a case where historical criticism proves unable to solve the problems it sets itself, the textual phenomena that give rise to these problems may be more satisfactorily integrated into a different reading perspective. However, since 'literary' readings such as this one are now commonplace, and since they do not in themselves meet the need for a theological perspective, the emphasis should perhaps fall on the negative dimension of the argument. The questions that historical-critical approaches raise are frequently open to multiple possible answers.[11] This multiplicity emerges gradually as scholarly investigation of an issue develops, and this gradual development creates the impression that what is taking place is *progress*. Such an impression is, of course, not necessarily false. After exhaustive testing over a prolonged period, more recent solutions may well be found to be more adequate than those that preceded them. Yet the impression of progress is illusory if what comes to light when scholarly solutions are tested is sheer multiplicity, as the combination of acute observation with speculative hypothesis proves in each case unable to command other interpreters' assent. What is remarkable is the tenacity with which the possibility of a convincing solution is maintained as one possible but unpersuasive solution is followed by another. But there must come a point at which the multiplicity of possible solutions undermines this tenacious faith. On what grounds do we believe that a final solution, so convincing as to bring to an end the multiplication of hypotheses, is actually attainable? Sooner or later, the zeal with which one catalogues attempted solutions and anatomizes their respective strengths and shortcomings must surely begin to flag? One would then begin to ask oneself how much has really been achieved by this prodigious expenditure of scholarly time and energy, and whether a solution is any nearer than when the initial question was first mooted. Yet no-one wishes to admit having laboured in vain, and there is therefore a certain pressure to preserve the place of a well-worn, time-honoured 'problem' on the scholarly agenda and a reluctance to consign it to the oblivion it may deserve. New recruits constantly come forward to testify that the problem, while extremely difficult, is also extremely important; that, while we are nowhere near a consensus, definite progress has been made; and that further investment of time and energy in this area is positively demanded.

   One of the merits of contemporary emphasis on the final form of the biblical text is that it breaks out of the vicious circles that revolve perpetually around the various so-called 'problems' acknowledged and licensed by the interpretative community.[12] One of its dangers is that it may lead its advocates to overlook the genuinely and permanently significant work that is still being undertaken within the historical-critical paradigm. The difficulty, of course, is knowing how to separate the wheat from the chaff (and from the tares).

Chapter 4

The Rhetoric of Oppression

A synchronic reading perspective is more appropriate to the status of the biblical texts as holy scripture than a diachronic one that locates them in the midst of an amorphous mass of uncertain, shifting, competing hypotheses.[1] But a synchronic perspective that understands the text as an aesthetic object, an enclosed and self-contained world, overlooks the fact that the text is also an entity in the public, socio-political domain. Within this public domain, holy scripture is, we might say, a blessing and a curse. It is the vehicle of the life-giving Spirit of truth, but it is also the letter that kills. An interpretative practice oriented towards the final form of the text must respond to the charge that, in ignoring this problematic reality, it fails to discharge its ethical responsibilities.[2]

Mark Allan Powell justifies as follows the self-contained text of much recent 'narrative criticism':

> As readers, we must accept the implied author's evaluative point of view even if it means suspending our own judgments during the act of reading. We may have to accept the notion that cowboys are good and Indians are bad... Readers are free, of course, to critique the point of view a narrative espouses. An initial acceptance of that point of view, however, is essential as preliminary to such criticism, for without such acceptance the story can never be understood in the first place. (*What is Narrative Criticism?* [1990], 24)

On this view, critique is voluntary and secondary; identification with implied author and/or reader is primary and obligatory, both for ordinary reading and for the interpretative practice that is here being delineated. This is in fact poor phenomenology of reading – readers can hardly avoid evaluating *as* they read – but an accurate statement of the priorities of narrative criticism. If a story represents native Americans as degraded, alien savages whose destiny is to be exterminated by the heroic white emissaries of civilization, narrative criticism will faithfully reproduce this representation without a murmur of protest. Underlying this refusal to engage in serious critical analysis of the rhetoric of oppression is not only the methodological self-limitation proper to any interpretative paradigm, but also an unquestioning faith in the revelatory power and pristine innocence of *stories*. The reader of a story is magically transported back to the Garden of Eden, and a reader tactless enough to criticize the story that is told there will immediately be expelled.

The continuation of the Joseph story of Gen.37–50 may serve to illustrate an interpretative perspective which combines a literary orientation (a concern with language and with close reading of the text as it stands) with a sensitivity to the text's ideological undercurrents. It is important to avoid the crudity of what Fredric Jameson has called 'those implacably polemic and demystifying procedures traditionally associated with the Marxist practice of ideological analysis' (*The Political Unconscious* (1981), 281).[3] Especially in the case of a text such as this one which is not currently used to legitimate oppression, the emphasis must fall on its indirect disclosure of the workings of a religiously-oriented rhetoric of oppression.

The sons of Jacob, arriving in Egypt to buy grain in time of famine, do not recognize their brother in the august figure of the governor with whom they must do business. He recognizes them, however, and an elaborate deception follows. Simeon is kept in prison as a hostage while the other brothers must return to their father with the demand that Benjamin – Rachel's second son who has taken Joseph's place in Jacob's affections – should be brought to Egypt. The money paid for the grain mysteriously reappears, and Jacob initially refuses to allow the favourite son to leave his side. Eventually, however, all the brothers duly appear before the governor. They feast with him, they are sent on their way with the grain they need, but Joseph has caused his silver cup to be hidden in Benjamin's sack so as to accuse him of theft when it is discovered there. Judah's intercession on his brother's behalf finally leads Joseph to abandon his concealment. He reveals himself to his brothers, and the whole family, reunited again, moves to Egypt to escape the famine.

What is it that motivates Joseph's strange conduct? As Hugh White has noted, his brothers' failure to recognize him means that 'he can now, in effect, "write" the ending [of the narrative] himself, and make them characters in a sub-plot of his own devising' (*Narration and Discourse in the Book of Genesis* (1991), 259). Why does Joseph exercise his authorial freedom in this way rather than another? This initial question leads on to a second. At the outset of the Joseph story its young hero dreams of absolute power, a dominance no less total for being confined, in childish fashion, to the circle of the family. The unfolding story shows how the hostility that the dream evokes becomes the very means of its fulfilment, and how this fulfilment ensures the reuniting of the family and its future wellbeing. The question is therefore whether Joseph's totalitarian power – exercised not just over his family but over the whole land of Egypt – enables his perspective to occupy the entirety of the narrative he 'writes', or whether this narrative also offers the means of undoing its own apparent glorification of dominance.

The logic of the strange strategies that Joseph adopts towards his family has been explored by Hugh White. The narrator points to the gap between the fiction Joseph is creating and the realities of the situation by focusing upon Joseph's thoughts, and especially the private tears (42.24; 43.30–31) that contrast so sharply with his public demeanour. 'The narrative purpose served by this portrayal is to reveal Joseph's growing feelings of compassion for his brothers behind his harsh facade, so that the reader can be aware that the meaning of Joseph's actions is not to be found in their surface appearance. This inner conflict serves to foreshadow the positive end to which this deception is leading' (*Narration and Discourse*, 259–60). Under-lying Joseph's fiction is the dilemma with which chapter 37 ended, 'the necessity yet impossibility of reintegrating Joseph into the family' (260). The purpose of Joseph's sub-plot is to ensure an authentic reconciliation arising from a transformation in the brothers.[4] He discovers from the brothers' response to the charge of spying that 'a crisis in Jacob's relation to the brothers has been avoided by the presence of Benjamin…, who could take his place in his father's affections… But there is one major change. Jacob does not entrust Benjamin to the brothers as he once entrusted Joseph. But no one questions this since beneath this change lies the truth which could destroy the family' (261). The demand that Benjamin should be brought to Egypt strikes at the heart of the *modus vivendi* that has been established, and the point is not lost on the brothers who are immediately reminded that 'in truth we are guilty concerning our brother, in that we saw the distress of his soul when he besought us, and we would not listen' (42.21). 'Joseph's demand thus returns the brothers to the primal scene of the crime' (262).

Joseph has reopened the old wound by exposing Jacob's distrust of the brothers, and he also intends 'to precipitate a crisis by ensnaring Benjamin, once in Egypt, thereby forcing the brothers to reveal whether they would sacrifice Benjamin as they once sacrificed him' (262). The money which is replaced in the brothers' sack is similarly related to the primal scene, again calling to mind their guilt over the sale of Joseph. But the conclusive re-enactment of that scene is still to come: Benjamin is singled out by his supposed theft of the cup, and the question is whether the brothers have learned from their past failures to maintain family solidarity. Once again the brothers have responsibility for the well-being both of a younger son of Jacob and of their father himself. 'In the earlier episode they were consumed by their hatred of Joseph without any regard for the feeling of Jacob', but Judah's long speech in 44.16–34 'makes it clear that now the brothers have come to be keenly aware of the significance and depth of Jacob's feelings about Benjamin' (266). Judah's willingness to sacrifice himself for the sake of Benjamin and Jacob means that 'the basis for trust now exists for Joseph, as does the possibility that the brothers can accept themselves and their own past without undue self-incrimination' (267).[5] Joseph attempts to ensure this self-acceptance by offering them not the humiliation of confession and forgiveness but the larger framework within which to understand what has happened: 'And now do not be distressed or angry with yourselves because you sold me here; for God sent me before you to preserve life' (45.5). Thus he 'invites the brothers to enter into the perspective of the transcendental Author who manipulates his characters on the stage of life to serve hidden ends as he had just manipulated them' (269).[6]

A drama of family conflict and reconciliation based on the transformation of the past and of memory through creative re-enactment: Joseph plays the role of the wise therapist who must sometimes appear cruel in order to expose and to heal the suppressed guilt which has distorted relationships within the family. Yet the treatment, if that is really what it is, seems to fail. The brothers – with the exception of Benjamin, who weeps – make no clear, unambiguous response to Joseph's emotional self-disclosure. At the outset, 'his brothers could not answer him, for they were dismayed at his presence' (45.3). At the conclusion, we are told only that 'he kissed all his brothers and wept upon them; and after that his brothers talked with him' (45.15). After Jacob's death, the brothers concoct a deathbed appeal that Joseph would forgive their sin, fearing that, in the absence of their father's restraining influence, 'Joseph will hate us and pay us back for all the evil which we did to him' (50.15). Thus 'the brothers' own perspective has not been collapsed into Joseph's cosmic "story"' (*Narrative and Discourse*, 273). These slight indications of the enduring possibility of a perspective that dissents from Joseph's may be read as an invitation to question the central character of this narrative rather more closely. According to Gabriel Josipovici, 'There are aspects of Joseph's self-revelation which should cause us concern. It is obvious that from the start of the story he at any rate is in no doubt that he is going to be the hero and saviour... It is not the narrator but *Joseph* who sees [his family's] lives in terms of a story or a drama with an initial prophetic dream, a catastrophe, a miraculous recovery, a revelation and a final reconciliation as all come to accept the truth of the prophetic dream' (*The Book of God*(1988), 83). Indications of the brothers' lack of enthusiasm for the narrative in which Joseph has located them raise the question whether an authentic reconciliation can ever take place within the framework established by the initial fantasy of dominance and its eventual realization.

For Joseph, the dissonance between his dreams of dominion and the fact of his enslavement is resolved by his accession in Egypt to absolute power. His brothers 'came and bowed themselves before him with their faces to the ground', and at that moment 'Joseph remembered the dreams which he had dreamed of them' (42.6, 9); he remembered, that is, how his brothers' sheaves gathered around his own and bowed down to it, and how even sun, moon and stars also bowed down to him (37.7, 9). His brothers bow down to him in his political capacity as 'governor over the land' (42.6), and Joseph underlines this by identifying himself as 'a father to Pharaoh' and as 'lord of all his house and ruler over all the land of Egypt' (45.8), and by instructing that his father be told 'of all my splendour in Egypt' (45.13). The message is not only that the ruler of all Egypt is Joseph, the long-lost son, but also that the long-lost son is ruler of all Egypt. Yet Joseph is also careful to incorporate into his narrative an element that was not found in the dreams. In the dreams, dominance and a corresponding submissiveness are represented purely as differences in personal fortune. Some attain prosperity and power while others do not, and the latter have no choice but to submit to the former: it is the casting of Joseph in the dominant role and his brothers in the role of suppliants that causes all the offence. The fantasy is fulfilled, but Joseph now attempts to play down the offence of this absolute contrast by inserting it into a more comprehensive narrative whose theme is the divine ability to use human evil in the service of the common good. 'God sent me before you to preserve for you a remnant on earth, and to keep alive for you many survivors. So it was not you who sent me here, but God' (45.7–8). The point is eloquently repeated after Jacob's death: 'You meant evil against me, but God meant it for good, to bring it about that many people should be kept alive, as they are today' (50.20). Joseph's exaltation no longer merely gratifies his will to power, nor is the continuing subject status of his brothers of any consequence to him in itself; for personal ambitions and achievements are effaced in the presence of the providential design for human welfare which subverts limited human purposes by directing them towards the general good.

The one who speaks so eloquently and reverently about divine omnipotence is still, however, the ruler of all Egypt, whose position of absolute power is not in the least diminished by his apparent self-effacement. When political authority speaks of God, one is impressed by the studied sincerity of the voice, which has learned to exploit even the power of tears (45.14–15, 50.17), and by the simplicity, humility and dignity of what is said. Yet the reality of the communicative situation should be sought not in the direction to which the rhetoric points us but, on the contrary, in the place of power and the will to power from which it proceeds. The good which is piously ascribed to God's providential ordering must in some sense be related to the interests of political authority.[7] How does the goodness of God function within this political discourse?

'God meant it for good, to bring it about that many people should be kept alive, as they are today' (50.20). This seems to represent a broader conception of the good than does the earlier reference to God's will 'to preserve for you a remnant on earth, and to keep alive for you many survivors' (45.7). It would be possible to understand 'many people' as a reference solely to the family of Jacob (which consisted of seventy persons, according to 46.27), just as it would be possible to limit the statement 'God sent me before you to preserve life' (45.5). But the context calls for a more comprehensive sense, for the Egyptians acknowledge that 'you have saved our lives' (47.25). The good willed by God is not only the preservation of the house of Jacob, it is the salvation of all the inhabitants of Egypt from the famine, a general salvation in which the house of Jacob as the chosen family must also participate.[8] Joseph's skill as an interpreter of dreams and as an administrator does not only preserve the life of his own family. The evil perpetrated by the brothers issues in the common good because Joseph was sold into slavery in Egypt, where his destiny as saviour of the people lay. The good that God intended is accomplished through Joseph; in speaking of the divine will to preserve life, Joseph is also speaking of himself as the incarnation of that divine will. He can speak, self-effacingly, of being sent by God (45.5,7,8), or, still more self-effacingly, he can speak of God's will to preserve life without any reference to himself (50.20). Yet the effect of his language is to clothe his own actions in the unimpeachable authority of the divine benevolence and omnipotence. In the very act of pointing away from himself to God ('Am I in the place of God?' (50.19)), Joseph represents himself as the wise, benevolent ruler who is the gift of God. God is manifested on earth no longer through the personal encounters with which the fathers were favoured (cf. Gen. 15, 18, 28, 32, and so on) but in the wise, altruistic actions of political authority. What is Joseph's 'glory' (*kābōd,* 45.13) but the earthly icon of the unapproachable divine glory? For this reason those who approach him must fall down before him (42.6).

God's benevolent rule of the world is exercised through political authority; political authority incarnates the divine benevolence. The dreams that signify the coming famine and open up the possibility of averting its worst effects are therefore granted to Pharaoh. The dream is from God: 'God has revealed to Pharaoh what he is about to do' (41.25, 28). God is the inscrutable power of fate that determines good and evil: 'The doubling of Pharaoh's dream means that the thing is fixed by God, and God will shortly bring it to pass' (41.32). Yet God as personal benevolent power makes available to humankind the means of guarding against the destructive decrees of his own *alter ego*, and it is for this purpose that political authority is instituted. Pharaoh, the embodiment of the divine benevolence, is naturally the recipient of the revelation that springs from that benevolence. However, the opacity of the dream means that Pharaoh's status as divine agent will have to be shared. God has revealed himself, but in concealed, enigmatic form; the revelation is still merely potential, and waits to be unlocked. Joseph's status as interpreter is therefore equal to Pharaoh's as dreamer. In response to Pharaoh's expression of confidence in his hermeneutic abilities, Joseph again makes the overtly self-effacing, latently self-aggrandizing transference of his own power to God which marks him out as a channel of divine power: 'It is not in me; God will give Pharaoh a favourable answer' (v. 16).[9] 'God has revealed to Pharaoh what he is about to do' (vv. 25, 28), and the real agent of this revelation, the interpreter who converts enigmatic symbols into revealed truth, asserts his own claims in the very act of refusing to speak of them. The unspoken assertion is successfully communicated, for Pharaoh is deeply impressed: 'Can we find such a man as this, in whom is the Spirit of God?' (v. 38). As Joseph had previously spoken of God's revelation to Pharaoh, so Pharaoh now returns the compliment: 'Since God has shown you all this, there is none so discreet and wise as you are; you shall be over my house' (vv. 39–40).[10] Like Joseph, Pharaoh reveals an ability here to speak self-effacingly about God at the same time as asserting himself as interpreter of God's action, and the fact that he now shares his own totalitarian power with Joseph suggests a possible correlation between the self-effacement that ascribes everything to God and the exercise of power.

Joseph's sudden exaltation to a position of dominance fulfils the will to power manifested in his childhood dreams. It is arguable, however, that his motivation is unimportant. His own insight, that the evil intended by human beings is turned by God towards the general good, might be applied to himself as well as to his brothers: the violence implied in the fantasy of dominance is contained and turned to good ends by the greater divine plan into which it is incorporated. A critique of his will to power would then be entirely beside the point. After all, what he says is apparently *true*, whatever his motivation: God indeed used Joseph as his providential instrument in ensuring 'that many people should be kept alive, as they are today' (50.20). They themselves acknowledge it: 'You have saved our lives' (47.25). If the organizational ability of the politician results in lives being saved in time of famine, only an utterly abstract, absolutist ethic would be concerned to expose a less than perfectly altruistic motivation. In such circumstances, the discourse of political authority about God would be true, even if at the same time it served its interest in maintaining its own power. The truth of the discourse would shine through its ideological conditioning.

The problem with this political truth-claim – that Joseph is the providential means whereby many lives are saved – is not that it is wholly false but that it is selective; and if this is the case, one can no longer hope to abstract the essential truthfulness of the discourse from its ideological functioning. Closer attention must be paid to Joseph's *exercise* of the power he is granted. Faced with the prospect of seven years of famine, his proposal sounds both intelligent and humane. The fifth part of the produce is to be gathered together during each of the seven years of good harvests, thus forming an adequate reserve during the seven lean years that will follow. Through practical wisdom such as this God accomplishes his saving will of preserving life. This proposal is immediately rewarded with the usual trappings of power: the signet ring from Pharaoh's own hand, expensive clothes, a gold chain, and a prestigious vehicle (41.42–43). 'You shall be over all my house, and all my people shall order themselves as you command; only as regards the throne will I be greater than you' (v. 40). More graphically expressed: 'I am Pharaoh, and without your consent no man shall lift up hand or foot in all the land of Egypt' (v. 44). How will this dangerously absolute power be exercised? Is it really compatible with the humane concern for the general welfare expressed in the initial proposal, or will its real purpose be the further extension of Pharaoh's control? The proposal is duly put into effect: 'And Joseph stored up grain in great abundance, like the sand of the sea, until he ceased to measure it, for it could not be measured' (v. 49). Coercive power is no doubt necessary for the accomplishment of this task, for the overseers appointed are to *take* the fifth part of the produce (v. 34); but no doubt the end justifies the means. The years of plenty pass, the years of famine come, and all Joseph's hard work comes to fruition. The starving people turn to him for help, the grain reserves are opened up – and Joseph *sells* the grain not only to foreigners but also to the Egyptians (vv. 56–57). The grain originally belonged to the people, it was taken from them and stored for their own future good – and now it is *sold* back to them. Joseph is God's providential instrument for keeping many people alive, but his humanitarianism proves to be compatible with the profit-motive. Gathering up surplus produce over a period of years, in the sure knowledge of a long period of acute scarcity during which one is guaranteed a monopoly: a safer and more lucrative business venture is hard to imagine.

Perhaps the political narrative of chapter 41 is of limited importance, serving only to set the scene for the resumption of the drama of family life that began in chapter 37? The delineation of the general situation – bread in Egypt, famine elsewhere – might be important only because it constitutes the mechanism whereby Jacob's sons are brought to Egypt, setting the family drama in motion again. Even after the moment of recognition, the narrator appears to be interested exclusively in the fortunes of the house of Jacob: the reality or otherwise of reconciliation turns out to be much less significant than the threat that the famine still poses to the survival of the family.[11] Yet, after the family is safely settled in Egypt, the narrator *returns* in 47.13–26 to the political narrative broken off at the end of chapter 41. The story of Joseph and his brothers is thus enclosed within the framework of the political narrative.[12] It is in 47.13–26 that the gap between religious rhetoric and political reality, already opened up by Joseph's exploitation of human misery, becomes a chasm. In God's providence Joseph ensures that lives are saved – but at such an appalling cost that his self-understanding in terms of a divine mission now rings hollow.

In 47.13–14 the narrator resumes the political narrative at exactly the point where it gave way to the familial narrative at the end of chapter 41. There Joseph was selling grain to Egyptians and foreigners. Now we learn that, as the famine worsened, 'Joseph gathered up all the money that was found in the land of Egypt and in the land of Canaan, for the grain which they bought; and Joseph brought the money into Pharaoh's house' (47.14). Since he has ensured a monopoly for himself, he is able to fix the price of grain as he wishes. There is plenty of grain left in the storehouses, yet Joseph is in possession of all the money in Egypt and Canaan. His prices must therefore have been exorbitant. Joseph's grotesque behaviour now leads us to suspect that the profit-motive is not just a minor appendage to the humanitarianism of the initial plan and its realization; rather, the exploitation of human misery has become his sole concern, exposing the apparent concern for human welfare of both Joseph and Pharaoh as a sham. Between them, Pharaoh and Joseph have come into possession of important knowledge about the future, but instead of using this knowledge in the service of the victims of famine they determine to exploit it ruthlessly. Yet this decision is never expressed. It is apparently taken for granted in chapter 41 that it is a duty to ensure that lives are saved in the forthcoming time of famine, but the reality of the situation – the achievement of a monopoly enabling the sale of grain at exorbitant prices – indicates a tacit agreement that the saving of life is not a priority in its own right but only in conjunction with the equally desirable aim that in this way all the money in the region should be 'brought into Pharaoh's house'.

Will the Egyptians be left to die, now that their money has all been spent? But they have other valuable resources which Joseph is determined to expropriate on behalf of his master. 'When the money was all spent in the land of Egypt and in the land of Canaan, all the Egyptians came to Joseph and said, "Give us food; why should we die before your eyes? For our money is gone"' (v. 15). The directness of the demand and the absence of the conventional polite formalities convey both the desperation of the suppliants and their illusionless grasp of the mechanisms of oppression to which they are being subjected. Joseph, however, is not impressed by the idea that food should be *given* in the form of a state hand-out. The suppliants must be made to recognize their responsibilities instead of loudly demanding their 'rights'. The usual rules of commerce still apply, and if there is no money left then something else must be given in its place. 'And Joseph answered, "Give your cattle, and I will give you food in exchange for your cattle, if your money is gone"' (v. 16). Joseph supplies them with enough grain to last the year, and in return gains possession of all their livestock – 'the horses, the flocks, the herds, and the asses' (v. 17).[13]

The following year the people no longer come to Joseph with truculent demands but in a suitably submissive frame of mind. They have learned to speak respectfully to those who control their destiny. There is no more subversive talk about the right to life, and the people have learned the hard lesson that grain will be exchanged but not given. 'And when that year was ended, they came to him the following year, and said to him, "We will not hide from my lord that our money is all spent; and the herds of cattle are my lord's; there is nothing left in the sight of my lord but our bodies and our lands. Why should we die before your eyes, both we and our land? Buy us and our land for food, and we with our land will be slaves to Pharaoh; and give us seed, that we may live, and not die, and that the land may not be desolate"' (vv. 18–19). Thus both land and people become Pharaoh's. Joseph gives them seed to sow, and concludes with them what is evidently supposed to be a most generous deal: 'At the harvests you shall give a fifth to Pharaoh, and four fifths shall be your own, as seed for the field and as food for your little ones' (v. 24). In Joseph's original proposal to Pharaoh, overseers were to be appointed who would take a fifth of the harvest during the seven good years, in preparation for the lean years that would follow (41.34).[14] Now, having reduced the people to a state of destitution, Joseph has devised a mechanism for institutionalizing what was originally supposed to be an emergency measure: the people are to give Pharaoh a fifth

of their produce *in perpetuo*. On that condition, Joseph is prepared to
permit their starving children to live. 'So Joseph made it a statute concerning the land of Egypt, and it stands to this day, that Pharaoh should have
the fifth' (47.26). So disoriented are the people by the disasters that have
befallen them that they are actually *grateful* for this normalizing of their
oppression. 'They said, "You have saved our lives; may it please my lord, we
will be slaves to Pharaoh"' (v. 25). Joseph too is still firmly convinced of his
own benevolence, for he is the appointed agent of the divine purpose of
human well-being, sent to Egypt 'to bring it about that many people should
be kept alive, as they are today' (50.20). The people's gratitude is a sign that
an illusionless understanding of the reality of oppression may be too heavy
a burden for its victims to bear. It is less painful to submit, internalizing the
rhetoric in which the oppressor represents himself as a benefactor, a gift of
God for the salvation of the people. The will to resist, which surfaced briefly
when an absolute right to life was asserted, proves impossible to maintain
in the face of famine and oppression, and oppression is thereby enabled to
normalize itself and to represent itself as part of the divinely-appointed,
providential order of things.

The political narrative of Gen. 41 and especially of 47.13–26 can
therefore be used to subvert the consoling, tranquillizing rhetoric of the
providence of God which the Joseph story holds forth as a possible master-
key to its own interpretation. Yet those interpreters – both historical-critical
and literary – who are almost exclusively interested in the family drama, and
who therefore marginalize the political narrative, cannot be criticized for a
blindness to a dimension of the text which should have been obvious to an
unprejudiced gaze; for the text itself ensures that the family drama is read
as the main plot to which the political narrative acts as a foil. The rhetoric
of the passage in chapter 47 itself ensures its own marginalization and the
repression of the possibility of a critical perspective on the story of Joseph.
Such a possibility remains technically open – for not even a canonical text
can finally exclude the possibility of a dissenting reader – but the text has
its own means of manipulating the reader in order to ensure that the
possibility is not actualized and that any attempt at actualization will seem
forced and overstated.[15]

The placing of this passage already aids the concealment of the gap
between Joseph's pious rhetoric and socio-political reality. It would have
been possible to locate it immediately after chapter 41, before the brothers'
first journey to Egypt. The opening of this section ('Now there was no food
in all the land; for the famine was very severe, so that the land of Egypt and
the land of Canaan languished by reason of the famine' (47.13)) brings us
back to the broader situation with which chapter 41 had closed ('Moreover,

all the earth came to Egypt to Joseph to buy grain, because the famine was severe over all the earth' (41.57)). This conclusion, with its emphasis on non-Egyptians, has been designed to prepare for the brothers' journey ('When Jacob learned that there was grain in Egypt...' (42.1)), but it would have been possible for the narrator to have included at this point the material found in 47.13–26, thus giving a unified account of Joseph's general strategy before returning to the family drama. This might have created some difficulties in the management of narrative time; by the end of this passage we have reached a somewhat later point in the seven-year famine than the point implied in 42.1. But the narrator has already inserted the story of Judah's family between Joseph's enslavement (chapter 37) and his fortunes in Potiphar's household (chapter 39), indicating that deviations from linear chronology are within his technical repertoire. Chronologically, 47.13–26 appears to run roughly in parallel to 42.1–47.12, for both relate to the first two years of the famine (45.6; 47.18). There is thus no technical reason why the material in the later section should not have been inserted immediately after chapter 41, thereby unifying the political narrative and displaying the full range of Joseph's political resourcefulness before focusing more narrowly on his family. Aesthetic reasons for the present ordering could no doubt be devised, but the most important point is that it serves to deflect attention from the political narrative. If its conclusion had been placed immediately after chapter 41, it would have disclosed and highlighted the oppressive nature of Joseph's 'wisdom' (41.39) and presented the manipulation of the brothers in a harsher light. The reader would carry over a sense of Joseph's ruthlessness into the resumed family drama. In the present arrangement, however, the Joseph who deceives his brothers is still the humanitarian Joseph of chapter 41, and only the unemphasized reference to his *selling* grain to the Egyptians hints at what is to come. The alternative order would run the risk of alienating the reader, displacing his or her sympathies too far in the direction of the brothers; it would encourage the reader to notice the possibility of an unfavourable judgement on almost all of Joseph's conduct. But Joseph must be protected from any such judgement, and in the present order the conclusion to the political narrative has therefore been relegated to the status of an appendix, to be read and noted but in isolation from the main linear outworking of the narrative. The narrator thereby signals that this material is to be deemed additional, tangential, not strictly necessary to the logic of the narrative although interesting in its own right. Its representations of character and action cannot easily be integrated into the main linear narrative, for that narrative is by this stage essentially complete. In the final note ('So Joseph made it a statute concerning the land of Egypt, and it stands to this day...' (47.26)), the narrator accounts for the existence of this passage in terms not of narrative logic but of antiquarian and aetiological interests, and its secondary, appended status is thus confirmed.

There are also factors internal to the discourse of this passage that ensure that its content will pass largely unnoticed. The harshness of the initial dialogue, where Joseph demands the people's cattle in return for food, is mitigated in the second dialogue, where the people *offer themselves* as slaves and where the final settlement looks, in this context, almost generous. While it is possible from a critical perspective to interpret this in terms of the internalizing and normalizing of the logic of oppression, that perspective is not the narrator's and therefore does not impose itself on the reader. Is Joseph really an agent of oppression? After all, in accepting the people's offer Joseph actually protects them from its possible consequences by allowing them to retain four-fifths of their produce for themselves. Perhaps, by dealing with Joseph rather than directly with Pharaoh, they are preserved from far worse oppression? Perhaps, within the constraints of his situation, Joseph does what he can to mitigate their sufferings? Oppression's ability to convince its victims of its own benevolence has insinuated itself into the texture of the narrative. All is well; strict justice is tempered with mercy in the most statesmanlike manner; a desperate threat to the people's life is skilfully averted, if at some cost to their freedoms; and to speak stridently of 'oppression' in this context is, to put it mildly, to commit an error of literary taste. The rhetoric of this passage seems designed to evoke some such readerly or literary-critical judgement.

Another rhetorical means of securing this favourable judgement is the presentation of the problematic material with relative brevity in an impersonal manner that leaves the reader uninvolved. The significance a reader ascribes to a unit of narrative will be dependent in part on the scope and complexity of its treatment in comparison to other units, and in a number of respects this narrative shows a simplicity and spareness of presentation uncharacteristic of the Joseph story as a whole. There are only two characters (Joseph and the crowd). No individuals are singled out from the crowd, as Reuben, Judah, Simeon and Benjamin are from the group of brothers; for that would imply a desire to unfold some of the potential pathos of the situation, something the narrator has no intention of doing. It is difficult to involve a reader imaginatively in the sufferings of a group rather than individuals, and the narrator exploits this fact by denying individuality to the Egyptians. The characterization of Joseph is entirely flat by comparison with the subtle presentation of private tears and public severity, concealment and revelation, which sustains the tension of the family drama; for this narrative unit is intended to be superficially interesting rather than demanding or involving. It occupies a single, unspecified narrative space, in contrast to the earlier use of the dual space of Egypt and Canaan, the homes of Joseph and of Jacob, with the potentiality for complex interaction that this opens up. In addition to the aetiology that concludes the passage (47.26), the reader's non-involvement is also promoted by a further antiquarian note in v. 22, where, having excluded the priests from the general sale of land and persons, the narrator explains that 'the priests had a fixed allowance from Pharaoh, and lived on the allowance which Pharaoh gave them; therefore they did not sell their land'. A narrative which must justify its existence by retailing miscellaneous historical-cultural 'facts' is clearly intended to be consumed dispassionately and with minimal engagement.

The nature of this carefully constructed non-involvement becomes still clearer when it is contrasted with the rhetoric of Exod. 1–2, where another situation of oppression involving Pharaoh and his subjects is now presented in a manner calculated to evoke the reader's sympathetic involvement. Here there are no antiquarian notes designed to promote distance. The suffering of the people is conveyed in emotion–laden terms as Pharaoh's pragmatic political rhetoric ('Come, let us deal shrewdly with them...' (Exod. 1.10)) is correctly translated into the vocabulary of oppression: 'Therefore they set taskmasters over them to afflict them with heavy burdens' (1.11); 'they made the people of Israel serve with rigour, and made their lives bitter with hard service...' (1.13–14); 'the people of Israel groaned under their bondage' (2.23). In contrast, the Genesis narrator derives the Egyptians' sufferings solely from the 'natural' event of the famine, seeking to withhold from the reader the knowledge that the famine is merely the occasion for the workings of oppression. Because oppression is in Exodus named as oppression, tales of heroic resistance can be narrated; but in Gen. 47 there can be no equivalents of Shiphrah and Puah, Jochebed and Miriam, Pharaoh's daughter and Moses, for the reality of the oppression to be resisted is denied. The perspective or point of view of the earlier narrative is that of the 'objective reporter' who merely records what was said and done by certain persons at a certain time and place, without any attempt at a multi-dimensional presentation which might begin to expose some of the realities hidden behind the so-called 'facts'. In Exodus, on the other hand, the narrator's point of view shifts constantly: from the initial scene-setting (Pharaoh's proclamation to his people (1.9–11)) and the consequent standpoint of 'the people of Israel' as a whole (1.11–14) to the more differentiated, individualizing focus first on the midwives (1.15–22) and then, still more concretely, on the family of Moses (2.1–10) and his initiation as an adult into the reality of oppression (2.11–15). Gen. 47

shows us little of the reality of hunger, destitution and enslavement, in either communal or individualized form. If it is the function of Exod. 1–2 to reveal the reality of oppression lying behind the facade of political rhetoric (1.10), it is the function of the earlier passage to conceal oppression by identifying rhetoric with reality. Any possibility of differentiating between the perspectives of oppressor and oppressed is ruled out when the oppressed internalize the self-presentation of the oppressor in the statement, 'You have saved our lives' (47.25). The reader who retains a sense of outrage at this point – stemming not least from the fact that such mechanisms are all too familiar – is left stranded as a lone dissenting voice which is allowed no recognition in the text. The counter-narrative which would recount the sufferings of the Egyptians with the rhetorical resources of the Exodus narrator remains a figment of the dissenting imagination.

It might seem pointless, and ludicrous, to criticize a text for failing to promote a positive attitude towards the ancient Egyptians. There are perhaps more appropriate objects for an excess of righteous indignation than the ideological deficiencies of a three-thousand-year-old narrative. The text in question is, however, communally acknowledged as canonical, and it is at least arguable that the entire history of biblical interpretation should be read as a history in which oppressive and liberating uses of the texts are ambiguously intertwined. If that is the case, and if this situation persists into the present, then an analysis of the texts in the light of this broader context is a theological imperative. It is not necessary to show that a particular text is directly and causally responsible for a still-current attitude or practice; only that, in an interconnected world, the rhetoric of the canonical text of a dominant religious community should not be abstracted from the contemporary context in which it still operates, but should be brought to light in such a way as also to disclose, indirectly, certain of the realities of this context. The function of religion in the concealment of oppression is a reality that unfortunately cannot be confined to the Joseph story, and to disclose its workings here is to contribute towards the broader analytical task. Thus, although criticism has necessarily been directed against the telling of the story as well as against its central character, the ultimate intention is not to criticize the text but to use it as an indirect means of exposing the workings of the rhetoric of oppression. In this sense, a 'positive' role is assigned to the text.[16]

A critical or resisting reading of this kind operates in accordance with a particular strategy which limits its concerns. It does not offer a 'balanced' reading which gives due weight to every part of the narrative; it accepts an inevitable one-sidedness as a price worth paying for its sharpness of focus. If, on the other hand, a 'balanced' reading does fuller justice to the text only by losing contact with the extra-textual world, then the loss outweighs the gain. A literary approach can perhaps be content to understand the text as an enclosed world, but the theological task is to understand not only the text but also reality in the light of the text. Because the relation between the text and reality is complex and manifold, a degree of selectivity is unavoidable.

Where, because of the nature of the reality that the text illuminates, resistance to the text is theologically necessary, it may be possible to find a measure of support for this resistance from within the broader canonical context. In the case of the Joseph story, for example, it has become clear by the end that Joseph's pre-eminence is strictly temporary and that he does not belong to the foundations of the history of Israel in the way that Abraham, Isaac and Jacob do.[17] When the time draws near for Jacob/Israel to die, Joseph is initially treated as though he were the first-born son, uniquely privileged. His father summons him and makes him promise to bury him in the family burial place (47.29–31). It is Joseph's sons who inherit the patriarchal blessing – although Joseph is displeased that Ephraim is given precedence over his first-born, Manasseh (48.2–20). The promise of the exodus is entrusted to Joseph (48.21), as is a piece of land: 'I have given to you rather than to your brothers one mountain slope which I took from the hand of the Amorites with my sword and with my bow' (48.22). Then all the sons are gathered together, and everything thus far has led the reader to suppose that on this occasion the pre-eminence of Joseph over his brothers will be finally, definitively asserted. Although Joseph has always been the paternal favourite, his dream of pre-eminence was initially rebuked by his father: 'What is this dream that you have dreamed? Shall I and your mother and your brothers indeed come to bow ourselves to the ground before you?' (37.10). And yet it is added that 'his father kept the saying in mind' (37.10). The book of Genesis will therefore surely end with Jacob, on his deathbed, confirming that Joseph is indeed pre-eminent over his brothers and that his dreams were therefore true. A reference from the end back to the beginning of the story will help to bestow on this narrative the unity approved by aesthetic theorists.

Reuben is addressed first: 'Reuben, you are my first-born, my might and the first fruits of my strength, pre-eminent in pride and pre-eminent in power' (49.3). And yet Reuben is unceremoniously and humiliatingly deprived of his primacy: 'Unstable as water, you shall not have pre-eminence, because you went up to your father's bed, then you defiled it – you went up to my couch!' (49.4). (The reference is to the occasion when 'Reuben went and lay with Bilhah his father's concubine' (35.22).) Simeon and Levi, the next sons, fare no better: 'Weapons of violence are their swords... Cursed be their anger, for it is fierce; and their wrath, for it is cruel!

I will divide them in Jacob and scatter them in Israel' (49.5, 7). (Simeon and Levi had once slaughtered the entire population of Shechem after the rape of their sister Dinah, having first incapacitated the males by tricking them into receiving circumcision (34.1–31).) Jacob's strategy is apparently becoming clear: addressing his sons in chronological order, he will find reasons for denying primacy to each of them until he reaches Joseph. Judah will no doubt be disqualified on the ground that he sold his own brother to the Ishmaelites (37.27), or because he lay with his daughter-in-law (38.12–19). Issachar and Zebulun, the fifth and sixth sons of Leah (30.14–20), never feature as independent characters and are therefore not serious candidates for primacy; still less are Dan, Naphthali, Gad and Asher, Jacob's sons by his concubines Bilhah and Zilpah (30.1–13). The beloved Benjamin, the second son of Rachel, may pose more of a threat to Joseph's chances. Joseph's displeasure at the precedence given to his own second son over his first-born (48.17–18) may stem in part from anxiety lest he too should be ousted in the same way.

In fact Jacob bestows primacy on Judah, the fourth son of Leah. 'Judah, your brothers shall praise you; your hand shall be on the neck of your enemies; your father's sons shall bow down before you… The sceptre shall not depart from Judah, nor the ruler's staff from between his feet, until he comes to whom it belongs; and to him shall be the obedience of the peoples' (49.8, 10). 'Your father's sons shall bow down before you': but they were supposed to bow down *Joseph* (37.5–10), and indeed actually did so (42.6). Joseph's hopes of fulfilling a central, permanently significant role in the history of Israel are dashed. It is true that he saved his family from the famine; but that is all. The God of Abraham, Isaac and Jacob is 'the God of your father' (49.25); despite the fulsome if vague blessings promised to Joseph (49.22–26), this God does not wish to be identified as the God of Joseph.[18]

In his role as lord of all Egypt, Joseph is known as Zaphenath-paneah, the name bestowed on him by Pharaoh; he is the husband of Asenath, the daughter of Potiphera priest of On (41.45). In this role and under this name, he is a figure of secular history who lies outside the true history of Israel. Opinions may vary as to his success in this role. Philo of Alexandria claims that 'after the famine, when the inhabitants were now rejoicing in the prosperity and fertility of the land, he was honoured by them all, who thus requited the benefits which they had received from him in the time of adversity' (*On Joseph*, 267).[19] But in treating the offending passage in Gen. 47.13–26, Philo has largely confined himself to praising Joseph for the honesty he displays in bringing 'all the money into Pharaoh's house' (v. 14) rather than his own, adding that 'the excellence with which he managed

Egypt... was beyond all words' (258–9). Philo is compelled to put a favourable gloss on this passage because of his mistaken assumption that the Joseph story is essentially the biography of a model politician (*bios politikou*). In its canonical form, however, the so-called Joseph story is introduced by the formula. 'These are the generations of Jacob' (37.2). Joseph has an important role to play in the history of Jacob's family, but it is not *his* history, and his political machinations are ultimately irrelevant to it. The narrator can on occasion play the role of court ideologue, so closely identified is he with Joseph's political perspective; but as the historian of Israel's sacred past, this cannot be his real concern.

Recent emphasis on the final form of the biblical texts is a hermeneutical shift with immense potential for the development of an interpretative practice oriented from the first towards theological concerns. The purpose of these first four chapters has been to outline some elements of the hermeneutical foundation upon which a theological superstructure is to be constructed. The decision to work with the final form of the biblical text is in keeping with its use of the narrative genre and with its functioning within an ecclesial context. It makes it possible to wrest the text from the grip of historical-critical hypothesizing. Although there is a danger that the text will now be construed as a self-contained and self-sufficient narrative world, it is possible to combine elements of a literary approach with a critical realism aware of the text's existence within the public, socio-political domain. While the specifically theological dimension of this hermeneutical proposal has not yet come into clear focus, we have at least taken a few steps along the way towards the theological goal.

PART TWO

THEOLOGY AND POSTMODERNISM

The next step is to begin to clarify the function of a more explicitly theological dimension within the argument. The term 'theological' is of course contested, but implies in my own usage an ability and a willingness to operate within a determinate form of ecclesial discourse: the tradition of self-critical reflection generated by the claims to truth, validity and adequacy inherent in Christian faith, or, more traditionally expressed, *fides quaerens intellectum*. A hermeneutic which claims to be 'theological' must therefore explore the possibility of an interpretative practice oriented towards self-critical reflection on Christian truth-claims. In the four chapters that follow, development of the theological dimension of the argument will proceed by way of dialogue with certain strands of postmodernist or poststructuralist theorizing. The route will of necessity be somewhat tortuous, and an extended introduction is required.

It has been forcefully argued by Stephen Moore (in his *Literary Criticism and the Gospels* (1989)) that biblical interpretation working within a 'literary' paradigm has usually been dependent on practices and theoretical beliefs, derived from literary studies, that have long been subjected to damaging attack within their native discipline. Banished from literary studies on grounds of superannuation, 'new criticism' takes refuge in the midst of a biblical scholarship which naïvely believes that the predicate 'new' is still applicable. The problems posed by this embarrassing belatedness can be overcome, Moore claims, by taking seriously the shift within literary studies from a theory of the (literary) text as self-contained, unified art-object to a theorizing of its indeterminacies that issues in the dissolution or deconstruction of the orderly, self-evident hierarchies and distinctions with which conventional criticism necessarily operates.[1]

One such self-evident distinction is the assumption that interpretation seeks to discover the meaning of a text and to demarcate it from the threat of a 'misinterpretation' that installs the text's non-meaning in the place reserved for its meaning. From a deconstructive perspective, the assertion that a text has a meaning, or meanings, tacitly assumes the transparency of language to that which lies behind it and which generates it; that is, it assumes that one can transcend language, eventually arriving at the reality to which language is merely a helpful sign-post. But – so the argument runs – we have at our disposal nothing but signs, and the idea that we can get outside language in order to attain to 'reality' is self-contradictory. What would 'the meaning' of a text be but a further set of signs, related to the first in supplementary rather than originary fashion? If it is objected that criteria are available for distinguishing 'the meaning' of the text from its non-meaning, the question arises as to where these criteria come from and how they could justify their alleged authority. Are we to postulate a stable, stabilizing 'authorial intention' as the final court of appeal? But the text refuses any such stability, engendering only the dispersal or haemorrhaging of its own (illusory) meaning as it proceeds out of the protective presence of its author into a realm in which real readers will never quite coincide with the ideal or implied reader it postulates. Even in the presence of its own author, will it be at one with its meaning? The author is not a pure point of origination but a site traversed by an uncontrollable, uncontainable variety of linguistic codes and practices, and the appearance of determinate meaning on the face of the text is a logocentric illusion concealing the heterogeneity out of which it is generated and which it vainly strives to master. The overt logic of the text will always already have been subverted by a covert logic or anti-logic, and the role of deconstructive analysis is to bring this paradoxical situation to light. This analysis cannot of course proceed from some privileged position outside textuality, for it proceeds from the denial that any such position is possible. It can, however, work from within, unable wholly to free itself from the old logocentric structures but nevertheless ceaselessly problematizing them.[2]

A dialogue between theology and deconstruction would have to recognize the 'anti-theological' dimension of the latter. The claim that there can be *logos*, rational speech, about *theos*, the source of all being and meaning, is treated as the founding gesture of logocentric illusion, and any and every claim to determinate meaning can thus be dismissively labelled 'theological.' There is perhaps not much benefit to be gained from the observation that 'theological' here is equivalent to 'metaphysical', which tempts one to differentiate the two and to claim support here for the resumption of traditional projects of anti-metaphysical theology: for the distinction of the God of Abraham, Isaac and Jacob from the God of the philosophers itself looks vulnerable to deconstructive dissolution.[3] Assuming, for the moment, that both dialogue partners – theology and deconstruction – wish to avoid simple confrontation, theology might see in its opposite number analogies with the *via negativa* adumbrated in certain mystical traditions, where a radical scepticism about the possibility of encapsulating *theos* in human *logos* is practised.[4] A more hermeneutically-oriented theology might welcome the new prestige accorded to texts, textuality, and an interpretative practice which, although in one sense it has abandoned the claim that interpretation can issue in truth, in another sense regards itself as the privileged site of a quasi-religious (anti-)epiphany in which the groundlessness of being fleetingly manifests itself in the dissolution of the systems of reference and meaning projected by or onto the texts. Might this abyss not be interpreted as a linguistically-mediated version of the *mysterium tremendum et fascinans*, encounter with which has been said to constitute 'religious experience'? The abyss inspires both the terror of vertigo and the exhilaration of play, and it is not some quasi-natural, non-textual encounter with the numinous that generates this irreducibly dual experience but an interpretative practice alive to the revelatory potential of textual indeterminacy.[5]

Alternatively, theology might choose – and we are still thinking in terms of options and possibilities and are not yet in a position to make a real, concrete choice – to construe the heterogeneous body of theoretical thought conventionally described as 'poststructuralist' or 'postmodernist' in a rather different fashion, as the highlighting not so much of indeterminacy as of *particularity*. (This distinction – which corresponds roughly to the distinction between Derrida and Lyotard – will be crucial to the structure of the following chapters.)[6] Where one strategy offers a critique of 'logocentrism', the other takes 'metanarrative' as its target. Grand theories or narratives attempt to encompass the whole of significant reality, and as such are fantasies of mastery and domination. Examples would include the Marxist thesis of the victory of the proletariat as the *telos* of the historical process, but also its opposite number which celebrates the world-historical triumph of capital as 'the end of history'. Metanarratives are characteristically formed out of a single totalizing concept: Progress, Evolution, Science, Reason, Secularization, Humanity – all such concepts imply variant forms of a metanarrative stemming from the Enlightenment, which arose in opposition to an earlier, Christian metanarrative that gave a totalizing account of reality from the beginning to the end, the earthly garden to the heavenly city, alpha to omega. Metanarratives are ideologies, and (it is said) we have reached the end of the era of competing ideologies. Our postmodern condition is irreducibly plural and irreducibly particular. Every particular social or communal location is the site of a variety of small-scale narratives, and it is these – rather than the old and defunct metanarratives – which enable us to make pragmatic if not theoretical sense of our world. We should abandon the metaphor of the 'foundation', with its suggestion that the various discourses that constitute our social world must be legitimated by some metadiscourse which assigns to each of them its predetermined place in the scheme of things. The 'foundation' is bound up with the metaphysical schema that claims to disclose *beneath* (or behind) appearance (the phenomenon, the manifest) an 'underlying' reality (the essence, the latent meaning): but appearance *is* reality, for we can identify nothing outside it. We thus return from the depths to the surface, finding there a bewildering, unmasterable network of relatively centred but not necessarily enclosed discourses, narratives, or language games which sometimes overlap or interact, sometimes compete, sometimes coexist harmoniously, and are sometimes indifferent to one another's existence.[7] Each has its own 'grammar', its own internal procedures and rules which participants must observe, but none of them has access to universal legitimating procedures transcending its own social limits.

If it is true that there are no longer any credible grand narratives but only small-scale narratives, it is also true that some of these small-scale narratives are considerably 'grander' – more powerful and influential – than others. The discourse of the market, currently extending its sway into more and more areas of the life-world, is not exactly a 'metadiscourse', for hardly anyone supposes that the market is able to subject the *whole* of the life-world to its logic. This is therefore another regional, particular discourse, competing, interacting, and coexisting with others. Yet this discourse, with its corresponding practices, has a remarkable capacity to infiltrate, to permeate and to transform other discourses and practices, subverting their autonomy and promoting a revolutionary global process of rationalizing and homogenizing while proclaiming the values of freedom, choice and difference. Faced with the phenomenon of this powerful, expansive discourse, the quasi-empirical identification of the postmodern condition as particularity converts itself into, or reveals itself as, an *ethic*: an ungrounded decision to promote and defend the autonomy of the particular, the local, and the marginal against the centralizing, homogenizing tendencies of metropolitan power and wealth.[8] It is this unstable relationship between the descriptive and prescriptive that, arguably, prevents this postmodern discourse of particularity from itself becoming a 'metadiscourse', the very genre it denounces as 'terroristic'.

The orientations in postmodern theorizing towards indeterminacy and towards particularity issue in rather different theological positions. Whereas the one gravitates towards negative theology or free textual play, the other can represent itself as a neo-conservatism, a move facilitated by the substitution of the term 'postliberal' for 'postmodern'. If there are no longer any credible metanarratives, then Christian metanarrative will have to be replaced by Christian narrative. The claim that this narrative is in a position to comprehend and master all other narratives has to be abandoned or – and this amounts to the same thing – deferred into an inaccessible eschatological future. Many strands of theological thought have long been distressed by the allegedly totalitarian and triumphalist tendencies of Christian metanarrative, and the loss or the problematizing of this universal dimension has seemed to offer a return to sanity which allows us to live at peace with our non-Christian neighbours. However, the universal claim is so integral to Christian faith that its loss or problematizing throws the whole structure into crisis. Is it possible to formulate an understanding of Christian faith which both moderates its universal claim and maintains a credible continuity with tradition? To this much-discussed problem, postmodern (postliberal) theology offers a strikingly novel and simple answer. Christian truth-claims are not to be understood as a metadiscourse but as *intrasystematic*.[9] Christian faith does not offer a set of true or false propositions about a chimerical, non-textual reality but a form of life which, like other forms of life, has its own language. A language, unlike a particular use of language such as a proposition, cannot in itself be true or false, and, as the social matrix that shapes and forms individual identity, it is relatively resistant to attempts at radical innovation. Christian doctrines are grammatical rules which set the limits within which 'true' – that is, intrasystematically acceptable – interpretative statements must operate. Interpretation is oriented here towards a 'reality' which is textually mediated or constituted, and the relevant texts are 'foundational' not in the sense that they can provide a generalizable legitimation for Christian discourse but in the sense that as *narrative* they are irreducible to any prior, non-narrative mode of discourse. The foundation, in other words, is intrasystematic.

In this perspective, other communities (religious or otherwise) have their own overlapping but incommensurable languages and narratives, and none of them has a right to prescribe the criteria by which the others are to be judged. The truth-claims of, say, the community of theoretical physicists remain intrasystematic, that is, they satisfy the criteria of validity and adequacy currently accepted within their discipline. There is no pressing need for the outsider to dispute the insider's claim that physics discloses aspects of the real, so long as it is understood that 'the real' here refers not to a Kantian *Ding an sich* but to a reality that has been filtered through communal interpretative procedures which determine in advance the possible modes of its appearance. The insider's talk about 'the ultimate building-blocks of reality', or whatever, must also be interpreted intrasystematically, and the tendency to construe this talk as a metadiscourse must be resisted. Within the discourse of the community of generals or of stamp-collectors, it would be meaningless to identify the ultimate building-blocks of reality with abstrusely-named subatomic particles.[10]

From a theological perspective, this emphasis on the irreducibility of particularity appears to offer the great advantage that Christian faith is rendered in principle invulnerable to criticism. The unbelieving philosopher who demonstrates the irrationality of belief in the existence of God participates, along with the anxious apologist who hastens to the defence of this belief, in a category-mistake. The fact that a particular set of procedures arguably returns a negative answer to a particular question tells us nothing about the situation in another discursive context. Even the question will not be the same: the deistic Deity that a particular philosophical tradition enquires after is not to be identified with the triune, narratively-encoded God of Christian faith. Any other attempt at a critique from outside will be similarly requested to mind its own business. Insiders too will be directed to look inwards and not outwards: outside they operate by different rules, and acknowledgement of that otherness is the corollary of the insistently *local* character of this style of theological reflection. A construal of individual and communal identity which might seem unbearably parochial may equally well be interpreted as a rejection of rootlessness and the determination to preserve the character of a particular locality as *home*. Socially located within the warm, maternal nurture of the Christian community, the theologian can enjoy the sense both of relief at the abandonment of an increasingly problematic Christian discourse of totality, and of an (almost) unbroken continuity with tradition. Postmodernism offers a solution to the modernist dilemma; the postliberal can combine a certain liberal poise with a conservative sense of place, thus gaining the best of both worlds. This is an elegant and economical way of cutting various Gordian knots.

A negative or a playful theology developed out of Derridean indeterminacy and a community-based theology of narrative are both characteristic although rather different products of postmodern theorizing. In my judgment, postmodern theorizing of both types must be *negotiated* and not succumbed to, and, if a fruitful dialogue ensues rather than a mere confrontation, the theological hermeneutic I am attempting to develop may establish its own theological location and its right to exist out of encounter with and resistance to this theorizing. No contemporary hermeneutical proposal can or should evade the impact of postmodern or poststructuralist theorizing in its various forms. At its best, it offers a heightened critical awareness of the constraints that structure the act of interpretation, strategies for subverting ossified hermeneutical dogmas that hinder creativity and innovation, and, in general, an extraordinary increase in the range of what it is possible for the interpreter to do and say. Why then is it necessary to speak of *resisting* this theoretical practice?

The necessity of resistance begins to come into focus as one observes the effects of postmodern theorizing on the concept of 'God'. [11] If, as Derrida puts it, there is nothing outside the text (if, that is, there is no encounter with pre-textual reality but an ungrounded succession of interpretations wandering from nowhere to nowhere), then it will be axiomatic that 'God', the transcendent signifier who was supposed to provide thought with its transcendent ground, is to be reinscribed as immanent within textuality.[12] He may be disclosed as the product of the futile though inescapable project of logocentrism, or honoured as a very important signifier within certain local languages; but the result of such an analysis is that the so-called metaphysical attributes of God are covertly transferred to textuality itself. Like God, textuality is unlimited and omnipresent, for there is nothing outside it. Like God, textuality is omnipotent: who can resist its will? Like God, textuality is omniscient, for all possible knowledge is contained within it. Like God, textuality is ultimately incomprehensible, and we can only submit ourselves to what we can never fully understand.

Perhaps this divinity can not only be acknowledged as fate but also celebrated as saviour? The gospel of textuality invites us to lay down our burdens, to abandon the struggle and the guilt of trying to differentiate truth and error, good and evil. According to one version, we are offered release from this work and a return to the blissful innocence of *play*: we renounce 'the Spirit of Gravity' and will believe only in 'a God who understands how to dance' (Nietzsche, *Thus Spoke Zarathustra*, 68). According to another version, *homecoming* is a more appropriate metaphor for the end of the work of truth-seeking. Returning to the particularity of home, the place in which we are rooted, we find everything exactly as it was when we left it. Our experience of the wider world has freed us from the childish illusion that the special language and rites of home are a direct transcript of ultimate reality, yet we do not wish the language and the rites to change, for they have become part of our identity. Exposing the theological undercurrents in these and other postmodern narratives of salvation shows not only how easily they can be converted into explicitly theological positions but also how difficult it is to find room for a genuinely different theological proposal in a situation where all the available space has already been occupied.

In developing such a proposal in the chapters that follow, I do not wish to give the impression that postmodern theorizing has been definitively overcome and that we can leave it behind us as we proceed on our way: it is too important a factor in our current context for such dismissive treatment. If, as Lyotard puts it, 'the postmodern condit on' is to be defined as 'incredulity towards metanarratives', then it is to be understood as a broadly-based cultural phenomenon and not just as a trend in certain sectors of the academy.[13] Admittedly, there are acute difficulties of definition here, but it seems reasonable to assume that the ironizing and relativizing that are so evident in current theoretical discourse have emerged not out of a vacuum but out of a complex of broader socio-cultural factors. If that is the case, contemporary theology must regard postmodern theorizing as an important dialogue partner which will assist in the shaping of its form and substance even as it is resisted.

In order to provide further orientation for what is inevitably a complex discussion, the argumentative strategy developed in the following four chapters may be outlined as follows.

First, I shall offer a reading of a Pauline text (1 Corinthians 14) from a perspective indebted to Derrida's textual practice (chapter 5). Whether this reading is, in itself, to be construed as imitation, parody or homage may be left ambiguous. Its function within my broader strategy is to disclose the *limitations* of this particular practice, which lie in its privileging of language over speech, *langue* over *parole*. An initially justified resistance to the logocentrism of a speech in which the individual is seen as the origin of meaning and truth loses its justification when one substitutes for it an impersonal, deterministic *language* rather than a communicative, relational and dialogical model of *speech*.

Second, with the help of recent theological appropriation of the work of Habermas and others, I shall outline an account of the social formation of persons through integration into linguistic community, intended as an alternative to poststructuralist linguistic determinism (chapter 6). This dialogical model of speech may be theologically grounded in the Genesis creation narratives, and it may also be employed in opposition to a monological, totalitarian conception of theological speech within the Christian community. This latter point is developed by way of a second reading of 1 Corinthians 14 which, in working from a different theoretical perspective, sheds further light on the limitations of the first one. The movement in chapter 5 from (deconstructive) exegesis to its theoretical assumptions is complemented in chapter 6 by a movement from an alternative theoretical proposal back to (theologically-oriented) exegesis.

Third, I shall offer further discussion of the postmodern theorizing not of indeterminacy (as in deconstruction) but of particularity (chapter 7). The contemporary emphasis on communally-located narratives, over against every metanarrative, has proved especially congenial to some theologians, and I shall explore the points of contact between non-theological proponents of this theorizing such as Lyotard, Fish and Rorty and 'postliberal' theologians such as Lindbeck and Hauerwas.

Fourth, the view that our world is created by means of language, on which this theorizing rests, will be criticized (chapter 8). Its theological non-realism results in an inward-looking, community-oriented perspective which can allow no place for the universality associated with belief in the world as already created by God prior to human linguistic practice. A symptom of this situation is the tendency to isolate the particular 'story of Jesus' from the universal horizons of creation and eschaton which constitute its canonical narrative context. A theological reading of Gen.1 is therefore developed in opposition both to the belief that language creates the world and to the removal of Christian narrative from its universal framework.

Chapter 5

The Musical Signifier

In the course of a major recent theoretical investigation of postmodernism as a broad cultural phenomenon, Fredric Jameson avails himself of Lacan's account of schizophrenia to point to the experience of language that lies at the heart of the various cultural practices he explores. Lacan, he writes, 'describes schizophrenia as a breakdown in the signifying chain, that is the interlocking syntagmatic series of signifiers which constitutes an utterance or a meaning... When that relationship breaks down, when the links of the signifying chain snap, then we have schizophrenia in the form of a rubble of distinct and unrelated signifiers' (*Postmodernism* [1991], 26). Personal identity is dependent on the ability to unify past and future with one's present, and this unification is the function of language, and especially the sentence; here, a determinate past from which the sentence originates is linked with the future which it projects. 'With the breakdown of the signifier, therefore, the schizophrenic is reduced to an experience of pure material signifiers, or, in other words, a series of pure and unrelated presents in time' (27). The temporal flow of meaning normally channelled through language suddenly drains away, leaving the channel empty, and the result is a certain atemporality in which words have become purely material objects – opaque, occult, resistant to penetration, as if floating in empty space. Commenting on a subject's account of the onset of schizophrenia, Jameson writes:

> The breakdown of temporality suddenly releases this present of time from all the activities and intentionalities that might focus it and make it a space of praxis; thereby isolated, that present suddenly engulfs the subject with undescribable vividness, a materiality of perception properly overwhelming, which effectively dramatizes the power of the material – or better still, the literal – signifier in

isolation. This present of the world or material signifier comes before the subject with heightened intensity, bearing a mysterious charge of affect, here described in the negative terms of anxiety and loss of reality, but which one could just as well imagine in the positive terms of euphoria, a high, an intoxicatory or hallucinogenic intensity. (27–8)

This displacement of the negative by the positive is important in Jameson's application of the model to postmodern cultural practices:

> What I have been calling schizophrenic disjunction or *écriture*, when it becomes generalized as a cultural style, ceases to entertain a necessary relationship to the morbid content we associate with terms like schizophrenia and becomes available for more joyous intensities, for precisely that euphoria which we saw displacing the older [existentialist] affects of anxiety and alienation. (29)

Freed from the burdens of reference and meaning and from the linear temporality that they create, postmodernism celebrates the 'pure and random play of signifiers', and therefore 'no longer produces monumental works of the modernist type but ceaselessly reshuffles the fragments of pre-existent texts, the building blocks of older cultural and social production, in some new and heightened bricolage' (96). A contemporary artistic manifesto speaks of an artistic practice along these lines in which 'meaning is bewildered, attenuated, made relative... There results a sort of mildness of the work, which no longer speaks peremptorily, nor bases its appeal on ideological fixity, but dissolves in multidirectional digression' (quoted, 174).

Although Jameson does not say so, the atemporal euphoria induced by the empty, material signifier, might be interpreted by its subject as a religious experience; that is, it might occur within a linguistic community in which experience is shaped and perceived in religious terms. The emptying of the signifier of first-order meaning might be experienced as the *ekstasis* of communion with the divine. While this possibility is not confined to any particular religious tradition, it corresponds within the sphere of Christian faith and practice to the phenomenon of *glossolalia*, the use by the worshipper of a 'language' whose meaning is unknown, that is, of a system of pure material signifiers, as a vehicle of ecstatic prayer: 'ecstatic' not in the sense of a complete loss of control, as in a trance or a fit, but in the sense of an intensification of experience which holds the normal structures of temporality in suspense without entirely eliminating them. Since the practice of *glossolalia* ('speaking in tongues') is a recent development in church life, it might be possible to interpret it as a genuinely postmodern phenomenon stemming, like other cultural practices of the material signifier, from what Jameson calls 'the cultural logic of late capitalism.'[1] In that case, the controversy that this practice has engendered in some church contexts would be a special case of the controversy engendered by all postmodern cultural practices insofar as they oppose or bypass the concept of meaning. Here, however, my interest lies in a theological assessment of the postmodern rejection of determinate linguistic meaning, taking *glossolalia* as a symbol of this general trend and basing the discussion on a reading of one of the crucial biblical texts appealed to in legitimation of this practice – 1 Corinthians 14, which is thus caught up into the postmodern problematic.

Speaking in other tongues is the primary manifestation of the Holy Spirit who descends upon the gathered disciples on the Day of Pentecost (Acts 2.1–21, cf. Mark.16.17). On this occasion alone, *glōssolalia* is said to be comprehensible to the hearers (although not to the speakers), for Jews from Parthia, Media and elsewhere confirm that 'we hear them telling in our own tongues the mighty works of God' (Acts 2.11). At a later point in the narrative, Gentiles' reception of the Holy Spirit is confirmed by their speaking in tongues (*lalountōn glōssais* (10.46)), as a sign that they are to be baptized (10.47–48) – although this phenomenon can also be presented as a *consequence* of baptism and of the laying on of hands, the 'normal' means by which the Holy Spirit is communicated (19.5–6). There is in these texts a tendency to assimilate speaking in tongues to prophecy (cf. 2.17–18; 19.6).[2] It is not clear whether, for Luke, speaking in tongues as the confirmatory sign of the gift of the Spirit belongs only to the early days of the church's mission or whether it is still understood as such in his own time – an ambiguity which is exploited in opposite directions by the present-day opponents and proponents of *glōssolalia*. In 1 Corinthians, on the other hand, the gift of the Spirit, conferred through baptism (1 Cor. 12.13) issues in 'all speech and all knowledge' (*panti logō kai panti gnōsei*, 1.5), a series of linguistically-oriented *charismata* (cf. 1.7) which include the utterance of wisdom (*sophia*), knowledge (*gnōsis*), prophecy (*prophēteia*), different kinds of tongues (*genē glossōn*) and interpretation of tongues (*hermeneia glossōn*) variously distributed to individuals by the one Spirit (12.4–11, cf. v. 30). This distribution occurs not for individual enhancement but for the common good, and it is the role of the metaphor of the body to underline this point. If a particular gift (speaking in tongues) is regarded as the only real proof of reception of the Spirit, then the result will be a distinction within the congregation between glossolalists and non-glossolalists, a division of the social space it occupies into an inside and an outside. But 'if the foot should say, "Because I am not a hand, I do not belong to the body," that would not make it any less a part of the body' (12.15). Correspondingly, 'the eye cannot say to the hand, "I have no need of you," nor again the head to the feet, "I have no need of you"' (12.21). There is to be no outside and inside within this social space, with the inside defined as the locus of the material signifier and the outside defined by its lack of this privileged non-meaning as the secondary, inferior, excluded locus of determinate meaning.

What is here rejected is a remarkable inversion of conventional evaluation which might have represented itself as flowing directly from the logic of the Christian *logos* (or *kerygma*), which inverts and is therefore 'foolishness' (*mōria*) to worldly discourse (1.18). In its place there is established in 1 Cor.14 a new hierarchy in which the entire social space is to be occupied by *prophēteia*, speech that is both disclosive and communicative. *Glōssolalia* is in contrast understood quasi-rationalistically as a simple, regrettable, avoidable breakdown in communication:[3]

> If even lifeless instruments, such as the flute or the harp, do not give distinct notes, how will any one know what is played? And if the bugle gives an indistinct sound, who will get ready for battle? So with yourselves; if you in a tongue utter speech that is not intelligible, how will any one know what is said? For you will be speaking into the air. There are doubtless many different languages in the world, and none is without meaning; but if I do not know the meaning of the language, I shall be a foreigner to the speaker and the speaker a foreigner to me. (1 Cor. 14.8–11)

The material signifier is banished from the centre to the margins ('In church I would rather speak five words with my mind, in order to instruct others, than ten thousand words in a tongue' (v. 19)). If allowed to occupy the centre, the non-communicative signifier will place the other 'in the position of an outsider [*idiōtes*]' who is unable to concur with what is said ('say the Amen', v. 16). A restricted space is still permitted to the material signifier ('Do not forbid speaking in tongues', v. 39), but in such a way that its threatening materiality is subjected to the constraints of disclosive, communicative speech: only two or at most three are to speak in a tongue, each in turn, and *there must be an interpretation* (v. 27) – that is, there must be a forcible imposition of a lucid signified onto the mysteriously opaque signifier, a conquest of the primal abyss by the *logos*, the rational word. If no interpretation is available, then glossolalists should keep silent, confining their subversive gift to the harmless privacy of individual devotion (v. 28).

In reconstructing the debate in this manner, I have tacitly assimilated it to the Derridean problematic of determinacy and indeterminacy, 'speech' and 'writing.' Once again, *logos* (in the guise here of *prophēteia*, a speech which discloses the secrets of the heart (v. 25)) seeks to depotentiate, to master and to control its opposite, indeterminacy (here, *glōssolalia*, the material signifier). Indeterminacy is a threat to the normal process of meaning in which the materiality of the signifier becomes translucent to a signified and to a referent established outside the secondary order of words in the primary order of things. Where indeterminacy arises, this hierarchical relationship of words and things is undermined and language becomes self-contained and self-sufficient, subverting its proper disclosive and communicative role and referring in an endless regress only to itself. Maintenance of this hierarchy, without which the *kosmos* collapses, requires an act of exclusion in which *logos* separates itself from its opposite. Although this gesture has to be repeated time after time and is never established definitively, it is always only a concrete, historical form of the gesture that is subjected to critical questioning. If, however, we focus attention on the gesture itself, we discover that it is not the originary movement it purports to be (the *logos* as the beginning of all things) but a secondary act of separation which supervenes upon something else which provides the conditions for the possibility both of *logos* and its excluded opposite and is itself not reducible to either. The origin of all things is the non-origin out of which reason and madness both proceed;[4] or, otherwise expressed, the separation is always already in place and cannot be circumvented, so that it is impossible to penetrate behind the duality to a unified origin which would enable the one finally to master the other;[5] or, in a more Saussurean formulation, the nature of language as a system of differences without positive terms points to the non-coincidence of sign and referent in every act of signification and suggests a primordial difference or rift between reality as constituted and reconstituted within speech and the inescapable but unattainable projection of a reality outside language.[6] Although the analysis does not show that non-reason is more original than reason, the fact that logocentrism pervades our western traditions of thought means that the main task of deconstructive analysis must be to expose its illusions and to undo its claims, showing that in the very act of defining itself over against its opposite the (non-)logic of the opposite is secretly present within its own boundaries, ensuring that the translucent 'truth' it strives for will always be deferred.

In rereading Paul's argument in the light of this Derridean problematic, my intention is both to illustrate the workings of a powerful and seductive contemporary interpretative proposal and also, ultimately, to show how the view of theological speech developed in the Pauline text evades Derrida's critique of logocentrism and exposes the strategic exclusions or blindnesses upon which the deconstructive critique itself is founded. We must, however, enter more deeply into the labyrinth; but not in such a way as ever to forget entirely that the purpose of entering it is to find the way out. The Derridean reading of Paul that I am proposing must, in the end, be placed within parentheses.

According to Paul, *prophēteia* is clear, comprehensible and therefore valuable for the furthering of communal life; *glōssolalia* is meaning-less and issues only in perplexity and the impairment of community. In prophecy voice and meaning coincide, and in Paul's text the single term *phōnē* therefore does duty for both. Thus, a faint analogy to prophecy may be discerned when even 'lifeless things (*ta apsucha*) give *phōnē*', the reference being to musical instruments (1 Cor. 14.7). If their notes are insufficiently distinct (that is, if they fall into the hands of an incompetent operator), their *phōnē* is mere 'sound' or 'noise', but when correctly handled it is closely analogous to the human 'voice'. Especially is this the case where music is integrated into a linguistic system, as in the case of the bugle (*salpinx*) whose *phōnē* fulfils a role exactly equivalent to the human voice when it issues the order to prepare for battle (v. 8). If, incorrectly played, the result is *adēlon phōnēn* (mere non-signifying sound), then the true function of this signifying instrument is to make something clear (*dēlos*), to convey a meaning. In the human voice, or its substitutes, sound becomes meaning. Thus, not one of the countless languages (*phōnai*) in the world is *aphōnos*, without meaning (v. 10) – a point so obvious as to be a tautology, for how can *phōnē* (language) lack *phōnē* (meaning)? This paradox becomes reality only for one who is in the unenviable position of the *barbaros* unfamiliar with the 'force [or meaning] of the language' (*dunamis tēs phōnēs*), but even such a person is aware from experience of a native tongue that the lack lies not in the foreign language but in him- or herself (v. 11). Through insertion into this broadly-based view of communication, *prophēteia* is seen as a special instance of the capacity of the human voice to transform sound into meaning.

From a Derridean perspective, we find ourselves here within the logic of a *logos* of which Aristotle can serve as a convenient symbol or symptom. 'Within this logos, the original and essential link to the *phōnē* has never been broken' (*Of Grammatology* (French original, 1967; ET 1976), 11). Here, the voice 'has a relationship of essential and immediate proximity with the mind... It signifies "mental experiences" which themselves reflect or mirror things by natural resemblance' (11). Thus logocentrism is here also phonocentrism: 'absolute proximity of voice and being, of voice and the meaning of being, of voice and the ideality of meaning'; the meaning of being as *presence* (12). The concept of immediate union with an absolute, present logos is a 'metaphysico-theological' notion, the essential characteristics of which may still be detected in the post-Christian philosophies of the Enlightenment and beyond: 'The age of the sign is essentially theological' (14). And (if we are willing to adopt this perspective, at least for the moment) this theological dimension could hardly be clearer than in the Pauline concept of *prophēteia*, in which the voice is engaged in a forth-speaking not of the fallible contents of one's own mind but of the thoughts of the divine mind. 'No-one comprehends the thoughts of God except the Spirit of God. Now we have received not the spirit of the world, but the Spirit which is from God, that we might understand the gifts bestowed on us by God. And we impart this in words not taught by human wisdom but taught by the Spirit, interpreting spiritual truths to spiritual people' (1 Cor. 2.11–13). Greek metaphysics is displaced here by a theory of revelation which reproduces its structures in the very act of resisting its claims: truth is communicated to the mind by logos or Spirit, whence it is passed on to those who are worthy to receive it by way of the human voice. The chain (logos/Spirit, mind, speech, reception) is unbroken, and – changing the metaphor – each element is perfectly contained in that which precedes it so that, as in a set of Chinese boxes, nothing extraneous can enter in.

However, this paradise of immediacy, transparency and luminosity is incapable of filling the entire discursive field, and its self-containment is possible only by means of an act of exclusion. There is a form of language that does not communicate to others the divine truth. In Plato's *Phaedrus*, that which is excluded is *writing*; the Judaeo-Christian spirit/letter contrast is closely modelled on the speech/writing hierarchy that here comes to expression. In a passage that is important for Derrida's idiosyncratic understanding of 'writing', Plato's Socrates argues that

> writing involves a similar disadvantage to painting. The productions of painting look like living beings, but if you ask them a question they maintain a solemn silence. The same holds true of written words; you might suppose that they understand what they are saying, but if you ask them what they mean by anything they simply return the same answer over and over again. Besides, once a thing is committed to writing it circulates equally among those who understand the subject and those who have no business with it; a writing cannot distinguish between suitable and unsuitable readers. And if it is ill-treated or

unfairly abused it always needs its father to come to its rescue; it is quite incapable of defending or helping itself. (*Phaedrus*, 275E)

Writing is cut off from the protective paternal presence, itself grounded in the divine logos, which would defend it against reproach. 'Wandering in the streets [so Derrida paraphrases], he doesn't even know who he is, what his identity – if he has one – might be, what his name is, what his father's name is. He repeats the same thing every time he is questioned on the street corner, but he can no longer repeat his origin' (*Dissemination* (French original, 1971; ET 1981), 143–4). This tale is saved from sentimentality by a gothic, Freudian twist: 'Writing can thus be attacked, bombarded with unjust reproaches... that only the father could dissipate – thus assisting his son – if the son had not, precisely, killed him' (146). The absence of the author and the absence of the referent are not accidental but constitutive features of writing, for 'writing is the name of these two absences' (*Grammatology*, 41). 'All graphemes are of a testamentary essence. And the original absence of the subject of writing is also the absence of the thing or the referent' (69).[7] 'The absence of the sender, the addressor, from the marks that he abandons, which are cut off from him and continue to produce effects beyond his presence and beyond the present actuality of his meaning, that is, beyond his life itself', this absence 'belongs to the structure of all writing – and... of language in general' (*Margins of Philosophy* (French original, 1972; ET 1982), 313). The absence or 'death' of the author, inscribed in the structure of the mark, is at the same time the absence or 'death' of the addressee, for writing must 'remain legible despite the absolute disappearance of every determined addressee in general' (315). 'To write is to produce a mark that will constitute a kind of machine that is in turn productive, that my future disappearance in principle will not prevent from functioning and from yielding, and yielding itself to, reading and rewriting... This essential drifting, due to writing as an iterative structure cut off from all absolute responsibility, from *consciousness* as the authority of the last analysis, writing orphaned, and separated at birth from the assistance of the father, is indeed what Plato condemned in the *Phaedrus*' (316). Writing is characterized as the absence of sender, addressee and referent. The deconstructive moment occurs when the structures of 'writing' are found within 'speech', thus subverting the hierarchy of speech and writing as metaphors of presence and absence. 'This structural possibility of being severed from its referent or signified (and therefore from communication and its context) seems to me to make of every mark, even if oral, a grapheme in general, that is..., the nonpresent *remaining* of a differential mark cut off from its alleged "production" or origin. And I will extend this law even to all "experience" in general, if it is granted that there is no experience of *pure* presence, but only chains of differential marks' (*Margins of Philosophy*, 318).[8]

What takes place here is that a quasi-empirical characteristic of writing (its relative autonomy) imperceptibly assumes the weight of the entire argument through assimilation to Saussurean *langue*.[9] For Saussure, *langue* precedes *parole* in the sense that the utterance of the individual is preceded and made possible by a system of linguistic signs which refer to 'reality' only by way of a primary reference to one another, a system composed of differences rather than positive terms that would give it a foundation, and thus centreless and indifferent to the 'truth' and 'falsehood' which can only be constituted within its own arbitrary but inescapable constraints.[10] The priority of language over speech is, in the structuralist and poststructuralist thought that avails itself of Saussure's insights, the death of the subject of speech, the unique individual conceived as the originary locus of meaning – as in the romantic theory of the artist or the existentialist conception of authenticity. In Derrida's version, the absence of the author that is constitutive of writing suggests that writing is structurally closer to *langue* than is speech; and this leads to an identification of language with writing (arche-writing) and so to the thesis of the priority of writing over speech. Thus, for Derrida, any empirical characteristic of writing that stems from its relative autonomy over against its author (or its addressee) can be inflated into a disclosure of Being. Writing, for example, may be difficult to understand, or illegible, and this fact occasions the following meditation:

> [What] if the Being of the world, its presence and the meaning of its Being, revealed itself only in illegibility, in a radical illegibility which would not be the accomplice of a lost or sought after legibility, of a page not yet cut from some divine encyclopedia?... The radical illegibility of which we are speaking is not irrationality, is not despair provoking non-sense, is not everything within the domains of the incomprehensible and the illogical that is anguishing. Such an interpretation – or determination – of the illegible already belongs to the book [as opposed to writing or text], is enveloped within the possibility of the volume... Prior to the book (in the nonchronological sense), original illegibility is therefore the very possibility of the book and, within it, of the ulterior and eventual opposition of 'rationalism' and 'irrationalism.' (*Writing and Difference* (French original, 1967; ET 1978), 77)

Here, the role of 'speech' or 'voice' elsewhere as the bearer of the claim to 'presence' is assumed by 'the book'. The book represents writing in a fixed, enclosed form, authored and therefore authoritative, which perpetuates, and may serve as a symbol for, the logocentric illusion. The appearance of fluidity in Derrida's terminology (here, for example, the speech/writing opposition is homologous to the book/writing opposition) is more apparent than real; for the fundamental problematic remains always the same, the subversion of determinate truth-claims by their subjection to precisely the indeterminacy, drifting and error that they claim to have mastered. Derrida's inventiveness lies in his ability to compose an endless series of variations on a single, monotonous theme.

This musical metaphor is, however, subversive of his position, which *at some level* appears to rest on the belief that this theme is not just *a* theme – a tune composed or chosen more or less at random that might just as well have been another or different – but *the* theme (the impossible idea of a master-tune out of which all music proceeds), the theme of Being itself. (What if the Being of the world revealed itself only in illegibility, etc.? But what if this theme revealed itself to be only a tune?) Thus the 'variations' on this theme – improvised by way of the demonstration that any chosen text is always already a variation on it – serve not only as a means of virtuoso display but also as *confirmations* of the fundamental truth-claim of the theme or thesis. The notion of a 'fundamental truth-claim' must, of course, be qualified and ironized in this context: thus, speaking of Being, one asks 'What if…?' rather than *asserting* the illegibility of Being. Yet the qualifications and ironizings are, I think, an attempt to *protect* from its own self-destructive tendencies something whose behaviour is elsewhere not unlike that of any other foundational philosophical thesis that seeks to establish itself.[11] If, however, the thesis is a theme and the theme is a tune, then Derridean deconstruction can be construed not as metadiscourse but as a more localized project which may well be judged ingenious, provocative, illuminating, and (for certain purposes) *useful*, but only at the cost of its grander pretensions.[12]

Returning to the 'orthodox' Derridean perspective which this exercise for the moment requires, we discover that in the Pauline text the counter-concept to a privileged speech (*prophēteia*) is not writing but *glōssolalia*, and this separation of one form of speech from another implies a homology to the Derridean speech/writing opposition. How, then, is *glōssolalia* like Derridean writing? Implicit in the very structure of writing is the absence of author, addressee, signified and referent, and *glōssolalia* is similarly a discourse of absence and therefore a form of writing. Here, there is no author or subject of speech, no centred self, secure in its own participation in the *logos*, to impose the tyranny of an allegedly universal meaning on an addressee. As a glossolalist, Paul complains, 'my spirit prays but my mind (*nous*) is unfruitful' (1 Cor. 14.14). The scandal of a spoken speech that bypasses and decentres the centred self, a colourless, neutral medium in which one participates but which one never masters, is the scandal of language itself. This medium is song-like, for in it one 'sings with the Spirit', the mysterious suprapersonal power that gives to be sung a melody or melodizing without beginning or end in which one may for a while take one's part. If this speech or song presupposes the absence of the centred self as the originator of meaning, it also presupposes the absence of an addressee. This, again, is part of its scandal: where this utterance of the material signifier is heard, *no-one understands what is said* – a point that is reiterated, in puzzlement and indignation, over and over again. The hearer, who would 'normally' fulfil the role of the addressee, finds him- or herself unable to do so. 'If you bless with the Spirit, how will the one who plays the part of the outsider say the Amen to your thanksgiving, if he does not understand what you are saying?' (v. 16) Outraged common-sense can only assume that the absence of the addressee is an unfortunate accident or breakdown that must be brought to the glossolalists' attention; it can only conceive of *glōssolalia* within the confines of a naïve model of language as the sender's intentional communication of a determinate message to an addressee.

A speech from which the addressee is structurally absent is inconceivable. Thus, here, an author ('Paul') sends a message to a certain addressee ('the church of God which is at Corinth' (1.2)). He does not do so in a strange language, for that would be to waste his breath by 'speaking into the air' (14.9), and his speech would then be 'unfruitful' (*akarpos*, cf. 14.14). This self-evident, common-sense, hierarchical model of language is, however, *paternal*, the language of the father: 'Though you have countless guides [*murious paidagōgous*] in Christ, you do not have many fathers [*ou pollous pateras*] – for in Christ Jesus, through the gospel, I fathered you [*egennēsa humas*]' (4.15). The paternal sower sows the word, and this seminal word is not unfruitful (*akarpos*) but begets the *ekklēsia*. How could paternal authority ever sanction that unfruitful dissipation of the precious seminal substance 'into the air'? *Glōssolalia*, like writing, is 'a nonviable seed' that 'overflows wastefully..., incapable of engendering anything, of picking itself up, of regenerating itself.' On the other hand, 'living speech makes its capital bear fruit and does not divert its seminal potency toward indulgence in pleasures without paternity' (*Dissemination*, 152). An emissary of paternal authority, the letter here takes the suggestive form of the scroll which in both form and content symbolizes and anticipates the paternal 'rod' (*rabdos* (4.21)) which will be inflicted if unlawful, oral textuality, perpetrated with the tongue (*glōssa*), does not immediately cease. And the paternal rod symbolizes, of course, the lawful generative power that issued in paternity.[13]

The absence of sender and addressee is also the al sence of the signified. The glossolalist, whom no-one understands, 'utters mysteries in the Spirit' (14.2), and the common-sense promulgated by the father can conceive this absence of a determinate signified only as a *lack*. 'Therefore, the one who speaks in a tongue should pray for the power to interpret' (v. 13): only so will the deficiency be remedied and legitimacy be restored, as the material signifier is compelled to open up its body to the lawful violence of phallocentric meaning. Yet the conquest is not total, for something has succeeded in eluding this violent mastery. If, says Paul, I speak in tongues without 'love' – that is, if the glossolalist rejects the model of language as communication and so fails to 'edify the church' with his or her meaningful speech – 'I am a sounding gong or a clanging cymbal' (13.1). What is meant by this? *Glōssolalia* is represented not as speech but as mere noise. Musical instruments in general are 'lifeless' (*apsucha* (14.7)), and the deadest of all are the ones that are not only formed from metal rather than from organic (vegetable or animal) substances but are also played by being *struck* rather than through the intimate warmth of human breath. *Glōssolalia* is an empty, hollow sound devoid of human meaning, and it is this sound that must be reintegrated into normal linguistic communication by way of interpretation, or forcible recoding (14.13). Like anything else, the sound of a gong *can* be turned into the bearer of a determinate signified (in a particular social context it may signify, for example, that a meal is ready to be served). Here, however, the use of this image necessitates the impossibility of any such integration into meaningful communication, for it is supposed to signify precisely the *absence* of meaningful communication, a form of speech that was no more than a hollow, ringing sound, as devoid of intentional meaning as a natural occurrence.

At this point, the act of repression on which this Pauline critique of the material signifier is founded begins to disclose itself. Here is a sound that cannot be integrated into speech and which must be banished to the outside. Loud metallic noises have no place in the Christian community. Yet the clanging cymbal (*kumbalon alalazon*) alludes to the very instrument which in Ps. 150.5 is employed in the praise of God: 'Praise him with loud cymbals' (*aineite auton en kumbalois alalagmou*). Here there is no question of an exclusion of *ta apsucha* in the name of *agapē* or *nous* or whatever, for this text continues (and concludes) by exhorting 'everything that has breath' (*pasa pnoē*) to 'praise the Lord' (Ps. 150.6). The metallic instruments are not only 'sounding' (*ēchon* (1 Cor. 13.1)) but 'well-sounding' (*en kumbalois euēchois* (Ps. 150.5a)), and their joyful sound is taken up into a worship of God which is communal and not merely private, although a rationalist with no ear for music might no doubt object that their sound is mere sound and does not communicate determinate meaning to the hearer. It is precisely in this absence of the signified that the praise of God takes place, and the linguistic artefact – the psalm – that accompanies and elucidates the instrumental music contents itself with announcing this situation and does not violate it by imposing an interpretation drawn from elsewhere. The praise of God in music is irreducible to any other language. Singing with the *pneuma* – circumventing *nous* and *logos* – must therefore be acknowledged as the vehicle of the praise of God, despite the initial attempt to disparage it as mere metallic noise, for singing and resounding metal belong together in a system of nonsignification. In this system, God is not a transcendent being outside a language which may be transcended in the act of silence, the withholding of speech out of an awareness of the all-too-human nature of this imperfect artefact which disqualifies it as a means of ascent into the divine sphere. Silence here is a mere act of violence imposed from outside (1 Cor. 14.28, 34), and the *utterance* of divine mysteries (*mustēria* (14.2)) is of their very essence. If *glōssolalia* is a way to the divine, it is no arbitrary vehicle which somehow transports us beyond its own limits but a participation in 'the languages of angels' (13.1) out of which the divine is constituted. *Glōssolalia* takes its part in the play of the divine music, evoking in the player or singer the ecstasy or *jouissance* that springs from the decentring and bypassing of subjectivity, freeing one from the nostalgic or guilt-ridden quest for a truth transcending textuality.

Paul the Apostle shares with Paul de Man the view that music is 'a pure system of relations that at no point depends on the substantive assertions of a presence, be it as a sensation or as a consciousness'; 'a mere play of relationships…, hollow at the core, because it "means" the negation of all presence' (*Blindness and Insight* (1983²), 128). The difference lies in the determination of the former, in pursuance of his vocation as a purveyor of absolutized speech, to subject the aberrant logic of music to the theo-logic of speech. Thus for him the trumpet (*salpinx* – another metallic instrument) is not engaged in a praise of God without signification, as in Ps. 150.3 ('Praise him with the sound of the trumpet'), but as an instrument of signification within the violent, hierarchical structures of the language of military conflict: 'If the trumpet gives an indistinct sound, who will prepare for battle?' (1 Cor. 14.8) The trumpet is here a surrogate for meaningful, imperative human speech, and its nonsignifying, musical character is suppressed. Music must be brought into the sphere of determinate meaning if the threat it poses is to be contained: the breakdown of meaning is represented as an accidental result of incompetent execution, rather than as inherent in the structure of music. 'If even lifeless instruments, such as the flute or the harp [*eite aulos eite kithara*], do not give distinct notes, who will know what is played [*to auloumenon ē to kitharizomenon*]?' (v. 7). But here the strain of protecting the stability of an inherently unstable position begins to show, for music refuses here to obey the model of meaningful communication to which Paul wishes to subject it, asserting, against his intentions, its own *self*-referentiality: the *aulos* communicates no meaning outside *to auloumenon*, any more than the *kithara* does outside *to kitharizomenon*. Again, it is claimed that *glōssolalia* is, as a breakdown in communication, analogous to playing the flute or the harp *badly*, so badly that no recognizable melody is forthcoming. But if the musical play of the flute or the harp issues only in what is fluted and in what is harped, then this play is analogous not to meaningful communication but to *glōssolalia*. The attempt to confine, to delimit and to master exposes only its own impotence in the face of that which is radically irreducible to, or untranslatable into, its own linguistic practice.

This *scherzo* could be indefinitely extended by devising further playful variations on its main themes, in accordance with the self-generative character of deconstructive analysis, a tendency to spread and to proliferate which precludes brevity and simplicity. Its musical play may, like many of Derrida's own texts, be seen as an attempt to actualize 'the Nietzschean *affirmation*, that is the joyous affirmation of the play of the world and of the innocence of becoming, the affirmation of a world of signs without fault, without truth, and without origin which is offered to an active interpretation' (*Writing and Difference*, 292). Asserting now a non-ironic stance outside the labyrinth, it is necessary to reflect on and to assess the experience of having been inside it. Deconstruction naturally claims that no such position outside the labyrinth is possible and that any discourse that asserts such a position will secretly fall victim to that which it denounces; but since that is all it ever says to anyone, friend or foe, it may be worth considering whether we are really condemned to this monotonous repetition in which every text is compelled to repeat the same thing, 'over and over again'. The appearance of playful and spontaneous inventiveness serves to conceal the harsh fate of the repetition to which deconstructive analysis binds us.

Where, then, are the limits and limitations of this extended gloss on the Pauline text to be found? We must search for that which belongs to its structure and not merely to its execution. As a performance, it may be judged a good, bad or indifferent mimesis of certain recognizable features of the style, conceptuality and ethos of the well-established, complex tradition of deconstructive analysis. Nothing in it is particularly innovative or unfamiliar. Apart from the relatively novel selection of a Pauline text on which to display its powers of execution, it belongs with the herd, and there is nothing in it which may not find support and legitimation in citations or proof-texts culled from the canonical texts of the established masters in this field. All that is necessary, however, is that the execution be tolerable enough to give an impression of the virtuoso performances of which others with greater technical mastery are capable – in order to establish where their limits lie.

Do the limits of this particular performance lie in the fact that it has imposed a modern philosophical problem onto the biblical text, suppressing the particularity of historical contingencies that interpretation should rather respect? In principle there is much to be said for a critique of deconstruction that contrasts the monomania that makes every text say the same thing with a respect for particularity. In a context, however, where an obsession with particularity is already overwhelmingly dominant, such a criticism functions only to perpetuate the old historical-critical ways with their own glaring limitations. In this context it would be appropriate to defend and to align oneself with Derrida's claim that writing – *écriture*, scripture – is the privileged locus of disclosure where Being in some sense gives itself to be known. For Derrida, the scriptures where the disclosure occurs belong to the philosophical and literary canons rather than to the biblical one,[14] and the disclosure itself is not something that Christian theology should recognize as such; yet the principle that scripture is of greater and more comprehensive significance than is supposed by the various scholarly orthodoxies is one that is worth defending. The deconstructive reading of the Pauline text has already secured for us a certain distance from the first-century contingencies that preoccupy the scholarly literature, thus helping to open up the further possibility of a theological reflection on the primary text in which a simultaneous, coinhering engagement with contemporary theological issues excludes a narrow biblicism in both its conservative and its historical-critical forms.

The limitations of deconstructive analysis may be found not in its treatment of texts *per se* but in its view of language in relation to the human person. The deconstructive reading offered two conflicting models of human speech. In one, a hierarchy was asserted in which human speech can become the earthly emissary of a heavenly, absolutized *logos* issuing from the mouth of God; this human speech must therefore call imperiously for submission and obedience. Over against this totalitarianism was placed a speech free from the tyranny of subject, addressee and referent, which served to subvert and to ironize the voice of paternal authority. What is overlooked, here and in deconstructive analysis generally, is the possibility that *language need not serve either authoritarian or libertarian ends but may be employed as a vehicle of dialogue between human persons*. The reason why the embeddedness of language in a shared social world is overlooked is a prior decision to exclude, so far as possible, the concept of the human subject who speaks to and is addressed by another. The priority of *langue* over *parole* is thought to rule out the possibility that an utterance might be significantly related to its speaker. Speech is supposed to share in the structure of writing, from which the author is absent, and it is therefore a logocentric illusion to believe that the individual human person is the originator and initiator of speech. There is no pre-linguistic, immaterial thought-substance which leaves the purity of its origin to become incarnate in the materiality of speech, for individual speech is merely a local manifestation of an impersonal language within which everything that can be said is already pre-scribed in advance. In this contemporary determinism, the individual person is now a mere site for the play of various discourses, and an instance of speech is thus to be traced back not to an individual speaker but to language itself. As the author is absent from writing, so the speaker is absent from speech. Language speaks, and the speaker is merely its mouthpiece. I do not speak a language, but the language speaks me. The human person is conceived as a machine for the receiving, decoding and transmitting of messages reaching it from outside. These machines are not identical, and the messages they transmit will depend in part on their respective locations and capacities; yet no privileged space of individuality is to be found in them, no power of originating messages, and no power of interaction. Yet they convey the illusion of individual origination, for does it not look exactly as though their messages proceeded wholly from *within* them?

Admittedly, Derrida does not describe human beings as machines. Yet writing (the absence of the subject, expelled by a mechanism which works of its own accord) is inscribed within human speech, and 'calculation, the machine, and mute writing belong to the same system of equivalences' (*Margins of Philosophy*, 107). Derrida is able to contain the mechanistic tendencies in his central philosophical themes by a self-identification with the Nietzschean *Übermensch* who laughs, dances and plays in active forgetfulness of Being (136), an image that may be applied to much of his textual production. But there is no basis in Derrida for the connotations of freedom, spontaneity and naturalness that would normally accompany this language, and therefore no freedom from the constraints of a writing-machine that operates in and through our speech. Derridean 'play' is the product of an *amor fati* which has learned to recognize and be happy in these constraints:

> I want to learn more and more to see as beautiful what is necessary in things; then I shall be one of those who make things beautiful. *Amor fati*: let that be my love henceforth! I do not want to wage war against what is ugly. I do not want to accuse; I do not even want to accuse those who accuse. *Looking away* shall be my only negation. And all in all and on the whole: some day I wish to be only a Yes-sayer. (F. Nietzsche, *The Gay Science*, §276)

While the confessional mode, with its suggestion of a still-intact subjectivity, is alien to Derrida, some such play-full acquiescence in the operation of the writing-machine is implied in his commendation of 'Nietzschean affirmation' or yes-saying. But, as for Nietzsche, accusation remains a necessity in the present, and the play of the *Übermensch* belongs properly to an unsayable future out of which one nevertheless strives to live in the present. Accusation is directed against those who do not understand that an anonymous writing traverses their speech and who believe that in their speech they utter a truth proceeding from outside of language.

Derrida's view of language thus entails a particular understanding of the human person which eliminates not only subjectivity, in the Kierkegaardian sense of the absolute priority of the existing individual, but also *relatedness*. The 'increasingly insistent and increasingly rigorous recourse to Nietzsche in France', in which Derrida participated, took place in reaction against a post-war context where, 'under the name of Christian or atheist existentialism, and in conjunction with a fundamentally Christian personalism, the thought that dominated France presented itself essentially as humanist' (*Margins of Philosophy*, 135, 115).[15] To speak of human relatedness, even in a quite different intellectual climate, would (for Derrida) still align one with the fundamentally Christian humanism to whose deconstruction or destruction he is committed. Since a Christian humanism which asserts the priority of human relatedness is indispensable for a politically-oriented theology, there can be no reconciliation or compromise at this point; nor can there be any dialogue on Derrida's own ground, for the concerns that would motivate such a dialogue have been excluded from that ground in advance.

It is therefore necessary simply to leave Derrida at this point, in order to seek in contemporary theological and non-theological 'humanism' a better understanding of the relation between language, human relatedness and the human person. Having achieved an alternative perspective, it will then be possible to offer a second, non-deconstructive, theological reading of the Pauline text that proceeds from the new perspective and also responds to the legitimate concerns of the first reading.

Chapter 6

Persons in Dialogue

What is required in response to poststructuralism is an approach which sees the human person as constituted and not eliminated by its socio-linguistic formation. A theological account of such a view of the human person has been developed by Alistair McFadyen in *The Call to Personhood* (1990), on which I shall be heavily dependent in the discussion that follows. McFadyen defends this view not against poststructuralism but against the individual-istic claim that persons precede relations, yet his theory of the person as formed within a social matrix can also be employed in the opposite direction to criticize the poststructuralist elimination of the concept of the person (or individual). What is required is a relational understanding of the human person which does not sacrifice its integrity as inalienably individual, and this contrasts with a perspective in which the concept of the person is so inseparable from the notion of the self-constituting ego that the counter-concept of a linguistically-mediated relationality simply eliminates personhood and individuality.

The more dialectical view is grounded in a relational, dialogical under-standing of the image of God: 'The Genesis creation narratives speak of human creation together in God's image in a way that should make impossible any Christian talk of individuals as isolated, individual entities' (McFadyen, 18).[1] In its vertical dimension, the concept of the image represents humankind as called by God's address to the autonomous response appropriate to dialogue, over against a 'pathological monotheism' in which God is conceived as the archetypal self-constituting individual, so that 'relations and communication must be a one-way (monological) exercise of determinating, manipulative and dominating power, which may affect others but which leave God untouched' (25). In its horizontal dimension, the image of God is closely related to the creation of humankind not in the form of an isolated individual but as male and female – that is,

107

as essentially (and not merely secondarily) relational.[2] The Yahwistic text which, unlike the Priestly, seems at first to posit a solitary individual goes on to show that 'it was not good for Adam to be alone, or at least only with the animals; in relation to them, to an animal Thou he could affirm only an animal I' (32). It is the creation of Eve which first makes reciprocity and personhood possible:

> If Eve only belonged to Adam without his also belonging to her, his isolation would not be broken. He would then have only another animal being and not one for whom he may also become a Thou. Adam can only say 'I' in the recognition that Eve is a human Thou before him and therefore an I for herself. The relationship between them involves the recognition both of her independence and that he becomes what he is only in relation to her; only, that is, through their mutual recognition or co-intention of each other as related but distinct Thou–Is. (33)

Gender-difference is to be seen as paradigmatic of human relationality in general, and does not imply that heterosexual marriage is the norm for true personhood.

These theological-exegetical points may, at least in their horizontal dimension, be readily integrated into the account of the person developed by Jürgen Habermas and others, which is oriented towards investigation of the socio-linguistic forces that determine and shape personal being.[3] Thus, for example, the relational view of the person may be demonstrated from the apparently simple phenomenon of the use of the first person singular personal pronoun in everyday communication. According to McFadyen,

> In using 'I', I am not referring to a thing (e.g. my 'self'), but to my position as a point location relative to others, and referring to that point as the location from whence communication may originate and with which communication may be conducted. 'I' does not indicate an internal entity or a static substance, but might be considered a portable means for contextualising oneself (a 'shifter'), a means for engaging in communication in various contexts, and constructing local personal (relational) identities... The under-standing of oneself as an I can then be the product neither of some internal experience nor of the possession of a static state or substance (e.g. 'self'); it can only be the product of engaging in processes of social communication in which others experience 'me' as 'you' and address and treat me as such. The 'I' is abstracted from experiencing

membership of a communication community in which one's status as a person (an I) is assumed. It is derived from being treated as a person within a given social (i.e. moral) order in which socially relative expectations are attached to the assumption that persons are continuous points of experience and of action and locations responsible for communication. (81–82)

The social formation of persons, their integration into a linguistic community through a gradually-acquired competence in its communicative procedures, creates a subjectivity which is to be understood in relational terms and not as self-constituting; but this does not amount to a view of the human person as a mere transmitter of anonymous messages which originate wholly outside itself. To use the pronouns 'I' and 'you' is to designate oneself and the other as originators of communication, and the fact that one makes use of pre-existent, prescribed communicative conventions is compatible with the relative originality and freedom with which they are deployed at any given juncture. (Thus the course of a communicative exchange will not be exactly predictable in advance by either dialogue-partner; a degree of openness and risk, within certain well-founded but not infallible expectations, is normal.) This originality is always only relative and never pure because it proceeds out of an internalized intersubjective network of communicative conventions which constitutes the social world within which all dialogue takes place. And yet the constitution of individuality within a determinate social world is no justification for the elimination of the pronoun 'I', with its claim to a relative autonomy, and the substitution of 'we' or 'they'. The 'self' that understands itself as self-constituting needs to be 'decentred' in the sense of recognizing itself not as a mere arena within which various anonymous discourses play and compete, but as always already a social product whose attainment of centredness occurs only through encounter with the reality of other centred persons. I can say 'I' only because I have previously been addressed as 'you' by other persons, in a manner that invites from me a response that reciprocally addresses them as 'you' and so acknowledges them as centred beings similar to yet other than the centred being I have now become; that is, an 'I' capable of initiating and receiving communication.

These objective or intersubjective structures of the social world are not as universally benign in their effects as the preceding paragraph may have suggested. The social world is not constituted solely by the mutual acknowledgement of I and Thou, as an apolitical theory of relationality would tend to suggest, for communication occurs only within a horizon in which massive, systematic communicative breakdown or distortion is also normal.[4] I become an 'I' because certain persons address me as a 'you' and because I reciprocate their address, but already in this small-scale primary social location distortions may occur. A serious and long-term discrepancy may develop between the 'I' I am expected or required to become and the 'I' that I wish to be; there is held out before me, like a set of clothes, an identity which others project for me but which I do not wish to assume. While this discrepancy may reflect contingent aspects of my individual situation, it may derive ultimately from elements in the broader social world which permeate, shape and constrain that individual situation. If I am addressed, for example, as a member of a marginalized group, the 'I' of my response will be distorted whether I submit to the imposed identity or attempt to resist it. I may experience material deprivation as, among other things, a form of communication in which my identity is projected by an anonymous other as unacceptable and worthless. Or, more comfortably situated at the other end of the social spectrum, the centred 'I' I become in being addressed and in addressing others may internalize the belief that there are certain classes of persons who are to be spoken *of* only in the third person plural, whose individual members are not to be regarded as possessing a subjectivity of their own and a right to engage 'us' in genuine communication. Thus, the social process by which persons are formed is at best only *relatively* undistorted. The social world whose existence is symbolized and enabled through the use of the personal pronouns is a complex space whose nature is largely opaque to all who inhabit it, a space in which communication takes place but is nevertheless everywhere *problematic*, with normality and routine perceptibly or imperceptibly intermingled with a violence, repression and falsehood in which one may be implicated as perpetrator or victim. The intersubjective matrix which forms individual, related persons also simultaneously *de*forms them. That which establishes me as a particular person may, as a constitutive element in that process, establish a perception of certain others as non-persons.

The opacity of the social world is such that the antithesis of genuine and distorted communication cannot be used to divide it neatly into two sectors, with perhaps an area of ambiguity between them. It does not seem particularly fruitful to apply this antithesis to much of the vast area of routinized interpersonal relations in which persons interact more or less adequately in accordance with well-defined roles. This is not to deny that systematically distorted communication may underlie and permeate the simplest interpersonal transactions; it is, rather, to seek for those areas of the social world in which this model of communication may most fruitfully be applied. The inability of this model to occupy the whole field is not really a problem, for it is neither possible nor necessary to summon the social world to give a full ethical account of itself.

McFadyen's identification of genuine and distorted communication with dialogue and monologue respectively is helpful in identifying the point at which the model may most fruitfully be employed. In monologue, the individual is manipulated or manipulates. One conversation-partner treats the other not as an autonomous subject but as an object, a means to an end:

> What is other is perceivable only as self-confirmatory and in terms of self-interest. Communication may intend the other only as an object, rather than autonomous subject, of communication. Otherness is reduced to a self-relation, real only as it appears in the subject's consciousness, as a repetition of a previously privately coordinated understanding: others cannot confront one as other, with their own reality and interests independent of one's own which establish both limits and claims on one. (26)

In dialogue, on the other hand,

> an address intends the other as a person, as an autonomous subject of communication... The form of the address intends the other as independent from this relation and this particular intention, and so acknowledges the other's freedom over against one. It is therefore recognised that the other may resist one's expectations and intentions in the relationship. For she or he is intended as an autonomous, self-centred subject of communication who may manufacture her or his own self-definitions and control appearance in public communication. To recognise and intend the freedom of the other in response is to recognise that the form and content of that response cannot be overdetermined by the address. (119)

In this undistorted communication, space is conceded to the other so that she or he may become not only a respondent to my questions but also an initiator who calls me to respond as well as to initiate:

> Making responsible answers to others cannot be a simple, mechanical response to a given stimulus which returns the intention in a way overdetermined by the other. That could hardly be called free or responsible. Yet neither may our responses be completely predetermined by our personal identities or intentions of these others which existed prior to their calls. That could hardly be called a response. Response must involve attending and returning to the other as she

or he is present in communication. This is a readiness to allow the calls of others to transform us in response. (121)

That does not mean, however, that undistorted communication requires a self-abnegation in which the other is intended as superior simply by virtue of his or her otherness, for that would entail not only the abandonment of one's own individuality but also the abandonment of dialogue and a self-subjection to the other's monologue. Just as the other is to be ceded space within which to resist my communication if she or he so chooses, so I must retain for myself the space which makes resistance possible. In addition, the reciprocity or equality thereby safeguarded is not to be understood in quantitative terms:

> In dialogue, equality refers to a formal identity between the partners, to the quality of their intersubjective engagement. It does not refer to their material identities, or to an equality in the quantity of the social space–time they occupy, or yet to their taking on the dialogue roles of I and Thou an equal number of times. A purely quantitative notion of equality issues in a tit-for-tat understanding of personal relationships where every communication has to return a response equal in quantity, where every gift has to be returned. As people are materially non-identical they have different needs and capacities for self-communication. A dialogical understanding of equality will be based upon and reflect these differences. (144)

Something similar is suggested by the Pauline image of the church as body, where the allocation of varying gifts and roles by the same Spirit establishes a formal equality– no-one is any more or less a member of the body than anyone else – within a diversity of roles which allows for hierarchical elements so long as these are understand in strictly reciprocal rather than monological terms.

This model may appear to be so closely bound up with small-scale, one-to-one relations that its broader political applicability is questionable, despite the emphasis on the social matrix of even the most intimate of relationships. In fact, however, the analysis is directly applicable to collective as well as to individual relationships.[5] A monological relationship occurs not only when an overbearing individual refuses to allow sufficient space to the other, but also when, for example, a hegemonic power ensures, through control of the media of communication, that an oppressed or dissident minority is never permitted the public space to question its monological definitions of self and other in such a way as to open up a dialogue which might help to secure change. Thus 'the dialogical form of the public sphere in which political objectives and interests are debated... functions as a normative referent for the exercise of political power' (208). 'Distorted socio-political structures which inappropriately exclude some people and their communication can only be tested . nd redeemed by the self-communication of excluded interest groups' (218). The attractiveness of this model is precisely its ability to operate in both the 'political' and the 'personal' spheres. As opposed to models of relationality that work almost exclusively in only one of these spheres, it is able to show that the social structures which produce the one also produce the other.

Exploring this theory of social relationships appears to have led us away from our starting-point in the critique of deconstruction. The intention, however, was to show the inadequacy of the poststructuralist elimination of the subject by outlining a theory in which subjectivity or personhood is not eliminated by the fact of its social construction but, on the contrary, constituted by that fact. This point lies at the heart of the critique of poststructuralism developed by Jürgen Habermas, most notably in *The Philosophical Discourse of Modernity* (German original, 1985). Habermas depicts modern philosophy as proceeding from a subjectivity construed in terms of the self-constituting ego. With reference to Derrida's critique of Husserl in *Speech and Phenomena* (French original, 1967), Habermas notes that Derrida ignores

> the point where the paradigm of linguistic philosophy separates from that of philosophy of consciousness and renders the identity of meaning dependent upon the intersubjective practice of employing rules of meaning. Instead, Derrida follows Husserl along the path of separating off (in terms of transcendental philosophy) every innerworldly thing from the performances of the subject that are constitutive of the world, in order to take up the battle against the sovereignty of ideally intuited essences within its innermost pre-cincts. (172)

In other words, the philosophy of consciousness or subjectivity that Derrida opposes with his theory of the originality of language and difference still controls his critique, which is a critique *from within*. Claiming to be a critique from within a very large entity, designated 'western metaphysics' and incorporating the entire western philosophical tradition, Derrida is in fact engaged in the self-critique of what had become, in his own context in the second half of the twentieth century, a rather more restricted and local philosophical tradition. Language is employed solely to combat the illusions of the philosophy of consciousness, and the fact – which could have been learned from Saussure's view of language as a social contract,[6] as well as from Wittgenstein or Austin – that language may be understood in terms of intersubjectivity is overlooked. Derrida's 'denial of this independently structured domain of everyday communicative practice' (204) in his debate with Austin stems from a systematic aestheticizing of language which induces an 'insensitivity toward the tension-filled polarity between the poetic/world-disclosive function of language and its prosaic, innerworldly functions' (205). In place of this aestheticism, Habermas offers

> a different, less dramatic, but step-by-step testable critique of the Western emphasis on logos [which] starts from an attack on the abstractions surrounding logos itself, as free of language, as universalist, and as disembodied. It conceives of intersubjective understanding as the telos inscribed into communication in ordinary language, and of the logocentrism of Western thought, heightened by the philosophy of consciousness, as a systematic *foreshortening* and *distortion* of a potential always already operative in the communicative practice of everyday life, but only selectively exploited. (311)

From a political–theological perspective, the theory of intersubjectivity or communicative practice has the advantage of operating, like any recognizably Christian theology, in the world of persons and not in the aesthetic fantasy-world of an enclosed textuality.

Theological versions of this theory will have to account for the role of the church in the midst of the social world and its structures of distorted and undistorted communication. If, as McFadyen claims, the church is 'any place where properly structured individualities and relations are co-present' (61), then it is conceived as a structural possibility of appropriate relations given in the creation of humankind in the image of God and not entirely eradicated by the fall. The difficulty with this is that, as we have seen, the relatively undistorted communication that calls forth personhood may occur within structures which effectively deny or constrain the personhood of others. Only where such distortions are *overcome* can one speak of a movement away from the old towards the new future of the kingdom of God, and only with reference to this movement can one speak of 'the church'. It is therefore preferable to retain (as McFadyen does elsewhere) the more conventional notion of the church as a specific historical community which not only incorporates (like any other community) the possibility of relatively undistorted communication derived from creation and fall but also relates its existence primarily to the eschatological vision of universally undistorted communication which lies at the heart of its gospel of the kingdom of God.[7] Any movement from distorted to undistorted communication is the redemptive movement of exodus of which the church speaks and whose universal, eschatological horizon it announces, thereby interpreting it as a movement with a genuine future even if in inner-historical terms it fails to come to fruition or is reversed.[8]

We have now reached the point from which a theological interpretation of the Pauline text earlier deconstructed can fruitfully begin. The theological issue that must be addressed, by way of the Pauline text, is as follows: *if the movement from distorted, monological communication to undistorted, dialogical communication is interpreted by the church as both redemptive and anticipatory of the eschatological future of the kingdom of God, then this process of interpretation must itself be dialogical.* The revelation of the dialogical nature of humankind's eschatological future cannot be bestowed in the form of a monological communication if such a communication is a denial of the autonomous personhood of the addressee, for the form of the revelation would then be radically at variance with its content. Yet the dialogical reception necessitated by such a revelation would not involve a simple, direct relation between God and a privileged human being, for in biblical tradition the revelation or word of God encounters human beings in the form of a human word. Even in the case of the prophetic 'Thus says the Lord', what is directly encountered is a human word with idiosyncrasies of style and content which mark it as simultaneously the word of a particular human being. The vertical dimension of the divine image is not prior to the horizontal in the sense that the relation of the individual to God is the primary source of his or her personhood, to which a horizontal, human relationality is then added. In the creation of humankind, in the image of God, as male and female, the horizontal and the vertical dimensions are posited as equally original, with the result that each is the mediation of the other. The individual who acknowledges God as creator and redeemer does not do so as a self-enclosed monad but as a member of a human community which is the social matrix within which his or her identity as a believer and a worshipper has been dialogically formed. The individual who seeks to engage the other in genuine dialogue acknowledges, in the act of doing so, objectively and perhaps also subjectively, the image of God and therefore the mediated presence of God in the other. If the image of God in the other constitutes a call to dialogue – rather than, say, a monologue addressed by either party to the other, or mutual indifference – then the same will be true when God's presence in the other is mediated not only in the universal form of the image of God but in the concrete form of the word of God. We will, in fact, have to relativize the idea that human utterance of the word of God is an *office* held on a permanent basis by certain individual members of the community – apostles, prophets, ministers, priests, bishops – whose role is to transmit a word which must simply be acknowledged by the rest of the community. Such a view is fundamentally monological (or logocentric). While particular office-holders can be the initiators of communication, it is more appropriate to see the revelation or word of God as located within the process of dialogue thereby initiated than to locate it solely in the statement that opens it. Criteria, deriving both from the revelation and the determinate social context of its reception, would naturally be deployed within the dialogical process for distinguishing undistorted from distorted communication of the word of God, and insofar as these criteria were correctly applied reception of the revelation or word of God would have occurred within the dialogue. The concept of dialogue does not imply either an easy consensus or an agreement to differ but necessitates a willingness to resist what one perceives as the distortions in the other's communications.[9]

The particular difficulty in establishing this point in this area lies in the belief that the apodictic quality proper to divine truth is more effectively presented in monological (or logocentric) rather than dialogical discourse. In other contexts, apodictic speech is not necessarily monological. It *may* take the form of a demand for submission which violates the addressee's autonomy, but it may equally be an invitation to a free acknowledgement that will not simply repeat it but which will apply, develop and integrate it in ways not foreseen or controlled by the initiator. Yet the idea that the mediation of the divine word through human speech should be monological rather than dialogical is deeply entrenched.[10] In returning to 1 Cor. 14, it is therefore necessary to ask whether this passage represents the speech appropriate within the Christian community as inherently dialogical.

At one point it seems that dialogue is conclusively excluded. 'As in all the churches of the saints, the women should keep silence in the churches. For they are not permitted to speak, but should be subordinate, as even the law says. If there is anything they desire to know, let them ask their husbands at home' (1 Cor. 14.33b–35). No amount of special pleading can conceal the fact that what occurs here is the violent suppression of dialogue in the name of a truth that is now to be experienced by women in a heteronomous and monological form which undermines their status as persons (for to be a person is to be a dialogue-partner). The primary locus of this truth is now to be the world of the male. Even the dialogue that is still permitted in the privacy of the home is deeply distorted, for in it women seek only to remedy their own deficiency of knowledge out of the superabundant understanding of the male. The rather strong exegetical arguments for regarding this passage as a post-Pauline insertion are less important than a recognition of the theological rationale for rejecting it whether or not Paul is deemed to be the author.[11] Having rejected this passage, we note that in v. 1 Paul exhorts *every* member of the congregation to desire the gift of prophecy, and this must include women. Even in chapter 11, in the course of an embarrassed, self-contradictory and undoubtedly Pauline argument for a degree of female subordination, it is assumed that women pray and prophesy within the congregation (v. 5). Women and men are initiators of communication in the church at Corinth.

A further reference to silence in this chapter relates to the glossolalists, who are to keep silent if there is no-one to interpret their mysterious utterances (v. 28). Is this a totalitarian, monological, logocentric silencing of the free, an-archic, musical discourse of the material signifier which, through the erasure of determinate meaning, participates in the divine discourse?[12] But their enforced silence is the mirror-image and the solution to the silence they impose on others who do not understand what is being said. 'If you bless with the spirit, how can anyone in the position of an outsider say the Amen to your thanksgiving?' (v. 16). Not only do others not understand, they are excluded, compelled to play the role of the *idiōtes* who can admire, envy but not participate in the performances of the initiates. The significance of the material signifier is to be traced not in its musical play *per se* but in the power it gives its performers to establish a structure of inside and outside within the community. The term *idiōtes* is in fact later used synonymously with 'unbeliever' (*apistos*), but there it designates real outsiders who stray into Christian worship, encounter the melodious babble of *glōssolalia* and dismiss it and Christian faith as nonsense (v. 23). *Glōssolalia* thus confirms unbelieving outsiders in their unbelief and establishes a new class of outsiders within the believing community. For the former it is simply non-communication, the refusal of a communication they had a right to expect; for the latter it is monological communication in its purest form. The glossolalists are speaking to God, they give utterance to divine mysteries, and yet the fact that they are also speaking in the hearing of the rest of the congregation means that a form of communication from inside to outside is nevertheless taking place. What is communicated is simply this structure of inside and outside in which the outsider is refused all participation while being expected to be present as a member of the audience. (Paul himself is powerfully drawn to this esotericism. He too speaks in tongues, *he* is no outsider (v. 18); among the initiates (*teleioi*) he utters divine mysteries that are beyond the understanding of the carnal Corinthians (2.6, 13; 3.1).)[13] The communication that emerges out of such profound hiddenness or descends from such a great height as to be perceptible only to an élite, who must be transported in the spirit above mere worldly realities, is, in one sense, dialogical: the élite begin to speak in response to what is spoken to them, whether they do so in the tongues of angels or of humans. Yet this esoteric revelation functions monologically for those who are present, who hear but do not understand, and who thus understand what they are intended to understand, which is that they are outsiders. The believer reconstituted as an *idiōtes* is the foot who says, 'Because I am not a hand, I do not belong to the body' (12.15). The glossolalist communicates no determinate meaning to the lowly foot except, 'I have no need of you' (12.21). Communication is distorted and this fact provides the criterion whereby the whole phenomenon can be judged and found wanting. Paul actually shares the glossolalists' self-understanding: they really do utter mysteries in the Spirit, their claim cannot be dismissed as nonsense in the cavalier manner of the real *idiōtai*, the unbelievers. And yet he believes that the true manifestation of the Spirit occurs in intersubjective understanding, in the light of which even the most impressive esotericism is a dangerous and distracting mystification which must be resisted. That which is truly divine gives itself to be *understood* in ordinary human speech, however much esotericists may deplore this view as a crude, rationalistic subjection of the ineffable heights and depths of the divine, which can only be glimpsed by those skilled in the tongues of angels, to the limited capacities of ordinary ungifted people.

If *glōssolalia* is an extreme, monological refusal of dialogue, then what of *prophēteia*? Prophecy too may take a monological form. If there is an absolute qualitative difference between God and humankind (if, that is, the concept of the image of God is drained of all meaning), then the appropriate human response to the overwhelming divine word, uttered through the mediation of the prophet, will be abject submission. Since the prophet attaches to his or her own words the claim, 'Thus says the Lord', an understanding of prophecy as monological and therefore as distorted communication might seem inevitable. The charismatic phenomenon of prophecy might then be considered a primitive enthusiasm which the church rightly abandoned and whose contemporary manifestations (along with speaking in tongues) should be rejected as a hindrance to dialogue and understanding. These judgements may be correct; but I am concerned here not with prophecy as a phenomenon of the history of religion but with the way in which, in a specific canonical text, prophecy is understood as paradigmatic of undistorted communication within the Christian community. If the position developed thus far is correct, it should be possible to find dialogical elements in Paul's representation of this phenomenon.

We note first that the text reflects a disagreement over whether prophets have *control* over their utterance. 'If a revelation is made to another sitting by, let the first [prophet] be silent. For you can all prophesy one by one, so that all may learn and all be encouraged. The spirits of prophets are subject to prophets, for God is not a God of disorder but of peace' (vv. 30–33a). The impression this gives of a parent reminding the children that they must take turns and not fight for control of the desire object is misleading (although prophecy is a phenomenon of childhood in 13.9–11): this is not an elementary lesson in good manners but a statement about the nature of prophecy. If all speak at once, it is not because they lack the normal social skills – they are adult women and men – but because they understand prophecy as an irresistible inrush of divine power which overwhelms their rational faculties and their inhibitions and compels them to give immediate utterance. When the spirit of prophecy falls upon several members of the congregation at once, then naturally they must all prophesy together, as the seventy elders did when the Lord took some of the spirit that was upon Moses and distributed it among them (Num. 11.25). The pentecostal promise is that 'I will pour out my Spirit upon all flesh, and your sons and your daughters shall prophesy' (Joel 2.28; Acts 2.17), and this implies that in this overwhelming, ecstatic event normal rules of decorum will be suspended. To describe the community's prophesying as a disorderly cacophony (*apokatastasia*, 1 Cor 14.33) is not to give a neutral description of an objective state of affairs but to reject the participants' view of the rationale and significance of this phenomenon. Prophecy and *glōssolalia*, the privileged modes of speech within the life of the congregation, are both subjected to a criterion which will transform the way in which they are understood: the purpose of speech is a communication from one person to another which evokes understanding and a response, and the insistence on the application of this criterion stems not from a common-sense view of language *per se* but from theological considerations. Human beings are created in the image of God, and if the distance between God and humankind is therefore not absolute and unqualified there is no justification for believing that God speaks through abnormal, ecstatic and irrational channels. God speaks only by way of one human person addressing another in intelligible language, for the vertical relation to God implied in the concept of the image is mediated in the horizontal form of an essential relatedness among human beings.

The prophetic word will therefore be a human word. It is not the case that a *theopneustia*, a powerful impulse falling into the *nous* from above, is secondarily 'translated' into the form of a determinate language to which, in its real being, it is alien. That would again imply a God who is wholly other and who addresses us, if at all, in monological fashion. If the Corinthians are eager for manifestations of the Spirit, they should find the Spirit in everything that contributes to the building of community (cf. v.

12). If the Spirit who inspires prophecy already indwells the congregation and builds community, then the prophetic word does not fall from an alien sphere or speak of that which is wholly new and unheard of. The Spirit, immanent within the congregation, guides individuals to comprehend and to communicate possibilities of truth and praxis, appropriate for a determinate situation, which are already potentially present in the discourse of the community. These possibilities may lie ready-to-hand in current discourse, or they may lie concealed in an earlier discursive stratum which more recent developments have covered up. The prophet is the person who, guided by the Spirit who indwells the whole community, discerns the disclosive potentiality of a particular conjunction between elements of existing discourse and the determinate situation. In the disclosure that occurs, truth and praxis are inseparable. When an unbeliever enters the assembly and encounters the prophetic word, 'the secrets of his heart are disclosed, so that, falling on his face, he will worship God and declare that God is really among you' (v. 25). The disclosure of the truth is at the same time the disclosure of a new praxis, incipiently present here in an initial act of worship that will lead in principle to the transformation of existing norms and practices.

The fact that the divine word is a human word not only in form but also in content is a necessary but not a sufficient condition for an understanding of it as dialogical communication. If the effect of the prophetic word is *always* to cause its addressees to fall on their faces, then it is an essentially monological discourse, for the physical gesture of prostration removes one from the fact-to-fact exchange necessary for normal dialogue. Yet this gesture is here predicated not of every addressee of the prophetic word but specifically of the outsider or unbeliever who hears that word for the first time. (It is, however, indicated here that the prophetic word is apodictic in nature and that it is therefore not a tentative suggestion, a contribution to an ongoing debate or a relevant point of view, but a truth-claim.) The formal equality of prophet and (Christian) addressee, as participants in the one Spirit, is compatible with a difference of role that may involve a hierarchical element. The relatively hierarchical relation of prophet and addressee does not, however, establish a one-way, monological channel of communication, for when the prophet speaks the hearers are to *weigh what is said:* 'Let two or three prophets speak (in turn), and let the others judge [*kai hoi alloi diakrinetōsan*]' (v. 29).[14] Prophetic speech is apodictic speech that implies a claim to divine authority, but as a fully human speech that aims at undistorted communication it must invite a free, personal response whose content it cannot determine or fully anticipate. The outsider who falls to the ground in response to the prophetic word does so only as an initial acknowledgement of a word which, as he or she begins to participate in the community, will increasingly be grasped as dialogical, not as demanding prostration but as inviting responsive speech.[15] The responsive speech in which one assesses the prophetic word may itself be a gift of the Spirit, whose gifts include not only prophecy but also 'the discernment of spirits' (*diakriseis pneumatōn* (12.10)), that is, the assessment of the productions of those who exercise spiritual gifts (*pneumata*, as in 14.12) with regard to their truth, validity and significance. Unlike monological or logocentric speech, the prophetic word is not complete is itself but subject to dialogical reception by the community, and appropriate reception is as much the gift of the Spirit as is the apodictic speech that initiates the dialogue.

This understanding of the prophetic word as mediating the word of God only as it is assumed into dialogue rules out the possibility that in it an imperious, dominating God speaks in such a way as to intimidate hearers of this human word into silence. Over against Paul's exhortation to assess the prophetic word, the *Didache* warns its readers to do no such thing: 'Do not test or examine [*oude diakrineite*] any prophet speaking in the Spirit, for every sin shall be forgiven, but this sin shall not be forgiven' (11.7). The application of Jesus' saying about blasphemy against the Holy Spirit to the prophetic word ensures that the prophet's communication will be entirely monological. Recognizing that submissiveness bestows enormous social power on the prophet, rules are established in order to limit the self-interested exploitation of this power: thus, 'No prophet who orders a meal in the Spirit shall eat of it, otherwise he is a false prophet' (11.9) On the other hand, more self-confident, articulate church members will see the danger of according such unquestioned authority to prophetic utterances, and will be tempted to reject the possibility of prophecy altogether. A church conscious of its orderly traditions and structures may have no place for the potentially disorderly ideal of a human speech which claims to mediate a present revelation of God. Against an over-reaction of this kind Paul warns, 'Do not despise prophecy' (1 Thess. 5.20). Beyond the alternatives of superstitious acquiescence to a numinous discourse and of rejecting this discourse as an all-too-human exercise of social power, a third possibility is proposed: 'Test everything, hold fast to what is good, abstain from every kind of evil' (1 Thess. 5.21–22). Prophecy becomes the divine word only as it is accredited as such in the course of the dialogue that it initiates. In the *Didache's* view, testing is inappropriate and impossible because one is in no position to assess whether or not a prophetic utterance fell directly from above into the prophet's mind or whether its origin was purely human. If prophecy is understood in terms of the *theopneustia* of the individual, then it is indeed safer not to test its utterances. If, on the other hand, prophecy derives not from above, vertically, but from *within* the congregation indwelt by the Spirit, then it must be subjected through the dialogical process to communally-acknowledged criteria. In other words, the apodictic prophetic word is subject to the same rules of reception as any other non-monological apodictic statement. Such a statement requires a context (a determinate situation and addressee) which it strives to restructure in some way. It speaks in the language appropriate to that context. If it is to be non-monological, then it will not simply impose itself in authoritarian fashion but will invite the addressee freely to accept it as the basis for a dialogue whose purpose is the investigation of the truth, relevance and further implications of the initial statement. Understood in such a way, prophecy can constitute an undistorted communication in which the revelation or word of God comes to expression in the present through dialogue.

If the prophetic word does not descend vertically from above but derives from within the community indwelt by the Spirit, then it must not only draw on the discourse of the community in general but also reactualize in a determinate situation in the present the word of the gospel upon which the community is founded. This points to the two norms whose application guides the dialogical process. One is the norm of truth, which assesses the conformity of the prophetic word to the founding word; the other is the norm of appropriateness, which assesses whether the alleged statement of the truth for the present answers the particular, legitimate demands of this present. An over-emphasis on the second may mean that the content of the prophetic word derives wholly from within the horizons of the present, depriving it of any significant relation to the founding word which it ought to reactualize. An over-emphasis on the first may mean that the prophetic word merely repeats past actualizations of the founding word, thus depriving itself of the contemporary responsibility and significance which is integral to its being as prophecy. Genuine prophecy is addressed to the present, but, if it is to have anything to say that cannot already be said from within the horizons of that present, it must remain rooted in the tradition generated by the founding word. This does not mean, however, that the dialogical process of assessment should move towards a point of balance, a compromise between two norms seen as competing with one another in which contemporary relevance and the need for conformity with the founding word mutually limit one another. Any attempt to lay down abstract rules for the application of the norms would risk turning the dialogical process into a monologue. It would suggest that possibility of an ideal procedure of assessment which could be applied by a sufficiently skilful individual without the inconvenience of dialogue. It would also suggest that the conjuncture of truth and appropriateness is always to be located in a *via media* between opposing claims, although it is just as likely that the conjuncture will occur at a point which within a given situation is widely regarded as an extreme. In other words, there should be no facile rejection of a claim to truth and appropriateness merely because it is closely related either to contemporary realities or to past actualizations of the founding word. There can be no circumventing of the need for dialogue by constructing a set of rules.

In response to the earlier deconstructive reading of this Pauline text, I have attempted an alternative reading which is no less sensitive than its counterpart to the issue of logocentric or monological truth-claims but which resolves this problem not by purporting to show the indeterminacy and instability at the heart of any determinate assertion but by developing the thesis that the manner of the communication of revelation of the divine word is essentially and inherently dialogical. This thesis is grounded in the claim that the revelation of the eschatological horizon of universally undistorted communication must itself be communicated in a dialogical form rather than imposing itself unilaterally in the form of a monological demand for credence and submission. Whereas the individual posited in poststructuralist theory becomes a mere field for the play of various conflicting discourses deriving from outside, in my preferred reading a relational understanding of the image of God prevents any such reduction while at the same time rejecting the notion of the self-constituting individual of which deconstruction is rightly so critical. It did not seem worthwhile, however, to attempt a point-by-point demolition of the claims and procedures of deconstruction, many of which will have been easily recognizable in the sample deconstructive reading I offered. Since the problem deconstruction addresses is ultimately a theological one, theological and exegetical resources were deployed to construct an alternative solution to this problem which makes better conceptual sense in face of the socio-political realities of the world outside the text.

Chapter 7

Narratives of Postmodernity

The encounter with deconstruction in the two preceding chapters issued in reflection on the dialogical *communication* of divine revelation, without direct consideration of its *scope*. A postmodern context poses acute difficulties for the claim of Christian faith to universal validity, stemming from the biblical notion of creation in the image of God together with the eschatological horizon that this projects. Earlier, I distinguished a tradition of postmodern theorizing that privileges indeterminacy from one that privileges particularity, and a critical dialogue with this latter tradition, especially in its theological forms, is required if the possibility of a non-totalitarian understanding of this universal validity is to be brought to light.

According to George W. Stroup, 'Communities, like individuals, have identities and these identities... assume narrative form, narratives which re-present and interpret the community's history and experience' (*The Promise of Narrative Theology* (1981), 91). This representative statement registers the recent entry of the term 'narrative' (or 'story') into the theological lexicon, a linguistic shift that signals and symbolizes the postmodern moment in contemporary theological discourse.[1] While the gulf between theological traditions and deconstruction may prove too wide for the latter to become a major participant in contemporary theological discussion, this is not at all the case with the postmodern theorizing of narrativity as a basic structure of human existence in the world, which is very much at ease in a theological context. Here, the term 'modern' represents the theological 'modern*ism*' more commonly if vaguely referred to as 'liberalism' or 'liberal theology', and postmodern theology may therefore prefer to designate itself as 'postliberal.' The term 'postliberal' indicates both a preoccupation with certain aspects of 'liberal theology', above all its alleged false universality and disdain for particularities, and a desire to re-establish contact with the 'orthodoxy' that a now-exhausted modernism or liberal theology once supplanted. The contact desired, however, takes the form of a re-entry into a tradition now seen as a language that one speaks within a particular community, and not as the bearer of divinely-revealed propositional truths. This ostensible neo-conservative tendency may appear to be at odds with the connotations of the term 'postmodern', suggestive for many of an extreme, relativizing libertarianism. But that is only one interpretation of the postmodern condition, and the term can in fact be usefully employed to highlight points of contact between contemporary theological and non-theological theorizing. Some examples of non-theological uses of 'narrative' or 'story' can shed light on the theological appropriation of this term.[2]

If, with Lyotard, the postmodern condition is defined as 'incredulity toward metanarratives' (*The Postmodern Condition* (French original, 1979), xxiv), then large-scale theories about the world (associated with science, the emancipation of the proletariat, wealth-creation, and so on) are strategically redefined as *stories*. Stories are not unrelated to reality; they may be 'true stories', they may use 'real' settings, their characters may be 'based on' real, historical individuals. But the term 'story' in this context posits a relation to external reality which is vague, impossible to systematize, and anyway rendered irrelevant by the story's foregrounding of its internal rules and operations. A 'metanarrative' is thus a story which, by way of a mistaken genre-categorization, has had its nature as narrative suppressed so as to enable it to assume the new function of offering a relatively complete, 'totalizing' explanation of reality. When they are true to themselves, narratives are heterogeneous and lack the totalizing aspirations of the grand theory in which a single narrative, alienated from itself, is erected as the source and criterion of all the others. The notion of a single originary narrative stems simply from a category mistake, as the collapse of the structuralist project of identifying just such a narrative or narrative-matrix clearly demonstrates. Thus, within the very definition of the postmodern condition there lies an assumption about the universal necessity of narrative for the formation of human identity within community. Pointing to the consensus in anthropological research that 'the distance separating the customary state of knowledge from its state in the scientific age' stems from 'the preeminence of the narrative form in the formulation of traditional knowledge' (19), Lyotard argues that scientific and non-scientific knowledge are just different: 'All we can do is gaze in wonderment at the diversity of discursive species, just as we do at the diversity of plant or animal species' (26). From the heights of enlightenment, the scientist classifies narrative statements as belonging to a different mentality – as 'primitive, underdeveloped, backward, alienated, composed of opinions, customs, authority, prejudice, ignorance, ideology…, fit only for women and children' – , thereby giving expression to 'the entire history of cultural imperialism from the dawn of Western civilization' (27). Christianity is obviously included in this indictment of every discourse of totality which legitimates the terrorizing and extermination of whatever is local and particular. But terror must be renounced, and the heterogeneity of communally authoritative narratives must be protected and celebrated.[3]

'Story' may also be strategically deployed as a synonym for 'interpretation'. The task of disciplines in which texts constitute the objects of study is said to be 'interpretation'; the reading experience will be facilitated and enriched if one avails oneself of the help offered by those who specialize in resolving the difficulties and obscurities encountered in reading. Here 'interpretation' is akin to 'explanation', but an ambivalence enters the term from the usage in which the phrase 'only an interpretation' is employed to reduce a truth-claim to the relatively arbitrary and subjective factors from which it is supposed to derive. The differences of opinion that arise in the course of textual interpretation make its assimilation to 'mere interpretation' relatively easy.[4] If a truth-claim is already problematized by the term 'interpretation', a further step is taken when interpretation is assimilated to 'story'. Whereas 'interpretation' problematizes an assertion of a correspondence to reality, 'story' almost eliminates it by construing an assertion of fact as non-referential and self-sufficient. Thus, in debate with John Searle and speech–act theory, Stanley Fish claims that Searle's arguments

> rest on a basic opposition: brute facts vs. institutional facts, regulative rules vs. constitutive rules, serious discourse vs. fictional discourse, the natural vs. the conventional. In each case, the left-hand term stands for something that is available outside of language, something with which systems of discourse of whatever kind must touch base – Reality, the Real World, Objective Fact. What I am suggesting is that these left-hand terms are merely disguised forms of the terms on the right, that their content is not natural but made, that what we know is not the world but stories about the world, that no use of language matches reality but that all uses of language are interpretations of reality. (*Is There a Text in this Class?* (1980), 243)

The procedure is similar to Lyotard's. A 'metadiscourse' (here in the more modest form of a philosophical thesis about language) attempts to establish a hierarchy in which certain uses of language are accorded privileged status whereas others are marginalized, and it does so by ascribing to the language it privileges a correspondence to reality which is then denied to the marginalized language. In opposition to this procedure, this metadiscourse must be shown to be a metanarrative – that is, a narrative which in asserting a correspondence to reality is alienated from itself – and one does this by arguing that the presentation of the 'facts' within an interpretative framework immediately makes them questionable (for interpretation is 'mere interpretation'), that no securely-grounded and neutral criteria are available for adjudicating the questions that arise from within an alternative framework, and that the resultant incommensurability and undecidability may be dramatized by redefining two rival interpretations as 'stories' neither of which can be reduced to the other. Some stories, indeed, 'are more prestigious than others; and one story is always the standard one, the one that presents itself as uniquely true and is, in general, so accepted' (Fish, 239). However, a strange thing happens when we stop theorizing about interpretation and start practising it: in interpretative practice, 'one cannot be a skeptic... because one cannot achieve the distance from his own beliefs and assumptions that would result in their being no more authoritative *for him* than the beliefs and assumptions held by others or the beliefs and assumptions he himself used to hold' (361). We cannot be consistent sceptics or relativists, for 'as soon as you descend from theoretical reasoning about your assumptions, you will again inhabit them' (370). The metaphor of 'descent' suggests a metaphysic in which the realm of mere appearances or facts is seen for the illusion it is only if one is able to ascend to the standpoint of *theoria*. Conversely, as soon as one descends one is again surrounded by the illusion that we can *know* certain things about texts or the world, and not merely tell stories about them.[5]

This results in interesting divergences from Lyotard's position. The problematic status of a theory which asserts the ubiquity of stories (is the theory itself just another story?) is acknowledged by Lyotard at points in his text where the theory appears to convert itself into an ethic, a call to defend heterogeneity against totality. This makes it possible for the inhabitant of a particular narrative-world to defend its particularity against encroachments from outside, while depriving him or her of the possibility of defending a position on the grounds that it is not 'just a story' but, in some sense, *true*, in correspondence with the way things really are. Fish, on the other hand, concedes that in interpretative practice beliefs appear to be true (while the theoretical standpoint now appears to be false), and he therefore acknowledges the rift between the standpoints of the theoretician and of the locally-situated participant, which Lyotard suppresses. The theory can thus explain resistance to itself, the incredulity with which it is received, at the cost of conceding to that resistance an inevitability and therefore a relative right to exist. Despite this structural instability, however, there is no doubt that the standpoint of *theoria* yields up the truth, which is that 'what we know is not the world but stories about the world'.

According to Fish, 'the entities that were once seen as competing for the right to constrain interpretation (text, reader, author) are now all seen to be the *products* of interpretation' (16–17). That is, 'the interpretative principles *produce* the facts' (341, my italics). Does this analysis apply only in the rather fuzzy realm of literary criticism, or may it be extended into those paradigmatic practices of discovery rather than production, fact rather than value: the natural sciences? Thomas Kuhn, whose notion of incommensurable paradigms has been influential in postmodern theorizing, argues that here too what occurs is production more than discovery: 'In so far as their only recourse to that world is through what they see and do, we may want to say that after a revolution [or paradigm-shift] scientists are responding to a different world' (*The Structure of Scientific Revolutions* (1970²), 111). 'What occurs during a scientific revolution is not fully reducible to a reinterpretation of individual and stable data' (121), for the data themselves change. Richard Rorty dissents from the idealism of such statements (also vestigially present in Fish), but on characteristically postmodern pragmatic–ironic grounds. The view of physics, for example, as finding rather than making is to be preferred

> not because of deep epistemological or metaphysical considerations, but simply because, when we tell our Whiggish stories about how our ancestors gradually crawled up the mountain on whose (possibly false) summit we stand, we need to keep some things constant throughout the story. The forces of nature and the small bits of matter, as conceived by current physical theory, are good choices for this role. Physics is the paradigm of 'finding' simply because it is hard (at least in the West) to tell a story of changing physical universes against the background of an unchanging Moral Law or poetic canon, but very easy to tell the reverse sort of story. (*Philosophy and the Mirror of Nature* (1980), 344–45)

Kuhn's philosophy of science, which by opposing one epistemology with another upheld the conventional notion that epistemology is a necessity within this particular genre of writing, is converted here into the strategic choice that confronts the novelist as to how to tell his or her story. In most fiction, a relatively stable background is constructed on the assumption that the reader will share certain conventional beliefs concerning, for example, the irreversibility of time and the impossibility of an individual's occupying several different places at once. A stable frame, recognizably similar to that within which the reader already lives, serves to promote the reader's involvement with the characters and interactions which are the story's real concern. For Rorty, the same is true of the stories we tell ourselves about the world. While a stable frame – the physical laws on the basis of which all reality is constructed – is a sensible strategic choice for the story-teller, there is no narrative law that precludes a different procedure. A story in which the conventional regularities of time and place are abandoned will, however, be harder to *sell* to one's target readership, and – since the story-teller's secret anxiety is always that he or she will find no-one willing to listen – this high-risk strategy is probably best avoided. Rorty appears here to be confirming Kuhn's claim that we *make* reality rather than discovering it; the notion of a 'discovery' that establishes the stable background to our stories is merely the invention of our most compelling story-tellers.[6]

While novelists and perhaps literary critics will continue to enjoy reasonable job-security in this narrativized world, the situation is more precarious for those who earn their keep on the understanding precisely that they are *not* telling stories. As a philosopher, Rorty is naturally concerned chiefly with the future employment prospects of philosophers. The role he rejects is that of 'the Platonic philosopher-king who knows what everybody else is really doing whether *they* know it or not, because he knows about the ultimate context (the Forms, the Mind, Language) within which they are doing it' (317–18).[7] The preferred role is that of 'the informed dilettante, the polypragmatic, Socratic intermediary between various discourses', in whose salon 'hermetic thinkers are charmed out of their self-enclosed practices' (317). Philosophy's sufficient aim is 'to keep the conversation going' (377). Philosophy, the perfect, ever-resourceful host, breaks up a repetitive dialogue that has been going on too long in order to introduce one of the participants to the shy individual who has so far been sitting embarrassedly in the corner with no-one to talk to. The occasional outbreak of a serious dispute must be gracefully defused; boring monologues must be deflected, pomposity deflated; and people must be taken out of themselves by the general atmosphere of animation, intelligence and wit. The role of the host will not only be to efface himself in making the necessary introductions, for from time to time he will be found at the centre of a conversation-circle, dazzling it with daring, sceptical talk which mocks every certitude and which would certainly scandalize the bourgeoisie were they to gain admittance. Above all, *story-telling* will be encouraged, and no-one here will be so gullible as to believe that any of the stories are 'true'. Seriously to claim that a story is 'true' is, in this company, simply *tasteless*. Stories are all the better for being invented, and those who do not accept this cardinal aesthetic dogma, by which the entire salon stands or falls, will be made to feel foolish and awkward.[8]

But will people really wish to attend Rorty's salon? Their discourses are incommensurable with one another: what will they have to talk about? If they attend it once, they will learn the fundamental lesson of incommensurability which determines its ethos.[9] Might they not now prefer to develop their own discourse in the company of the like-minded, establishing with other discourses a tacit non-interference pact? Rorty's salon is based on a belief in the natural gregariousness of incompatible people with little or nothing in common. In these circumstances, how can even the most resourceful and charming of hosts persuade them to keep coming back? Is his desire to do so motivated by a reasonable appraisal of what is desirable and possible, or is it motivated by his own secret anxiety about being left without a role, with only himself for company? In practice, theologians who have adopted a view of narrative or story similar to these non-theological accounts do not usually draw the conclusion that animated conversation with non-theological story-tellers is now their chief task. On the contrary, the link between story and community, suggestive of a relatively closed social context, creates, if anything, a withdrawal from other discourses, a respectful abandonment of them to their otherness.

A relatively coherent central claim (that all we have is stories about the world) can therefore be expressed not only in different disciplinary contexts but also in the service of very different attitudes towards the world. In Lyotard, the defence of heterogeneity against totality is a matter of real ethical seriousness. As an ethical commitment, indeed, it is not without severe problems. (Must we really defend the integrity of the small-scale narrative worlds within which child prostitution or clitoral circumcision are practised, regarding resistance to such practices as the imposition of an alien, terroristic totality?)[10] But at least it *is* an ethical commitment, and it is not hard to envisage circumstances in which it would serve as a valuable corrective. By contrast, the ethical commitments of Fish and Rorty are rather more limited. Fish is committed to gracefully exposing the groundlessness of all language, and specifically of all literary criticism, which in fact writes the texts it claims to read. Since practitioners of various modes of criticism tend to believe in the existence of the objects of their study, the theory asserts its own non-credibility and leaves everything as it was before; it is another way of understanding the world without changing it. Rorty is committed to the sufficiency of a civilized conversation which might, perhaps, change some things in some ways but which is basically uninterested in such utilitarian considerations. Like everything else, ethics is aestheticized, turned into a matter of style, the area in which we are free to invent ourselves; for moral beliefs turn out to be as ungrounded as epistemological ones.[11] The important point, however, is that a very similar belief about the narrativity of our social worlds runs through these rather different theoretical discourses. This means that theologians may adopt this central belief, in suitably christianized form, while appearing to have little in common stylistically or temperamentally with this heterogeneous postmodern theorizing.

By what route might a theologian arrive at the conclusion that the postmodern theory of narrativity is a suitable conceptual tool for Christian theology? It is of course impossible to generalize about the genealogy of such a position, but the earlier work of Stanley Hauerwas in the field of theological ethics is an instructive illustration of one possibility. Hauerwas gradually moves towards the view that the specificity of Christian ethical thinking is to be found in the communal and narrative matrix in which it is shaped and from which it should never be severed. Thus, in a typical formulation, 'the "political" question crucial to the church is what kind of community the church must be to be faithful to the narratives central to Christian convictions' (*A Community of Character* (1981), 2). The metadiscourse to which this is opposed is that of 'liberalism', which 'presupposes that society can be organized without any narrative that is commonly held to be true' (12). Moving back a few years to an article on 'Theology and the New American Culture' first published in 1972, we can identify the pre-postmodern theological stance from which the postmodern emphasis on irreducible particularity in this case derives. Here, the alignment of the church with secular political causes such as opposition to racism or the Vietnam War is said to commit the error of 'confusing the demands of the gospel with the reigning idealities of culture' (*Vision and Virtue*, 244). In opposition to this error, 'it is only as the church becomes a community separate from the predominant culture that she has the space and rest from which to speak the truth to that culture... The church's task... is not to choose sides among the competing vitalities of the current culture, but to speak the word of truth amid warring spirits' (245). Political radicalism, in its secular form, fails to realize that, however zealously we may 'manufacture "moral–political" causes', 'the emptiness of our lives cannot long be filled with such goods' (260). Christians who understand their vocation as participation in these causes are in fact surrendering their birthright, participation in a community separated from the world.

This somewhat conventional emphasis on the separation of the church from society is the initial point of contact with postmodern theorizing. In *Truthfulness and Tragedy* (1977), the term 'story' (or 'narrative') is used systematically in the now-familiar postmodern manner as a means of resisting totalizing theories and promoting a particularity and communal rootedness which cannot, however, be grounded in extra-textual reality. Thus, 'ethical objectivity cannot be secured by retreating from narrative, but only by being anchored in those narratives that best direct us toward the good' (17). Whatever this 'objectivity' may be, it no longer refers to the possibility of intrasubjective consensus, for while 'Christians may have common moral convictions with non-Christians,... it seems unwise to separate a moral conviction from the story that forms its context of interpretation' (203n). Christian 'facts' are now created out of a narrative matrix: the notion of 'story as the grammatical setting for religious convictions' means that 'Christian convictions are not isolatable "facts", but those "facts" are part of a story that helps locate what kind of "fact" you have at all' (73). Metanarrative succumbs to irreducible narrative plurality: 'There is no story of stories, i.e. an account that is literal and that thus provides a criterion to say which stories are true or false. All we can do is compare stories to see what they ask of us and the world which we inhabit' (78–79). The metadiscourse that is opposed here appeals to an ethic grounded in universal human nature rather than in particular narratives, and this opposition provides a new context for Hauerwas's rooted dislike of Christian socio-political engagement. Thus we are everywhere confronted with a choice: *either* we remain faithful to the Christian narratives and concentrate on the quality of life within the Christian community, *or* we pursue a secular 'justice' with no roots in those narratives. Christian social ethics is concerned not with attempts 'to make the world more "just", but with the formation of a society shaped and informed by the truthful character of the God we find revealed in the stories of Israel and Jesus' (*A Community of Character*, 92). Christian narrative legitimates withdrawal from the world.[12]

The main themes of this theological–ethical proposal are characteristically postmodern: the universal narrative formation of individual identity within a communal matrix, the irreducible particularity of such a formation, the ensuing incommensurability of discourses, and the opposition to totalizing metadiscourse. While it is possible for postmodern theorizing to emphasize the groundlessness not only of metadiscourse but also of every local, particular narrative world (Fish and Rorty both do so), it is also possible to emphasize that particular narrative worlds legitimate or ground themselves in ways which are *internally* adequate (the view of Lyotard). The difference is a difference of emphasis and of ethos, for each view implies the other. In a theological perspective, however, the question this raises is whether a particularizing theology of narrative such as Hauerwas's entails a denial of any correspondence between the community's narrative of divine engagement with the world and extra-textual reality. While that might seem to represent the logical outcome of Hauerwas's position, his interest lies more in establishing the separation between community and world than in eroding the community's truth-claims. If a certain erosion also occurs, as I think it does, this is an unintended side-effect of the theological proposal. We might identify here a 'weak' non-realism which will be uneasy about its own apparently relativizing tendencies and which may deploy a variety of expedients in order to contain them.

George Lindbeck's *The Nature of Doctrine* (1984) is, by contrast, an extended exploration and defence of theological non-realism. As we have seen, postmodern theorizing is dependent on a prior discourse which makes, or seems to make, totalizing claims which fit it for the role of the metadiscourse to be subverted, and in Lindbeck's presentation this normally clear duality is complicated by the fact that two opposing positions share this role. The first is the 'propositionalist' position which 'emphasizes the cognitive aspects of religion and stresses the ways in which church doctrines function as informative propositions or truth claims about objective realities' (16). The second, which bears the brunt of Lindbeck's critique, is the 'experiential–expressivist' approach which – in reaction against the first – 'interprets doctrines as noninformative and nondiscursive symbols of inner feelings, attitudes, or existential orientations' (16). The alternative is the 'cultural linguistic model' which accepts the view of religion as a language and form of life found in anthropological, sociological and philosophical contexts. 'The function of church doctrines that becomes most prominent in this perspective is their use, not as expressive symbols or as truth claims, but as communally authoritative rules of discourse, attitude, and action' (18). As an approach to the study of religion this is familiar enough: Lindbeck's list of predecessors includes Marx, Weber, Durkheim, Geertz and others (20), not figures generally thought to be in the vanguard of postmodernism. The postmodern moment occurs not in the theory itself but in the theologian's acceptance that it represents an adequate and sufficient statement of the nature of Christian doctrine. The usual efforts to show that Christian faith is *not only* a sociological reality, and indeed that this is not its most significant dimension, are conspicuously absent, and there is no need even for the cautious proviso of much recent sociology of religion that the discipline must place in parentheses the truth-claims of the religion in question. The postmodern or postliberal theologian understands mainstream sociology of religion as a challenge to construe the reality of Christian faith wholly within Christian language. It is language rather than 'truth' that is primary; for language can be used for many purposes, only one of which is the making of statements about reality. One of these functions is story-telling, for 'to become a Christian involves learning the story of Israel and of Jesus well enough to interpret and experience oneself and one's world in its terms' (34).

The experiential–expressivist approach tends to suggest that the various religions are symbolizations of the same core experience of the Ultimate, and that they must therefore respect and learn from each other. It behaves, in other words, exactly as a metadiscourse ought to, subjecting heterogeneity to sameness in totalitarian fashion. By contrast, the cultural linguistic approach is highly particularist: 'One can in this outlook no more be religious in general than one can speak language in general' (23). Metadiscourse believes that it can transcend language and gain access to a 'core experience of the Ultimate', whereas in fact language precedes experience: 'The means of communication and expression are a precondition, a kind of quasi-transcendental (i.e., culturally formed) *a priori* for the possibility of experience' (36). Since religions correspond to different language and different cultures, they are incommensurable and there is no common framework within which to compare them. But do they not all assert truth-claims which, *prima facie* at least, conflict with one another and require some form of adjudication? The answer is that truth is intrasystematic, that is, dependent on the grammatical rules for correct and incorrect utterance that happen to be in force in a given locality. 'Utterances are intrasystematically true when they cohere with the total relevant context, which, in the case of a religion when viewed in cultural–linguistic terms, is not only other utterances but also the correlative forms of life' (64). It follows that 'intrasystematic truth is quite possible without ontological truth', that is, without correspondence to reality (64). The statement that 'Denmark is the land where Hamlet lived' is intrasystematically true even if its ontological status may be questionable (65), and the same is true of the resurrection of Jesus (67). Doctrines are regulative, and Ockham's razor indicates that propositional interpretations are superfluous: 'If doctrines such as that of Nicaea can be enduringly normative as rules, there is no reason to proceed further and insist on an ontological reference' (106). The consistent and almost obsessive dismantling of the various ramifications of a correspondence theory of truth is typical of postmodern theorizing. It induces a sense of mild euphoria as apparently stable structures prove to be ungrounded, composed of nothing more substantial than words, as if suspended in the air.

Doctrines, as grammatical rules, are secondary reflections on a primary datum, 'the biblical narratives interrelated in certain specified ways (e.g., by Christ as center)' (80). These narratives are not the products of prior experiences but are themselves the matrix within which experience is formed: thus, while the expressivist model may identify love as what is truly Christian, for rule theory 'it is the Christian story which alone is able to identify what for Christians is true love' (83). Once again, an alleged universal (love) is reinterpreted in particularist terms that make it specific to a single linguistic community. The movement is one of contraction for the sake of concretion. Preference is given to that which is small-scale, local and sharply defined, and no room is permitted for the possibility that, when due allowance has been made for the claims of particularity, the Christian narrative might still be *about* something of rather more than local significance. Narrative, on this view, cannot be *about* something any more than language can: like language, its role is to give us the *means* to talk about things. Christians must allow themselves 'to be molded by the set of biblical stories that stretches from creation to eschaton and culminates in Jesus' passion and resurrection' (84).

We have here, in other words, a further version of the self-contained text of Frei and others. It is not 'that believers find their stories in the Bible, but rather that they make the story of the Bible their story... Intratextual theology redescribes reality within the scriptural framework rather than translating Scripture into extrascriptural categories. It is the text, so to speak, which absorbs the world, rather than the world the text' (118). The world absorbed by the text is not the world that, in Christian belief, is *already* God's creation but an enclosed world that arises out of communal self-absorption in the presence of a text whose possibilities for interaction with the wider human community have been systematically erased. But this does not matter, for 'religious communities are likely to be practically relevant in the long run to the degree that they do not first ask what is either practical or relevant, but instead concentrate on their own intratextual outlooks and forms of life' (128). Intratextuality is introspection. As soon as we look outwards, we risk losing the precious, fragile story around which we have gathered. But what if the story itself directs us to look outward? The restriction of the text's sphere of significance to the gathered, self-contained, introspective community represents a low doctrine of scripture rather than the reverse. Alternatively, if it is a high doctrine of scripture it is so only relative to the low view of doctrine within which it is inscribed.[13]

This emphasis on the irreducibility of narrative within its small-scale communal context, over against every totalizing metadiscourse, Christian or otherwise, recalls Lyotard's view of the postmodern condition. While Lyotard represents narratively-shaped particularity as the universal human condition, Lindbeck is primarily concerned with the particular particularity of the Christian community and its narrative: the predictable, characteristic difference of location between philosopher and theologian. Lindbeck is less enthusiastic than Rorty about the possibilities for conversation offered by postmodern groundlessness, although he thinks that here too his cultural linguistic model is preferable to the experiential–expressivist one. Particularity must focus on itself, preserving the difference. Lindbeck agrees with Fish that language creates the facts, and not the other way round. In other words, his model derives its power of attraction not primarily from its ability to solve specifically theological problems but from a widely diffused ethos which it faithfully reflects. That is no doubt true of any theological proposal, but it is worth pointing out in this case because of the specific tension it creates: the plea for a return to the particularity and concretion of the Christian communal and linguistic matrix is dependent for its credibility as a theological proposal on the non-theological, postmodern view of particularity as a universal.

Chapter 8

Language, God and Creation

For the perspective I am here attempting to develop, the dilemma created by the theological versions of the postmodern privileging of particularity is as follows. On the one hand, the rediscovery of the irreducible narrative dimension of many of the biblical texts seems to offer a valuable and much-needed point of contact between biblical interpretation and theology. On the other hand, by denying that theological, ethical and political assertions are matters of universal, extrasystematic truth or falsehood, it deprives a more politically-oriented theology of the ground on which it would have to stand. Theology must reject a hermeneutic that condemns the biblical texts to narcissistic self-referentiality. What is needed, however, is not a return to non-narrative theology but a better theology of the Christian narrative, and this will inevitably remain indebted to earlier work in this field even as it attempts to remedy its deficiencies. Hence the appropriate procedure is to attempt to show that a claim to universality is inherent in Christian narrative, and that this particular narrative therefore refuses the particularity which is here imposed upon it.

Narrative theologies sometimes display a tendency towards christomonism in their preoccupation with 'the story of Jesus'. Even if its roots in the Hebrew scriptures are formally acknowledged, this story, as the climax and culmination of the earlier story of God's dealings with Israel, may be seen as self-contained and as self-sufficient for the formation of the communal identity of those who respond to the call that issues from it. The story is the story of the foundation of the community within which it is preserved, and it is therefore a story of fulfilment and presence, the story of a transcendent and eschatological event that has occurred already. (The language of transcendence and eschatology can of course be understood intra-systematically.) This story need not be understood as a metanarrative. Like other stories, it can hold together a community because people remain attracted to the attitudes that it inculcates and the form of life that it generates; and for these purposes it does not need to be a 'true' story – let alone *the* true story – in any ontological sense. The gospel story is no longer anchored, as it were, in the way that things really are. It floats, adrift, as one of an indefinite number of communally-sanctioned narrative worlds which, according to circumstances, people may either choose or be compelled to inhabit.

All this is quite possible, and no doubt correlates to some extent with the realities of contemporary church life. It is possible, for example, to understand one's Christian commitment in terms of the Marcan model of discipleship, where '"following me" is not so much believing certain things about Jesus as it is a form of life, a way of being in the world, in which the cross becomes the primary symbol and one seeks to be "last of all and servant of all"' (George Stroup, *The Promise of Narrative Theology,* 163). Perhaps it does not matter that one is unable satisfactorily to account for this choice, for example through a theological account of the nature of human being in the world? In a consumer society, we are not normally called upon to answer for our choices. We simply choose, and, so long as our choice falls within the boundaries of what is currently defined as acceptable, our social world will absorb our choice back into itself without comment.

Whether or not the gospel story is anchored in extra-textual reality, it is certainly located in a broader canonical context which it is possible but not obligatory to ignore or downplay. In this canonical context, the particular story of Jesus functions as the mid-point between the universal horizons of creation and eschaton: against the background of the one it points towards the other. The beginning of the biblical narrative presupposes an ending which is equally universal, and the story of Jesus' ministry in Galilee and his death and resurrection in Jerusalem cannot in itself be an adequate conclusion to a narrative which begins with the creation of the world. If one accepted this view of the location of the gospel story, the universal horizons of the Christian narrative would have to be seen as the indispensable hermeneutical framework within which the story of Jesus must be set.[1] The story of the creation of the community is set within the story of the creation of the world and its final destiny.

This does not yet entail any real difficulties from an intrasystematic perspective. In the beginning, God creates the heavens and the earth, and in the end God brings his creation to its intended goal in the new heavens and the new earth: this is simply to assert that the God of the biblical narrative is Alpha and Omega, the beginning and the end, and tells us nothing about extra-textual reality. Creation and eschaton are textual realities in just the same way as are the ministry, death and resurrection of

Jesus. At most, one could say that the 'full' Christian narrative is *formally* a metanarrative which purports to contain all reality within its scope; this would make it different in scope but not in kind from most of the other narratives which shape identity within determinate cc nmunal contexts. In opposition to this, however, my intention here is to show that the narrative of creation, and by implication the whole of the narrative that flows from it, cannot be satisfactorily accommodated in the intrasystematic Procrustean bed without violence to its integrity.

In both its non-theological and its theological forms, the postmodern privileging of particularity is bound up with an account of language as constitutive of the multiple social worlds we variously inhabit. World is created through the word, in apparent agreement with the biblical creation narrative; but the word here is not the divine word but human language. Is God language, and is language God? If so, there would then be no need to preface the assertion that 'the Word was God' with the more cautious claim that 'the Word was *with* God'. This divinizing of language is explicitly asserted by Don Cupitt, a theologian of a rather more libertarian postmodernity than Lindbeck's or Hauerwas's. In his *Creation out of Nothing* (1990), Cupitt outlines a postmodern view of God as 'a symbol for the continuously upsurging creative movement of language itself, in which we live and move and have our being... The flow of the common language through us structures the world' (151). God here is no longer an *intra*systematic entity; God is the totality of the system of language itself. This view of God is a postmodern version of pantheism, and this 'heretical' provenance will make it unacceptable to an intratextual theology which works within the particularities of the Christian community. But if it remains 'heretical' – that is, against the rules of the prevailing grammar – to assert that language is divine, then we shall have to see language as a purely human product. To say that our world is formed out of the communal, linguistic, narrative matrix into which we are socialized is to say that language-users (that is human beings) have created that world. But if we create the world through language, it is also the case that we create the (intrasystematic) creator-God through language. The claim that God created the world is intrasystematically true but extrasystematically false in that it was we human beings who created both the world and this intratextual God by means of our language and stories. Intrasystematically, God is still the creator, but if one examines the operations of the system itself this God is subjected to a Feuerbachian reversal as he himself turns out to be the creature of language and therefore a human product: *an idol.* In a non-theological postmodernism this would be no problem at all, for there Feuerbach's fundamental claim – that we talk God into being – is accepted without question, with the proviso that it should also be extended to the rest of reality. In a theological context, however, such a finding is rather more embarrassing. It cannot be evaded by claiming that, for the individual, language is a pure given into whose origins one simply does not enquire, for it may well be perfectly clear to the individual language-user that the semantic, grammatical and syntactical conventions that he or she observes originate solely in the collective decisions of prior language-users.

This anomaly suggests that, from a theological perspective, the doctrine that language constructs or creates the world that we inhabit requires a rather more critical scrutiny. Perspectives that appeal to this doctrine often disclose hitherto hidden dimensions of our socio-linguistic worlds, and as a methodological delimitation rather than an ontological claim it retains its value. But when the methodological delimitation which guides the procedures of various interpretative practices is surreptitiously converted into a metadiscourse, theology is confronted with a choice either to conform and to rewrite itself as a purely intratextual enterprise, or to resist.

Taking the latter route, the theological reading of Genesis 1 that follows is motivated by two fundamental concerns. One is to delineate one of the universal horizons between which the story of Jesus is located. Our understanding of the world as divine creation is indeed textually mediated, but to regard its extra-textual truth or falsehood as a matter of indifference is to deny precisely the universality that is integral to the narrative. The other is to underline the priority of the world as divine creation to the human speech which, within limits, subjects it to a secondary shaping. Although speech (divine speech) is involved in the initial production, divine action as represented here is by no means confined to speech.

If the act of creation is accomplished through speech, then speech and act are identified; and this results in what we may call the *speech–act model* of divine creativity. In the gloss on Gen. 1 that occurs at the beginning of the Gospel of John, this model is apparently regarded as definitive: 'Through him [that is, the divine word] all things were made, and without him was not anything made that was made' (John 1.3). Although it is possible that *logos* here is more closely associated with 'reason' than with 'speech', or that it is used synonymously with *sophia*, the intertextual links with Gen. 1 and the frequent use of *logos* in connection with (revelatory) speech elsewhere in the gospel make the speech–act interpretation plausible here. The earlier text of course lacks the Johannine hypostatization of speech; but less often noted is the fact that Gen. 1 does not present the notion of creation through the word in the unified manner implied in the Johannine text. In fact the speech–act model occurs unambiguously on only three occasions in this chapter. The first and best known is the command, 'Let there be light', which immediately produces the desired effect – 'and there was light' (v. 3). In the second case, the utterance concerning the separation of sea and dry land is followed by the words, 'and it was so' (*wayᶜhî kēn* (v. 9), cf. *wayᶜhî ᵓ ōr* (v. 3)). In the third case, the same words announce the immediate fulfilment of the command that the earth should put forth vegetation (v. 11). The specific speech–act implied in all three cases is that of the command, a strange command addressed to entities that do not yet exist and whose coming into being is their act of obedience to it: 'For he commanded and they were created' (Ps.148.5).

However, the account of the creation of the firmament on the second day employs a different model. Throughout Gen. 1, the coming into being of an entity is always preceded by a divine word – in this case, 'Let there be a firmament in the midst of the waters, and let it separate the waters from the waters' (v. 6). Here, however, it is not said that 'it was so'. The word does not immediately call the intended entity into being, for it still has to be *made*: 'And God *made* the firmament and separated the waters which were under the firmament from the waters which were above the firmament.' Only at this point does the now-redundant 'and it was so' recur (v. 7). The model employed here is not the speech–act one of instant obedience to the divine command. Unlike the light, the firmament does not immediately spring into being; it has to be constructed. The preceding saying is thus to be understood not as a command which suffices to bring into being the desired state of affairs but as the decision which constitutes its necessary but not its sufficient condition. In order to bridge the gap between the decision ('Let there be…') and its fulfilment ('And it was so') an act of fabrication has to occur. This model may therefore be described as the *fabrication model*. Grammatical similarity ('Let there be…' (*yᶜhî*)) conceals the presence of different models of divine action. In order to create, God commands; but he also decides and makes. The fabrication model is used to account for the creation of humankind, where the reference to making in the preceding divine speech shows unambiguously that this speech is a decision and not a command ('Let us make man in our image…' (v. 26)).[2]

The two models may appear in combination. When God says, 'Let there be light in the firmament of the heavens to separate the day from the night', his utterance is apparently identified retrospectively as a command by the formula 'and it was so' that follows (vv. 14–15). Yet the account continues by saying that 'God made the two great lights, the greater light to rule the day, and the lesser light to rule the night; he made the stars also' (v. 16). Reference to making (or creating) now identifies the preceding saying not as a command but as a decision. The apparent contradiction is resolved by understanding the saying as both command and decision, performatively sufficient and insufficient, at one and the same time, an indication that we are not dealing here with different occasions (on one occasion God commands, on another he decides and makes) but with models which – for reasons that have yet to become clear – must be applied simultaneously in their reference to divine action despite incompatibility in their more 'normal' sphere of human action. The two sides of this antinomy are reflected in the psalms. Ps. 33.6 employs the speech–act model: 'By the word of the Lord the heavens were made, and all their host by the breath of his mouth.' On the other hand, Ps. 8.3 employs the fabrication model: 'When I look at thy heavens, the work of thy fingers, the moon and the stars which thou hast established...'

A further complication appears as a third model is employed simultaneously with the other two. The saying, 'Let the earth bring forth living creatures according to their kinds: cattle and creeping things and beasts of the earth according to their kinds', is followed both by 'and it was so' and by a reference to making (vv. 24–25), in close analogy to the account of the creation of the heavenly lights. But the command/decision 'Let there be lights' differs from the command/decision 'Let the earth bring forth.' In the former case, the reference is to a coming into being *ex nihilo*, in the midst of a prior vacancy. In the latter case, the reference is to a coming into being out of the matrix of a prior plenitude, that is, to a *mediated* coming into being. God creates immediately by command and by fabrication, but he also and simultaneously creates mediately in employing one of his creatures as the womb out of which others proceed. This *mediation model* is also evident in the saying, 'Let the earth put forth vegetation, plants yielding seed and fruit trees bearing fruit in which is their seed, each according to its kind, upon the earth' (v. 11). Here it is employed simultaneously with the speech–act model: 'And it was so' (v. 11) is followed not by 'And God made', in accordance with the fabrication model, but by 'The earth brought forth vegetation', in accordance with the mediation model (v. 12). But the mediation and fabrication models too can occur simultaneously: 'Let the waters bring forth swarms of living creatures' is followed by God's creating the sea monsters and every living creature with which the waters swarm (vv. 20–21). 'Let the earth put forth' is followed by 'The earth brought forth', whereas 'Let the waters bring forth' is followed by 'And God created'. Mediation is here the mode of God's fabrication, but not in such a way that the fabrication model could simply be abandoned in favour of a less anthropomorphic alternative. Mediation is also to be the mode of God's future creative action: plants and trees are created as containers in which is preserved the precious seed which will propagate the species (v. 11), and the divine blessings that command or promise the fruitfulness of sea creatures and humans alike suggest a similar situation of mediation (vv. 22, 28).

The creation narrative thus makes use of three interconnected but distinct models in order to represent the act of divine creation. Each has a different role, but the full meaning of each emerges only in combination with the others. The speech–act model indicates the creator's transcendence over his creation: where a mere word accomplishes its utterer's will so that there is no need for a more direct intervention, a transcendent power is postulated which encounters no resistance from the sphere into which the command is directed. The fabrication model indicates a much closer involvement with the sphere of created being, a contact that occurs not only in the medium of speech uttered from afar but also in the more intimate form of touch, the contact between the creator's hands and the matter out of which sun, moon and stars are to be moulded. Fabrication also implies skill, one of the senses of the biblical term 'wisdom': the almost supernatural skill of the craftsperson who creates structures of extraordinary delicacy and intricacy out of common materials. The exalted potentate who commands (commissions?) and the artisan who labours are, in this case, one and the same, the latter perhaps a kenotic version of the former. The transcendent God, the creator of the ends of the earth, does not grow weary (Isa. 40.28), but the labouring God is exhausted by his exertions and must rest on the seventh day (Gen. 2.2).[3] Anthropomorphic language is necessary here insofar as the doctrine of the image of God asserts a fundamental likeness between humankind and God which bestows on human language the capacity to speak meaningfully of God. Anthropomorphism is not a mere accommodation to human weakness which must be negated in the soul's ascent to a God conceived as wholly other. Language is, however, barred from too straightforward an access to the mystery of divine creation by the superimposition onto one another of incompatible models drawn from human experience, and a further restraint is imposed by the model of mediation. To say that God makes is also to say that the waters bring forth in response to his call, and to originate life – and not merely to reproduce it – is beyond human power. Yet the role of the mediation model is not simply to reinforce, from the side of the creature, the transcendence implied in the speech–act. The creation that brings forth life does so because of the prior presence of God in the mode of indwelling. The waters bring forth because the Spirit of God from the beginning hovered dove-like over the face of the waters (v. 2): the waters, and earth which will be separated from them on the third day, are represented from the beginning not as a neutral location but as the predestined site of the origin of life. The divine spirit or breath is the spirit of life immanent in creation in the form of the breath of the living creature. When God takes away their breath/spirit, they die and return to the dust; when he sends forth his breath/spirit, they are created (Ps. 104.29–30). Their spirit and God's are one. In the creation narrative, however, the divine spirit is mediated by way of the matrix of earth and sea which she (*ruaḥ*, a feminine noun) indwells, and this immanentist perspective balances the more transcendentalist view that the bestowal and the withdrawal of the spirit derive from direct interventions of God.

As represented in this narrative, God does not merely create through the word. God as creator is triune: one, but also threefold.[4] This God is, first, transcendent, but the function of this concept is still to express something of the *relationship* between creator and creation, and not to postulate a deity who is so wholly other as to be incapable of creating. Second, this God is wholly involved in his creative activity, and his involvement takes the intimately bodily form of labour; God acts not only through the immaterial medium of speech but also in the corporeal work of making and shaping things with his hands. ('His *hands* formed the dry land' (Ps. 95.5).) God is not so wedded to his spirituality as to be incapable of bodily exertion. Third, in the most intimate relation of all, this God indwells her creation, not in the form of a passive, static presence but in an active, dynamic, self-transcending movement towards the emergence and reproduction of life and breath first in the creatures of sea and land and finally in human beings. Present to them in their very life and breath, she is closer to them than they are to one another. In her we live and move and have our being. Without the divine breath or spirit, the fruitful earth is merely lifeless dust (Gen. 2.7).[5]

At some points in the narrative, there appears to be an appropriateness about the mode or modes of the relation between creator and creation adopted by the narrator in order to represent a particular event of coming into being. Light, an immaterial entity, is appropriately summoned into being through the equally immaterial medium of speech, the word of command; but the firmament, which needs to be solid enough to prevent the upper waters from deluging the earth, must be laboriously constructed. While narration of the coming into being of the land creatures uses the model of mediation ('Let the earth bring forth living creatures') as well as the model of fabrication, the latter model is used exclusively in representing the creation of humankind ('Let us make humankind in our image, after our likeness'). 'Let the earth bring forth humankind in our image, after our likeness' would suggest a smooth continuity with what has preceded, whereas the reference to the image and likeness implies a new and transcendent event which is more appropriately conveyed by the model of fabrication. Humans acknowledge their origins in the earth: they are formed out of 'dust of the ground' (*ᶜāphār min-hāªdāmāh*, Gen. 2.7), and to it they return (3.17). But it is more important that they should acknowledge their origins in God: 'Thou didst form my inward parts, thou didst knit me together in my mother's womb' (Ps. 139.13). Thus it is appropriate that, in both creation accounts, humans are said to be *made.*

Elsewhere in the narrative, however, the models seem to be applied arbitrarily. The use of all three models simultaneously (as in the account of the creation of land creatures) does not imply a greater complexity or value in the entity created than when a single model is used (as in the account of the creation of light, the firmament, and humankind). The earth is to bring forth vegetation and the waters swarms of living creatures: but in the one case it is said that 'the earth brought forth vegetation', continuing the use of the model of mediation, whereas in the other it is said that 'God created the great sea monsters and every living creature… with which the waters swarm', switching from mediation to fabrication. Traditional trinitarian terminology helps to clarify this situation. Specific appropriations of a divine act to a divine person may be made, but only within the constraints of the principle that *opera trinitatis ad extra sunt indivisa*: the triune God is wholly present in each of his/her acts, and we are not to think of three separate agents who sometimes work in concert and sometimes separately. Thus every act of creation involves the word of command issuing from God's mouth, the wisdom or skill (*ḥokmāh*) and the strength of God's hands, and the dynamic indwelling of God's breath.[6]

According to this narrative, transcendence, bodily involvement and indwelling are the three different modes in which creator relates to creation. But this use of the concept of relation is limited to the circumstances of creation's coming into being; nothing has as yet been said of the *telos* of these various creative acts. The narrative is, in fact, a strictly objective account of what happened, and it does not indulge in speculation about the creator's motives or purposes. However, in reading any account of a series of actions carried out by an agent, it is natural and legitimate for the question *why?* to arise in the reader's mind, whether or not the narrative acknowledges the question by providing an explicit answer to it. If God's action is comprehensible to the extent that this narrative presupposes, then it should provide indications of his purpose for the reader to develop.

One such indication occurs in the refrain, 'And God saw that it was good' that follows the creation of light (where 'the light' is specified (v. 4)), the separation of dry land from sea (v. 10), the creation of plant life (v. 12), the heavenly lights (v. 18), the creatures of sea and air (v. 21), and the land creatures (v. 25). At the end of the day's work, the labourer steps back from the now-completed artefact, surveys it from outside, and discovers a conformity between the final product and the original intention. The emphasis here is on the relatively autonomous 'goodness' of the individual productions. At the end of the working week, however, the divine creator surveys the entire field of his labours and discovers that it not only contains a diversity of entities that in each case correspond to the maker's intentions (he already knew that) but also that the diversity is no mere heterogeneity but an interrelated whole which may itself be pronounced 'very good' (v. 31), corresponding to an intention which has not been directly expressed.

The affirmation of the parts as good serves to establish their relative autonomy. It is not said that trees, birds and animals are good merely in relation to the humans who will eventually be given 'dominion' over them (v. 28), for they are already affirmed as good before humans arrive on the scene. This relative autonomy of every non-human creature is best seen in the creation of entities that have no obvious human purpose. While the sun and the moon have a function in relation to humans (the giving of essential light, the demarcation of various units of time), the stars do not: yet 'he made the stars also' (v. 16). (The narrator knows nothing of their possible roles in cultural products such as navigation, astrology or science fiction.) The stars are good quite apart from any humanly-oriented purpose. The same is true of the great sea monsters. Like the stars, these call simply for a human contemplation as other and as good with no consideration of utility: thus the psalmist, contemplating the sea and all that dwells in it, acknowledges the existence of 'Leviathan which thou didst form for play with him/ in it' (Ps. 104.26).[7] Play, whether God's or Leviathan's, is the antithesis of utility: it is an end in itself and not a means to an end. Throughout this psalm the psalmist practises the spiritual discipline of contemplating God's works as good in themselves, and although considerations of human utility are not excluded they occur only alongside references to the use-value of created entities for non-human members of the living community. 'Thou makest springs gush forth in the valleys, they flow between the hills, they give drink to every beast of the field... By them the birds of the air have their habitation, they sing among the branches' (Ps. 104.10–12). The uniquely privileged role of humans is retained in the sense that it is a human (and not, say, a bird) who here joins in the creator's contemplation of all created works as good and who addresses the creator as 'Thou'. But this contemplation simultaneously involves a decentering of humankind in recognition of the relative autonomy of non-human creation. Thus, even where an entity has – unlike the stars or Leviathan – use-value for humans, its existence is not exhausted in that use-value. The dominion over all living things granted to humans (Gen. 1.28) must be balanced by the recognition that these things are pronounced to be good in themselves and not just in their human use-value.[8] Indeed, the relative autonomy of animals is confirmed by the fact that no permission is given to humans or to other animals to engage in the morally questionable practice of killing them in order to consume their flesh: plants provide food for humans and animals alike (1.29–30). Permission to consume meat is a concession to the violence of fallenness (9.1–7), and even here the irreducible otherness of the slaughtered creature is acknowledged in the command to abstain from its blood, in which is its life (9.4, cf. Lev. 17.10–11; Deut. 12.23). Human acts which treat the non-human creation simply as the sphere of use-value or market-value, refusing the acknowledgement of its autonomous goodness, are acts of terrorism in direct opposition to the intention of the creator as interpreted in the Genesis narrative.

The narrator's emphasis on the goodness not just of the whole but also of the parts indicates that the relationship established through command, fabrication and creative indwelling has as its goal the establishment of relatively autonomous entities which are of value for their own sake. But if the various created entities are 'good', then as parts of an interrelated, hierarchically-constructed whole they are collectively pronounced to be 'very good'. Created entities do not come into being at random, according to the inspiration of the moment, but in accordance with a tacit design for the whole. Three titanic acts of separation are represented as foundational for the entire enterprise: the separation of light and darkness, with their regular, predictable alternation; the separation of the waters above from the waters beneath (that is, the creation of a giant air-bubble in the midst of the watery waste); and the separation of dry land from sea. The dry land and the sea are pronounced good not only as objects of contemplation ('Yonder is the sea, great and wide' (Ps. 104.25)) but also because of their correspondence to a divine intention which views them as a means as well as an end: earth and sea are to be the womb out of which every kind of living creature is to spring. The vegetation and the fruit trees are similarly created to be both good in themselves and good for others: humans, animals, birds and reptiles, as yet uncreated, stand in need of the sustenance that only these created entities can provide (1.29–30). The sun and the moon are good in themselves, and as such praise their maker: 'Praise him, sun and moon, praise him, all you shining stars!' (Ps. 148.3). Yet they are also good for others in structuring time in ways on which both animal and human life depends. Sea and earth, plants and trees, sun and moon belong to a 'lower' level of the hierarchy in the sense that their role is to be good for others as well as for themselves. These creatures of the second to the fourth day must necessarily be installed before the animal and human creatures of the fifth and sixth days, for while the former can exist without the latter the latter are wholly dependent on the former. But there is also a certain hierarchy within the creatures of the fifth and sixth days, for it is humans who uniquely resemble God and who are entrusted with dominion over all living creatures (vv. 26, 28 – a role which, as we have seen, does not include killing and eating them) and who form the apex of the pyramid-like creative process.[9] It is human existence that constitutes the ultimate *telos* of the six-day act of creation, and it is only as a hierarchically-structured whole oriented towards the creation of humankind that the outcome of six days of hard work is pronounced to be very good.[10]

The relative anthropocentricity of the Genesis account of creation has for over two centuries led to its inclusion among those biblical narratives which are said to be especially problematic for 'modern thought'.[11] Although the task of creation is superhuman, the time-scale is all too human; all is completed within a single working week. Anthropocentricity also entails geocentricity, and this latter difficulty is brought to a head in the parenthetic remark, 'he made the stars also' (v. 16) – a relatively unimportant event which perhaps does not occupy very much of the fourth day. In contrast to this, the grand but bleak narrative of modern science, within which the occurrence of the human is a fortuitous although interesting epiphenomenon, postulates an inhuman scale of times and distances which seems to render redundant the earlier narrative of the origin of things that it displaced. Perhaps the earlier narrative should now be regarded as a kind of poem, evoking a religious attitude towards the world, or as a text whose function is purely intrasystematic? Can it still maintain any claim to tell the truth? The assumption of the present treatment of this text is that it can, and that its much-criticized geocentricity and anthropocentricity are not to be dismissed along the lines of modern scientistic ideology, with its totalitarian talk of primitive mentalities which we have now outgrown. The earth is at the centre of the universe and humans are the pinnacle of creation not because the priestly writers had the misfortune to live before Copernicus or Darwin but because such a presentation is indispensable within a non-alienated, theological account of human existence in the world and before God. From this standpoint, one can only judge the far more prestigious scientific narrative, which conceives of the human intrasystematically as fortuitous and extrasystematically as the site and origin of the inhuman knowledge propounded in the narrative, as alienated and alienating. That is not, of course, to reject this scientific narrative or to deny that a nuanced assessment of it would be necessary within a more broadly-based theological reflection on the doctrine of creation than this one. The point here is simply that the theologically-grounded humanism of the Genesis creation narrative is indispensable for a politically-oriented theology that wants to be able, modestly and within limits, to give an adequate account of itself. The theological damage caused by positivistic disparagement of this text can hardly be over-estimated.[12]

The theological reason for the privileging of the human, which must be understood in a way that is compatible with the relative autonomy and otherness of non-human creatures, is the unique resemblance of human-kind to God. God calls into being a created entity that is like himself and to that extent unlike fruit trees, stars or beasts of the earth. The absolutely clear distinction between creator and creation which has hitherto been maintained is complicated here by the emergence of a created being who appears to belong in a certain proximity to the divine sphere. And yet humans, created in the image and likeness of God and as male and female, also seem to be fully integrated into the rest of creation. They too are the object of a divine act of making, and (unlike the second creation narrative that is to follow) this account devotes no special attention to the manner of this divine act. In addition to the more common '*āsāh* ('make'), the verb *bārā'* ('create') is employed (vv. 26–27), but since God also 'created' the great sea monsters (v. 21) this verb does not seem to confer any special distinction. The blessing, 'Be fruitful and multiply' (v. 28) recalls the blessing of sea creatures and birds (v. 22). Together with the ability to propagate themselves, humans share with animals the need for constant sustenance (vv. 29–31). Thus, the being who is given dominion over the earth is not alien to the creatures over which that dominion is exercised. Fish, birds and animals submit to one who is like themselves, for God did not choose to bestow dominion over the earth on the angelic inhabitants of the heavenly world, suitably adapted for corporeal, terrestrial existence. (The Genesis narrative, locating humankind firmly within the material world, is opposed to every version of this dualistic anthropological myth, whether ancient or modern.)[13]

How then are we to understand the notion of the image and likeness of God, so critically important both within the Genesis narrative and for any credible politically-oriented theology? Earlier discussion has already suggested that the answer is to be found in the concept of relatedness. On the horizontal plane, it is not the human monad who is created in the image and likeness of God but the human being formed in and by social relations to others, of which the pairing of male and female is here paradigmatic.[14] Does this mean that God too is inherently a communal being, a community of persons? Contemporary trinitarian theology tends to answer this question affirmatively and to discover here the close analogy between God and humankind that the doctrine of the image of God seems to require.[15] The incipiently trinitarian view of God in Gen. 1, as worked out above, would seem to favour such a view, along with the remarkable plural, 'Let *us* make', which has established Gen. 1.26 as an important trinitarian proof-text.[16] Rather than following Barth in finding the image or likeness in a strict duality (male and female corresponding to Father and Son),[17] it is preferable to speak of an *open* community at both the divine and the human levels. The triune God seeks communion with the human other; correspondingly, male and female do not remain self-enclosed but are fruitful and multiply. We must therefore add that the divine movement here is an outward one in search of a dialogue partner, and it is in this movement that the likeness between God and humankind is to be found in its vertical dimension.[18] We speak with those who are similar enough to ourselves to speak back to us; we do not speak to rocks, earthworms or vegetables. God, likewise, seeks in the created order a being similar enough to himself (created in his image, that is, in his likeness) to be able to speak back to him, to answer his Thou with a reciprocal Thou.[19] This does not return us to the view of the monadic human person alone with God in an exclusive I–Thou relationship, for humankind is in this narrative not created as a solitary individual but in social form. It is as shaped by membership of a human community that the individual person responds to God's address, and conversely that address is mediated through the human community. In the somewhat different presentation in Gen. 2, the relation between God and the solitary *'ādām* is insufficient: aloneness is still aloneness (and therefore 'not good' (v. 18)) even when one is alone with God, and the being of this solitary creature must be complemented by another like himself. One might perhaps say that, as in Gen. 2 it is not good for Adam to be alone, so in Gen. 1 it is not good for God to be alone: both narratives would then describe the quest for a dialogue partner, a quest that in both cases involves the formation of animals and birds (cf. 2.19) but which only reaches its goal with the emergence of 'a helper corresponding to him': Eve in the one case, humankind (male and female) in the other. The two narratives culminate in the moment in which one recognizes in that which is other a likeness to oneself that offers the possibility of dialogue. 'So God created humankind in his own image, in the image of God he created them... And God blessed them, and God *said to them*...' – the first time that God's words are addressed *to* a creature, on the assumption that they will be understood. Adam similarly recognizes in Eve the other who is like himself (cf. *kᵉnegdō*, 2.18, 20): 'This at last is bone of my bones and flesh of my flesh' (2.23). In both cases the idea of 'likeness' occurs in the context of the quest for a dialogue partner. It is true that in Gen. 1 there is no sign of the anxiety of solitude implicit in Adam's situation in ch. 2. As the trinitarian reading of Gen. 1.26 indicates, the plural, 'Let *us* make' rules out the possibility that

God is lonely, or bored with eternal solitude. Yet God, like Adam, seeks dialogue with the other outside himself, and it is in the fulfilment of this quest that the creation narrative reaches its goal.

The purpose of this discussion of Gen.1 was to develop the outlines of a positive theological response to the challenge of the postmodern privileging of particularity, community and narrative, in both its theological and its non-theological forms. There are three main areas of this postmodern discourse that I have sought to address:

(1) A contrast has been developed between the postmodern theory that the world comes into being through speech and the Genesis account of the creation of the world. I have argued that, despite the Johannine prologue, Gen. 1 does not present the world as the simple production of the divine speech–act, but employs a much more complex, incipiently trinitarian conceptuality. While advocates of the view that (human) speech creates the world will perhaps not be greatly upset to learn that their conviction is not shared by this text, there are elements here that point to the limitations of their view. Thus, adopting the speech–act model, we may note the differences between the productions of divine speech–acts and of human ones. If human speech–acts can be said to create our world, the world they create is radically unstable because always subject to contestation by other speech–acts which strive to project a different world. As Copernicus's heliocentric model is gradually accepted, the world itself changes. But the productions of divine speech–acts are not subject to this instability; for trees, birds and humans are not representations which a change in discourse will convert into a quite different set of representations. In other words, these productions possess in their materiality a kind of intransigence capable of resisting the tendencies of human discourse to arbitrary representations. This is, of course, a statement of faith and not an attempt at a refutation from some common, neutral standpoint. Yet it coheres with certain features of our 'everyday' understanding of the world: for example, with the fact that we tend to say that, in a given situation, I and another person experience *the same reality differently*, rather than that we are so locked into our separate narrative worlds that we experience *different realities.* The former assertion expresses a belief in the relative autonomy or transcendence of the object experienced over the various experiences of it, and also coheres with the belief that our common humanity gives us the basis for a dialogue in which we might attain a consensus formed in part by the object itself. These beliefs may or may not be true; but they are certainly very common, so common that the postmodern idealist will have to exercise unwearying vigilance in order to elude them.

(2) Theology has always been intratextual in the sense that its knowledge of the objects of its investigation is mediated in large part through texts. In 'natural theology', it is true, one evaded this textuality by employing pure reason; yet this non-textual theology was until the Enlightenment normally subordinated to an emphatically textual 'revealed' theo ogy. But this theology was not intratextual in the sense that its objects were constituted wholly by the text and lacked any reality outside it. The epistemological situation, that reality is textually mediated and that there is no independent access to it, is not reducible to the ontological claim that there is nothing outside the text. In other words, one may envisage a hermeneutic guided by an intratextual, theological–exegetical *realism*: here, one would seek to identify and elaborate the *truth-claim* of a text, within a determinate contemporary situation, while acknowledging that this truth-claim comes not in the form of a pure transcript of reality but in an irreducibly textual form that necessitates an interpretation that will always itself be subject to contestation. One need not be so overawed and intimidated by the difficulties of the task that one begins to contest the very concept of the truth-claim. If one does so, and practises intratextual theology in its pure, postmodern form, one simply replaces one set of difficulties with another. The God who may be said, intrasystematically, to have created the world becomes, without remainder, the product of human linguistic practices. It is intrasystematically false but extrasystematically true that the creator conforms to the intrasystematic definition of an idol. This means that a purely intrasystematic reading of the creation story, which carefully denies that 'propositional' claims are within its remit and claims to be speaking wholly from within the text, is impossible without doing violence to that text. A text that begins by asserting an absolute beginning and a divine creative action in that beginning establishes for its reader a boundary beyond which it is impossible to pass without doing violence to the text. Yet the intrasystematic reading, which recognizes itself as such and is therefore capable to some extent of viewing itself from outside, is committed to the view that this beginning is only a relative limit which establishes a starting-point for the system but which is preceded by the real beginning in which human linguistic practice creates the God of the system out of nothing. Interpretative violence is not necessarily a problem in itself, for interpretation has never been a conflict-free zone; but is a problem for a theology which claims to respect everything and to leave it all in place, exactly as it was before.

(3) Theological exegesis of the creation story also serves to establish the scope of the entire biblical narrative that follows from it. If the triune God

brings the world into being for its own sake but above all for the sake of human beings, made in his likeness to engage in dialogue with him, then this beginning must determine the theme and the scope of the story that follows. The 'beginning' referred to at the outset is *also* the beginning of a book, and engenders in the reader's mind the expectation that, through all subsequent detours and displacements, some semblance of a coherent plot will be preserved which will lead eventually to an end which is not a mere cessation but a goal and a resolution. The expectation might be disappointed; for example, the book might be unfinished, as postulated by a now-unfashionable view of another book that begins with an *archē*, the Gospel of Mark. It might be open-ended, failing or declining to resolve the problematic it seemed to set itself. But a book that begins with the assertion that 'In the beginning God created the heavens and the earth' establishes, through the comprehensiveness of its scope, the expectation that the narrative will lead eventually to an equally comprehensive goal – as indeed it does, in the creation of new heavens and a new earth at the close of the book of Revelation.[20] The universal horizons of this narrative do not permit the extraction of 'the story of Jesus' to serve as the legitimation-myth of a small community in its self-imposed exile from the world. Over against the apolitical parochialism of some postmodern narrative theology, the story of Jesus must instead be interpreted as the midpoint of time, deriving from the universal horizon of the creation of the world and of humankind in the likeness of God, and pointing towards the universal horizon of an eschaton in which the human and non-human creation together reach their appointed goal. Interpreted in this way, the story of Jesus should cause the small community of those who seek to live in the light of it to look outward into the world, fearful of losing through narcissistic self-absorption the precious possession entrusted to it.

PART THREE

HOLY SCRIPTURE AND FEMINIST CRITIQUE

In chapters 6 and 8, the use of biblical texts for the purpose of theological construction was occasioned by the need to resist certain facets of poststructuralist theory, and at the same time facilitated by its privileging of textuality over against every claim to unmediated access to the truth. In dialogue with this theorizing of *écriture*, it was possible to begin working with the biblical texts as, once again, 'holy scripture' – an approach beyond the range of the literary–critical perspectives explored in chapters 3 and 4. The concept of holy scripture does not inevitably lead to a neo-conservative hermeneutic which denies the legitimacy of the exposure and critique of inner-biblical ideological constructions. It calls instead for an attempt, never completed and always provisional, to distinguish the biblical witness to the liberating gospel from its entanglement in the oppressive law, resisting the latter not for the sake of the satisfactions of negation but as a contribution to the appropriate contemporary expression of the gospel. If the historical-critical paradigm for biblical interpretation is still marked by the dissolution of 'holy scripture' that stemmed from the Enlightenment's hostility to textuality, then a postmodern or postliberal context may help to rehabilitate this concept.

The historical-critical challenge to the concept of holy scripture is no longer the primary one, although exegetes often still assume that it is. Over the last two decades, in parallel with the development of literary paradigms for biblical exegesis, there has developed a feminist critique of the biblical texts which has begun to expose the hitherto unsuspected extent and depth of their androcentrism. Thus, there has gradually come to light a new dimension of the oppressive law whose presence within these texts and the interpretative traditions they have generated is such a crucially important hermeneutical factor. The oppressive law is, in one of its aspects, the law of patriarchy, the law of the Father, which defines the human place in God's world in terms which privilege men and marginalize women. If 'holy scripture' does not also offer the theological basis for resisting the law of the Father, then this concept should be rejected as an irredeemable ideological construct, however propitious the current climate may otherwise seem for its rehabilitation. The biblical texts would have to be desacralized and secularized still more rigorously than under the historical-critical paradigm, and at best it might be possible to salvage some usable fragments and suggestive possibilities from the ruins.

Why have these alarming prospects suddenly come to the fore in ways which until recently would have seemed inconceivable? The initial problem, rightly raised by some feminist exegetes with considerable frankness, is that the field of biblical interpretation has, like so many others, been dominated by men. Interpretative fashions come and go; each one both promises and withholds the final unveiling of the true meaning; source, form and redaction criticism develop their routines which surpass even the old allegorical methods in subtlety; but one thing has changed hardly at all, and that is that the debate is carried on over the centuries almost exclusively by men. Biblical scholarship has been a matter of men arguing with men. The social changes of the past century have gradually made it possible for a number of women to participate in the field at a high level – fewer than in other humanities disciplines, no doubt because of the ambivalent status of women in many areas of the church. Women biblical scholars, entering the previously all-male club, were encouraged to believe that gender is irrelevant to the tasks of scholarship and to conform to the rules and codes of conduct laid down by the male authorities.

Up to a point, this arrangement still works quite well, assisted by the impersonality that academic convention imposes on scholarly discourse. But only up to a point, for, as the older understanding of 'objectivity' gradually loses credibility, the beliefs have come to the fore that gender can and does make a great deal of difference, that academic impersonality is often a mask for male interests,[1] and that a woman's perspective might produce radically different results and assessments.[2] These opinions have received some striking confirmations in recent work. But feminist interpretation of the Old and especially of the New Testament is still at a relatively early stage in its development, and it has not yet attained the institutional recognition achieved by feminists in disciplines where women scholars are more numerous. It may or may not be true that in literary studies, as one male critic believes, 'some feminists... exaggerate the difficulties of their task in order to develop in one another a sense of heroic solidarity in the face of overwhelming odds' (K. K. Ruthven, *Feminist Literary Studies* (1984), 6). In biblical studies, however, feminists might well claim that a sense of solidarity in the face of opposition and indifference is entirely justified.[3] And this raises the difficult and sensitive question of the nature and the extent of male participation in this particular discussion. How can male interpreters participate in an enterprise which is supposed to bring women's perspectives to the fore?

Feminist analysis in all fields does not aim simply to offer a women's perspective to complement or offset the dominant male one. Its claim is more critical and more far-reaching: that the cultural worlds we inhabit are marked far more deeply than we had ever imagined by socially-constructed gender differences. According to Rosemary Ruether, 'Sexism is not just a female problem. Indeed, it is primarily a male problem that men have imposed on women. Sexism cannot be solved by women alone. It demands a parallel male conversion' (*Sexism and God-Talk* (1983), 189) If this is true, then feminist analysis in all fields, and specifically feminist biblical interpretation, is in some sense a challenge to male scholars as well as to women. A challenge demands a response, and, if this challenge is valid, the response should take the form at least of a developing critical awareness of the extent to which gender constructions have marked both the biblical texts and the work of interpretation. Much that still passes without comment as innocent and self-evident is in fact nothing of the kind. Once they have begun to internalize these perceptions, men too are capable of the unease in the presence of androcentric assumptions that generates feminist critique, even though their experience will not coincide with that of the primary victims of those assumptions. And to engage in critique is also to turn one's mind to the positive possibility of a new, different interpretative practice.

Even if this is true, however, the apparently separatist language of much feminist discourse must be acknowledged. If, as Mary Ann Tolbert suggests, what matters is that women should learn to read 'the old androcentric texts of the Bible *as women*, out of the experience of being women in a patriarchal world' ('Protestant Feminists and the Bible' (1990), 16), this would presumably not be an endeavour in which even the best-intentioned males could or should participate. Yet other projects might be devised which would not require this necessary exclusion. It is possible to envisage a critical and reconstructive theological project, open also to male interpreters, capable of learning from and responding to feminist analysis of the textual construction of gender, which is after all equally applicable to maleness, femaleness, and their interrelations. Clear lines of demarcation between what is appropriate to a male and to a female interpreter would, within such a project, be unnecessary.

Feminist biblical exegesis seems to have formed around a basic polarity. In the field of the Hebrew Bible or Old Testament, the orientation has been primarily towards what are described as 'literary' approaches. Thus Phyllis Trible and Mieke Bal can give two of their books the respective subtitles, 'Literary-Feminist Readings of Biblical Narratives' and 'Feminist Literary Readings of Biblical Love Stories'. The status of the term 'literary' is still fairly clear within biblical studies despite the controversy it has engendered within recent literary theory. Negatively, a 'literary' approach will mean that the range of historical issues that has for so long dominated the discipline is set aside. Positively, 'literary' denotes an interdisciplinary orientation towards older or newer forms of literary–critical or literary–theoretical inquiry: a 'new critical' interest in unity as an aesthetic category, for example, or a more contemporary concern to deconstruct the illusions of textual stability and of the single sense. Literary-*feminist* readings of biblical narratives will tend to favour destabilizing reading modes, since they reject the assumption of the texts' ideological innocence projected by more 'aesthetic' approaches. The feminist hermeneutic of suspicion threatens to undermine the remarkable rehabilitation of biblical texts which has recently taken place under the rubric of their literary 'artistry'. [4]

If 'literary–feminist readings of biblical narratives' mark one pole of feminist exegesis, continuing engagement with traditional exegetical and historical issues marks the other. In the New Testament field the major work is at present Elisabeth Schüssler Fiorenza's *In Memory of Her* (1983), which, despite its hermeneutical sophistication, still works with relatively conventional exegetical methods. Fiorenza's main aim is to recover the original experience of a 'discipleship of equals' which she believes lies behind the largely androcentric New Testament texts, an experience to which these texts still bear witness in fragmentary fashion, as it were despite themselves. Since the historical-critical method has long occupied itself with precisely this project of reconstructing historical realities from fragmentary textual evidence, much of Fiorenza's exegetical discussion fits comfortably within this interpretative paradigm. She also offers a reading of the New Testament texts which explores the process of patriarchalization which gradually changes the original 'discipleship of equals' into its opposite, and here too conventional exegetical techniques are employed. Hermeneutically, Fiorenza calls for a radical change of ethos away from the ideal of detachment towards a more committed stance;[5] yet her exegetical work is best seen as the product not of a wholly new interpretative paradigm but of a mutation within the old one.[6] The historical-critical tradition is (at best) not a static entity but a developing, self-critical process, and there is no reason why it should not adapt and reform itself in the light of feminist insights, as it has done with other innovative perspectives.

Much of the more popular writing about women in the New Testament has also adopted the mode of conventional exegetical and historical argumentation, and this may also be extended back into the Old Testament. The contemporary social setting of the body of work I have in mind is the ongoing controversy about the role of women in the church, which gives it a more precise focus than that of the 'literary–feminist readings' mentioned above. The aim is to show that, despite appearances to the contrary within the interpretative tradition and even within the New Testament itself, the Christian tradition offers in its foundational texts sufficient theological resources for a reconstruction of church practice based on the premise of women's equality. This argument is directed both against the defenders of traditional Christian patriarchy and against the radical feminist claim that women's only authentic response to the church is to leave it. While I sympathize with the intentions that here come to expression, I shall point in the following chapter to the inadequacy of many of the interpretative strategies that are currently employed in this area.

Chapter 9

Strategies of Containment

New Testament texts, or biblical texts generally, are – so we are told – to be read in the light of their historical contexts. This claim is of course the cardinal dogma of the historical-critical method, but it is may be asserted with a particular focus: to explain, and perhaps to justify, the apparent presence of objectionable androcentric elements in the texts, and to highlight the presence of more positive, egalitarian elements. Positive elements, lying overlooked and unnoticed in the background, are to be foregrounded, potentiated as weapons in the contemporary ideological conflict. Negative elements – for example, texts subjecting women to their husbands or otherwise silencing them – are to be reassigned to an 'original context' constructed in such a way as to limit their influence. They are to be *depotentiated*, removed from the grasp of those on the right and on the left who wish to defend or to expose the church's patriarchal heritage.

This might be described as the method of *contextualization*. It can take both negative and positive forms, depotentiating some texts and highlighting others. A basic feature of contextualization as a strategy of containment is indicated by Susanne Heine when she writes that 'statements in the ancient texts which must be offensive to any feminist interest become understandable once we set them in the conditions of their time' (*Women and Early Christianity* (1987), 147). According to this hermeneutical model, to be offended is to fail to understand, and historical reconstruction thus offers itself in the apologetic role of advocate for the integrity of the text. (To understand all is to forgive all: is it self-evident that this maxim adequately represents the *telos* of historical reconstruction?) However, 'understanding' in this context is above all an understanding of limitations. The text, growing out of particular, specifiable conditions, cannot without distortion be transplanted into a quite different set of conditions; its claim, falsely understood as universal, is in fact purely local and should not be

161

permitted to constrain our own present. This hermeneutic emphasizes 'that these passages [the Pauline texts relating to women] have to be understood in relation to the situations for which they were written. All too often they have been hooked out of their contexts, and applied to totally different social situations, or to issues which lie beyond their concern' (Ruth Edwards, *The Case for Women's Ministry* (1989), 69).

One popular use of the method of contextualization is to ascribe objectionable elements in biblical texts to external influences alien to what the texts are essentially seeking to communicate. According to Mary Hayter,

> the Christian ideal…, frequently manifested in practice in the earliest days of the Church, was equalitarian and counter-cultural. Membership in the Body of Christ was defined by 'faith commitment', not by sexuality. But internal and external pressures upon the Church, pressures which were largely culturally conditioned, led Christian leaders to resort to Jewish interpretations of Old Testament teaching on woman's place and to reimpose ancient subordinationist views about family order and rules of conduct for females. Much of the equalitarianism of primitive Christianity was lost. (*The New Eve in Christ* (1987), 143)

If both 'internal and external pressures… were largely culturally conditioned', then even 'internal' pressures originating within the church are 'external' in the sense that they are external to the church's gospel. The model therefore presupposes a pure 'essence of Christianity' which can be sharply differentiated from the distortions and deviations superimposed by alien influences. We have here not only a narrative of creation and fall but also a hermeneutical grid to be applied to all the relevant texts: egalitarian texts are the product of the origin, subordinationist texts are the product of alien influence. Hayter refers in particular to the pressure of 'Jewish interpretations', drawing on the long tradition of seeing Judaism as the primary threat to the purity of the gospel. In 1 Tim. 2.13ff, for example, 'the Adam and the Eve image are interpreted and applied in Jewish fashion and according to the cultural assumptions of the day' (133). New Testament authors 'could not merely ignore the ideas which formed part of the contemporary world-view' (122).

Any cultural influence, and not just a Jewish one, can constitute an 'external pressure' in this model. Thus Elisabeth Schüssler Fiorenza, who is far more aware of the need for critique of ideology than most other writers in this field, traces the social arrangements prescribed by the *Haustafeln* of

Ephesians, Colossians and 1 Peter back to Aristotle's grounding of hierarchical arrangements within the household in the natural order (*Memory*, 254–9). However, pressure was exerted not by pure ideas but by social contexts, and in particular by the infringement of the general view 'that slaves as well as wives [should] practice the religion of their masters or husbands and preserve the religious ancestral customs of the house' (263). 'Whenever slaves or wives converted to Judaism, to the Isis cult, or to Christianity, the order of the household was endangered and with it, therefore, the political order of the state' (264). 1 Peter is particularly alert to this criticism: 'The author "spiritualizes" or "internalizes" the Christian calling as a purely religious calling that does not disrupt the established order of the house and state… Naturally this "defense" could not establish that Christians did *not* disrupt the Greco-Roman order of the patriarchal house and state, since, by abandoning the religion of their masters and husbands, they in fact *did* so. However, this strategy for survival gradually introduced the patriarchal–societal ethos of the time into the church' (266). The 'external pressure' which distorts the original vision of equality is here a complex entity comprising *(a)* a general ethos, to which Aristotle gives 'classic' expression, and *(b)* the resultant pressure on a counter-cultural group which leads *(c)* to a compromising 'strategy for survival'. The adaptation to a hostile environment which, in this view, underlies the subordinationist texts denies them any legitimate function in our own more egalitarian social environment, and Fiorenza is critical of modern attempts to 'justify on theological grounds the historical and contemporary discrimination and oppression of those whose "nature" predisposes them to be "ruled" in patriarchal structures' (*Bread not Stone* (1984), 83).

This position has the effect of introducing a discrepancy between what the texts say and what they mean. What they mean is, roughly, as follows: we must be prepared to compromise some of our original ideals for the sake of good relations with society at large. A pure essence reluctantly submits to distortions originating from outside itself in order to ensure its survival in some form. But if that is what the texts mean, it is not what they say: what they say of themselves is that they are the product of internal Christian ideology. In 1 Peter, slaves are to submit to their masters because in doing so they imitate the suffering Christ, and the interest lies not in avoidance of suffering but in God's approval of suffering meekly endured (2.18–25). In Ephesians, the subordination of wives to their husbands is derived not from external social pressures but from the central Christian image of the exalted Christ (1.19–23), whose maleness is here brought into symbolic focus (5.22–33).[1] Returning to Hayter's alleged 'Jewish interpretations', the hierarchical language of 1 Cor.11.2ff derives not from Judaism but from christology (vv. 3–5), and it is from this base that the subordinationist reading of Genesis proceeds in vv. 7–9. There is no indication in the two passages silencing women (1 Cor. 14.33b–35 and 1 Tim. 2.13ff) that this measure was intended as a temporary response to local difficulties, for both passages express deeply-held convictions about what is and is not fitting to woman's nature. Concrete social pressures there surely were, but the texts refuse to acknowledge them and indeed conceal them so effectively that the modern interpreter is reduced to informed guesswork. Subordinationist statements are always derived from what represents itself as an inner-Christian logic, a matter of theological principle rather than practical expediency, so that these texts are perfectly fitted for their historical role of reinforcing patriarchal order in the later church which holds them to be canonical. Their complicity with their own subsequent reading is so close that it is very difficult to see the latter as a simple misreading.[2] The limited context constructed by the strategy of contextualization is just what these texts appear to refuse, and they should be 'depotentiated' not by reference to external pressures of which they say almost nothing but by exposing and criticizing the Christian ideologies to which they give expression. Naturally these Christian ideologies did not develop in isolation from social ideology in general but in complex interaction with it. Yet the fact that a christianized ideology is objectionable does not prevent it from being Christian, since the definition of what is 'Christian' is in the New Testament not a given but a process inseparably intertwined with ideological factors.

The hypothesis of external pressures does not only attempt to depotentiate subordinationist texts; it paradoxically uses the externality to which these texts are assigned as positive evidence of an original discipleship of equals. Where there is an outside, the product of external pressures, there must also be an inside as well, the product of the pure origin, even if no trace of this is to be found in the texts concerned. Thus subordinationist texts, far from constituting a purely negative entity, are put to positive use in delineating and reinforcing the inside to which they are the outside by the very fact of their opposition to it. Where ideological pressures are construed as external, then inside everything is at peace. Negative contextualization, a strategy initially constructed for the purpose of depotentiation, turns out to contain its positive counterpart.

Another, less paradoxical, use of the hypothesis of external pressures to enhance the purity of the original essence is to be found where the alleged pressure is said to be *resisted*. Ruth Edwards, commenting on the story of Mary and Martha (Luke 10.38–42), states that 'Jesus here is clearly affirming a woman's right to be a disciple and not to be solely concerned with domestic affairs. It is hard to think of a greater contrast with contemporary

Jewish attitudes' (*The Case for Women's Ministry*, 44). Jewish tradition is again an alien influence, but here that influence is countered by a different practice represented as distinctive, admirable, and Christian. Hermeneutically, what occurs here is that a particular practice – Jesus teaching a woman – is highlighted by way of intertextual linkage with another 'text', that of 'contemporary Jewish attitudes'. Significance is bestowed upon a text which, in itself, might not seem especially noteworthy, by way of its conversion into a counter-text to a previously hidden proto-text. The meaning of the text is to be found not in itself but in this encounter with that which it is said to contradict, and the contrast serves to heighten it and to reinforce the idea that Jesus was, after all, very remarkable in his 'attitude towards women'. [3]

What do we actually learn from the story of Mary and Martha? That, rather than being wholly absorbed by 'domestic affairs', women must above all be pious, receptive to religious instruction emanating from males? If the maleness of Jesus is construed as hermeneutically significant, the story is open to such a reading. 'If the story were to be useful to feminists one would have thought that it would have to show role reversal. It would need to concern on this occasion a man sitting at a woman's feet and learning from her. But that is unthinkable in the context. The story does not even portray a dialogue between two equals. The image we are given simply serves to confirm the picture of teacher and listener given to men and women respectively within a patriarchal order' (Daphne Hampson, *Theology and Feminism* (1990), 104). It will not do to complain that these suggestions are hopelessly anachronistic, patiently explaining that such a scenario would have been inconceivable in Jesus' time and culture; for that would confirm Hampson's claim – that Jesus, kind to women though he may have been, was nevertheless part of a patriarchal order that must be rejected. If it was impossible in Jesus' culture for women to exercise what we now regard as appropriate roles, that might be a sign of Jesus' limitations as well as his culture's. [4]

In Edwards' comments on Luke 10, the purpose of contextualization was to enhance the distinctiveness of Jesus' conduct by contrasting it with the alleged contemporary norm. The (relatively) good, which one might otherwise take for granted, is made to appear exceptional through contrast with the bad norm whose rhetorical function is to provide a negative backdrop against which the good can be displayed to best advantage. This strategy is also deployed in Ben Witherington's treatment of 1 Tim. 2.14, the passage where Eve is burdened with sole responsibility for the Fall: '*Adam* was not deceived', as the male author virtuously remarks. On this Witherington comments: 'There is nothing in this exposition which

implies Eve's sin was sexual. Our author is considerably more constrained
[sic] in his assertions than some of his rabbinic counterparts' (*Women and
the Genesis of Christianity* (1990), 195). This image of rabbinic voyeurs
fantasizing about Eve's sexuality makes it possible for a viciously misogynistic
text to represent itself as a model of sobriety and decorum. What is of
interest is not whether the factual assertion about rabbinic tradition is
correct but the use to which it is put: the victims of 'textual harrassment'
are offered the assurance that their oppressor is actually being kind to them
in refusing to use the cruder means of harrassment at his disposal.[5]
Contextualization claims to show the text resisting the pressure of external
circumstances or traditions, and by this means serves rhetorically to
enhance the text and to divert attention from its objectionable features –
thereby protecting and perpetuating the opinion that the New Testament
'has something vital to say about women and their roles in society in general
and in the Church in particular, even today' (xiii).

The natural *Sitz im Leben* for the hypothesis of external pressures, succumbed to or resisted, is the church debate on women's ministry. The
debate has been constructed in part around matters of exegesis, and the
postulate of what is called 'biblical authority' constitutes the common
ground which is not itself taken up into the discussion. But the debate about
women and the Bible need not take the form of controversy with conservative defenders of the old patriarchal order. There is an opposition of the left
as well as of the right: non-Christian or post-Christian claims that a religion
based, however tenuously, upon the Bible is so incurably androcentric that
it should simply be abandoned. The debate opened up by this attack is a
sporadic, informal affair which operates without the institutional structures
that generate and focus its inner-churchly counterpart. It is, however, felt
by participants to be in the long run at least as significant as the church
debate, for what is at issue here is not just the reform of ministry but the
future moral credibility of Christian faith.

The response of Christian exegesis to these attacks from outside or from
the margins is again likely to take the form of an appeal to contextualization:
this strategy will enable one to deploy specialist knowledge and thus to shift
the debate from the Christian/non-(post-)Christian polarity towards the
more advantageous polarity of professional and amateur. A debate between
a Christian and a non-Christian might be carried out on equal terms, but
the Christian who is also a professional exegete should be in a position to
refute the merely amateur critic foolhardy enough to venture into his or her
professional domain. In this construction, the subordinate status of the
amateur is defined by inability or refusal to play the exegetical game

according to the rules laid down by the professional institution. Amateurs, it is held, enter the field with strong and fully-formed convictions, searching for whatever seems to confirm their convictions and overlooking evidence to the contrary. They are hasty and lack the patience to learn and respect the rules. They are strangers to the subtle mechanisms which the institution has devised in order to make expressions of conviction ppear naïve and awkward, mechanisms which can dissolve any and every simple opinion into a relativizing manifold of possibilities. In a word: amateurs lack *balance*. The balance that insists that there are at least two sides to every question represents itself as the cardinal virtue of the professional institution. The Christian exegete who speaks in defence of Christian faith against its feminist critics therefore speaks as representative of the institution, and hearing that institutional voice is for our purposes more important than individual traits.

According to Susanne Heine, what is taking place in the debate over feminist theology is 'the working out of terrifyingly simple prejudices' (*Women and Early Christianity*, 2). 'One of the greatest problems of feminism and feminist theology seems to me to lie in the fact that women form a negative theory out of their hurt and their negative experience and claim universal validity for it. It is then the "nature" of the male to be destructive, the "nature" of the Christian tradition to damage people, to eliminate women from history, to demonize the feminine' (3). Scholarship is necessary in order to restore the balance: 'There is no doubt that a history of negative Christian attitudes towards women can be written, but so too can a history of positive Christian attitudes towards women' (5). It is, then, the 'nature' of feminism to be one-sided, and empirical examples of poor scholarship are to be construed as symptomatic and typical. The position attacked is a seamless whole, and there is no space permitted to a self-criticism *within* feminist analysis.[6]

To take a simple example of feminist one-sidedness and scholarly redressing of the balance: texts can be collected which represent Eve as chiefly responsible for the Fall and so for all subsequent human misery. We gather together passages from 1 Timothy, Ben Sira, the Apocalypse of Moses, the Life of Adam and Eve and Tertullian, and, if we sum up what is said in these texts, 'we get the following picture: "woman" is the first and often the only one to bear the blame for the coming of sin and disaster into the world. Covetous and easily led astray, she constantly succumbs to temptation and is responsible for the continuation of the disaster' (Heine, 17). Feminism rests its case at this point, but scholarship has more work to do. 'This tradition..., which has also found a way into the New Testament, contrasts with another which says that *Adam* is responsible for everything'

(17). By assembling texts from 4 Ezra, 2 Baruch, Rom. 5 and 1 Cor. 15, 'it is possible to compile a "horror picture" of the male, as we did earlier in the case of Eve' (19). A tradition that can be so critical of men can hardly be represented as biased against women, and the methodological mistake is to assume that the statements about Eve are automatically representative.

This vignette of the triumph of scholarship over prejudice identifies a problem (that of selectivity) and responds to the ensuing dissonance by offering a wider range of contextual material whose function is to restore harmony and to foster reconciliation. But is it possible that the initial dissonance is a symptom of something deeper than lack of acquaintance with the full picture? What if one enquired further about the interests served by the canonical passages cited? In the case of 1 Tim. 2, the function of the reference to Eve is to disqualify women from active ministry within the church and to return them to their traditional role as child-bearers subject to male authority. In order to offer the requisite balance, the relevant passages in Rom. 5 and 1 Cor. 15 would need to argue that *males* are excluded from positions of authority by virtue of their relation to Adam, the author of all our misery. That would constitute a true biblical even-handedness. But even amateurs who need to look up the passages will know for certain that Paul cannot possibly have said that. Paul, wishing to find a precedent for his claim that human destiny is dependent on a single man, Christ, cannot refer us to both Adam and Eve without complicating his already complicated analogy still further. He could have offered an analogy between Eve as source of sin and death and Christ as source of righteousness and life, but his reason for omitting to do so is not that he is prejudiced against men and wishes to exonerate women. The point is that the maleness of Adam answers better to the maleness of Christ, or rather it allows the issue of gender to be concealed under an androcentric inclusivity: 'As one man's trespass led to condemnation for all men, so one man's righteous act leads to justification and life for all men' (Rom. 5.18). *Anthrōpos* is used to refer both to maleness and to humanity inclusively, thereby constituting the male as the norm and the female as the aberration who can only be returned to the norm by becoming silent and invisible, that is, by absorption. Adam can represent Eve, but Eve cannot represent Adam. In the later construction, the antitype of Eve is not Christ but Mary, and as Christ is superior to Mary so Adam is superior to Eve. Salvation history is the history of two (inclusive) men, silently supported by two (exclusive) women. The only balance here is the balance of patriarchal hierarchies.

Far from restoring the balance, contextualization can serve to further a feminist critique: texts about Eve whose naïve misogyny lies on their surface led us to uncover the concealed androcentrism of texts about Adam.

Contextualization is a double-edged weapon. We may draw another example of the breakdown of its one-sided use from a different attempt to contextualize Eve which refers the Genesis story to a particular life-setting in ancient Israel. From the time of Solomon, according to Heine, 'the queens of Israel brought with them the religious cults with which they were familiar, so that Yahweh, the God of Israel, became one among many gods and goddesses. The prophetic history-writing sees this apostasy to the alien idols as the occasion for punitive judgment by Yahweh, which finally leads to the destruction of the kingdom and the dispersion of the people. Thus Genesis 3 and Eve make Solomon's "wicked wives" into wicked women generally... Genesis 3 was written from the perspective of a man living in the first millenium BC under the rule of David and Solomon in Israel, in particular political and social conditions, with the problems and questions to which they gave rise. So what the text says must be read in the light of a particular historical situation and from the perspective of the author' (22).

Wicked woman seduces a righteous but too gullible man into disobedience to Yahweh's command: Solomon corresponds to Adam, and the wives who led him astray correspond to Eve. The structural homology is worth exploring further, whatever the historical relation between the two narratives. Solomon's reign is paradise. 'Judah and Israel dwelt in safety, from Dan to Beersheba, every man under his vine and under his fig tree, all the days of Solomon' (1 Kings 4.25). Even here, however, the presence of Yahweh's command indicates that possession of the earthly paradise is contingent: 'If you turn aside from following me, you or your children, and do not keep my commandments and my statutes which I have set before you, but go and serve other gods and worship them, then I will cut off Israel from the land which I have given them...' (1 Kings 9.6–7). As long as Solomon is alone, the monarch of all he surveys, there is no problem; and equally there is no problem so long as women confine themselves like the Queen of Sheba to acknowledging his magnificence (1 Kings 10.1–10). But: 'King Solomon loved many foreign women, the daughter of Pharaoh and Moabite, Ammonite, Edomite, Sidonian, and Hittite women... When Solomon was old, his wives turned away his heart after other gods; and his heart was not wholly true to Yahweh his God, as was the heart of David his father. For Solomon went after Ashtoreth the goddess of the Sidonians, and after Milcom the abomination of the Ammonites' (1 Kings 11.1, 4–5).[7] Woman, dangerous especially as incarnating the power of the goddess, draws Man out of the all-male relationship on which the security of paradise rests, and a painful encounter between Man (Adam/Solomon) and his Overlord is necessary in order to formalize the breach. 'Therefore Yahweh said to Solomon, "Since this has been your mind and you have not kept my covenant and my statutes which I have commanded you, I will surely tear the kingdom from you and will give it to your servant.'" Concessions follow: 'Yet for the sake of David your father I will not do it in your days, but I will tear it out of the hand of your son. However, I will not tear away all the kingdom; but I will give one tribe to your son, for the sake of David my servant and for the sake of Jerusalem which I have chosen' (1 Kings 9.11–13). The vertical breach between Solomon/Adam and Yahweh is reproduced horizontally in the division between Israel and Judah, Cain and Abel. A process of decline gathers speed and finally plunges into the catastrophe of national destruction or cosmic deluge.

The event which precipitates this process is instigated by Woman as the locus at which two rival ideological systems meet. On the one hand, she is at the base of the hierarchical structure whose two upper levels are occupied by Man and Yahweh respectively. So long as she maintains that rightful position she is largely silent and invisible. Yet she is also drawn towards an alien ideological system in which she encounters a supernatural being (Ashtoreth, the serpent) who mocks Yahweh's patriarchal pretensions to exclusive authority. She is herself other and different, and is therefore strongly attracted to the alien being who shares her exclusion from the dominant order and seems to promise her autonomy. Man, powerful so long as he maintains the bond with Yahweh but a slave to his sexuality in the presence of Woman, is easily led astray.[8] Thus the instability of the base makes the entire hierarchical structure unstable. Its stability is dependent not on the top but on the bottom level, and Yahweh himself is impotent in the face of Woman, who possesses the real power to preserve or to destroy. Woman is therefore to be feared, and this fear is expressed in the disproportionate violence both of Yahweh's vengeance and of the misogyny underlying these texts.[9]

In Heine's reading, the 'historical context' of the Genesis story in the political circumstances of Solomon's reign was supposed to limit and contain that story, subverting the attempts of 'naïve' interpreters to draw universal conclusions from a text whose significance is purely local. Older interpreters sometimes drew opinions hostile to women from the representation of Eve; modern feminist critics attack both text and interpretation; yet both sides 'remain caught up in that naïve attitude which begins from a biblical text as it stands' (20). Biblical scholarship, however, 'has established a more sophisticated range of methods' involving above all the recognition that 'texts are composed by people who live in a society at a particular time in a particular situation and have particular problems which they attempt to solve' (20). Once it has been contextualized, the text is depotentiated. Misogynists cannot claim it for their own and feminists need no longer worry about it, for it is concerned with a long-forgotten problem in a far-away time and place. Balance is restored. Over against this characteristic product of historical-critical apologetics, my counter-reading of these texts emphasizes that the so-called 'historical circumstances' are textually mediated to us only through the veil woven by the mythicizing and ideologizing process.[10] In this form they are already structured by precisely the mythical patterns which they were supposed to contain and limit, so that, far from limiting the Genesis story and its potentially misogynistic traits, the later historical text rewrites it on a grand scale.

The interpretative practice of *contextualization* sets alongside a text a second text, a *con*text – the prefix (derived from an archaic form of the Latin *cum*) signifying 'together with', 'in combination with'. The text does not bear its meaning in itself, nor does it acquire a plurality of meanings through the activity of its readers; its meaning comes to light when it is placed 'together with' its originating con-text. The context, secondary in the sense that it has to be supplied by the interpreter, derives its rhetorical force from an apparently indisputable ontological priority which gives it the right to control the meanings and significances of a text in perpetuity. The task of interpreters is to police the limits of the text in order to prevent interpretations foreign to the context from gaining access and to expel those that have previously eluded their vigilance.[11] In many interpretative situations the typical historical-critical gesture of restoring a text to its originating context retains its usefulness. Yet alongside this well-known 'historical conscious-ness' there must also develop an increasing consciousness of the means by which 'historical contexts' are constructed by interpreters out of the mass of available raw material, in pursuance of interpretative strategies with which one may or may not wish to align oneself. In this sense the context remains secondary to the text, and its function as guarantor of stable, ojectified meaning collapses.

In the exegetical discussion of the role of women, the social function of the strategy of contextualization is to assert the need for women to play a fuller and more equal part in the life of the church and to resist the suggestion that they should simply leave it. The assignment to a text of a context is intended to minimize the damage done by androcentric or misogynistic texts, and to reach positive conclusions by highlighting contrasts. The Christian tradition, in its biblical origins, must be shown to offer resources which will further the project of women's participation in the church, and, conversely, counter-indicators mist be shown to be containable. A fundamental harmony must be demonstrated between contemporary concerns and the spirit if not always the letter of the Bible.

What would happen to interpretation, then, if one set aside this emphasis on context? Far from signalling a flight from history, this would be to take history *more* seriously by acknowledging that, as a matter of fact, the biblical texts have not been confined to their originating contexts but have for centuries been instrumental in shaping ideological systems in which women have been subordinated to men. The incalculable historic power of the Bible creates an existential need to understand how texts which promise liberation can have functioned as agents of oppression, and this is one of the main concerns underlying the 'literary–feminist' readings of Old Testament narrative to which we turn in the following chapter.

Chapter 10

Hebrew Narratives and Feminist Readers

Perhaps we should face the *possibility* that the biblical text (or most of it) is basically inimical or indifferent to the project of the equality of men and women? That is essentially the view of non-Christian or post-Christian feminists and probably of many others who remain within the Christian tradition in spite of the Bible rather than because of it. However reluctant one may be to accept fundamental criticism of the sacred text, it is valuable to have to confront the claim that the extent and the depth of the problem is far greater than anyone had previously imagined. To focus on the *extent* of the problem would lead us into a general survey;[1] but more significant, perhaps, is current work on individual passages which aims to disclose its *depth*, to develop strategies of resistance to the text's dominant ideological perspective, and to rehabilitate figures and perspectives marginalized by the text. This approach is being successfully applied to the study of narrative in the Hebrew Bible, and we shall reflect upon this body of work not only because of its intrinsic importance but also in preparation for a theological–hermeneutical response which takes its challenge seriously without allowing negation and disillusion to have the final word (chapter 11).

Phyllis Trible's *Texts of Terror* (1984) is representative of a broad approach to Hebrew narrative developed by a number of women scholars.[2] Trible wishes to recount 'tales of terror *in memoriam,* to offer sympathetic readings of abused women' (3), and the texts she selects tell of Hagar, the second Tamar, the Levite's concubine, and Jephthah's daughter. In what sense are these stories designated 'texts of terror'? The 'terror' is located initially in the events that the texts narrate: banishment, rape, ritual murder. Put simply: the Bible, which among other things is a repository of stories, contains 'sad' stories as well as 'happy' ones, and the exegete reflects upon some which belong in the former category not least because 'ancient tales of terror speak all too frighteningly of the present' (xiii). Yet these may also

173

be said to be 'tales of terror' in a more subtle and a more sinister sense, if it can be shown that the stories collude in the manner of their telling with the agents of the terror they relate. 'Terror' would then no longer be located only in what is related, and so kept at a comparatively safe distance; it would also have insinuated itself into the rhetorical presentation, and the texts themselves would need to be exposed and resisted as agents of terror. This seems to me to be the most significant hermeneutical issue raised by Trible's approach, and it will therefore be worthwhile to consider its further ramifications. To what extent do these texts collude with the terror they relate?

Hagar enters the biblical narrative because Sarah 'seeks to counter divine action with human initiative' (2): 'And Sarai said to Abram, "Behold now, Yahweh has prevented me from bearing children; go in to my maid; it may be that I shall obtain children by her"' (Gen. 16.2). But when Hagar conceived, 'Sarai dealt harshly with her, and she fled from her' (v. 6). The verb translated 'dealt harshly' (*ᶜnh*) is also used in Exod. 1.11, 12 to describe the people of Israel's oppression under the Egyptians; but, 'ironically, here it depicts the torture of a lone Egyptian woman in Canaan, the land of her bondage to the Hebrews' (13). No deity intervenes on her behalf, and she has to claim her own exodus, fleeing to the wilderness as Israel was to do (13–14). In the wilderness, however, she encounters the angel of Yahweh, who brings her the comfortless message: return and submit. 'These two imperatives, return and submit to suffering, bring a divine word of terror to an abused, yet courageous, woman. They also strike at the heart of Exodus faith.' God inexplicably identifies with the oppressor (16). This reversal of the exodus faith recurs when Hagar and her son are finally expelled at Sarah's demand: 'Whatever Sarah says to do, do as she tells you,' says God to Abraham (Gen. 21.12). God is on the side of Israel in the wilderness, but 'with Hagar the reverse happens. God supports, even orders, her departure to the wilderness, not to free her from bondage but to protect the inheritance of her oppressors' (25). The promise that follows – 'I will make a nation of the son of the slave woman also, because he is your offspring' (Gen. 21.13) – ensures the divine help that enables the child to survive the rigours of the desert (vv. 18–20). Yet here too the narrative subtly reinforces Hagar's exclusion, for the recipient of the promise is not Hagar but Abraham, and God even echoes Sarah's contemptuous language ('the slave woman', cf. v. 10). 'The deity identifies here not with the suffering slave but with her oppressors' (22). The narrative revolves around the vertical Abraham–Yahweh axis ('Behold, my covenant is with *you*' (Gen. 17.4)), and the possibility of a quite different perspective (Hagar's) cannot be acknowledged. 'Belonging to a narrative that rejects her, Hagar is a fleeting yet haunting figure in scripture' (27).[3]

It is not only that the narrative relates Hagar's rejection; the narrative itself rejects her. This rejection is enforced above all by the narrator's use of the figure of Yahweh. Yahweh is, in one sense, a character in the narrative, issuing instructions and even appearing in visible form (Gen. 18.1). In another sense, however, he *contains* the narrative rather than being contained by it, for he controls not only the outward course of events but also the perspective within which they are to be comprehended. 'Shall not the judge of all the earth do right?', asks Abraham (Gen. 18.25), and the infallibly right and just judgement of Yahweh is the controlling perspective of the narrative which ensures that apparent ambiguities, deviations, and alternative points of view are held firmly in check. Thus, in highlighting an inconsistency in Yahweh's judgement, the discrepancy between the present identification with the oppressor and the later identification with the oppressed, Trible is offering a resisting reading, a reading against the grain of the text: oriented towards the motif of exodus, the text here denies the exodus faith. 'Literary–feminist' readings of narratives from the Hebrew Bible typically seek to develop strategies of resisting the text, and one reason why resistance is necessary is the dual use of the figure of Yahweh both as an actant within the text and as a means of enforcing and stabilizing a dominant ideological perspective; a perspective which, in this case, reproduces the exclusion of Hagar in the manner of the telling.

Is this ideologically-motivated dual use of the figure of Yahweh characteristic of the Hebrew narratives in general? Do they not often display a reticence in speaking of the deity, a reluctance to subject the ambiguities and complexities that they relate to the false clarity of explicit judgements, even an incipient 'secularity' that prefers to represent the interaction of character and event on a purely human plane? In the story of Jephthah and his daughter in Judges 11, according to Robert Alter, 'the narrator's extreme reticence in telling us what we should think about all these conflicts and questions is extraordinary, and, more than any other single feature, it may explain the greatness of these narratives. Is Jephthah a hero or a villain, a tragic figure or an impetuously self-destructive fool?' ('Introduction', 22). The explicit divine involvement in the Abrahamic narratives is, in fact, exceptional, together with the clear judgements thus imposed upon the reader. 'In more typical biblical tales, where the perspective is not the vertiginous vertical one between man and God but a broader horizontal overview on the familial, social, erotic, and political interactions among human figures, the crucial consequence of reticence is the repeated avoidance of explicit judgement of the characters... Man, made in God's image, shares a measure of God's transcendence of categories, images, defining labels'(23).

Yahweh's narrative function in the story of Jephthah and his daughter is obviously not the same as in the case of Hagar. He is silent; he does not instruct, nor does he judge. The foreground is populated by purely human agents. Yet the bare fact of Yahweh's non-utterance in this story need not be given privileged treatment as an indication of an aesthetic of 'reticence', for this same motif can equally well be subjected to ethical criticism. Thus Mieke Bal writes: 'Attempts to argue that his silence is evidence for his condemnation of the sacrifice do not seem convincing. If he does not speak for it, he does not speak against it either. In his alleged omniscience, he could have foreseen the outcome of the vow. If Jephthah accomplished the victory, it was, in the eyes of the *gibbor*, thanks to Yhwh's help. And, finally, while Yhwh knew how to prevent Isaac's sacrifice, he refrains from preventing Bath's' [Jephthah's daughter's] ('Dealing/With/Women' (1990), 30).

Pursuing the ethical issue further, we may investigate the possible connections between the crucial events of vv.29–34: Jephthah's empowerment by the Spirit of Yahweh, his vow to offer sacrifice in the event of victory, the actualization of that victory, and the appearance of his daughter as sacrificial victim. It is no doubt possible to argue that the divine empowerment has to do only with military prowess and offers no guarantee of the soundness of Jephthah's judgement, that victory would have been granted even without the vow, and that Jephthah was mistaken in treating the vow as binding, offering 'a sacrifice neither sanctioned by the law nor well-pleasing to God' (Josephus, *Antiquities* 5. 266).[4] Yet the structure of the Old Testament institution of the vow implies the efficacy of the conditional promise to offer life in securing a benefit such as victory: 'And Israel vowed a vow to Yahweh, and said, "If you will give this people into my hand, then I will utterly destroy their cities." And Yahweh hearkened to the voice of Israel, and gave over the Canaanites; and they utterly destroyed them and their cities' (Num. 21.2–3). The absence from Judges 11 of the corresponding phrase, 'And Yahweh hearkened to the voice of Jephthah', is less significant than the lack of any indication that the normal structure of the vow is here put into abeyance. Although the text does not explicitly exclude Josephus's reading, it is more plausibly understood as implicating Yahweh by implying a causal relationship between the vow and the ensuing victory.[5] The victory is the infallible evidence that Yahweh hearkened to the voice of Jephthah and accepted his vow, just as disapproval would have been signalled by defeat. A vow is structured in such a way that ensuing events become divine words (a yes or a no), and this makes problematic the assumption that Yahweh is truly silent in this story.[6]

Yahweh is therefore an actant in the story of Jephthah and his daughter just as he is in the story of Hagar. Once again, he has a dual function: he is contained by the story as one character among others, and yet he also contains it by establishing its dominant perspective. Yahweh, we recall, is the judge of the earth who always does what is right, and his perspective therefore coincides with and identifies the narrator's.[7] The vow secured the victory, and the sacrifice of Jephthah's daughter was therefore necessary and right. Perhaps Jephthah would have been victorious even without a vow; but, granted that he did vow, the consequences of that vow for good and ill are manifestations not of ambiguity or chaos but of divine order. The story is not a tragedy, for it involves no outrage to the moral order of the universe necessitating a long struggle to re-establish that order. In the divine realm which constitutes the background to this story, all is well, whatever the human pathos of the foreground events.

As in the case of Hagar, the function of divine order as a narrative device is not only to secure the expulsion or destruction of women but also to represent such events as legitimate and right in particular circumstances. Resisting readings which seek out the weak points in the ideological structure of this ancient tale are likely to be more creative than simple expressions of outrage. Starting from the formal analogy between Hagar's (double) exodus into the wilderness and Israel's, Phyllis Trible was able to establish a set of contrasts between the two narratives which disclosed a flaw or weak point in their ideological structure. Comparable reading strategies can be applied to Judges 11; analogies may be found, for example, which subvert the naïve trust in the righteousness of the judge of all the earth that the narratives seek to communicate. Thus Mieke Bal links this passage with Judges 1.12–13, where Caleb gives his daughter Achsah to Othniel in reward for the capture of Kiriath-sepher. 'The victor is entitled to the chief's daughter as a bride': just as Othniel deserves Caleb's daughter, so Yahweh deserves Jephthah's ('Dealing', 20). This analogy highlights the dependence of the story in Judges 11 on the patriarchal assumption that daughters are property to be transferred from one male to another.[8]

Alternatively, or additionally, one might link this story with the events of Judges 19.22–26, where the Levite's concubine is 'sacrificed' – expelled, subjected to multiple rape, then murdered – to appease the citizens of Gibeah. According to Anne Michele Tapp (who also relates these passages to Gen. 19), 'In each fabula confrontation between two male parties concerned with either the acquisition or protection of a desired object preludes the offering of virgin daughters for sacrifice' ('Ideology of Expendability' (1989), 168). Jephthah wishes Yahweh to grant him victory over the Ammonites, the Levite's host wishes to protect his guest from homosexual rape, and the outcome in both cases is a father's offering of a virgin daughter to the male addressee: 'Behold, here are my virgin daughter and his concubine; let me bring them out now. Rape them and do with them what seems good to you, but against this man do not do so vile a thing' (19.24). In fact, in Judges 19 only the concubine is expelled and raped, and the virgin daughter proves surplus to the requirements both of the men of Gibeah and of the narrative. Her presence is perhaps the result of assimilation to Gen. 19.8 (the offer of Lot's daughters in a similar situation), but we might also see her as signalling a connection with the story of Jephthah in which a father again shows himself willing to sacrifice his virgin daughter. 'In each fabula, virgin daughters, as the property of their fathers, are sacrificially offered to protect male honor and status' – Jephthah's military prowess, the Levite's bodily integrity (169). Another point of contact: 'In each fabula, a doorway separates safety from danger. Actants located inside the spaces separated from the outside by doorways are threatened by actants located outside. The only actor safely able to transgress the boundary of a doorway is the patriarch of the house' (170).

According to Tapp, Jephthah enacts the roles of both the townsmen and of the host: he issues the initial request or demand, and he offers his daughter in response (169). It may be more revealing to develop the comparison along different lines, asking how it affects the narrative role of Yahweh in Judges 11. Two fathers offer to sacrifice their virgin daughters: to whom? In the one case, to the guarantor of narrative order and stability, in the other, to a collective rapist. In which case, having noted a series of similarities which enable the two stories to break out of their respective boundaries and to begin to mingle with one another, we find Yahweh endowed with the features of the rapist. He and his collective *alter ego* in Gibeah share a predilection for converting young women into bodies, autonomous subjects into violated objects. If, with Bal, we regard the transaction between Jephthah and Yahweh as a transfer of property from one male to another along the lines of Judges 1.12–13, then Yahweh can still function as guarantor of order, although the patriarchal structuring of that order has now been highlighted. But if we emphasize that this particular transfer takes the form of a violent sacrifice, then the identification with the rapists of Gibeah seems to set Yahweh's character in a quite different light.

There is, however, a danger that a critique of patriarchal ideology will overlook the possibility of a *self*-critique within the text or its broader context. Signs of this possibility are evident when the stories of apostasy and violence that conclude the book of Judges are punctuated by statements dissociating the narrative past from the implied reader's present. In Judges

17.6, in connection with Micah's silver image, it is said that 'in those days there was no king in Israel; every man did what was right in his own eyes'. The same sentence concludes the book in 21.25, and its first half is also repeated in 18.1 and 19.1. The narratives immediately covered by these apologetic statements depict not only the religious crime of apostasy but also examples of inhumanity such as the Danites' massacre of the people of Laish ('a people quiet and unsuspecting' (18.27)), the rape and murder of the Levite's concubine, the appalling civil war that ensued between the tribe of Benjamin and the rest of the people, and the kidnapping of the young women of Jabesh-gilead and Shiloh to replace the Benjaminite women who had been massacred. By including the four references to the anarchy of those pre-monarchic times, the narrator gives the reader permission to disapprove of these atrocities from the relative security of a present where they seem unthinkable. Even if there is no king, however, Yahweh is involved. The death of the Levite's concubine leads to a holy war being declared against the tribe of Benjamin, and Yahweh assumes or is assigned the role of commander-in-chief. He orders that Judah should be first into battle against the Benjaminites (20.18); he orders the resumption of battle after initial defeats (20.23,27–28); and, in the end, 'Yahweh defeated Benjamin before Israel, and the men of Israel destroyed 25,100 men of Benjamin that day' (20.35). The massacre of the inhabitants of Jabesh-gilead and the kidnapping of their young women stems from a combination of the people's vow to give none of its women to Benjamin and their 'compassion on Benjamin because Yahweh had made a breach in the tribes of Israel' (21.15). The four hundred women obtained in this way prove insufficient for the needs of the men of Benjamin, and they are therefore instructed to seize the unmarried women of Shiloh during their annual festival (21.16–24). Despite Yahweh's involvement, however, the narrator signals his disapproval of a situation in which 'every *man* did what was right in his own eyes' (21.25), notably in the treatment of women as disposable property. The issue here is not loyalty to Yahweh rather than the Baals, as at the beginning of the book (Judges 2); it is, to a large extent, the treatment of women.

The use of the figure of Yahweh to stabilize the ideological perspective of a narrative is therefore not as straightforward as one might expect. The narrator is capable of reinterpreting events in which Yahweh is directly involved as the product solely of human lawlessness, and a tension opens up between narrator and narratives.[9] Since they derive from a situation of human lawlessness, one cannot expect the traditional narratives to speak the truth about Yahweh as it is now apprehended; Yahweh was understood and worshipped differently 'in those days' (20.27, 28). While the narrator does not explicitly signal that this is also a possible approach to the Jephthah story, his ambivalence about Yahweh's role at the end of the book indicates that a critical perspective on the earlier stories is retrospe⟨ tively permitted.

Another mode of feminist reading reflects on biblical portrayals of women in the light of the concept of the 'stereotype'. The 'realism' of biblical narrative is qualified by the demonstration that certain of its characters are the bearers of gender-related generalizations as well as being 'individuals'. However, this does not mean that biblical 'realism' fails to be 'true to life'. Both inside and outside texts, individuals are subjected to generalizing stereotypes, primarily on the basis of gender, and the identification of stereotypes therefore has the effect of showing both textual and extra-textual reality to be constructed rather than natural.

Feminist analysis discloses the operation of stereotypes in the textual representation of three of David's wives – Michal, Abigail and Bathsheba. Stereotypical elements may be present even when, as in the case of Michal, they coexist with individualizing elements. In other words, individuality gives no immunity from the stereotyping process.

David kills Goliath, Saul becomes violently jealous, and into this unstable and dangerous situation enters 'Saul's daughter Michal' who 'loved David' (1 Sam. 18.20). Hoping to secure David's destruction by demanding a hundred Philistine foreskins as a marriage present, Saul has his servants communicate to David the message that '"the king delights in you and all his servants love you; now then become the king's son-in-law"… And when his servants told David these words, it pleased David well to be the king's son-in-law' (vv. 22, 26). Cheryl Exum comments: 'From Saul's perspective, Michal's love for David may be convenient but is otherwise largely gratuitous. I think it is largely gratuitous from David's perspective as well. The situation is one in which the men's political considerations are paramount, while regarding the woman, we hear only that she loves. Already the text perpetuates a familiar stereotype: men are motivated by ambition, whereas women respond on a personal level' ('Murder They Wrote' (1990), 50).

We pass rapidly over Michal's subsequent story: her outwitting her father in order to save her husband (1 Sam. 19.11–17), her enforced separation and remarriage to Palti the son of Laish (1 Sam. 25.44), and her equally enforced return to David (2 Sam. 3.13–16, where it is poignantly noted that her husband 'went with her, weeping after her all the way to Bahurim', although nothing is said of her own feelings). There follows one final episode, where Michal comes out to meet David as he accompanies the ark into Jerusalem, dancing before Yahweh as he does so (2 Sam. 6.20–23), and says: 'How the king of Israel honoured himself today before the eyes of his servants' maids, as one of the vulgar fellows shamelessly uncovers himself.' David denies any exhibitionist intent: 'It was before Yahweh, who chose me above your father, and above all his house, to appoint me as prince over Israel – and I will make merry before Yahweh.' He will make himself still more contemptible in her eyes; and the fact that 'Michal the daughter of Saul had no child to the day of her death' may indicate, as Exum suggests, that the additional dishonour referred to is abstention from sexual relations (52–3).

Michal is a victim of the text's ideology. 'The rejection of Saul's house requires that Michal have no children... The woman provides an opportunity for narratively displacing a strategic and embarrassing problem at the political level onto the domestic level, where it offers less of a threat' (Exum, 53–54).[10] Although she is a king's daughter and a king's wife, 'Michal appears not as a regal figure, but rather as a jealous, bitter, and worst of all, nagging woman' (55). Her leaving the safety of her house to confront the king is symbolic: she 'opposes the system that would have her remain inside, in her place, doubly subordinated as subject to her king and as woman to her husband. Here the message is: refusal to submit leads to rebuke and humiliation. Michal speaks out against the figure of authority – the husband/king – and is silenced.' And yet, 'the muted female voice provides the means for deconstructing the dominant, male narrative voice' (59). Female characters need not remain buried for ever under the weight of ideologically-motivated stereotypes. It is true that 'the narrator lets her protest but robs her of her voice at the critical moment, allowing her no reply to David and no further speech'. Yet, 'her protest can be used against the narrator to bring to light the crime, to expose the gender bias of the story... Her protest thus serves as an indictment of the phallogocentric world view represented in and reflected by the narrative' (61).[11]

Nabal was churlish and ill-behaved but his wife Abigail was of good understanding and beautiful (1 Sam. 25.3). Nabal refused to give David the supplies he needed, but Abigail defied her husband in order to protect him from David's wrath, coming in person with asses laden with good things. She prophesied David's future greatness and asked him to remember her when her prophecy was fulfilled. He praised her discretion and, since Nabal promptly died when told what had happened, made her his wife; at which point she vanishes from the biblical story.

Abigail and Nabal are both, according to Adele Berlin, 'exaggerated stereotypes' (*Poetics and Interpretation of Biblical Narrative*, 30). As his name indicates, Nabal is the proverbial 'fool', and as with the fool of the wisdom literature it is simply his nature to be obstinate, boorish, and drunken. Abigail, on the other hand, epitomizes the model wife; she is 'a narrative interpretation and expansion of the qualities attributed to the good wife of Proverbs 31, who provides food for her household and "opens her mouth with wisdom, and the teaching of kindness is on her tongue'" (Alice Bach, 'The Pleasure of her Text' (1990), 30).[12] Although David loses no time in marrying her, there is hardly a hint of sexuality in the way she is portrayed. This story thus makes a revealing contrast with another story in which a woman 'rushes from the security of home to halt the destructive action of a male': Judith takes with her the same items of food as Abigail does – a skin of wine, barley cakes, loaves, dried fruit (Judith 10.5) – but her purpose is 'to fool her enemy into believing that she is preparing for a sexual banquet and that she has come to lead him to victory' (Bach, 'Pleasure', 32). There is nothing of this in the story of Abigail, although one might have expected a sexual element in a plot in which '"fair maiden" Abigail is freed from the "wicked ogre" and marries "prince charming"' (Berlin, *Poetics* 31). The text distributes to Michal, to Abigail, and to Bathsheba respectively the various wifely functions needed to satisfy unbounded male ambition: 'First, the connection with the royal house, then the acquisition of personal wealth and the assurance of kingship, and finally a pleasurable sexual liaison' (Bach, 'Pleasure', 33).

The model wife is distinguished not only by her intelligent concern for the welfare of her present and her future husband, but also by her modesty. 'This is clearest, and most exaggerated, when she addresses David as lord and refers to herself as his maidservant. This might be interpreted as correct etiquette, or the politic thing to do when trying to convince David not to harm her husband, but it is out of all proportion at the end of the story when David proposes marriage. The widow of the wealthy rancher answers the young upstart by saying: "Behold, your handmaid is a servant to wash the feet of the servants of my lord!"' (Berlin, *Poetics*, 31). In sum, Abigail 'is much more of a type than an individual; she represents the perfect wife' (32).

Judges 9.50–57 tells how the citizens of Thebez, besieged by Abimelech, shut themselves into a strong tower. Abimelech drew near to the tower, intending to burn it down. 'And a certain woman threw an upper millstone upon Abimelech's head, and crushed his skull. Then he called hastily to the young man his armour-bearer, and said to him, "Draw your sword and kill me, lest people say of me, A woman killed him." And his young man thrust him through, and he died.' Abimelech's prompt action to preserve his good name was unsuccessful. In a later siege, close to the city, 'some of the servants of David among the people fell. Uriah the Hittite was slain also' (2 Sam. 11.17). Careful instructions are given by Joab to the messenger: 'If the king's anger rises, and if he says to you, "Why did you go so near the city to fight? Did you not know that they would shoot from the wall? Who killed Abimelech the son of Jerubbesheth? Did not a woman cast an upper millstone upon him from the wall, so that he died at Thebez? Why did you go so near the wall?" then you shall say, "Your servant Uriah the Hittite is dead also' (2 Sam. 11.20–21).

Mieke Bal sees operative here certain types of male solidarity in the face of woman. Uriah's solidarity with his comrades at the front leads to his refusal to sleep with Bathsheba and ironically occasions his death when, on his return from the female domain of the city to the male domain of the front, those same comrades withdraw from him in a gesture of 'desolidarity' (*Lethal Love* (1987), 30). Uriah had been tacitly required to help David out of his difficulty, and 'in refusing this negative male solidarity Uriah in fact excludes himself from the ideological community to which he belongs' (31). The rhetorical question Joab places in the mouth of David, relating recent casualties among the besiegers to the death of Abimelech, appears to overlook the deep discrepancies between the two cases: for example, between the professional, male competence of the soldiers shooting arrows from the wall and the amateurish, female incompetence of the woman with her millstone. Yet in mentioning the threat posed by a woman, Joab indicates that (unlike Uriah) he understands the requirements of the situation and is willing to obey the law of male solidarity in face of this threat. 'It is only when we assume such an intuitive identification, based on the common interest men have when facing women, that we can fully understand… the inconsistency of the rhetorical question' (33). The question springs from an unconscious fear of women, and expresses the awareness that 'one dies a shameful death as soon as one is so foolish as to fight woman when she is defending her wall/entrance from her mighty position as the feared other' (33). An interpretation that blames one man but exonerates the other, on the grounds that he is only obeying orders, 'eliminates the most painful sting of patriarchy: the solidarity *against* the other' (36). This fear-induced solidarity is at the root of the stereotyping process.[13]

Further reflections on the ideological functions of this stereotyping process are offered in Esther Fuchs' study of 'The Literary Characterization of Mothers and Sexual Politics in the Hebrew Bible' (1985). Fuchs' starting-point is the 'annunciation type-scene' identified by Robert Alter and consisting of three main thematic components: 'the initial barrenness of the wife, a divine promise of future conception, and the birth of a son' (Fuchs, 119). The examples studied relate to Sarah (Gen. 17–18, 21), Rebekah (Gen. 25), Rachel (Gen. 30), Manoah's wife (Judges 13), Hannah (1 Sam.

1), and the Shunammite woman (2 Kings 4).

In Gen. 17.5, the name 'Abraham' is bestowed on the individual formerly known as Abram in recognition of his role as 'the father of a multitude of nations'. His childless wife Sarai is similarly to be 'a mother of nations', and is renamed as 'Sarah'. Yet the two are treated unequally, for the divine promise made directly to Abraham reaches Sarah only by way of her husband, and the covenant is with him (and his male descendants) and not with her. In keeping with the impression that fatherhood is a more exalted destiny than motherhood, the child to be born is said to be Abraham's: 'I will give *you* a son *by her*' (v. 16). The woman 'bears a child', but the child 'is born *to a man*...' (v. 17); 'Sarah your wife shall bear *you* a son' (v. 19). The woman is, apparently, a receptacle or conduit for the male seed. 'Sarah's status as primarily the *means* of reproduction, the instrument through which God will keep his promise to Abraham, cannot be gainsaid' (120).

Sarah is likewise only marginally present at the annunciation scene itself (Gen. 18.1–15). 'Unlike Abraham, who is implicitly praised for his generosity and eagerness to please his guests, Sarah, who is not privy to what is happening outside the tent, receives no credit for her work [cf. v. 6], since she functions as her husband's adjunct' (120). 'Abraham's activity outside the tent is contrasted with Sarah's passivity. Seventeen verbs predicate Abraham's dedication to his guests... Sarah, on the other hand, is the subject of four verbs, none of which demonstrates a high level of exertion: to hear, laugh, deny, and fear... Sarah emerges from this scene as confined, passive, cowardly, deceptive, and above all untrusting of Yahweh's omnipotence' (121). When, eavesdropping from inside the tent, she laughs incredulously at the promise of a son, she is initially reprimanded through her husband: 'Why did Sarah laugh...?' (v. 13). In Gen. 21.2–3, it is three times emphasized that the promised son was born to Abraham, and it is accordingly Abraham who names him (v. 4).

However, to assume that these features are 'typical' of the sexism of Hebrew narrative is to invite the charge of one-sidedness and lack of balance, for many of them are not replicated in later exemplars of the annunciation type-scene. In Gen. 25.23, the text reports Yahweh's response not to Isaac but to Rebekah: 'There is not so much as an allusion to a moral discrepancy between the man and his wife, at this point' (122). In Gen. 30.22, it is said that 'God remembered Rachel, and God hearkened to her and opened her womb', in contrast to the need for the husband's prayer in 25.21 (123). In Judges 13.3, the angel of Yahweh appears to Manoah's wife as she sits in the field (cf. v. 9): 'The open field points up metonymically the woman's independence, just as the tent underscored Sarah's confinement'

(124). Manoah's wife demonstrates a superior intelligence to her husband's by her insight into the visitor's identity (v. 6) as compared with his ignorance (v. 16), and by her calm and logical refutation of his terrified exclamation, 'We shall surely die, for we have seen God' (vv. 22–23). According to v. 24, 'The woman does not bear a son "to" her husband; neither does she consult her husband about their son's name' (124). Whereas 'the first scene uses Abraham's hospitality to enhance his upright-ness, the latter exposes Manoah's hospitality as maladroitness... Sarah emerges from the first scene as a skeptical and parochial housewife, vastly overshadowed by Abraham's magnanimity. Manoah's wife, on the other hand, is perspicacious, sensitive, and devout, outshining her inept husband' (124–25).

Similar deviations from the Abrahamic prototype can be seen in the other two stories. In the case of Hannah, 'the potential father is pushed even further away from the focus of the story', for, 'unlike Rachel, Hannah does not turn to her husband, Elkanah, for help. She decides to address her plea directly to Yahweh' (125). 'In his capacity as Yahweh's representative, Eli promises Hannah God's help. Fulfilling his role as husband, Elkanah has intercourse with his wife, but neither of these male characters is shown to have any awareness of the special significance of his actions. Both Eli and Elkanah are excluded from the privileged point of view of Hannah, the omniscient narrator, and the implied reader' (126). In 2 Kings 4.14, the reason for the Shunammite woman's childlessness is not that she is barren but that 'her husband is old' (127). Whereas the first type-scene links the wife's miraculous conception with the husband's righteousness, here the woman conceives as a reward for her righteous conduct in caring for Elisha, Yahweh's emissary (127).

A feminist analysis confining itself to the surface content of a narrative's 'attitude towards women' would find here a number of 'positive' elements to offset the 'negative' ones. If a certain negative stereotyping is visible in the case of Sarah, the later childless women of the Bible are united in rejecting it and in establishing new norms of their own. Yet, according to Fuchs, 'the growing recognition of the potential mother figure suggests an ever increasing emphasis within the biblical framework on the institution of motherhood' (128). 'What seems to be a sentimental narrative about the happy transition from emptiness to fullness and from failure to victory is a carefully constructed story intended among other things to promote the institution of motherhood' (129). Despite the growing emphasis on the figure of the potential mother, the message is that 'woman has no control at all over her reproductive potential'. The maleness of Yahweh and his angelic or human messengers 'dramatizes the idea that woman's reproductive potential should be and can be controlled only by men' (129).

Thus Tamar would have been burnt if she had sought children outside the family. Ruth is extolled not merely 'for her ability to survive physically in adverse circumstances…, but for her success in finding and marrying a direct relative of Elimelech, her father-in-law, and giving birth to children who would carry on the patrilineage of her deceased husband' (130).[14] Artistry is the tool of ideology: 'It should be ascribed to the imaginative and artistic ingenuity of the biblical narrator that one of the most vital patriarchal concerns is repeatedly presented not as an imposition on woman but as something she herself desires more than anything else' (130). We must recognize, however, that this representation is the product of patriarchal ideology rather than of psychological insight into woman's nature (131). Further confirmation of this ideological function may be found in the representation of a motherhood relatively independent of male control in 1 Kings 3, the story of the judgement of Solomon: here, 'the message seems to be that when woman gives birth outside of wedlock, there is bound to be trouble. Not only will she suffer, but her baby's life may be jeopardized. Motherhood uncontrolled by man is dangerous and some-times fatal. King Solomon, who resolves the conflict with breathtaking brilliance, stands for the male master who alone can restore order in a world come undone by woman's unreliable nature and what appears to be her natural tendency to compete against her own sex' (131). The same association of motherhood and rivalry is apparent in the cases of Sarah and Hagar, Rachel and Leah, Hannah and Peninnah: 'By perpetuating the theme of women's mutual rivalry, especially in a reproductive context, the narrative implies that sisterhood is a precarious alternative to the patriarchal system' (132).

Fuchs thus draws attention to an 'ideology of motherhood' at work in various otherwise contrasting narratives, and objects to their tacit assump-tion that childbearing is essential to woman's identity and status, and that it is therefore 'natural' for childless women to long for children. Underlying this argument is the assumption that this desire is not natural but socially constructed and therefore revisable. But if this desire (whatever its origins) has been thoroughly internalized, as in the case of the biblical women but also of many contemporary women, then to ascribe it to a false conscious-ness or self-alienation will be to attack the immediate subjectivity of the persons concerned. The point is not that Sarah and Hannah are wrong to desire children, but that their stories can be used communally to represent childbearing as woman's normative role. In representing the desire for children, the narratives reflect a common experience of women and only become destructive when that common experience is regarded as universally normative, so that divergence from it is treated as deviancy and perversion. Oppression thus attaches not so much to the narratives themselves as to an interpretation in which certain experiences or attitudes they express are treated as normative.

On the other hand, it is important to feel the full weight of the claim that the biblical texts are entangled in a marginalization of women that in different ways and degrees encompasses the past, the present and the foreseeable future. This situation justifies the sharpness of the critique of patriarchal ideology developed by feminist scholarship, even if this critique has no more uttered the final word on these texts than has any other mode of interpretation.

Chapter 11

The Limits of Patriarchy

The preceding discussion of 'literary–feminist' interpretation of narratives from the Hebrew Bible has drawn upon the work of women scholars from Christian, Jewish and secular backgrounds who are united in their perception of the biblical texts as deeply problematic from a feminist perspective. What is at issue is not just one or two stories (Jephthah's daughter, or the Levite's concubine) but the representation of women across a very wide range of biblical material. In itself, the representation of Abigail or Michal may not matter very much; but as a symptom of a far more extensive problem it matters a great deal, for the biblical texts have been read in ways that perpetuate an unjust understanding of gender roles in the religious communities that acknowledge their authority. It is this fact that justifies the unmistakable note of personal engagement that one everywhere detects in feminist biblical interpretation. To argue that the biblical texts have been unfairly treated through subjection to a modern perspective unavailable to their authors is simply to reinforce the familiar historical-critical inability to recognize the hermeneutical significance of these texts' continuing impact on the present. Historical critics can remain indifferent to the implications of their findings for church or synagogue, but feminist interpreters cannot afford the luxury of this disengagement. Assuming, then, that feminist interpreters' analysis of the problem of patriarchy in Hebrew narrative is broadly correct, what implications are to be drawn from this?

One possibility, open to Christians although not to Jews, would be to understand these findings in the light of an already-existing assumption of the superiority of the New to the Old Testament. In the Old Testament, it is popularly believed, God is capricious and wrathful; in the New Testament Jesus proclaims him as a loving heavenly Father. In the Old Testament God is the God of the Jews alone; in the New Testament he cares for all of his children. In the Old Testament he commands the extermination of his people's enemies; in the New Testament we are told to love our enemies. These popular antitheses – ill-informed, one-sided and pervasive – make it easy enough to add a further antithesis contrasting Old Testament representations of women unfavourably with 'Jesus' attitude towards women'. The fact that the silencing of women in the worship of God occurs in the New Testament and not the Old is no difficulty for this theory, which will promptly ascribe it to residual 'Jewish attitudes' within the church. But the antithetical approach is unacceptable not primarily because it cannot be sustained but above all on theological grounds. It is the product of an unreflecting, *de facto* Marcionism which both deprives the gospel narrative of its essential hermeneutical context and reproduces within the Christian view of the Jewish community precisely the self-righteous superiority that it ascribes to its opposite number.

From a feminist perspective, however, the representation of women in both Testaments might imply the need for a radical rejection of the concept of 'holy scripture'. To speak of the Hebrew Bible/Old Testament as 'holy scripture' is to accord it an authority and a prestige which ultimately transcend the feminist critique. If this body of scripture or writing generally represents women from the standpoint of an unholy patriarchal ideology, then why should it still be described as 'holy'?[1] Perhaps, indeed, the very concept of authoritative scripture is an inherently patriarchal one, stemming from a projection of masculine notions of hierarchically-ordered power onto the deity? A feminist critique from this perspective might be located alongside similarly critical feminist approaches to the 'classics' of the various secular canons. It would be compatible with a refusal to participate in the life of a conventional religious community, signalled perhaps in the self-definition as 'post-Christian' – a self-definition which is significant not only existentially but also as symptomatic of the scope of the problem exposed by feminist analysis.[2] Since the expression 'conventional religious community' covers a wide variety of social phenomena, however, the critical rejection of the concept of 'holy scripture' would not necessarily entail a definitive refusal or departure. In defence of the decision to stay in, it might be argued that the Old Testament does not present a uniformly patriarchal perspective. It offers us some feminine imagery for the deity, an egalitarian view of creation in which man and woman alike are created in the divine image, stories of relatively independent women such as Deborah, Ruth and Judith, and, overall, a small, fragmentary but significant series of passages or texts which offer the beginnings of an alternative to the dominant patriarchal perspective. We are encouraged to use what we can and discard the rest, a principle that can also be extended to the New

Testament. This programme of sifting through religious traditions (biblical or otherwise) in search of what is still usable is characteristic of much contemporary feminist theology, and the biblical texts are thus placed on the same level as non-canonical texts as sites where valuable building-material may still be found in the midst of all the patriarchal rubble.[3] There is, however, no justification here for the pre-eminence implied by the expression 'holy scripture'. The demolition called for by feminist consciousness seems at least as comprehensive as the one that historical consciousness claims to have achieved.

Is this the only approach compatible with a recognition of the seriousness of the problem and a refusal to adopt the usual apologetic expedients? We must reflect further on the positive basis of beliefs and commitments from which the feminist critique proceeds. Insofar as such a critique was able to make constructive use of the biblical texts, it would then derive its criteria not only from outside, from the demands of the present, but also from *within* the texts. 'Feminist consciousness' would then not be a purely extra-textual entity stemming from various contemporary social forces, and secondarily applied to biblical texts to which it is essentially alien. It would be informed and nourished both by contemporary perceptions and by elements of the biblical message, and these two factors would mutually condition and shape one another. In a circular process with no discernible starting-point, contemporary perceptions enable one to recognize previously overlooked aspects of the biblical texts, but only as the biblical texts simultaneously give a particular focus and shape to contemporary perceptions. At best, contemporary perceptions enable us to see what has been there all the time: elements in the texts that resist what is now rightly recognized as the presence of oppression within the same texts. If these resistant elements are construed merely as scattered fragments, then one is acknowledging that, in their native context, their power of resistance is low; they are usable in themselves, but they cannot restore the concept of the Old Testament as holy scripture. If, on the other hand, they belong to the fundamental structure of Old Testament narrative, then an *internally* grounded critique becomes a possibility. Criticism would then be not an extraneous imposition but an interpretation of the text's own capacity for *self*-criticism.[4]

In the Christian canon, the paradigmatic expression of this biblical self-criticism is the Pauline law/gospel antithesis, which asserts that 'gospel' (that which points towards liberation) and 'law' (that which oppresses) are both to be found in holy scripture, but that the former is somehow more fundamental than the latter. Thus in Gal. 3 the law which brings a curse is enclosed within the prior promise of blessing and the fulfilment of that promise in Christ, to indicate that 'law', despite its formidable presence in holy scripture, does not have either the first or the last word. Whatever the difficulties posed by Pauline elaborations of this theme, the framework seems worth preserving over against both the biblicism which will always seek to mute any protest that is raised against the texts, and the hardening of that protest into a comprehensive rejection which permits the salvaging only of a few fragments.[5]

This framework suggests the following hypothesis: that in the Old Testament the manifold oppression of women does not have either the first or the last word. This hypothesis, if it could be established, would substitute the qualitative approach proper to a theological hermeneutic for the quantitative approach which concludes that, in the Old Testament representation of matters of gender, there is much more 'negative' than 'positive' material. To demonstrate that the oppression of women does not have the first word, it is necessary to show that in the nexus of creation and fall there occurs a transition from an egalitarian intention to patriarchal reality. Patriarchy is not grounded in the ultimate order of things; it contravenes the creator's intention. The biblical assumption is, however, that the tension between divine purpose and human reality is not permanent. The fundamental Old Testament paradigm of the divine act which points towards the elimination of the tension is the exodus from oppression in Egypt, which, through both Old and New Testaments, serves as the prototype for further, perhaps greater and more comprehensive divine acts of liberation. If the liberation of women and men from the constraints of patriarchy is to be credibly grounded in the exodus prototype, then this theme would have to be acknowledged in some way within the exodus narrative; and this proves to be the case, for the narrative opens with an account of women's acts of resistance to tyranny (Exod. 1.15–2.10) and closes with their song of thanksgiving for deliverance (Exod. 15.20–21). In so far as the Old Testament, like the New, closes in the expectation of the universal, as yet unfulfilled act of deliverance, the inner-historical event of the exodus can be seen as an (admittedly fragile) anticipation of the event in which divine intention and human reality are definitively reunited. Patriarchy may fill up the interim, but it does not have either the first or the last word, and inner-historical anticipations of its final overthrow are to be expected.[6]

The narrative in Gen. 2–3 of the creation and fall of the first man and woman is open to diverse assessments. The fact that in Gen. 2 woman's creation is subsequent to man's may be taken to imply her congenital inferiority, as it is by the deutero-Pauline author: women should not have authority over men in church, 'for Adam was formed first, then Eve' (1 Tim.

2.13). On the other hand, the incompleteness of the man (*hā-'ādām*) in his solitude, which is specifically described as 'not good' (Gen. 2.18), might be seen as stemming from his lack of an *equal*, a being *l*negdô*, 'corresponding to him' in a way that the animals cannot. [7] The hypothesis that the creation/ fall nexus marks a transition between an original intention and a secondary, fallen reality finds support above all in two statements that can relatively easily be put to dogmatic use. First, it is said in Gen. 1.27 that 'God created *'ādām* in his own image, in the image of God he created him, male and female he created them.' Second, the Lord God, speaking to the woman about her husband after their transgression, tells her that 'he shall rule over you' (3.16). The participation of humankind, male and female, in dominion over all living things (1.28) is destabilized and complicated by the subsequent subjection of women to their husbands. The rule of men over their wives is, in the perspective of this story, a *secondary* development.[8]

Phyllis Trible has pointed to the way in which, in Gen. 3.22-24, the woman is subsumed under the masculine expression *hā-'ādām*: 'Then the Lord God said, "Behold, *the man* has become like one of us, knowing good and evil…"', and thus 'he drove out *the man*'. What is significant is what happens to 'the man', and the woman need not be mentioned. Thus, 'what God described to the woman as a consequence of transgression [that is, that the man would rule over the woman], the story not only reports but actually embodies' (*God and the Rhetoric of Sexuality* (1978), 135). Something similar occurs in the case of the image or likeness of God. A certain patriarchal colouring is admittedly already evident in Gen. 1.27, where the statement that 'in the image of God he created *him* [that is, *'ādām*]' precedes the statement that 'male and female he created *them*', Yet, as Trible points out, 'the formal parallelism between the phrases "in the image of God" and "male and female" indicates a semantic correspondence between a lesser known element and a better known element' (17), so that it is humankind in its twofold form that is 'in the image of God'. Within the constraints of an inescapably patriarchal language that knows only the masculine *'ādām* as a generic term for the species, the writer nevertheless asserts the equality of man and woman before God. (Paul, wishing to assert their *in*equality, is therefore forced to ascribe the image of God to the male alone (1 Cor.11.7).) In Gen. 5.1-3, on the other hand, the theme of the likeness of God returns in a context where *'ādām* has become the proper name of the first male. 'And *'ādām* knew his wife' (4.25) is soon followed by 'This is the book of the generations of *'ādām*' (5.1a). This formula is everywhere else in Genesis linked to a proper name (cf. 10.1; 11.10, 27, etc.), and, especially in the light of 4.25, the term should undoubtedly be translated 'Adam'. This then affects the sequel (5.1b): 'When God created *ādām*, he made him in the likeness of God.' Is the likeness of God now predicated exclusively of Adam? The reference to male and female is, indeed, repeated: 'Male and female he created them, and he blessed them and named them *'ādām* when they were created' (5.2). But the two synonymous parallel statem᷎ ᷎nts of 1.27bc have drifted apart in 5.1b–2, for in the interim *'ādām* has come to function as the proper name of the first male, and the concept of the likeness (or image) of God is therefore related far more closely to the male than in the earlier passage. Thus, in 5.3, *'ādām* is again a proper name, linked with the notion of the 'likeness': 'When Adam had lived a hundred and thirty years, he became the father of a son in his own likeness, after his image, and named him Seth.' The inclusive usage, still maintained in 5.2, now seems awkward and out of place. The participation of woman in the image or likeness of God is not formally denied, but what is actually affirmed is that *Adam* is in the likeness of God and that his son is in his own likeness. The result is a patriarchal chain of transmission: as God makes Adam in his own image and likeness, so Adam passes on his own image and likeness to Seth, even though the original command to 'be fruitful and multiply' was addressed to both male and female (1.28). As in 3.16–24, a gap has opened up between the original intention and the subsequent reality, and the text not only *describes* that gap but also *enacts* it. The transition occurs at the moment when the woman is told, 'He shall rule over you' (3.16), and this dominance, with its implied silencing of an originally independent voice, *is accomplished by textual means.*

The statement, 'He shall rule over you' faces in two directions, forwards and backwards. In its forward reference, it is a performative statement which ensures that the future of which it speaks will come to pass. That future is decreed not only for the first man and woman but also for their descendants, for Man/Adam is clearly a representative figure, as is Eve, 'the mother of all living' (3.20). All the complex ramifications of patriarchy stem from this sombre divine decree: the fate of Hagar, Jephthah's daughter, the Levite's concubine, Bathsheba and many others is already sealed. As Adam and his sons must endure the curse of the ground, so Eve and her daughters must submit to the curse of the law which makes them the property of males. Yet the decree also has a backward reference, in the sense that it speaks of a state of affairs that is not original. It would have been straightforward enough to narrate the decree in connection with Eve's creation. ('And the rib which the Lord God had taken from the man he made into a woman and brought her to the man, saying, "Your desire shall be for your husband, and he shall rule over you." Then the man said…' (cf. 2.22–23, 3.16)). The creation of the man was immediately followed by a brief homily ('You may freely eat…' (2.16–17)): why not also in the case of the woman? Patriarchy needs to be reassured about its own foundation in the order of things, and surely has a right to expect a clear divine instruction to the woman at the outset, putting her in her place. Why then is patriarchal order in fact given this equivocal, unstable, secondary status which represents it as a necessary evil along with poisonous snakes, birth pains and backbreaking labour, evils which one seeks to minimize so far as possible? The Hebrew narrators were somehow able to transcend the all-embracing, self-evident patriarchal context in which they no doubt lived and worked, in order to assert that 'in the beginning it was not so.' [9] If in its forward reference the decree determines the future, in its backward reference to a quite different divine intention manifested at the point of origin it places patriarchal ideology in potential crisis.

Thus the biblical texts achieve a certain self-transcendence. They are not, as it were, taken by surprise by contemporary feminist critique; on the contrary, they offer it a theological grounding which will take from it the reproach that it anachronistically imposes modern sensibilities upon the sacred text. Critique can locate itself *both* in contemporary realities *and* within the text. It can thus evade the dilemma – *either* contemporaneity *or* the text – constantly posed by an unreflective conservatism which believes that the fact of contemporaneity is already and as such a proof of alienation from the text. In the beginning God created humankind, male and female, in his own image and likeness, to share equally in the project of converting the world into their home. Men and women fall out of the dialogical relationship to the creator that their participation in his image and likeness opens up for them, and from this aporetic rift between divine intention and human reality there grows the complex, pervasive phenomenon of patriarchy, a phenomenon whose reality is reflected in and reinforced by precisely the biblical texts which, in their representation of the beginning, also serve to problematize it by depriving it of the ideological foundation it desires.

If the beginning represents the divine intention and the secondary reality springs out of a rift between God and humankind, then the depiction of the beginning does not refer us to a golden age which recedes further and further into an unattainable past even as we nostalgically long to return to it. This bittersweet, conservative pessimism is entirely alien to the biblical world (even Qoheleth knows nothing of it). In the Pauline presentation, the beginning that precedes the secondary curse of the decree is characterized as *promise*, temporarily held in abeyance by a decree deriving from non-divine powers (cf. Gal. 3.19–20; 4.1–10), but nevertheless destined for fulfilment. The universal content of the promise ('In you shall all the nations be blessed' (Gal. 3.8)) suggests an analogy with the original blessing given to a humankind in which male and female are created equally in the image of God (Gen. 1.27–28), and for that reason this blessing too must be construed as a promise. The fulfilment of this promise coincides with the fulfilment of the Abrahamic promise with which Paul is here directly concerned. Christ is the promised seed of Abraham, and the universality of this fulfilment is indicated here by reference to the abolition of the hierarchical barriers that separate Jew from Gentile, slave from free, and also male from female: 'There is neither male nor female, for you are all one in Christ Jesus' (3.28). The eschatological vision of an undivided humanity, in fulfilment of the original promise, is anticipated in fragmentary and problematic fashion within the Christian community. But it is also antici-pated in the history of Israel; for here too, in the realm of the oppressive, non-divine law, it is possible to live by faith in the divine future projected by the promise. As Habakkuk classically expresses this possibility, 'The righteous shall live by faith' (Hab. 2.4, quoted in Gal. 3.11). Applying this Pauline hermeneutic to the secondary, non-divine law of patriarchy, bounded by the prior promise and the future fulfilment, it will now be possible to reinterpret the apparently random, scattered passages in the Hebrew scriptures where patriarchal ideology is partially eluded as anticipations of a future in which the original promise is to be fulfilled.

According to Paul, God sent his Son to liberate those who were enslaved to the non-divine powers that divide Jew from Greek, slave from free, male from female; slavery to the powers entails slavery to their law of patriarchy (cf. 3.28; 4.1–8). The references to slavery (*doulos* (v. 1), *dedoulōmenoi* (v. 3), *edouleusate* (v. 8)) relate this event back to the paradigmatic saving event of the exodus, in which God liberated Israel 'from the house of slavery' (*ex oikou douleias* (Exod. 13.3, 14, etc.)). The sending of the Son (*exapesteilen* (Gal.4.4)) thus recapitulates the sending of Moses: 'I send you [*apostello se*] to Pharaoh' (Exod. 3.10; cf. v. 12, 'the sign that it is I who send you [*hoti ego se exapostello*]'). The exodus is therefore the prototype of the divine act that liberates from the oppressive law and that fulfils the promise given in the beginning.

It is significant that the sending of Moses as the agent of God's redemption is prepared for by women's acts of resistance to oppression.[10] The king of Egypt attempts to gain the co-operation of the Hebrew midwives, Shiphrah and Puah, in carrying out his genocidal plans; 'but the midwives feared God, and did not do as the king of Egypt commanded them, but let the male children live' (Exod. 1.17). Called to account for their actions ('Why have you done this, and let the male children live?' (1.18)), Shiphrah and Puah are quite unabashed – unlike Moses, who was fearful of speaking in Pharaoh's presence (4.10–16) – and respond with an outra-

geous lie which succeeds both in clearing them from blame and in denting
Egyptian national pride: 'Because the Hebrew women are not like the
Egyptian women, for they are vigorous and are delivered before the midwife
comes to them' (1.19). The note of sarcasm is perceptible to the reader if
not to Pharaoh. One response to the oppressor may be to laugh at his
stupidity, and on this occasion it pays off: 'So God dealt well with the
midwives' (1.20, cf. v. 21).[11]

The refusal of Shiphrah and Puah to co-operate with the policy of
genocide makes it possible for the infant Moses to survive the experience of
birth, but his plight is still desperate, for Pharaoh has commanded his
people to drown Hebrew male children in the Nile. His mother, Jochebed
(the name is given in 6.20), shows a wisdom equal to that of the midwives,
although her action is initially mystifying to the reader: 'When she could
hide him no longer she took for him a basket made of bulrushes, and covered
it with bitumen and pitch and placed it among the reeds at the river's brink'
(2.3). The basket (*tēbāh*) incongruously recalls Noah's ark (*tēbāh* (Gen.6.14,
etc.)), which was also covered with pitch to make it waterproof. It is not clear
to the reader why Jochebed expects this small imitation of the ark which
once saved a remnant of humankind from the flood to save her own son
from drowning. Jochebed leaves her son in this flimsy craft, while the child's
sister, Miriam (cf. Num. 26.59; 1 Chr. 6.3) stays behind to watch (Exod.
2.4). When, in the following verse, we are told that 'the daughter of Pharaoh
came down to bathe at the river, and her maidens walked beside the river',
the rationale for Jochebed's actions begins to emerge, although it is left to
the reader to deduce. It is no coincidence, surely, that Pharaoh's daughter
bathes at the precise spot where the basket has been placed among the reeds.
She always bathes there, and the basket has been placed there in order that
she should notice it. And since Jochebed's intention is obviously to save her
beautiful child (*tôb* (2.2)), then her act is a mode of communication, an
appeal from a Hebrew woman to an Egyptian woman to be an ark to shelter
the child from the waters of oppression in which he will otherwise be
drowned. Why does the child Miriam stay behind 'to know what would be
done to him' (2.4)? Obviously because Jochebed has given her too a part to
play in the drama of her communicative act. The basket is duly discovered,
and when Pharaoh's daughter opened it 'she saw the child, and lo, the baby
was crying'. Her recognition of the baby as 'one of the Hebrews' children'
is preceded by a reference to her pity for it, and the virtual simultaneity of
pity and recognition already assures the reader that Jochebed's stratagem
will be successful. The verb (*ḥml*) that tells of Pharaoh's daughter's 'pity' for
the child refers not only to her feelings but to her decision to 'spare' him;
not to leave him to his fate, or to order one of her attendants to drown him

so as to be able to return to the palace and inform her father of an unpleasant but necessary duty obediently carried out. In other words, her immediate, spontaneous decision to spare the child accepts without question Jochebed's challenge to enter into complicity with her in resisting her own father.

Now it is time for Miriam to play her part. The reader must assume that her mother has instructed her, although the narrator maintains the mask of reticence that corresponds to the furtiveness of the events.

> Then his sister said to Pharaoh's daughter, 'Shall I go and call you a nurse from the Hebrew women to nurse the child for you?' And Pharaoh's daughter said to her, 'Go.' So the girl went and called the child's mother. And Pharaoh's daughter said to her, 'Take this child away, and nurse him for me, and I will give you your wages.' So the woman took the child and nursed him. (2.7–9)

No questions are asked about the identity of the small girl with her helpful if presumptuous suggestion to the princess, and likewise no questions are asked about the identity of the nurse with whom she returns. While the narrator does not exclude the possibility that Miriam and Jochebed deceive Pharaoh's daughter by concealing their own prior relationship to the child, it is more plausible to understand the subterfuge as transparent from the start. Pharaoh's daughter knows who these Hebrews must be (and they know that she knows), but instead of compelling a confession that will then enable her to display her royal magnanimity, she willingly participates in their subterfuge, tactfully refusing to expose it as such. She is on their side, and their solidarity as women committed to the preservation of life over against its destroyers bridges the social and racial gulf that otherwise divides them.

The solidarity of women in resisting the oppressor – Shiphrah, Puah, Jochebed, Miriam, Pharaoh's daughter and her servants – preserves the life of the child and is thus a necessary condition for the future liberation that Yahweh will later accomplish through him.[12] It is inappropriate to distinguish too sharply between human acts and divine acts here. Yahweh is the author of the exodus event, but he accomplishes it through human agency: 'I brought you up from the land of Egypt, and redeemed you from the house of bondage; and I sent before you Moses, Aaron and Miriam' (Mic. 6.4). Correspondingly, the women's acts of resistance, which preserve the life of the primary human agent of liberation, derive not only from their own courage and compassion but also from the divine agency which is already secretly at work for the ending of oppression. The series of divine/human acts that accomplish the exodus does not begin with the call of Moses or with the spectacular, violent trial of strength that occurs in the plague sequence, but with the solidarity of the women in preserving life and resisting death. In order to interpret their actions theologically, we may recall the discussion in chapter 8 of the triune God of Gen. 1, and specifically of the Holy Spirit who indwells the created order. But what justification is there, exegetical or theological, for saying that the women's actions were inspired by the Holy Spirit?

In *The Wisdom of Solomon*, a writing on the fringes of the Christian Old Testament, the Holy Spirit is identified with Wisdom.[13] 'Who has learned thy counsel, unless thou hast given Wisdom [*sophia*], and sent thy Holy Spirit from on high?', asks the speaker at one point [9.17], indicating the identification through the synonymous parallelism and thereby confirming the appropriateness of feminine pronouns in speaking of the Holy Spirit. Wisdom (or the Holy Spirit) is divine: she is 'a breath of the power of God', 'a reflection of eternal light' (7.25, 26). She is 'the fashioner of all things' (*technitis pantōn* (7.21)), but she fashions them not from outside the created order but from within, as a child is fashioned in the womb. 'Because of her pureness she pervades and penetrates all things' (7.24); for 'the Spirit of the Lord has filled the world' and 'holds all things together' (1.7). Such statements are necessary affirmations of the universality of her indwelling presence, but lest we should think in terms of an undifferentiated, static immanence we should also note the particularity of her presence. The balance between her universal and her particular presence is expressed in 7.27: 'Though she is but one, she can do all things, and while remaining in herself, she renews all things; in every generation she passes into holy souls and makes them friends of God and prophets.' In chapter 10, the author gives an account of the biblical narrative from the creation to the exodus, discovering at every point the particular presence of Wisdom. Over against a straightforward, literalistic monotheism which makes God one agent among others, the author construes divine agency as the immanent inspiration of particular human acts. Thus, 'a holy and blameless race she delivered from a nation of oppressors. She entered the soul of a servant of the Lord, and withstood dread kings with wonders and signs' (10.15–16). The reference is, of course, to Moses (no women are referred to in this text). But, as we have seen, Shiphrah, Puah, Jochebed, Miriam and Pharaoh's daughter also withstood a dread king, with the protection not of signs and wonders but of their own courage, imagination and compassion. They too belong among the agents through whom Wisdom delivered Israel from a nation of oppressors, and their actions stem from her no less than do Moses'; for 'in every generation she passes into holy souls and makes them friends of God and prophets'. Shiphrah and Puah become God's friends (cf. Exod.

1.20); Miriam becomes a prophet (Exod. 15.20); but the assertion encompasses them all, and also gives the assurance that in every generation divine Wisdom inspires women and men to comparable acts of courage, imagination and compassion in the face of oppression in its manifold forms.[14]

The concept of divine Wisdom or the Holy Spirit as the immanence of God within her creation makes possible a theological interpretation of human actions of resistance and liberation, thus overcoming the conventional dilemma in which autonomous human capacities or acts are set in opposition to divine acts over which God exercises exclusive control.[15] What this concept cannot do in itself, however, is to show that the women's acts *anticipate a future free from oppression*. But that is implied in the Exodus text, where the participation of the child Miriam in the women's resistance at the outset of the story is complemented by the aged Miriam's song of triumph at its conclusion:

> Then Miriam, the prophetess, the sister of Aaron, took a timbrel in her hand; and all the women went out after her with timbrels and dancing. And Miriam sang to them: 'Sing to the Lord, for he has triumphed gloriously; the horse and his rider he has thrown into the sea.' (Exod.15.20–21)

In the exodus, women's liberation is acknowledged; and they participate in it not as passive beneficiaries, as the emphasis here on the miracle at the sea might suggest, but as active participants whose deeds were inspired by divine Wisdom. Elsewhere in the Hebrew scriptures, as we saw in the preceding chapters, a more sombre picture is given in which the texts both represent and enact the manifold oppression of women. Yet, if the hermeneutical hypothesis derived from Paul is correct, the patriarchal order which the texts generally promulgate and reinforce represents neither the first nor the last word. The non-divine law of patriarchy occupies the interim between the blessing of man and woman, created in the image of God to be equal – a blessing construed now as a promise – and the fulfilment in which the patriarchal male–female hierarchy will be no more, along with other hierarchies of oppression. Holy Scripture possesses an all-too-real capacity to oppress its addressees by subjecting them to a law that contravenes the divine intention, but it also transcends itself by pointing to a quite different end, fulfilling what was promised in the beginning and already making its presence felt, in fragmentary and anticipatory form, in those inner-historical events and actions to which the future belongs. The exodus is the paradigmatic biblical act of salvation, and future acts, including the eschatological one, must take an analogous shape. If the narrative which recounts this event speaks of a liberation of women in which women themselves actively participate, then it is possible to see here a biblical indication of a future beyond the law of patriarchy.

Such an interpretation of the exodus narrative is dependent on a *hermeneutic of hope*. Passages from the book of Isaiah offer the rudiments of such a hermeneutic of the exodus:

> Thus says Yahweh, who makes a way in the sea, a path in the mighty waters, who brings forth chariot and horse, army and warrior; they lie down, they cannot rise, they are extinguished, quenched like a wick: 'Remember not the former things, nor consider the things of old. Behold, I am doing a new thing; now it springs forth, do you not perceive it? I will make a way in the wilderness and rivers in the desert... to give drink to my chosen people, the people whom I formed for myself that they might declare my praise.' (Isa. 43.16–21)

The command, 'Remember not' ('*al-tizkᵉrû*) appears to contradict Moses's command, 'Remember (*zākôr*) this day, in which you came out from Egypt, out of the house of slavery, for by strength of hand Yahweh brought you out from this place' (Exod.13.3).[16] Yet the expectation of new things is shaped not only by the contemporary situation but also by the memory of the former things. The memory that God *once* made a way in the sea, a path in the mighty waters, makes it possible to describe him as the one who *makes* a way in the sea (*hannōthēn bayyam dārek* (Isa. 43.16)) and to base one's hope for 'a new thing' on this memory. The same is true of the fragmentary narrative presentation of women's part in the divine act of liberation: it can be seen as pointing beyond biblical or contemporary patriarchy towards the new future that divine Wisdom is preparing through her human agents, now, in the so-called 'secular' world which remains her creation, beyond the world of the sacred text.[17] The difference between this form of remembering and that which is excluded is that the one generates hope and the other is a substitute for hope. One is oriented towards the world of the secular present, and is occupied with the past not for its own sake but in order to discern with its help God's new future breaking into that present. The other is oriented towards the sacred past as an escape from the contradictions and the complexities of the present, and is distrustful of all talk of divine action in the secular world, outside the pages of the sacred writings. These same sacred writings are, however, capable of a self-transcendence which calls the reader to look up from the page and outwards into the world to discern there the liberating action of 'the everlasting God, the Creator of the ends of the earth' who 'does not faint or grow weary' (40.28). The self-transcendence of the writings answers to the transcendence of the Creator who – as they themselves acknowledge – is not bound by these writings; but nor is liberating divine action to be discerned apart from them.

These hermeneutical reflections are intended as a response to contemporary feminist critique of the representations of women in Hebrew scriptures. I have accepted the claim that these texts pose major difficulties for feminist appropriation, and have argued that this finding should be regarded as one of the central theological–ethical issues of our current hermeneutical situation. Rather than adopt the selective approach which exhorts us to use the fragments that are usable and to reject the rest, I have sought to maintain a critical–theological estimation of these texts as 'holy scripture', which has led to an exploratory attempt to discover structurally significant standpoints within the texts from which critique of their own patriarchal ideology might proceed and from which, still more importantly, a constructive theological alternative to that ideology might be outlined. These 'internal' standpoints do not exist in some hermetically-sealed textual sphere but are only attainable because contemporary feminist analysis enables us to discover facets of the texts which are otherwise concealed. But, conversely, that which is thereby uncovered illuminates our own largely obscure hermeneutical situation, and shapes and directs our perceptions in unforeseen and unforeseeable ways.

Chapter 12

The Father of the Son

In chapter 9, I criticized the assumption that the strategy of contextualization (understanding texts against the background of their historical context) is the appropriate way of containing the damage done by patriarchal texts and of highlighting the positive potential of supposedly egalitarian ones. The main reason for criticizing this strategy was that it fails to recognize the seriousness of the problem that texts from the New Testament as well as the Old pose for feminist appropriation. Its answers are too easy. It is one of the merits of the literary–feminist paradigm that it is beginning to expose the depths of this problem. Yet if the result of this exposure is the reduction of the Old Testament or Hebrew Bible to a heap of patriarchal rubble from which only scattered fragments can be salvaged, this would obviously entail the rejection of any normative status, however attenuated, for these texts, and a consequent tension with the communities in which normative status is still formally maintained. The theological proposal in the preceding chapter was therefore motivated by the desire to maintain the sense of a communally normative status, in accordance with the general emphasis here on the community of faith as the proper sphere for the biblical text and for its interpretation.

When transferred to the New Testament, these concerns encounter a somewhat different interpretative environment. In the New Testament story, a father sacrifices not a daughter but a son, and the role of sacrificial victim is willingly accepted. Women in the New Testament are not expelled, raped, murdered, or dismembered. Its chief protagonist, a male, addresses other males in far harsher tones than he ever uses with women. It is normal for him to side with women against male oppressors: the doctors who enrich themselves at the expense of the haemorrhaging woman (Mark 5.25–34), the woman denounced by the Pharisee as a sinner (Luke 7.36–50), the woman caught in the act of adultery whose male accusers are shown to be operating a double standard (John.8.2–11) – in each case Jesus sides with the oppressed against her oppressors. The way into the kingdom of heaven is wide open for prostitutes, victims of multiple oppressions, whereas for the righteous rich it is as narrow as the eye of a needle is to a camel.

Yet the New Testament texts do indeed represent the saviour of the world as a *male*, and this means that the structural possibility of their co-option into the service of Christian patriarchal ideology is always present. (Already in Eph. 5.21–33, the maleness of Christ makes it possible to transfer the unequal relation between him and the (female) church to the husband–wife relation.) The possibility and reality of the oppressive use of the Christ-symbol leads Mary Daly to ask: 'If the symbol [of Christ] *can* be used in that way [that is, oppressively], isn't this an indication of some inherent deficiency in the symbol itself?' (*Beyond God the Father* (1973), 72). Its deficiency is, precisely, its maleness: 'It is most improbable that under the conditions of patriarchy a male symbol can function exclusively or ad-equately as bearer of New Being... The role of liberating the human race from the original sin of sexism would seem to be precisely the role that a male symbol *cannot* perform' (72). For Daly, the situation would be still worse if one preferred the traditional language of the Father and the Son to the Tillichian conceptuality that her own language evokes.

The problem that the person of Jesus poses for feminist theology is exacerbated by the fact that it is he who is responsible for the language of God as 'Father' (and thus, at least indirectly, for the concomitant 'Son'). Rosemary Ruether believes that the early Jesus movement used Father-language 'to liberate the community from human dominance–dependence relationships based on kinship ties or master–servant relationships' (*Sexism and God-Talk* (1983), 64). Thus, 'because God is our king, we need obey no human kings. Because God is our parent, we are liberated from dependence on patriarchal authority' (65). Yet when the community becomes part of the established order of society, 'God as father and king can be assimilated back into the traditional patriarchal relationships and used to sacralize the authority of human lordship and patriarchy' (66). Ruether's conclusion is that 'in order to preserve the prophetic social relationships, we need to find a new language that cannot be as easily co-opted by the systems of domination' (66). In other words, Jesus' God-language is inadequate, although its intention should be respected. For many Christian as well as post-Christian feminists, there can be no going back on the path 'beyond God the Father', although it is acknowledged that a non-patriarchal understanding of God as father remains a possibility. It is puzzling, however, that this possibility is not more actively exploited.

Elisabeth Schüssler Fiorenza's major work, *In Memory of Her* (1983) offers much the most important and thorough investigation to date of Jesus' praxis and God-language from a feminist perspective. The theological and exegetical heart of the book is its second main section, devoted to 'women's history as the history of the discipleship of equals'. In its three chapters, Fiorenza explores the place of women within the Jesus movement, the early Christian missionary movement, and the Pauline churches in which the egalitarian baptismal formula of Gal. 3.28 was in process of modification in a patriarchal direction. It is argued that in the earliest days of the Christian movement space was permitted for the practice of a 'discipleship of equals', and it can therefore be asserted that 'radical feminism has rediscovered the "equality from below" espoused by the Jesus movement in Palestine without recognizing its religious roots' (132). Fiorenza prefers to speak where possible of 'the Jesus movement' rather than of 'Jesus', and 'discipleship' is understood as a communal praxis rather than with exclusive reference to Jesus. In this way, the problem of the male saviour is contained. Revelation is to be encountered not only in 'the life and ministry of Jesus' but also in 'the discipleship community of equals called forth by him', in which women actively participated (34). With regard to the earliest community's view of God, Fiorenza also develops an important argument based on Jesus' allusions to *sophia*: the discipleship of women is said to be grounded in a feminine image of the deity as wisdom. Thus Fiorenza is able to relegate the problematic image of God as Father to the margins and to relate 'the basileia vision of Jesus as the praxis of inclusive wholeness' primarily to 'the Sophia-God of Jesus' (118, 130).

In the parable of the lost coin, Jesus 'images God as a woman searching for one of her ten coins, as a woman looking for money that is terribly important to her' (131). The use of this image is not unique, for 'the earliest Jesus traditions perceive this God of gracious goodness in a woman's *Gestalt* as divine *Sophia*... The very old saying, "Sophia is justified [or vindicated] by all her children" (Luke 7:35[Q]) probably had its setting in Jesus' table community with tax collectors, prostitutes, and sinners... The Sophia-God of Jesus recognizes all Israelites as her children and she is proven "right" by all of them' (132, parentheses original). It is Sophia who speaks in the promise, drawn from the wisdom tradition, of the light yoke which is easy to bear (Matt. 11.28-30), just as she is explicitly the speaker in Luke11.49: 'Therefore the Wisdom of God said: "I will send them prophets and apostles, some of whom they will kill and persecute"' (the Matthean version omits the reference to the Wisdom of God). Thus Sophia laments the murder of her envoys: 'O Jerusalem, Jerusalem, you slay the prophets and stone those who are sent to you. How often have I wanted to gather your children as a mother bird collects her young under her wings, but you refused me' (Luke 13.34(Q)). To the passages Fiorenza cites we might also add the parable of the woman and the leaven (Luke 13.20–21 = Matt. 13.33), which in its pairing with the parable of the man sowing mustard-seed reproduces the pairing of the male shepherd with the woman as images of deity in Luke 15.3–10. 'To sum up, the Palestinian Jesus movement understands the ministry and mission of Jesus as that of the prophet and child of Sophia sent to announce that God is the God of the poor and heavy laden, of the outcasts and those who suffer injustice. As child of Sophia he stands in a long line and succession of prophets sent to gather the children of Israel to their gracious Sophia-God' (135).

Fiorenza concedes that 'the Q traditions not only image the gracious goodness of the God of Jesus as divine Sophia but also call this God "father"', and therefore asks: 'Do they thereby indirectly legitimize patriarchal structures and the "second class" status of women in such structures, or does their androcentric language have a critical impulse that radically denies any religious authority and power for the structures of patriarchy?' (140). The view of familial structures presented in Jesus' sayings on discipleship indicates that the latter view cannot be correct, and the saying preserved in Matt 23.9 is evidence that the notion of God as father criticizes patriarchy rather than reinforcing it: 'Call no one father among you on earth, for you have one heavenly father' (150). Thus, 'the "father" God of Jesus makes possible "the sisterhood of men" (in the phrase of Mary Daly) by denying any father, and all patriarchy, its right to existence' (151). Despite the great scandal which the term 'father' has caused to many Christian feminists, 'the monotheistic fatherhood of God, elaborated in the Jesus traditions as the gracious goodness usually associated with a mother, must engender liberation from all patriarchal structures and domination if it is to be rescued from the male projection of patriarchy into heaven' (151). That is, the theme of God as father is to be saved from patriarchal misappropriation by being redeployed in the critique of patriarchy, in accordance with the important Matthean saying. Yet scarcely more than two pages of Fiorenza's long book are devoted to this issue, and she would seem in practice to agree with Ruether that this term stands in permanent danger of being co-opted by patriarchy and that an alternative God-language must be found. For Fiorenza, Jesus' Sophia-God is sufficient: 'The earliest Christian theology is sophialogy' (134).

Any assessment of Fiorenza's exegetical position must also take account of her extensive hermeneutical reflections. In exegetical practice she normally appears to be working within the constraints and criteria of the historical-critical method, and yet she repeatedly and vigorously attacks its claim to 'objectivity' or 'value-free neutrality'. If 'objectivity' is understood as the validity of a truth-claim apart from the circumstances in which it is asserted, then Fiorenza clearly asserts the objectivity of her conclusions: Jesus really did understand himself as Sophia's agent and this claim does not stem from the wishful thinking of the modern fer. inist theologian. In this sense, Fiorenza claims to be *more* objective than male exegetes who, because of their androcentric biases, make all kinds of historically unjustified assumptions about the New Testament texts and early Christian history. The 'objectivity' that is rejected must therefore be the notion that the exegete should at all times remain personally disengaged from the issues that arise from the texts. But it is quite possible for non-feminist New Testament scholars to work out through their scholarship a commitment, for example, to oppose fundamentalism or distorted Christian views of Judaism (commitments which Fiorenza shares). In that case, her emphasis on personal engagement is not different in kind from that which the historical-critical paradigm already permits. This means that, despite the elaborate and sophisticated hermeneutical reflection within which it is set, Fiorenza's historical reconstruction still allows itself to be assessed in conventional historical-critical terms, so long as one heeds her warnings about the blindnesses caused by androcentric bias.

A conventional exegetical critique of Fiorenza's historical reconstruction would be inappropriate here. In preparation for a theological-exegetical response to her marginalizing of the image of God as father that will also address the christological issue, a single historical-critical point will be sufficient. It is a problem for Fiorenza's attempt to displace the masculine image of God as father with the feminine sophia-image that in the oldest strata of tradition the father-image is the more frequent. Fiorenza's argument is dependent upon the hypothesis of Q, and in the material so designated there are at best only two direct references to Sophia (Luke 7.35, par. Matt. 11.19; Luke 11.49?) as against nine references to God as father (Luke 6.36/Matt 5.48; Luke 10.21–22/Matt. 11.25–27 (five times), Luke 11.2/Matt. 6.9; Luke 11.13/Matt 7.11; Luke 12.30/Matt 6.32). Matt. 23.8–9, a non-Q text, whose importance Fiorenza rightly emphasizes, may also be added to this list of early uses of the father-image. The ratio might be altered if we removed the fivefold reference to 'the father' in Luke 10.21–22 and par. from this list, on the grounds that this passage may belong to a comparatively late stratum in the Q tradition. But this would still leave us with references to the divine father as 'merciful' or 'perfect', as the addressee of prayer, as the giver of good things to those who ask, as knowing the disciples' needs, and as the one upon whom the disciples must call. It is therefore difficult to accept Fiorenza's claim that 'the earliest Christian

theology is sophialogy' (134). The women and men who were Jesus' first
followers may have worshipped God as Sophia, but they certainly worshipped
God as father. Rather than ignoring this fact or following Ruether's advice to
search for new models elsewhere, it seems preferable to exploit to the full the
anti-patriarchal possibilities in the father-image that Ruether and Fiorenza
both somewhat cursorily acknowledge.[1] This preference is rooted in the
hypothesis that to speak in an anti-patriarchal manner of God as father is to
say something important about God, although this image should not be
isolated from other images such as 'wisdom' or 'spirit' and 'son'.[2]

The image of God as father may create difficulties for feminist theology, but
the maleness of the image is not in itself a sufficient reason for refusing to
work with it. Mary Daly speaks of a 'cosmosis', the coming into being of an
integrated, healed cosmos, which 'will require in men as well as in women
a desire to become androgynous, that is, to become themselves… If they do
not shrink from the good news because it means loss of undeserved privilege
and prestige or because it means setting forth on a long and perilous trip into
uncharted territory, [men] might succeed in becoming human' (*Beyond
God the Father*, 172). If men are not beyond redemption (if, in other words,
feminism resists the temptation to become Manichean), then neither is the
image of God as father. If the redemption of this image from patriarchal
misappropriation is to take place, it must shed the privileges unjustly
ascribed to divine and human patriarchs and, in some sense, become
androgynous. The theological question guiding the Lucan exegesis that
follows is whether and how the anti-patriarchal possibilities of this image
are exploited within the New Testament itself.

In Luke 10.21–22 we are told that Jesus

> rejoiced in the Holy Spirit and said, 'I thank thee, Father, Lord of
> heaven and earth, that thou hast hidden these things from the wise
> and understanding and revealed them to children; yea, Father, for so
> it was well-pleasing before thee. All things have been delivered to me
> by my Father and no-one knows who the Son is except the Father,
> or who the Father is except the Son and anyone to whom the Son
> chooses to reveal him.'

The naming here not only of the Father but also of the Son and the Holy
Spirit raises the possibility that, in attempting to formulate a theological
understanding of God in the light of feminist theological critique, trinitarian
conceptuality may prove to be richer and more adequate to the subject-

208   *Text, Church and World*

matter than the undifferentiated, singular deity of 'Christian monothe-ism'.[3] One who is addressed as 'father' is said to have revealed something ('these things') not to high status, elite males but to children. What this father reveals is presumably himself, his own presence and action. Yet this revelation, which initially appears to be general in scope, is in the second sentence closely related to the one who is cryptically referred to as 'the son'. If 'all things' (*panta*) are related to 'these things' (*tauta*), then the father's revelation to children occurs by way of the speaker ('me'). The father is 'my father'. The effect is to introduce a complication into the relatively straightforward depiction of God as 'father, lord of heaven and earth'. The father is identified now not only as lord of heaven and earth but also as the father of the son, and the son is identified as 'me', the speaker – Jesus. Yet this identification of Jesus as the son is not made explicit, and it is left to the reader to connect the reference to 'my father' with 'the son'. To say that, according to this passage, Jesus is the son is true, but overlooks the reticence with which this identification is suggested rather than asserted. The reticence stems from the initially closed circle in which only the father and the son know each other's identity. The father may indeed be lord of heaven and earth, but true acknowledgement of the God who answers to that description is not at all as straightforward as the language may initially suggest. But, if the relation of father and son is a secret, known only to the two participants, how then does the father's revelation to children take place? It takes place when the son chooses that it should. Jesus gives thanks for a revelation to children that ultimately stems from the good will of the father, but he himself – as the son – participates in the event of this revelation.

If we regard this passage as the hermeneutical key to the use of the father-image elsewhere in the gospel narrative, then this image is not simply a manifestation of a male-oriented monotheism. The lord of heaven and earth is not the god who self-evidently upholds the patriarchal status quo; he is not 'the Father' in some generalized sense, a projection of socio-political exigencies, he is the father of the son. His identity is initially known to the two of them alone, and the wise and understanding males who construct the lord of heaven and earth in their own image, in order to preserve the unjust order of which they are the beneficiaries, are guilty of idolatry. But the father is the father of the son, and he can only be revealed by the son. For the patriarchal Father, all such esoteric language is an irrelevant mystification. He does not need to be 'revealed' in some occult way, and an exclusive revelation to 'children' from which the wise are excluded is a ridiculous idea. As patriarchy is self-evident, so is the patriarchal Father. It follows that the non-self-evident revelation of the father of the son, which occurs through the son, will reveal the *difference* between this father and the heavenly patriarch. And, if it is Jesus – the protagonist of this narrative – who opens up the relation of father and son to others, then this will take place not in the privacy of some gnostic inner space but in the narrative itself. Thus, a few chapters later, the narrator represents Jesus as uttering the best-known biblical passage about the divine fatherhood, the so-called 'parable of the prodigal son' (Luke 15.11–32). Might this be an occasion for Jesus the son to reveal his father as different from the heavenly patriarch? If an absolute qualitative difference is not discernible here (if the parable turns out simply to reinforce patriarchal order), then the constructive use of the gospels' imaging of God as father will probably prove impossible. I shall argue, however, that this difference is in fact the central theme of the parable.[4]

This passage initially looks vulnerable to feminist ideology-critique. Three males occupy the centre of the stage, and women exist only in the negative, marginalized form of the prostitutes in the far country. Is this story simply a vivid image of male dominance?[5] Refutation of this understandable conclusion can occur only by way of the exegesis as a whole. It is, however, inadequate merely to point to the maleness of the three main characters, and then to rest one's case. The intricacies of their interactions must be carefully observed.

At the heart of the parable is a discrepancy between the expectations that both sons have of their father when the younger one returns home in disgrace, and the actuality of the father's conduct. In the far country, the younger son rehearses the speech he will utter on his return home: 'I will arise and go to my father, and I will say to him, "Father, I have sinned against heaven and before you; I am no longer worthy to be called your son; treat me as one of your hired servants"' (15.18–19). The decision is taken with reluctance, only at the point of starvation; the humiliation of returning and being treated like the servants is thinkable only because they 'have bread enough and to spare, while I am perishing here of hunger' (v. 17). The encounter with the Father will be a terrifying ordeal, and the abject submission planned by the son will at best issue only in menial employment. What is at issue is simply the extent to which he will be disowned. The harsh treatment that is to be expected stems from the Father's authority as the surrogate of 'heaven': to sin against the Father is to sin against God, and to return to this figure is therefore to walk voluntarily into an earthly day of judgement. Strangely, however, the expected harsh treatment does not materialize. The father does not even listen to the prepared speech, and since he is not listening the son does not get as far as the main point, the request for employment. As a character, the younger son disappears from view in the midst of the celebrations of his return, and the spotlight switches to his older brother.

On being informed of the reason for the celebrations, the older brother too immediately senses a discrepancy between the father's conduct and the norms he might have been expected to observe. His complaint stems in part from personal chagrin; despite his years of dutiful service, no such celebrations have ever been held in *his* honour. But accompanying this personal grievance is also the sense that a patriarchal norm has not been upheld. 'When this son of yours came, who has devoured your living with harlots, you killed for him the fatted calf!' (v. 30). Is that any way for the patriarchal surrogate of 'heaven' to behave? His worthless son (he is no longer worthy to be called 'my brother') has, after all, dissipated the paternal *property*, and since patriarchal power and status are defined largely in terms of property its dissipation amounts to a form of castration, an attack on the male person at its most intimate and vulnerable point. Thus the Greek terms used here to represent the concept of 'property' are *bios* ('life', the elder brother's term (v. 30)) and *ousia* ('being', used twice by the narrator in vv. 11, 13). In patriarchy, property or wealth is not some external entity which can be added to or subtracted from without affecting the 'being' of the person to whom it belongs. If wealth is diminished, the person diminishes; if it increases, the person increases. The person who loses or gains in this way does not remain the same person, for his personhood is not a private, autonomous 'self' but is produced, sustained and constantly redefined by the social relations in which he is enmeshed; and against the redefinition occasioned by loss of property there is no appeal. Thus it is the Father's very being or life that has been impaired by the younger son whose return is so strangely being celebrated. It is because the younger son understands perfectly the nature of his crime as an act which mortally wounds his Father that he is so reluctant to return and so sure of a hostile reception which will at best issue in lifelong humiliation. Indeed, his acts have threatened the Father with death. If the transfer of *ousia* and *bios* from Father to sons is successfully accomplished, then the Father's being, substance and life will live on through his male heirs even after his decease, and he will have acquired a kind of conditional immortality. But where, even before his decease, his substance is dissipated, then his power to survive is drastically diminished.

A naïvely realist reading of the parable might find a difficulty in the fact that both brothers are so badly mistaken about their father's character. (On the elder brother's testimony, he was normally not a man much given to celebration (cf. v. 29).) The explanation is that the logic of the narrative requires this discrepancy between expectation and actuality or between patriarchal and non-patriarchal images of fatherhood, and that the problem of grasping the father's 'character' as an integrated, lifelike whole does not exist for this narrator.[6] The brothers' expectations are in fact an actualization in narrative form of an understanding of the father/son relation rooted in the wisdom tradition. According to Prov. 28.7, 'A wise son observes the law, but one who keeps riotous company [*poimainei asōtian*, LXX] shames his father.' The meaning of the younger son's decision to live *asōtōs* (Luke 15.13) is thus clear to both brothers. According to Prov. 29.3, 'He who loves wisdom makes his father glad, but one who keeps company with harlots squanders his substance [*plouton*, LXX].' Will the son who keeps company with harlots and squanders his substance nevertheless make his Father glad? That is precisely the elder brother's question (cf. Luke 15.30), and it gains a momentary poignancy from the preceding reference to the total lack of celebration in his own life: 'Lo, these many years I have served you, and I never disobeyed your command; yet you have never given me a kid that I might make merry with my friends.' According to scripture, 'The father of the righteous will greatly rejoice, he who begets a wise son will be glad in him' (Prov. 23.24); but in the elder brother's case there has been no outward token of any such joy. Yet we should not acquiesce in his self-pity, for, as the father reminds him, he benefits from living dutifully within the patriarchal system. 'You are always with me, and all that is mine is yours' (Luke 15.31): there has been no waste, no profligacy, and the elder son has been the beneficiary of this fact. To the elder brother, the Father has been the patriarch concerned primarily with the acquisition, preservation and transmission of property. To the profligate younger brother, the father manifests his own profligacy as one who cares nothing for the doubtful privileges of patriarchal status.[7]

In recognizing the returning son when he was still some way off, in running to him, in embracing and kissing him, ignoring his prepared speech in his eagerness to prepare the celebrations, the father renounces the patriarchal order. The son who lives *asōtōs* shames his Father, but this father shows not the slightest concern for any damage done to his honour. He is not thinking of himself at all but of 'my son' (v. 23), or, as he pointedly puts it in response to the elder brother's disparaging 'this son of yours' (*ho huios sou houtos* (v. 30)), 'this your brother' (*ho adelphos sou houtos* (v. 32)). The son who keeps company with harlots dissipates his Father's substance, but the father is so unconcerned that he orders further celebratory dissipation of that substance and ignores the elder brother's remark about the impairment of his 'life' (*bios* (v. 30)). Nor does the reference to 'harlots' evoke any response, although in the wisdom tradition it is one of the Father's chief tasks to inculcate a horror of those loose women who entrap inexperienced youths with the promise that 'stolen water is sweet, and bread eaten in secret is pleasant' (Prov. 9.17) and with other similarly seductive talk (cf. Prov. 7.13–21). Both sons in their different ways address their father in his patriarchal role as preserver of his own substance, but he hardly seems to hear them. His behaviour is a kind of kenosis of patriarchy; he sets aside the status, power and wealth that belong to him as a Father by virtue of his intimate relation to 'heaven' or God (Lk.15.18, 21). He follows precisely the programme for men proposed by Mary Daly ('If they do not shrink from the good news because it means loss of undeserved privilege or prestige…, they might succeed in becoming human' (*Beyond God the Father*, 172)). Does he also manifest the 'desire to become androgynous, that is, to become themselves' that Daly recommends to men and women (172)? His behaviour is not gender-specific. It is certainly not characteristic of the Father, but nor is it characteristic of the mother – for biblical tradition seems not to know of the stereotype according to which Fathers are stern and unbending whereas mothers forgive their children no matter what. His behaviour is 'human', but it is also divine. From a patriarchal perspective, on the other hand, it is suicidal folly, the self-inflicted death of the Father.

This is the father – a father who hardly even understands patriarchy – revealed by Jesus, the son, through the parable. That the Pharisees and scribes to whom the parable is addressed will probably reject it is a sign of its truthfulness, for it is a matter of thanksgiving that the revelation of the father through the son does not coincide with the Lord of heaven and earth whom wise and understanding males employ to legitimate an unjust social order, but rather unmasks this figure as an idol. The revelation of the father through the son occurs, however, not only through the son's speech but also through his action. The parable arises out of criticism of Jesus' behaviour: 'This man receives sinners and eats with them' (v. 2).[8] As in the parable ('let us eat and celebrate' (v. 23)), this shared meal, like any other, is a sacrament of acceptance and community. The limits of acceptance and community are normally rather clearly circumscribed, for the meal is shared between family members, friends and associates of approximately equal status. Thus, when Jesus goes to dine one sabbath 'at the house of a ruler who belonged to the Pharisees' (Luke 14.1), the narrator indicates that, although he is regarded with suspicion, Jesus' social status still places him within the small circle of those who qualify as potential dinner-guests at the house of a ruler. Even within that circle there are gradations, for seating is arranged in order of rank from 'the place of honour' down to 'the lowest place' (14.8–9); yet the range of status-gradations thus traversed is small when measured on a broader social scale. Jesus, however, exposes the ideological dimensions of this socio-political construct when he says to his host: 'When you give a dinner or a banquet, do not invite your friends or your brothers or your kinsmen or rich neighbours, lest they also invite you in return, and you be repaid. But when you give a feast, invite the poor, the maimed, the lame, the blind, and you will be blessed, because they cannot repay you. You will be repaid at the resurrection of the just' (14.12–14). A guest attempts to defuse the tension generated by this astonishingly tactless speech by uttering a platitude suggested by the reference to the resurrection: 'When one of those who sat at table with him heard this, he said to him, "Blessed is he who shall eat bread in the kingdom of God!"' (v. 15). But Jesus is not bound by the social rules of the shared meal, since his initial transgression was precisely to offer a radical criticism of these rules; and he therefore adds another transgression to the original one by refusing to allow the fellow-guest's statement to remain in the genre-category of the platitude, instead taking it absolutely seriously. Who are those persons who will eat bread in the kingdom of God and be blessed? The wealthy, high-status males who are Jesus' fellow-guests have their property to attend to (fields, oxen, wives to supervise) and therefore make excuses for non-attendance, using the politest possible terms in conformity with the rules: 'I pray you, have me excused' (vv. 18, 19). Those who will eat bread in the kingdom of God are precisely those whom the host should have invited on this occasion: 'the poor, the maimed, the lame, the blind' (vv. 13, 21). If in future he follows this advice (but obviously he will not), his meal will be an anticipation of the great banquet of the kingdom of God, the meal-symbolism denoting the utter destruction of the currently impregnable social barriers which so drastically limit the possibilities for human community. Unlike his host, however, Jesus does practise in his eating-habits a form of community which makes the nature of the existing system visible and questionable by refusal to conform to it, thus signifying and anticipating the future. And so, inevitably, he is criticized by those who like the existing system and who see the future as simply an extension of the present and the past: 'This man receives sinners and eats with them' (15.2, cf. 5.30, 7.34, 19.7). To them, he is the prodigal who dissipates his Father's substance in the far country. What Jesus discloses, or what the father reveals through the son, is hidden from wise and understanding males; and this is a matter for thanksgiving, for it offers the possibility of a future which is not the extension and perpetuation of present injustice but radically new. What is at issue in all this is not a pietistic concern with a forgiveness of the individual 'sinner' which derives from the depths of the Father's all-embracing paternal love; such a concern is ultimately a concern of the present system. What is at issue is the system itself, and especially the radical difference between it and the kingdom of God. In Jesus' praxis, the light of the future shines on the present in judgement and promise, and in this way the son reveals the father whom he alone knows to those whom he chooses.[9]

It is this praxis that is defended in the 'parable of the prodigal father'. In eating with sinners, the son enacts the kenosis of the father who, scandalously disregarding the usual patriarchal obsessions with property and status, embraces his younger son and orders that the fatted calf should be killed so that there might be feasting and celebration.[10] Thus, the tension between Jesus' and his critics' understanding of meal-symbolism is disclosed in the parable as a tension between the truth delivered by the father to the son ('All things have been delivered to me by my father' (10.22)) and the falsehood of a system *here disclosed as that of patriarchy.* Jesus' diagnosis of his critics' position is that it stems from their devoted service of the Father. Their boast that they diligently accomplish a hard, demanding, divinely-imposed duty (cf. 15.29) is deflated by the reminder that they serve the system because they benefit from it: 'All that is mine is yours' (15.31).

In the praxis of Jesus, by deed and word, the son enacts the kenosis of the Father. But this assertion, the result of superimposing Jesus' praxis onto the parable, is of course a mythological one, for the father of the son has never been the Father of the patriarchal system. The father in the parable renounces the system in which, on the evidence of both of his sons' expectations, he has previously operated; but no such renunciation is necessary for the father of the son. The father and the son are known only to one another, and this father is related to the patriarchal deity as the true God is to an idol. From the divine standpoint, the idol in no sense represents God's own past, which must now be renounced; the parable's representation of this renunciation or kenosis is an accommodation to the perspective of the addressees ('the Pharisees and the scribes'), and the only kenosis that might really take place is their own renunciation of the patriarchal system in order to participate in the praxis of Jesus. Perhaps, in doing so, they might become human – through the restoration of the impaired image of God in which they were created, that uniquely human characteristic whereby women and men are able to engage in dialogical communication with one another and with God. Jesus' entire ministry is to be understood as a praxis calling and enabling people to embrace this possibility, and thus in word and deed the son reveals the father to those with ears to hear and eyes to see. 'The words that I say to you I do not speak on my own authority, but the father who dwells in me does his works' (John 14.10). In the two short parables that immediately follow the complaint of Jesus' critics (Luke 15.1– 10), the actions of the shepherd and the woman do not represent the action of either the father or the son in isolation. Jesus does not intend a one-to-one correspondence between the protagonists in the stories and either his own action or that of God. The parables represent the work of father and son *as a unity*, and thus offer a theological defence of Jesus' controversial praxis. In his acts, the divine father and the divine/human son are together working for the restoration of the image of God in humankind and for the creation of anticipations of the true community of the future kingdom of God over against the counterfeit community of the past and present. Because patriarchy characterizes the counterfeit community and not the true one, it is a matter of indifference in these parables whether the united action of father and son is represented by means of a male protagonist (the shepherd searching for his lost sheep) or a female one (the woman searching for her lost coin).

The action of father and son in the praxis of Jesus is profoundly hidden. All that is directly visible is a man behaving unconventionally. How then does the disclosure of the truthfulness of his words and deeds take place? Evidently the father is the source of this revelation: he is thanked because he has 'hidden these things from the wise and understanding and revealed them to children' (Luke 10.21). The son also participates in the disclosure: no-one knows 'who the father is except the son and anyone to whom the son chooses to reveal him' (10.22). But the revelation for which the father is thanked is not completed by the words and works of the son, although these constitute the site at which revelation must take place. Pharisees and scribes see what is done and hear what is said, but there is no sign in the text that they retract their complaint that 'this man receives sinners and eats with them', as they would have done had revelation occurred in its subjective as well as its objective dimension. The fact that the 'sinners' are the victims of the dominant system may make them more likely to listen to a message that proclaims the reversal of that system, but victimhood is ultimately neither a necessary nor a sufficient condition for the occurrence of the revelation. This possibility is ruled out by the statement that the son reveals the father *to whomever he chooses*. The problem of how the meaning and the truth-content of Jesus' praxis can ever come to light within a system closed to it is acknowledged by Jesus himself:

To what then shall I compare the people of this generation, and what are they like? They are like children sitting in the market place and calling to one another, 'We piped to you, and you did not dance; we wailed, and you did not weep.' For John the Baptist has come eating no bread and drinking no wine, and you say, 'He has a demon!' The son of man has come eating and drinking, and you say, 'Behold, a glutton and a drunkard, a friend of tax collectors and sinners!' Yet Wisdom is justified by all her children. (Luke 7.31–35)

The system assimilates that which fundamentally questions its legitimacy to the existing concept of a dangerous space beyond its limits whose inhabitants – the deranged, addicts, scapegoats of various kinds – do not observe its laws. The system has in fact constructed this space, which is therefore not really 'outside' itself at all, in order to contain the problems posed by those persons unable or unwilling to conform to its demands; but ideology demands that the fact that this space is a social construct be concealed so that its inhabitants' marginal existence under the disapprobation of the righteous may be deemed to be 'natural'. This strategy of containment also serves to defuse the more fundamental challenge posed in their different ways by John the Baptist and by Jesus. Jesus' challenge need not be taken seriously, for it stems from a prior repudiation of the way of righteousness so as to share in the pleasures of life among the unrighteous. He is a disobedient son who left the Father in order to squander his wealth amidst the subhuman population of the far country, and who now returns impenitently to trouble those who continue to dwell righteously in the Father's house.

'Yet Wisdom is justified by all her children' – despite the apparent omnipotence of the system. Wisdom is the divine mother who gives birth to children whose wisdom enables them to recognize the inspiration and presence of their mother in the praxis of John and of Jesus, who are also among her children. It is she who enables all her children to see through the lies of the system, and it is she who thus ensures that the revelation of the father in the words and works of the son does not go entirely unacknowledged. As Jesus speaks and acts, she is there with him; he carries out her will as well as the father's, for her will and the father's are one.[11] Her presence in others too gives them the ears to hear and the eyes to see when he speaks and acts.[12] If it is Wisdom who inspires the praxis of Jesus as well as its acknowledgement, then she is to be identified with the Holy Spirit who descended upon him in the form of a dove at his baptism (Luke 3.21–22), accompanying the voice of the father which acknowledged him as his beloved son. Wisdom may on occasion lead her children to eat no bread and drink no wine, as in the case of John the Baptist (7.33); thus, Jesus, full of the Holy Spirit, is led by the Spirit into the desert to fast for forty days (4.1–2). She is under no illusions about the response her children will receive, as Jesus is aware: 'Therefore the Wisdom of God said, "I will send them prophets and apostles, some of whom they will kill and persecute"' (11.49). She suffers the pain of their rejection, not only for their sake but also for the sake of those who reject them: as Jesus says, speaking in her name, 'O Jerusalem, Jerusalem, killing the prophets and stoning those who are sent to you! How often would I have gathered your children together as a hen gathers her brood under her wings, and you would not!' (13.34). Yet she persists in her appeals, knowing that in the end they will come to fruition. 'To what shall I compare the kingdom of God? It is like leaven which a woman took and hid in three measures of flour, till it was all leavened' (13.21).

The father anoints the son with the Spirit to empower him for his ministry of revealing the father by preaching good news to the poor and liberating those who are oppressed (cf. 4.18; 10.22); but the Spirit is not the son's exclusive possession, for Wisdom must also give birth to the 'children' (*panta ta tekna autēs* [7.35]), especially among the poor and the oppressed, who will recognize her presence in his otherwise ambiguous ministry. The wisdom she bestows on her 'children' (*nēpioi*) is diametrically opposed to the male-oriented wisdom of the 'wise and understanding' (10.21), out of which a patriarchal system is constructed which can know neither the father nor the son. The wise and understanding are therefore strangers to the reality of Wisdom. Theirs is a wisdom which is so sensitive to gradations of status that the guests' places at a wedding feast all have to be arranged in order of rank, from the place of honour down to the lowest place, to the shame of anyone who strays from his appointed station (cf. 14.7–11). Hers is a wisdom which inspires Jesus to feast with the poor, the maimed, the lame and the blind as a sign and sacrament of the contradiction of the present order by the future kingdom of God.[13]

Thus, when Jesus thanks the father for disclosing himself to children, a disclosure in which he as the son also participates, he 'rejoices in the Holy Spirit' (10.21). The inclusive celebration of community that she inspires is a sign of contradiction but also an occasion for joy, just as the contradiction of the elder brother stems from the joy of the father. Spirit, son and father participate in the joy attending the liberation that anticipates the coming kingdom of the triune God.

The (so-called) parable of the prodigal son has been read here in the light of the representation of Jesus' person and praxis in its narrative context, and a final hermeneutical and theological problem that remains to be addressed arises from this intermingling of parable with history-like, realistic narrative. The parable refers us obliquely to Jesus' own narrated praxis, but it remains unclear precisely what significance is to be ascribed to this fact. Is the gospel narrative itself to be understood as a parable, an enclosed textual world which nevertheless sheds oblique light on the realities of our contemporary world? Or is the primary referent of the story of Jesus not itself or our world, but Jesus himself, a historical person whose significance for Christian faith is more than merely historical? An understandable desire to escape from the obscurities and ambiguities of history might lead us towards the former conclusion. On this view, we may concern ourselves with Jesus solely as a narrative figure, and our findings are therefore independent of questions as to what may or may not have been true of the historical Jesus. The assumption that Jesus may be enclosed within the text is deeply embedded within much contemporary narrative.criticism, and it is difficult to formulate objections to it without losing its valuable emphasis on the final form of the text. If we assert on theological grounds that our concern must be with the real Jesus and not with a merely literary figure, we are in danger of succumbing to the doubtful hypothesis of a fundamental rift between the real Jesus and the gospel texts, the hypothesis from which 'the quest of the historical Jesus' set out. If, on the other hand, we assert as a conviction of faith the identity of the real Jesus with his narrative embodiment, the danger is that this issue will be removed from the sphere of public discussion and become essentially irrelevant. One engages in some form of narrative criticism and announces the conviction that the narratively-embodied Jesus coincides with the real Jesus; but unless this conviction significantly affects interpretative practice, it is of no real significance. How are these dangers to be avoided? The issue will be addressed at various points in the following chapters, but some preliminary reflections are appropriate here.

The father and the two sons in the parable are unnamed; neither their own country nor the far country is identified; and there are no indications that a specific historical period is intended. However, the father and the son of the main Lucan narrative are precisely identified as, respectively, the God of Israel, now revealed as the father of Jesus, and Jesus himself. The story is set within a clearly specified space – Galilee, Judea and Jerusalem – which is continuous with the space in which the evangelist's envisaged readers are located (as the geography of Acts demonstrates). Its main action begins 'in the fifteenth year of the reign of Tiberius Caesar' (Luke 3.1), a historical time located on a chronological continuum with the time that the evangelist shares with Theophilus. Its author's expressed intention is that 'you' – Theophilus as representing every subsequent reader – 'may know the truth [*asphaleia*] concerning the things about which you have been instructed' (1.4). It is presupposed that the reader is already familiar with traditions stemming from 'those who from the beginning were eyewitnesses and ministers of the word' (1.2), and is therefore aware that, at a time still within the memory of older contemporaries, and in a place that is distant but not too distant, a certain Jew by the name of Jesus of Nazareth lived, worked, taught, died and was raised, thus founding the community in which these facts are preserved and passed on. On discovering that the main character in the narrative that ensues is also named Jesus of Nazareth, the reader will naturally identify this narrative figure with his historical namesake, about whom he or she has already been instructed. The invitation into the world of the text is at the same time an invitation into the real world beyond the text, to which the text refers.[14] (The authorial persona that briefly appears here, before disappearing behind an impersonal mask, seems unaware of modern scruples over the notion of 'the real world'.) In the term *asphaleia* is contained the assertion that the narrative and the referential worlds ultimately coincide: *ultimately* rather than immediately, because 'the things which have been accomplished among us' are open to many different narrative embodiments (1.1; cf. John 20.30; 21.25) and not to a single master-narrative which merely transcribes successive facts in positivistic fashion.

Two important points follow from this. The first is that to see this or any canonical gospel as 'a literary creation with an autonomous integrity' over against 'the life of Jesus' is a major error of literary judgement.[15] The second is that, where in the preceding discussion 'Jesus' is referred to, the referent is the historical bearer of that name – not as someone to whom we may gain independent, unmediated access but insofar as that historical person is mediated to us in and through the text. A corollary of this is that the interpretation of elements of Jesus' praxis offered here is open to challenge from those whose working hypothesis is not the *asphaleia* of the text but the rift between the text and the historical Jesus. Any such challenge would have to be answered, and could not be ruled out of court on the grounds that the reading offered here relates only to an autonomous narrative world.

All this immediately exposes the theological reading offered here to the charge that it anachronistically imposes modern concerns and insights onto the historical figure of Jesus. Sensitivity to 'the peril of modernizing Jesus' is regarded as one of the most important achievements of historical-critical scholarship, although there is much less sensitivity to the peril of archaizing Jesus. If Jesus can only ever by spoken about within the medium of contemporary discourse, then it will be impossible to avoid 'modernizing' him. The question is whether this is done in ways that retain a sense of his own historical particularity, and the obvious presence of 'modern' priorities and insights does not necessarily mean that an awareness of Jesus as living within a different socio-cultural world to our own has been lost. Far from distorting whatever they touch, these elements of contemporaneity may offer insights into aspects of Jesus' person, praxis and teaching which have otherwise gone unrecognized. And if Jesus is not simply a Jewish 'prophet' but 'the saviour of the world' (John 4.19, 42), then there is no sphere available for his saving activity other than the one which is always already occupied by discourses and practices which differ, to a greater or lesser extent, from those of early first-century Galilee.

PART FOUR

THEOLOGY, HERMENEUTICS, EXEGESIS

Throughout the preceding chapters, the fundamental concern has been the development of a hermeneutic and a corresponding exegetical practice oriented towards theological questions. In Part One, various contemporary versions of the hermeneutic of the final form of the text were explored, with the intention of establishing the foundation upon which a theological hermeneutic for biblical interpretation can be constructed. In Parts Two and Three, in dialogue with poststructuralist or postmodern theory and with feminist theology respectively, I began to develop an exegesis oriented from the start towards specifically theological issues. I offered a non-logocentric (or non-monological) understanding of the divine word; a reading of the creation narrative which was intended to broaden the horizons of 'narrative theology' and to illustrate the possibility of a hermeneutic of intratextual realism; an application of the law/gospel antithesis to Old Testament androcentrism, showing how a transcending of their own androcentrism is inscribed within these texts; and a trinitarian response to the feminist critique of New Testament father/son language.

A common thread running through these theological readings of biblical texts might be found in the doctrine of the Spirit, located within a broad trinitarian perspective. Yet these readings were occasioned by particular problems arising from contemporary hermeneutics and theology, and were inevitably somewhat piecemeal in character. A final step, which must be taken in the remaining chapters, is to attempt to formulate in more systematic fashion some of the elements of a *theological hermeneutic*, intended as a framework within which exegesis may proceed. To develop a theological hermeneutic would be, first, to offer a theological justification for particular hermeneutical decisions. In previous chapters I have assumed the appropriateness of working with the final form of the text, the legitimacy of criticizing and resisting the text at certain points, and the need to draw upon secular insights originating outside the sphere of theology and the church. Theological hermeneutics must reflect upon such decisions from within a theological perspective, and I shall offer a reflection of this kind in the chapter that follows. But it is also important to recognize that a theological position can itself function as a hermeneutic. In the reading of the creation narrative in chapter 8, for example, the doctrine of the trinity fulfilled a hermeneutical function, disclosing facets of the text that would otherwise have been overlooked. Christian doctrine initially offers an interpretation of scripture, but in a second moment constitutes a hermeneutic which will affect subsequent scriptural interpretation.

The relation between exegesis and theology is, in fact, a manifestation of the hermeneutical circle or spiral, in which whole and parts are dialectically related.[1] Exegesis of the parts (individual biblical texts) presupposes some sense of the whole (an interpretation of the basic content of Christian faith). Yet this sense of the whole is not brought to the texts from outside them but stems, at least partially, from prior exegesis. Exegesis can serve to develop, clarify and correct a given theological position; and conversely a given theological position can serve to give exegesis an orientation and a relevance that it would lack if pursued in merely random fashion. This dialectical formulation points to a middle course between two extremes. It enables one to maintain the relative autonomy of the biblical texts, over against every attempt to impose on them a doctrinal framework (whether traditionalist or modernist) which determines and fixes their meaning in advance, thereby rendering itself immune to criticism and correction. It also enables one to maintain the relative autonomy of a given interpretation of Christian faith, over against every biblicistic attempt (traditionalist or modernist) to subject it to the tyranny of the letter. Exegesis and theology must proceed in dialogue with one another, and chapters 14–16 therefore offer some samples of such a dialogue.

Chapter 13

Theological Hermeneutics

Engagement with contemporary hermeneutical discussion is an essential prerequisite for any attempt to rethink the relationship between exegesis and theology. Yet much of this discussion takes place in non-theological contexts, and the significance for theology of, for example, debate about authorial intention or the role of the reader is not self-evident. It is therefore necessary to engage in further theological reflection on some of the main hermeneutical assumptions of earlier chapters. Three theses will serve as a starting-point for the discussion.

1. Access to the reality of Jesus is textually mediated.

This thesis is, of course, a truism: we would know little or nothing of Jesus were it not for the mainly Christian texts that speak of him. Yet as a theological–hermeneutical thesis this statement has certain important functions within current debate, and the first of these stems from its conceptual distinction between the reality of Jesus and its textual mediation. Even in the absence of written texts, it would remain true that Jesus of Nazareth was a Galilean who achieved some popular success as a teacher, healer and exorcist before being crucified in Jerusalem by the Jewish and Roman political authorities. The reality of Jesus is not, however, exhausted by such straightforward historical statements, for the beliefs about himself that he wittingly or unwittingly engendered are also part of that reality, and they are still widely held to be (in some sense) true. While controversy about the nature and significance of his reality has been unceasing ever since his public ministry began, it is uncontroversial that this reality is mediated (satisfactorily or otherwise) by written texts, above all by the gospels. Contemporary hermeneutics can hardly deny this, whatever scruples it may have about terms such as 'reality' and 'fact', but its emphasis on the autonomy of the text in its final form can easily lead to the conclusion that

223

the 'pre-textual' reality of Jesus is hermeneutically irrelevant. Instead of claiming that the reality of Jesus is textually *mediated*, ought we not to state that it is textually *constructed?* The word became not flesh but text. But the denial of the enfleshment of the word has been characteristic of every form of docetism, and the almost embarrassingly material term 'flesh' has functioned historically as a criterion whereby docetism can be identified and rejected. The detection of an ancient christological heresy in contemporary understanding of textuality will not cut much ice in the broader debate but cannot be so easily dismissed in a theological context.

The word became text: Hans Frei's argument in *The Eclipse of Biblical Narrative* can be read as favouring such a view, especially if one emphasizes what this text actually says and does not say, rather than its author's probable intentions.[1] As we saw in chapter 1, Frei argues for the inviolability of the final form of the gospel narratives, in opposition to every attempt to penetrate to some allegedly deeper meaning or truth (whether historical or theological) some way beneath the surface of the text. In understanding the gospels as realistic narrative, Frei assimilates them to the genre of the realistic novel and rejects the assumption that they belong to the genres of myth, allegory or historiography. In breaking up the surface of the text in quest of some deeper level of truth, one merely destroys the text; for realistic narrative is irreducible. Frei highlights the irony that the development of the illegitimate modern reading of the gospels coincides historically with the rise of the realistic novel: theological polemic and apologetic ensured that the analogy between the realistic narrative of the gospels and that of the novel was almost universally overlooked.[2] But this means that it becomes hard to differentiate Jesus from a character in a novel. The referential function of the gospel narratives is consistently played down; and when, at the end of *The Identity of Jesus Christ*, Frei suddenly asserts that the fundamental truthfulness of the resurrection narratives is actually very important, he has no conceptuality available for making this assertion plausible and is reduced to gnomic utterances about the mysteriousness of faith.[3]

My own argument has also assumed fairly consistently the appropriateness of working with the text in its final form. Is a docetic tendency inevitable in such a view? In the discussion of language, God and creation in chapter 8, I argued that the claim that the doctrine of divine creation is only intrasystematically true has the effect of making language, and therefore human beings, the creator of the deity, who thus conforms to the intrasystematic definition of an idol. I argued instead for an *intratextual realism* which would understand the biblical text as referring beyond itself to extra-textual theological reality, while at the same time regarding that reality as accessible to us only in textual form, in principle and not only in practice. Theological reflection would therefore have to understand itself ultimately as textual interpretation. On the other hand, Jesus is a purely linguistic creation if the word became text rather than flesh. As a character in a realistic narrative, he is represented as the son of another character, God. Yet the real, extrasystematic 'father' of Jesus is the (collective) author who constructed this memorable narrative character out of certain prior communal linguistic resources; Jesus is the only-begotten son of the evangelists or of the early Christian community. If one wishes to avoid this conclusion while maintaining the irreducibility of the final form of the text, it is necessary to speak of the text as *mediating* the reality of Jesus rather than as *constructing* it.

Working with the final form of the text makes it possible to marginalize many of the diachronic issues that arise within the historical-critical paradigm. It might be argued that, whatever the problems of appropriating the historical-critical perspective on the gospels for theological use, nothing is gained by eliminating them by arbitrary hermeneutical decree. I argued in chapter 3 (taking source-critical study of Gen. 37 as a test-case) that historical criticism's current crisis of confidence stems not from arbitrary hermeneutical decrees but from *within itself,* and especially from its persistent inability satisfactorily to answer many of the questions it sets itself. These questions are open to an indefinite number of answers which, in the absence of secure criteria, are possible but not compelling. Rather than acknowledging this uncomfortable situation, the tendency is to take short-cuts in order to attain the reassuring closure of a provisional preferred solution, which may derive much of its persuasiveness from the rhetorical skill with which it is presented, the dictates of fashion, and the advocacy of prestigious names. To take an example from the gospels, the problem of the origin and usage of the phrase 'son of man' in connection with Jesus appears to be open to an indefinite number of possible solutions. Various criteria are employed (pre-Christian usage, double dissimilarity, and so on), and any given application of such criteria may be judged more or less appropriate in subsequent discussion. At one stage in the discussion, some scholars found it plausible to claim that sayings in which Jesus appeared to speak of an apocalyptic son of man as someone other than himself must be 'authentic', whereas sayings in which he refers to himself as the son of man are 'secondary'. At another stage, 'son of man' is seen as a straightforward Jewish circumlocution for 'I', employed by Jesus without any dogmatic import but subsequently converted into a christological title by the ever-inventive early church.[4] Yet to the critical non-participant in this debate, the reasons adduced for preferring either solution to any other seem less than overwhelming, even if at individual points progress may be detected.

Detailed investigation is needed of the institutional factors which perpetuate the illusion that the historical-critical method has the resources to solve the problems which it sets itself.

If the irreducible plurality of possible solutions to historical-critical problems offers a pragmatic reason for working with the final form of the text, this situation is also suggestive theologically. It accords with the sense that the texts are abused when they are subjected to a type of question they were never intended to answer. In response to an earlier style of scholarship, preoccupied with Jesus' intellectual and personal growth, Martin Kähler pointed out that 'the New Testament presentations were not written for the purpose of describing how Jesus developed' (*The So-Called Historical Jesus and the Historic, Biblical Christ* (1896), 51). Historical research can of course 'help to explain and clarify particular features of Jesus' actions and attitudes as well as many aspects of his teaching' (54); yet these partial clarifications do not satisfy the critic's inner need to put forward comprehensive solutions. Thus one adopts a general hypothesis which determines the shape of one's research: that Jesus was an unremarkable figure in the context of his own time and place, that his teaching differs at point after point from that of the early church, that the value of an element of tradition is determined by whether it can be shown to be 'original' and 'authentic' rather than 'secondary' and 'inauthentic', that religious experience is more important than dogma.[5] 'Disguised as history, the historian's theory passes imperceptibly into our thought and convictions as an authentic piece of reality' (56). A similar sense that in much historical research the interpreter is at odds with the orientation of the texts is expressed by Karl Barth.[6] Referring to the difficulty or impossibility of deriving a history of Israel from the Old Testament or a life of Jesus from the New, Barth argues that

> the sources always have to be wrested to yield a result of this kind. And what they have yielded under compulsion has never been of a kind to rejoice the heart of a historian. Of course, with many other things they do give us something which is recognisable as history, human history in itself and as such, but always incidentally, and with all kinds of strange abbreviations and extensions and twists which derive from the fact that they are really trying to tell us about happenings of quite a different nature, so that in face of them the historian is always confronted with a painful dilemma: either to let them say what they are trying to say, and not to have any history at all in our sense of the term, or to extract such a history from them at the cost of ignoring and losing what they are really trying to say. (*Church Dogmatics*, IV, 1 (1953), 505)

Returning to the case of Jesus as 'son of man', this would suggest that the texts are unwilling and unable to provide the comprehensive developmental schema that is desired, and that, where they are nevertheless forced to serve as evidence for one or another hypothetical schema, what they might have to say when they represent Jesus as speaking of himself as 'the son of man' remains unheard.

Elsewhere Barth expresses the same point in terms of the inseparability of form and content in the biblical texts. 'As the witness of divine revelation the Bible also attests the institution and function of prophets and apostles. And in so doing it attests itself as Holy Scripture, as the indispensable form of that content. But because this is the case, in this question of divine revelation the Church, and in and with it theology, has to hold fast to this unity of content and form... In this question of revelation we cannot, therefore, free ourselves from the texts in which its expectation and recollection is attested to us. We are tied to these texts' (*Church Dogmatics*, I, 2 (1938), 492). These assertions are directed against the view that 'in the reading and understanding and expounding of the Bible the main concern can and must be to penetrate past the biblical texts to the facts which lie behind the texts' (492). That is to overlook 'the universal rule of interpretation... that a text can be read and understood and expounded only with reference to and in the light of its theme' (493). 'If we have a particular interest in antiquities, we can read them [the biblical texts] in this way at our own risk, at the risk of failing to serve even our own interest and missing the real nature and character of the writings.' But theology should have 'the tact and taste, in face of the linking of form and content..., to resist this temptation, to leave the curious question of what is perhaps behind the texts, and to turn with all the more attentiveness, accuracy and love to the texts as such' (493–94).[7]

This approach is perhaps best elaborated in terms of the genre of the biblical texts. If genre is a function of communal reception and usage as well as of inherent characteristics, then the genre of the biblical texts is that of 'holy scripture': that is to say, these texts function in a peculiar way in the life of a determinate community or set of interrelated communities.[8] When the community gathers for worship, these texts (above all, the gospels) are read and reread in the expectation that, when heard within this liturgical and sacramental context and interpreted through the medium of preaching, they will serve to clarify and to reinforce the community's beliefs, values and practices and assist its members to respond appropriately to the challenges of a world which generally operates on the basis of very different beliefs, values and practices. A certain level of historical understanding will assist their response, not least in giving them a critical distance from an over-anxious, defensive biblicism. Yet in the last resort historical understanding is a very minor component in the more comprehensive understanding that is desirable. The frequent complaint that preachers do not show sufficient zeal in communicating to their hearers the results of historical-critical scholarship, fearful of the outrage they would cause were they to do so, is only justified in a limited sense; for this reticence also betrays an awareness that in this context the Bible and its interpretation is expected to offer something different from the latest historical-critical hypotheses.[9]

It is possible for professional biblical interpreters to regard this expectation as none of their business. Indeed, this is not simply a matter of personal choice, for the institution imposes some such self-understanding on its members as a condition of membership. If they wish to understand themselves as responsible to the church, that is their private concern which they must learn to locate at the margin of their public responsibilities. The (historical) truth about Jesus and about the texts which bear (fragmentary) witness to him is, in this view, almost inevitably distorted when brought into the sphere of the church and its range of expectations.[10] The real Jesus must be rescued from the church; he must be raised from the deadness of his ecclesiastical incarnation by the life-giving power of historical scholarship.[11] This task can take on some of the characteristics of a mission or vocation: historical scholarship believes itself to be justified not only in its own right but as a means of exposing and resisting churchly obscurantism in its manifold forms. The results of this scholarship tend to reflect this understanding of its social location. Its chief aim is to establish that Jesus (the historical Jesus, that is, the real Jesus) differed significantly from the images of him set up by the early church and perpetuated ever since; and the relationship between Jesus and the early church is thus the result of a projection or retrojection of the relationship between the scholarly and ecclesial communities back into the past. As Jesus may be distinguished from the early church, so the scholarly community which aims to rediscover and revive him distinguishes itself from the ecclesial community in which he is entombed. The quest of the historical Jesus is, in important respects, the quest of a non- or anti-ecclesial Jesus who will serve the interests of a community which wishes to assert its distinctiveness over against the ecclesial one. Insofar as the products of this mode of scholarship are endorsed by more 'liberal' or 'radical' members of the ecclesial community, the sociological function of such an endorsement is to locate oneself on the frontier at which the church meets the modern, secularized world, thereby setting oneself at a distance from the main body of the ecclesial institution.[12]

Ecclesiastical obscurantism and bad faith do indeed need to be exposed and resisted. The (post-)modern, secularized or pluralistic world may indeed be a source of genuine insight for critical theological appropriation, as I have tried to show in previous chapters and will underline again in this one. What is at issue is whether the interpretative task is best undertaken on the basis of a relative or complete separation from the beliefs, values and practices of the ecclesial community, or whether it would be possible to take seriously, from the start, the expectations that accord with the genre of the biblical texts as the holy scripture of a worshipping community. To understand the interpretative task in such a way is of course no guarantee that one will perform it well, just as the alternative, separatist self-understanding does not preclude the production of insights that prove ecclesially and theologically fruitful. Yet there seems no valid theoretical reason why one should not practise a mode of interpretation responsive both to the traditions of the ecclesial community and to the demands of the world beyond the community, for the church is itself related diachronically to its own past and synchronically to the wider world, and must be faithful to the requirements imposed by both dimensions of its location. Historical knowledge and research will not be excluded from such a programme; but the decision to work with the text in its canonical, communal form will serve to relativize the still-dominant obsession with the circumstances of the texts' origins, which wilfully disregards these same texts' communal role.

As for the presupposition that normative theological 'truth' is to be apprehended by way of the canonical form, this is a claim that could only be justified by the quality and persuasiveness of the interpretative practice that proceeds from it. But one further clarification must be made. Choosing to work with the canonical form of the texts does not entail a denial or a downplaying of their referential function, in the manner of narrative criticism, for (as we have seen) the outcome of such a position would be docetism, the denial of the historical humanity of the incarnate word. But the assertion that the gospel texts refer us to historical–theological reality, and that these texts are the irreducible means of access to this reality, should not be understood as necessitating a precise, detailed correspondence between the narratives and the course of historical events. Barth uses the term 'saga' to point to the peculiar genre of biblical narratives, sharply differentiating this from 'myth', in which general, ahistorical truths are clothed in narrative form: 'Saga in general is the form which, using intuition and imagination, has to take up historical narration at the point where events are no longer susceptible as such of historical proof. And the special instance of biblical saga is that in which intuition and imagination are used but in order to give prophetic witness to what has taken place by virtue of the Word of God in the (historical or pre-historical) sphere where there can be no historical proof' (*Church Dogmatics*, IV, 1, 508). Thus the resurrection narratives, like the account of the creation, might be described as 'saga' or 'legend'; but this does not mean that the resurrection did not happen in time and space in the same way as the crucifixion. 'Even accounts which by the standards of modern scholarship have to be accounted saga or legend and not history – because their content cannot be grasped historically – may still speak of a happening which, though it cannot be grasped historically, is still actual and objective in time and space' (336). The texts may or may not render faithfully the details of empirical history; but they do render faithfully the history of the relation of God and humankind, and it is in the light of this function that they must be interpreted. Barth thus postulates an 'intratextual realism' in which one regards the text in its final form as the irreducible witness to a divine–human history which occurs prior to and beyond the text, but which can only be known in its textual mediation. The labours of conservative apologists to demonstrate the 'historicity' of the biblical narratives are thus largely beside the point, but so too are the labours of historical sceptics to find 'inauthenticity' and 'secondariness' at every turn.

It is worth pursuing this issue a little further by glancing at a pre-modern form of the debate about historicity which, as Hans Frei has shown, dominates modern biblical interpretation. In his *Contra Celsum*, Origen takes issue with Celsus's denial of the historicity of various aspects of the gospel narrative (for example, the descent of the dove at Jesus' baptism and the story of the wise men and the star, discussed in 1.40–61). Origen notes that 'the attempt to show, with regard to any history, however true, that it actually occurred, and to produce an intelligible view of it, is one of the most difficult undertakings that can be attempted, and is in some cases impossible' (1.42). In the *De Principiis*, however, this difficult undertaking has lost much of its significance. It is now acknowledged that, for the sake of its witness to unseen realities, scripture may include within historical narrative 'some feature which did not happen; sometimes the event is an impossibility, sometimes, though possible, it actually did not happen' (4.2.8). This is true of the gospels as well as of the Old Testament; for example, in the claim of Matthew's temptation story that all the kingdoms of the world could be seen from the mountain-top. 'The thorough investigator can find enough similar instances to convince himself that stories which happened according to the letter are interspersed with other events which did not actually occur' (4.3.1). Although 'no one should suspect us of generalizing and saying that because a particular story did not happen, no story actually happened' (4.3.4), the interpreter will often find it difficult to determine whether a given event happened or not (4.3.5). The believer is able to agree with the unbeliever about the presence of non-historical elements in the narrative, although they disagree sharply about the significance of this fact. For the unbeliever, these elements disclose the untruthfulness of the whole. For the believer, they are irreducible, indispensable ways of speaking about the divine–human history, and since interpretation is oriented towards the text in its canonical form, it is often unnecessary to decide whether and how far events occurred as narrated.[13]

2. Since theological interpretation must distinguish the law from the gospel within the biblical text, the decision to work with the canonical form does not render the text immune from criticism.

Barth's insistence on the unity of form and content in the biblical text is open to the objection that it commits the theologian always to defend the text, taking its side when it is impugned, in strict adherence to the principle of biblical authority. Barth is not a biblicist in a conventional sense, for in his view dogmatics 'does not ask what the apostles and prophets said but what we must say on the basis of the apostles and prophets' (*Church Dogmatics*, I, 1, 16). Yet he is capable of insisting, in response to Bultmann's suggestion that he should exercise more discrimination, that it is impossible 'for an interpreter honestly to reproduce the meaning of any author unless he dares to accept the condition of utter loyalty' (*The Epistle to the Romans* (1922[2]), 18). The outcome of such language is that Barth reinforces the conservative, biblicistic tendency to polarize submission to the authority of scripture and an allegedly arrogant refusal of that submission engendered by loyalty to one or other of the passing trends of the modern world. H. Thielicke's judgement on Bultmann's demythologizing programme is a typical expression of this point. According to Thielicke, 'Wherever a non-biblical principle derived from contemporary secular thought is applied to the interpretation of the Bible, the Bible's *facultas se ipsum interpretandi* is violated, with fatal results' (in H. W. Bartsch (ed.), *Kerygma and Myth* (ET 1954), 149). The dualistic assumption that text and world are mutually exclusive will be criticized below, but the issue in the present context is whether a critique of aspects of the biblical text can be justified on inner-biblical, theological grounds. The critical discussion of the biblical representation of women in chapters 9–11 raised this question in acute form, and I have already suggested that the Pauline law/gospel antithesis is helpful at this point. I shall here develop this suggestion further, with reference to Luther's interpretation of this antithesis in his 1535 commentary on Galatians.[14]

According to Luther's reading of Paul, the Christian does not in this life finally leave the sphere of the law. Whereas Paul states that the law kept us under restraint only 'until faith should be revealed' (Gal. 3.23), and not thereafter, Luther claims that we should apply this 'not only to that time but also to experience [*ad affectum*]; for what happened historically and temporally when Christ came – namely, that he abrogated the law and brought liberty and eternal life to light – this happens personally and spiritually every day in any Christian, in whom there are found the time of law and the time of grace in constant alternation [*subinde per vices*]' (*WA* 40/ 1. 523.32–524.16; *LW* 26. 340).[15] We are subject again to the time of law in the condition of *Anfechtung* ('temptation'), when we are terrified by the thought of God as judge, hating and blaspheming him and fleeing from his countenance. But we also experience the time of grace, for the conscience 'is always encouraged by the daily coming of Christ, who, just as he once came into the world at a certain time to redeem us from the harsh dominion of our custodian, likewise comes to us spiritually every day, causing us to grow in faith and in knowledge of him' (*WA* 40/1. 536.25–28; *LW* 26. 349– 50). What for Paul is an irreversible linear movement (the time of the law is superseded by the time of the gospel) has become for Luther a circular movement from law to gospel and (by implication) from gospel back to law.

The duality in Christian experience represented by the law/gospel distinction becomes hermeneutically significant when interpreted as a twofold relation to the biblical text: for the twofold relation to God as the harsh judge to be feared and as the merciful redeemer to be loved is textually mediated.[16] It is holy scripture that both repels and attracts, and a simple, undivided affirmation of its entire content is therefore a sign that one is deceiving oneself. The conflict of law and gospel represents an irreducibly dual response to the text which occurs in reading and which may therefore underlie formal interpretation. Yet the scope of this conflict is not yet fully uncovered where the law which repels and the gospel which attracts are assigned to Moses and to Christ respectively. This would suggest that, with minor qualifications, the Old Testament is to be identified wholly with law and the New wholly with gospel, a view which, along with its other obvious drawbacks, preserves the notion of irreversible linear movement which Luther does not accept. What makes the conflict over the biblical text really serious is the fact that, for Luther, 'Moses' can function as a surrogate, euphemism or mask for Christ himself. Christ is experienced as the embodiment of law as well as of gospel; he is the centre of scripture, and as scripture is irreducibly dual so is he.

The Christ who embodies the oppressive law and who appears to conflict with the Christ who embodies the grace of God is the creation of Satan. Satan is the Accuser, and there is thus an inward affinity between him and the oppressive law. Our subjection to scripture as oppressive law is his work, and in particular it is his practice 'to set against us those passages in the gospel in which Christ himself requires works from us and with plain words threatens damnation to those who do not perform them' (*WA* 40/1. 50.16–18; *LW* 26.10–11). The result is that Christ ceases to be a saviour and becomes a lawgiver. If Moses alone is the lawgiver, and if Christ is unambiguously the bringer of grace, our situation is not so serious, for Moses is too distant a figure to pose an immediate threat. But if Moses is a mask for Christ, the situation becomes desperate: we are faced with an alien Christ who by issuing harsh demands in the plain words of the scriptural texts threatens to take from us what we believed we had gained from the Christ who, in other texts, promised us divine grace. It has long been known that the devil is capable of quoting the divine word (he does so to Eve in the garden and to Jesus in the desert), but he normally gives himself away either by contradicting it or by drawing obviously false conclusions from it. What is so sinister in this case, however, is that he presents us with Christ's 'plain words', in which Christ himself really does seem to threaten us. We may wish to believe that the threatening words proceed from the devil, but there are no objective signs of his presence and it appears to be truly Christ who is speaking; for the words are the words of Christ and the sense seems to be the literal sense.[17] Satan 'makes a practice of frightening us by transforming himself into the person of the mediator himself. He cites some passage of scripture or some saying of Christ and thus suddenly strikes our hearts and gives the impression of being the true Christ. So strong is this impression that our conscience would swear that this is the same Christ whose saying he cited.' Satan skilfully presents us with a Christ who is quite orthodox – the Son of God, the son of man, born of a virgin – but then 'he attaches something else to this, some saying in which Christ terrifies sinners, as in Lk.13: "Unless you repent, you will all likewise perish." By adulterating the genuine definition of Christ with his poison he produces this effect, that although we believe that Christ is the mediator, in our conscience he remains a tyrant and a tormentor. Thus deceived, we lose the pleasant sight of Christ, our high priest and mediator, and dread him no less than Satan' (*WA* 40/1. 92.20–93.17; *LW* 26.38–39). 'Therefore we should be on our guard, lest the amazing skill and infinite wiles of Satan deceive us into mistaking the accuser and condemner for the comforter and saviour, so that we lose the true Christ behind the mask [*sub larva*] of the false Christ, that is, of the devil, and make him of no advantage to us' (*WA* 40/2. 13.27–30; *LW* 27.12).[18]

Despite these warnings and exhortations, temptation constantly returns. Whenever temptation is overcome, it may seem clear that the speaker of the accusing words was Satan and not Christ; but when the scriptural text ascribes sayings to Christ such as 'If you would enter life, keep the commandments', it is hard to see why we should ascribe it to a satanic counterfeit when it is brought home to the conscience. Luther claims that 'Christ also interprets the law, to be sure, but this is not his proper and chief work' (WA 40/1. 91.28–29; LW 26.38); yet this suggests, at the very least, a strange complicity between Christ and Satan. Why does Christ utter sayings that are so useful to the accuser in his struggle against grace? Why does he not confine himself to his proper work, which is to give himself for our sins? Why does he not keep silent, instead of toying with the role of Moses despite the confusion that this was bound to cause? Can the distinction between the true Christ who 'also interprets the law' and the false Christ who is a lawgiver be maintained?

One is inclined to dismiss these agonized dilemmas as the pathological products of the protestant 'introspective conscience'. Yet Luther's distinction between the true and the false Christ of holy scripture is of genuine hermeneutical significance, for it provides theological justification for the interpreter who wishes to resist the plain, literal meaning of scriptural texts where that meaning is oppressive and tyrannical, where a demand is addressed to will or intellect which cannot and perhaps should not be fulfilled. A more conventional exposition of the protestant scripture principle urges upon us a submission to the text at all costs, but the theological hermeneutic outlined here by Luther enables us to recognize the oppressive text and to resist its literal meaning, not because the latter is a simple misunderstanding but because the authority of the gospel is greater than the authority of the text. The possibility of resisting the law for the sake of the gospel is, of course, grounded in the Pauline text which Luther is interpreting, for in Galatians the circumcision of Gentiles is rejected even though there is the best possible scriptural authority for regarding it as the indispensable sign of the covenant between God and his people. After Paul, resistance to certain features of the Law of Moses is a commonplace of Christian hermeneutics, but it is Luther who, by distancing the concept of law from its Old Testament roots, makes it theologically possible and necessary to be willing to resist even the gospels. If even the words of Christ are not immune from this possibility, no other part of scripture will be so sacrosanct as to claim exemption

How does a scriptural text become oppressive? What is it that makes some texts law and others gospel? Luther's language may suggest that the distinction is fixed, inherent in the texts. Jesus' saying, 'Unless you repent, you will all likewise perish' is law; Paul's reference to the Christ 'who gave himself for our sins' is gospel (WA 40/1. 93.18–27; LW 26.39). The one text is a demand, the other a promise. Yet, if Luther tends to assign sayings of the synoptic Jesus to the law and the assertions of the major Pauline epistles to the gospel, we are not compelled to follow him in this: for whether a text is experienced as contrary to the gospel is determined not only by its objective content but also by the way it is understood in the community to which one belongs. The recognition of a text as oppressive does not proceed from a contextless encounter between a hypersensitive reader and a pure, uninterpreted text, but from the contemporary interpretative context within which the reading takes place.

Luther is well aware of this fact. Thus he uses Paul's language about 'the Son of God who loved me and gave himself for me' (Gal. 2.20) as an occasion to attack once again the idea that the true Christ is Moses, a hard taskmaster and a lawgiver, and discloses as he does so the reason why this is such a critical point for him:

> It is very hard for me, even in the great light of the gospel and after my extensive experience and practice in this study, to define Christ as Paul does here. That is how much this teaching and noxious idea of Christ as the lawgiver [*de Christo legislatore*] has penetrated into my bones like oil. On this score you younger men [the students who are listening to his lectures] are much more fortunate than we older ones. You have not been imbued with these ideas with which I was imbued from boyhood, so that even at the mention of the name of Christ I would be terrified and grow pale, because I was persuaded that he was a judge. Therefore I have to make a double effort: first, to unlearn, condemn and resist this ingrown opinion of Christ as a lawgiver and a judge, which constantly returns and drags me back; secondly, to acquire a new idea, namely trust in Christ as the justifier and saviour. If you are willing, you can have much less difficulty in learning to know Christ purely. (*WA* 40/1.298.24–299.14; *LW* 26.178)

A few lines later Luther again warns how 'the devil comes, disguised as Christ [*sub larva Christi*] and harassing us under his name' (*WA* 40/1. 299.19–20; *LW* 26.178), and it is now clear that the real basis for this temptation lies not in the texts which speak of Christ as lawgiver and judge considered in isolation, but in these texts insofar as they entered the discourse surrounding the young Luther and were internalized by him. These texts are law for Luther because of their role in a religious discourse which he now repudiates as oppressive and contrary to the gospel, and it is this contemporary situation that give his resistance its critical hermeneutical significance.

The fact that this distinction relates to the texts as they function within a fluid contemporary discourse indicates that the law and the gospel are not fixed entities, inherent within texts and therefore easily identifiable and subject to our control. It would be mistaken to regard Luther's difficulty with certain of the sayings of Jesus as a timeless theological problematic with which we must struggle in essentially the same way as he did. The theological–exegetical attempt to distinguish the law from the gospel should be genuinely contemporary, originating in the role of the scriptural texts in the religious and theological discourse of our own time. The criterion by which the 'plain meaning' of certain texts must be resisted and rejected is the gospel itself; but since the gospel is not accessible to us in transparent, uninterpreted form, the process of discrimination will not be a mechanical one but a constant struggle for discernment, taking place above all in dialogue with others.

3. Insights originating in the secular world outside the Christian community can have a positive role in assisting the community's understanding of holy scripture.

This thesis is implicitly denied when a given interpretation is opposed on the grounds that it betrays the influence of modern secular thought and encroaches upon the Bible's capacity to interpret itself (as in Thielicke's statement, quoted above). On this view of the Bible, interpretation occurs or should occur in a self-contained sphere uncontaminated by external influences. Brevard Childs argues (as I do) that biblical interpreters should see themselves as responsible to the community of faith and finds the historical-critical tradition deficient at this point; but when he argues that the community of faith does not need the assistance of insights proceeding from outside itself, in that it has within itself the resources necessary for understanding the biblical texts as sacred scripture, he too assumes a sharp distinction between church and world. To regard the church as a self-sufficient sphere closed off from the world is ecclesiological docetism, and it also makes impossible an adequate theological understanding of the world and its alleged secularity.

It is, however, easier to assert or assume the positive and inescapable role of insight proceeding from outside the Christian community than it is to justify this assertion theologically. A starting-point may be found in the interpretation in chapters 8, 11 and 12 of the role of the Spirit within the world both of creation and of human society. The Spirit is, according to Gen. 1, the creative matrix out of which all living beings proceed; and, as Wisdom, 'she passes in every generation into holy souls and makes them friends of God and prophets' (Wis. 7.27) – and not just within the restricted sphere of the covenant. It is true that in the New Testament the presence of the Spirit is largely confined to the Christian community. The Spirit 'was not', until Jesus was glorified (John. 7.39), and it is said of 'the Spirit of truth' that 'the world cannot receive him, because it neither sees him nor knows him' (John. 14.17). This perspective on the person and work of the Spirit remains important in its refusal of any easy accommodation between the church and the world and in its legitimation of a christologically-based prophetic critique: 'When he comes he will convince the world concerning sin and righteousness and judgement' (Jn. 16.9). Yet the broader canonical context suggests that the Spirit dwells within the created and human world as well as within the church, in which case truth may proceed from the world to the church as well as from the church to the world. 'The wind/spirit blows where it wills, and you hear the sound of it, but you do not know whence it comes or whither it goes' (John. 3.8). The wind cannot be confined within the walls of an institution, and neither can the Spirit.

In developing this assertion, I shall make use of a work stemming from a tradition not normally noted for its 'liberal' openness to the world beyond the confines of the community: the extensive and important treatise on the Spirit by the English Calvinist theologian John Owen, published in 1674.[19] Owen's main concern is to reflect upon the New Testament's presentation of the Spirit in connection with the community and the individual, and the emphasis of the *Pneumatologia* as a whole is on the presence of the Spirit as that which differentiates the community from the world. Owen is predictably hostile towards the growing tendency to derive all necessary religious and ethical truth from an undifferentiated, universal human faculty of reason – that is, towards the secularizing tendency now referred to as 'the Enlightenment'. [20] Yet there are genuine theological reasons why the presence of God the Spirit in the world beyond the church must be affirmed, and Owen is too conscientious and competent a theologian to overlook them. A trinitarian framework – unpopular then, as now [21] – means that the Johannine assertion of the non-existence of the Spirit prior to and outside the church (John. 7.39) cannot be taken in an absolute sense, and the representation of the Spirit in the Old Testament thus becomes an important issue. Arguing against the anti-trinitarian claim that vague Old Testament language about God's spirit should be differentiated from New Testament assertions about the Holy Spirit, Owen avails himself of the Pauline statement that there are various workings but one Spirit, implying that the working of the Spirit is more diverse and comprehensive than is generally believed (*Pneumatologia*, 59). But how are we to understand the 'peculiar work of the Holy Spirit in the first or old covenant'?

In the doxology that concludes Rom. 11 we are told that 'from him and through him and to him are all things' (v. 36), and Owen adopts the patristic trinitarian reading of this text. The Father is the originator of created entities, the Son upholds them (Col. 1.17; Heb. 1.3), 'and the finishing and perfecting of all these works is ascribed to the Holy Spirit' (94). God the Spirit is involved in the *perfecting* of the heavens and the earth. The heavens are described in Ps. 8.3 as 'the work of thy fingers', and the Spirit is identified as 'the finger of God' by the interchangeability of that phrase with 'the Spirit of God' in Luke 11.20 and the parallel Matt. 12.28 respectively. We therefore conclude that 'by him [the Spirit] were the heavens, as it were, curiously wrought, adorned, garnished, rendered beautiful and glorious, to show forth the praise of his power and wisdom. Ps. xix.1' (97). The teleology implied in Rom. 11.36 is, however, clearer in the case of the creation of the earth, where it is the Spirit of God, moving over the face of the deep, who must transform the initial unformed mass into an orderly and harmonious whole (Gen. 1.2). (Owen rejects the translation of *ruaḥ elohîm* as 'a mighty wind' – later adopted by the New English Bible – not only because of its Socinian provenance but also on the philological grounds that the verb *rḥp* signifies an easy, gentle motion, as in the reference in Deut. 32.11 to the eagle who 'fluttereth over her young' [AV]). Thus, in Gen. 1.2, 'the whole matter being created out of which all living creatures were to be educed, and of which they were to be made, he [the Spirit] takes upon [himself] the cherishing and preservation of it; that as it had its subsistence by the power of the Word of God, it might be carried on towards that form, order, beauty, and perfection, that it was designed unto' (98). The seeds and principles of life are communicated by the Spirit: 'Without him all was a dead sea, a confused deep, with darkness upon it, able to bring forth nothing, nor more prepared to bring forth any one thing than another' (98).

According to Ps. 104.30, 'When thou sendest forth thy Spirit they are created, and thou renewest the face of the ground.' The reference here is clearly not to the first creation but to a continual creative activity, and the act of life-giving creation out of the initial dead waste is constantly re-enacted as new living creatures are brought into being. 'Whereas the earth itself, the common nurse of them all, seems in the revolution of every year to be at an end of its use and work, having death brought upon the face of it, and oft-times entering deep into its bowels, the Spirit of God, by its influential concurrence, renews it again, causing every thing afresh to bring forth fruit according unto its kind, whereby its face receiveth a new beauty and adorning' (99). Owen is well aware that what he describes is in one sense a natural process, but he rejects the absolutizing of this modern insight: 'As we would own the due and just powers and operations of second causes, so we abhor that atheism which ascribes unto them an original and independent efficacy and causality, without a previous acting in, by, and upon them of the power of God' (103).

The human person is especially closely related to the creator Spirit. According to Job 33.4, 'the Spirit of God has made me, and the breath of the Almighty gives me life'. The creation of humankind is here and in Gen. 2.7 assigned to the Spirit in that the Spirit perfects the work of creation (101). This perfection consists not only in the biological life that humankind shares with animals and plants but also in the unique relation of humans to God: human knowledge of, inclination towards and ability to perform God's will were brought about by the Spirit, and it is therefore the Spirit who is operative in the restoration of these abilities (102). The fact that Adam lost this knowledge of God through the fall does not remove him from the sphere of the Spirit's operation; for the immanence of the life-giving Spirit within the created order must surely also imply the Spirit's presence within the realm of human society, since biblical language knows of no firm distinction between the two (compare the uses of the term 'world' in John 1.10). Thus Owen speaks of a secret work of the Spirit 'in things natural, civil, moral, political, and artificial' (6), and states that 'in all men, from first to last, all goodness, righteousness, and truth are the "fruits of the Spirit", Eph. v.9' (103). The biblical text – 'the fruit of the Spirit is in all goodness and righteousness and truth' (AV) – associates the Spirit not only with goodness, righteousness and truth within the congregation but with *all* manifestations of these qualities, at all times and in all places. No time or place is ultimately able to absent itself from the omnipresence of the Spirit. 'Whither shall I go from thy Spirit? Or whither shall I flee from thy presence?' (Ps. 139.7).

Thus even Cyrus may be described in Isa. 45.1 as the Lord's anointed (103), and his anointing implies the action of the Holy Spirit (cf. Isa. 61.1). Although Cyrus is personally ignorant of Yahweh (45.4, 5), his task is to be the agent of divine redemptive and disclosive action which has as its goal 'that people may know, from the rising of the sun and from the west, that there is none besides me' (45.6). It might therefore be said of Cyrus, Yahweh's 'shepherd' who is to 'fulfil all my purpose' (44.28), that 'I have put my Spirit upon him, he will bring forth justice to the nations' (42.1), just as this was said of Yahweh's 'servant.' Cyrus thus represents a question addressed to the people of the covenant community: are they able and willing to acknowledge the redemptive and disclosive action of the Spirit in this apparently secular figure and the historical movement that he represents? To make this acknowledgement is fraught with risk; Cyrus may prove a disappointment, or worse. Yet to refuse the acknowledgement for which the prophet appeals may also be risky. Refusal to recognize divine action beyond the bounds of approved tradition may be a subtle form of denial of 'the everlasting God, the Creator of the ends of the earth' who 'does not faint or grow weary'; for the tradition refers us precisely to this transcendent God ('Have you not known? Have you not heard?' [40.28]). Thus the Lord complains: 'Who is blind but my servant, or deaf as my messenger whom I send?... He sees many things, but does not observe them; his ears are open, but he does not hear' (42.19–20; cf. 43.8). Israel, the Lord's servant, is blind and deaf above all to the announcement of divine creative-redemptive action through Cyrus, who has been anointed by the Spirit even though he does not know the Lord. The sphere of creation–redemption encompasses the whole world, and the indwelling creator Spirit may also act as the redeemer Spirit, redemptively present in all goodness, justice and truth. To permit disclosures of goodness, justice and truth originating outside the community to impinge upon the interpretation of the sacred texts is not to contaminate them.

Movements within the world beyond the ecclesial community continually pose a question to the community. They bring before it the question whether particular aspects of its existing self-understanding, beliefs and practices are still to be regarded as authentically Christian, or whether they require critical reappraisal or outright rejection. This process of questioning from outside is one of the ways in which the Spirit leads the community out of distorted and inadequate positions into all the truth (cf. John.16.13); and it is one of the ways in which oppressive law is distinguished from life-giving gospel as holy scripture is read and interpreted.

Chapter 14

Christology and Community

In the preceding chapter I summarized and defended theologically several of the hermeneutical decisions on which this book is based. Theological hermeneutics, as practised above, comprises that part of the theological task that reflects on the appropriate principles of textual interpretation in this field. Yet there is a further step that must be taken at this point, which is to recognize that a theology may itself constitute a hermeneutic. The hermeneutical principles underlying the theological exegesis undertaken in previous chapters are not exhausted by the explicitly hermeneutical themes discussed above (preference for the final form of the text, and so on); they also include the themes of Christian theology, which guide and shape the form and content of the exegesis no less clearly than distinctively hermeneutical concepts, while themselves being clarified and corrected by the progress of the exegesis in accordance with the inescapable workings of the hermeneutical circle. *Christian doctrine thus has a hermeneutical function.* In the theological discussion that will occupy the remainder of this book, we will therefore not be leaving the sphere of hermeneutics. And since theology is involved in a circular relationship with exegesis, further exegetical discussion will be required at every stage. Hermeneutics, theology and exegesis flow into and out of each other with no fixed dividing-lines; on occasion they may be practised simultaneously.

I have chosen to illustrate the interrelatedness of hermeneutics, theology and exegesis by reflecting upon certain issues of christology (chapter 14) and praxis (chapter 15). Different themes might have served this illustrative function equally well; but these ones were not selected at random, as they clarify positions I have outlined in earlier chapters.

1. The doctrine of the person of Christ cannot be adequately developed without consideration of his transformation of human relations and of the eschatological goal of perfected community towards which this is oriented.

241

The inseparability of christology and soteriology means that christology will be affected if salvation is understood as involving present and future communal transformation, and as individual reorientation only within this communal context. Exegesis of a passage from the Epistle to Titus (2.11–3.7) suggests the three theological criteria that will guide the subsequent discussion.

According to Tit. 3.4–5, 'When the kindness [*chrēstotēs*] and the love of humanity [*philanthrōpia*] was manifested [*epephanē*] of our saviour God, not because of works which we performed in righteousness but in accordance with his own mercy, he saved us through the bath of rebirth and the renewal of the Holy Spirit.' Jesus Christ is thus the epiphany of the divine philanthropy or love of humankind. Did we or did we not perform at least some 'works in righteousness' prior to the epiphany? Either way, the epiphany originates solely in the divine mercy. Any righteous works that were performed were partial and inadequate, for the background to the account of the epiphany is the near-breakdown of human relations that preceded it: 'We ourselves were once foolish, disobedient, erring, enslaved to various desires and pleasures, passing our time in malice and envy, hateful, and hating one another' (3.3). The divine *philanthrōpia*, manifested in Jesus Christ, thus has as its goal the creation of human community where previously there was conflict, and that is the significance of the bath of rebirth and the renewal of the Holy Spirit, whereby one is initiated not into an individual experience of enlightenment but into a community. Divine philanthropy is mediated through human community, and it extends through the ecclesial community into the wider society; for Christians are 'to speak evil of no one, and to show consideration [*prautēs*] to all people' (3.2). The epiphany of the divine humanism in Jesus Christ is potentially universal in scope; for 'the grace of God has been manifested [*epephanē*] as bringing salvation to all people, teaching us to reject irreverence [*asebeian*] and worldly desires, and to live disciplined, just and reverent lives in this age, awaiting the blessed hope and the epiphany of the glory of our great God and Saviour Jesus Christ, who gave himself for us so that he might redeem us from all lawlessness and might purify for himself a people of his own, eager to perform good works' (2.11–14). To claim that in this passage the gospel is 'reduced to the level of ordinary morality' is to miss the point that the gospel is about the recreation of community out of divided human existence, a transformation grounded in Jesus Christ as the epiphany of the philanthropic God and oriented towards a further, final epiphany which will perfect the re-creation that has already begun.[1] The apparently mundane, prosaic emphasis on performing 'good works' (2.14) takes on a new significance when one recognizes that the context of these acts is the recreation of human relationships through Jesus Christ.

This modest and unassuming passage offers three criteria to guide the development of a christology which may itself function as a hermeneutic within which exegesis of other New Testament passages may proceed. First, Jesus Christ is not only 'our great God and Saviour' (2.13); as such, he is also the divine *philanthrōpia*. Christology must therefore speak of him from the start as the incarnate word who discloses the divine commitment to and affirmation of humankind. He is Immanuel, God with us. Second, the humanity of Jesus Christ indicates that God's commitment to us is mediated in the form of human community. God does not merely send a human to tell us of God's love for humankind; he himself comes *as* a human, and his love is not known apart from the human love in which it is manifested. Thus the calling of a community marked by the praxis of *philanthrōpia* is the purpose of the incarnation. This praxis cannot be limited to the Christian community, for the object of the divine–human love is *anthrōpos*, humankind in general. Third, the limits and limitations of this communal praxis indicate that this purpose has not yet been fulfilled and point towards a fulfilment or perfecting of community that lies in the future. The future *epiphaneia* of Jesus Christ (2.13) cannot have a different purpose or content to his past appearance (3.4); thus, his past appearance in love for humankind should not be contrasted with his future appearance in judgement. The love that he embodies will not be divine only but divine–human, inseparable from the love of humans for one another within perfected community. A brief dialogue with two modern christological proposals will help to clarify these points.

According to Barth, Jesus Christ as God with us is the heart of the Christian message, which is primarily about God and only secondarily about humankind (*Church Dogmatics*, IV, 1 (1953), 4–5).[2] Yet we are not thereby made mere objects, for God with us implies that we are with God (14); God with us is the establishing of our humanity, not its extinction (14–15). God has become human in order to take up our case. In his omnipotence, he is able to be human in a quite different way to our way, suffering the consequences of our transgression for our sake and being his own human covenant partner in our place (12). God with us is a matter not only of ideas and concepts but above all of the story of the bearer of a particular name (16); everything depends on the gospel being *about* Jesus Christ in the fullest sense (21). An understanding of grace according to which God is everything and humans nothing is nonsensical, for 'in the giving of his Son... God is indeed everything but only in order that man may not be nothing, in order that he may be God's man, in order that as such he, too, may be everything in his own place, on his own level and within his own limits' (89). Since in Jesus Christ God became human, 'we cannot think or demand or expect too much or too high things of man' (91). This theology of the divine humanity is sharply differentiated from Barth's own earlier view of God as 'Wholly Other', with its concomitant christology; such a view is shown to be 'untenable, and corrupt and pagan' by God's revelation of himself in Jesus Christ. It makes God in the image of 'our own unreconciled humanity' (186).[3]

Jesus Christ here embodies the divine love for humankind, in accordance with our first criterion. However, there are problems with the other two criteria – communal transformation as the immediate and as the eschatological goal of the divine *philanthropia*. Barth recognizes that Christ's call is not to a private relationship, as Kierkegaard believed along with pietism, but first and foremost to membership of a community (687–9). But the idea that should follow from this – that the community is the sphere of transformed human relations – is left curiously abstract. Barth is perhaps inhibited by his emphasis on Jesus Christ alone as God's truly human covenant-partner. As such, he is our representative; but in the relationship of representation those who are represented are not only present in the person of their representative but also, in an important sense, absent. He acts in their place, and they are thus absent from their place. The covenant consists in the relation to God of this one, representative man, in his relative solitude. But to be human is precisely not to be solitary; it is to be with other humans, not just in physical proximity but in relationship to them at the deepest possible level. When the word became flesh, he dwelt *among us*, not apart from us like John the Baptist in the desert, for only so could the divine love for humankind be mediated in human form and with a human face. The problem is compounded when the community is presented as 'the earthly–historical form of existence of Jesus Christ himself' (661). This interpretation of the theme of the body of Christ emphasizes the singleness of the church at the expense of the inner-ecclesial love which binds together its very diverse members in the one Spirit, losing the Pauline sense of community in order to maintain the narrow christological focus.

The curious apartness from other humans of Barth's representative human also leads to an exaggerated sense that the divine–human relation is consummated and fulfilled in the life, death and resurrection of Jesus Christ, and that all that remains thereafter is the recognition and acknowledgement of that which is already the case. Yet, according to our third criterion, the consummation and fulfilment of the divine–human relation does not occur apart from the perfection of human community, and the limits and the limitations of the ecclesial community indicate that the goal of God's becoming human has in no sense already been fulfilled and that the future is a real future. It is symptomatic of this problem that, at the outset of Barth's presentation of the doctrine of reconciliation, creation and eschatology are placed on the 'circumference' of the Christian message whereas 'the covenant fulfilled in the atonement is its centre' (3). What is significant about this image is that it is static. The linearity of historical time is abolished as creation and eschatology cease to represent a true beginning and end but exist only as a single unbroken periphery, everywhere equidistant from a still centre at which the divine–human relation is fulfilled by a single, representative man.[4]

It may be that the persistent failure to recognize the communal dimension and implications of salvation derives from the demarcation between 'faith' and 'good works' established by the Reformation. Barth is thus able to write about christology almost as though the communal sphere of interpersonal relations did not exist, so complete is his preoccupation with a purely vertical understanding of the divine–human relation which fails adequately to relate humans to one another. John Howard Yoder's book, *The Politics of Jesus* (1972), marks an important step forward in this respect, although its modest scope precludes a full engagement with the christological tradition. Yoder's chief target is the claim that the ethical teaching of Jesus is largely irrelevant for Christian ethics. There are a number of versions of this claim in circulation. Jesus, we are told, called for an 'interim ethic' whose stringent requirements were made on the assumption that the end was very near; or, Jesus was a simple, rustic figure whose personalization of all ethical problems is of little use in our reflection on power relations in the contemporary world; or, his message was ahistorical, dealing with spiritual and not social matters; or, he was a radical monotheist who in pointing to the will of God relativized all human values and ethical teaching, including his own; or, he came not to teach but to give his life for the sins of the world (Yoder, 16–19). Such approaches also affect the reading of the rest of the New Testament. Thus, Paul is often commended for his 'emphasis on the priority of grace and the secondary significance of works', which ensures 'that ethical matters could never be taken too seriously' (21). These approaches also ensure that Christian ethics will be an autonomous activity, appealing only to the general principles and not to the concrete realities of Jesus' praxis and teaching.

Working with the text in its final form, Yoder is concerned to oppose the 'spiritual', apolitical understanding of Jesus that ascribes to him a mission to restore the vertical, divine–human relation which leaves more or less unaffected the horizontal plane within which humans relate to one another. This drastic restriction of the significance of Jesus is the product of modernity: 'In line with the personal appeal which has been so central in

Protestant faith since Luther, even more since Pietism, and especially since
the merging of Protestant existentialism with modern secular personalism
– and even more especially since Freud and Jung imposed upon everyone
in our culture the vision of man as a self-centered reacting organism – it has
seemed quite evident that the primary message of Jesus was a call most
properly perceived by the individual, asking the h_arer for something that
can be done most genuinely by an individual standing alone' (135). Yet, in
the great manifesto in Luke.4.18–19 ('The Spirit of the Lord is upon
me...'), it is clear that what is in mind is a visible, political restructuring of
human relations (39). The widespread, tacit acceptance of S. G. F.
Brandon's assumption 'that Jesus could have constituted a political threat
only by being violent' (59) corresponds to a distortion at least as serious as
Brandon's thesis that Jesus was a Zealot, the essentially docetic view that
Jesus was 'above' politics.[5] In fact, 'the events in the temple court and the
language Jesus used were *not* calculated to avoid any impression of insurrec-
tionary vision. Both Jewish and Roman authorities were defending themselves against a real threat. That the threat was not one of *armed*, violent
revolt, and that it nonetheless bothered them to the point of their resorting
to illegal procedures to counter it, is a proof of the political relevance of
nonviolent tactics, not a proof that Pilate and Caiaphas were exceptionally
dull or dishonorable men' (59). The crucifixion was not a misunderstanding of a figure whose claims were purely spiritual, and is to be seen as 'the
punishment of a man who threatens society by creating a new kind of
community leading a radically new kind of life' (63). Jesus' commitment to
non-violence is a political rather than a purely personal choice, for it entails
a communal life which discerns and resists 'the idolatrous character of
political power hunger and nationalism', as Jesus did when invited to bow
down before Satan (32).

Yoder's theological ethics does not quite succeed in breaking out of the
antithesis between doctrine and praxis, faith and works, theology and
ethics. The justified preoccupation with what Jesus came to do is not
sufficiently grounded in the basic christological question of who Jesus is, a
question that here remains unasked. The communal practice of *philanthrōpia*
and a corresponding non-violent resistance to violence might simply be
traced back to Jesus of Nazareth, in which case it is one human possibility
among others. But if Jesus of Nazareth is himself the divine–human Son
who embodies the *philanthrōpia* of God, then this communal practice issues
from God's own saving activity. If so, it must also have a universal goal, the
perfection of human community, in which case Yoder's somewhat Ritschlian
identification of community and kingdom would have to be qualified. Yet
Yoder's work is valuable in pointing out that the gospels in their final form

represent Jesus' ministry as inescapably and essentially political. He does not need to engage in detailed research into the socio-political background to Jesus' ministry, following this with speculative suggestions about how 'the historical Jesus' might have been located in relation to this background. He simply reads the gospels as they stand, but with a certain awareness of the distorting effect of generations of apolitical, 'spiritual', individualistic reading.

A christology which combined Barth's emphasis on Jesus Christ as incarnating the divine humanism, Yoder's recovery of the political and communal dimensions of his ministry, and an orientation towards the eschatological future, might achieve the appropriate balance.[6] In this context, however, my intention is to illustrate the interrelatedness of theology, hermeneutics and exegesis, and it is therefore necessary to demonstrate in the discussion that follows that the christological position I have outlined is capable of producing distinctive exegetical insights.

2. The actions of Jesus, as narrated in the gospels, must be interpreted not as isolated events but against the background of the soteriological, christological and eschatological claims of the narratives as a whole.

This is, in fact, a hermeneutical application of the christological thesis discussed in the previous section. The actions of Jesus are to be understood as oriented towards the restoration of authentic human community in situations where it is distorted or absent. These actions thus shed light on the humanity of the Son – both his becoming human and the divine *philanthrōpia* that he incarnates. They also offer anticipatory images of the perfected community of the eschatological future. An interpretation of Mark 5.1–20 (the story of the Gerasene demoniac) serves to illustrate the application of this hermeneutic to exegetical practice, although some preliminary analysis of this story will be necessary before the application takes place.

No explanation is given for the sea journey that takes Jesus to the country of the Gerasenes. At the end of a day of parabolic teaching, he simply announces his intention – 'Let us go across to the other side' (Mark 4.35) – and the opening of chapter 5 tells of his safe arrival after the stilling of the storm: 'They came to the other side of the sea, to the country of the Gerasenes' (v. 1). Why did he go? 'When he had come out of the boat, there met him a man with an unclean spirit' (v. 2). This strange, apparently fortuitous meeting proves to be the key to Jesus' journey to these parts, for as soon as it has reached a satisfactory conclusion he returns to the other side of the lake (v. 18). Is this really the chance meeting that it appears to be, or does Jesus travel to these parts precisely in order that this unfortunate individual should be freed from the powers that torment him, in accordance with the Father's will and the guidance of the Spirit? The Father's direct involvement in the narrative at two crucial points – the baptism and the transfiguration (1.11; 9.7) – indicates that nothing in the rest of the narrative takes place without him; and the same may also be said of the Spirit, who not only impels Jesus into the wilderness (1.12) but leads him wherever he goes and empowers his activity (cf. Luke 4.14). Yet the presence of the Father and the Spirit with the Son is not directly mentioned, in accordance with the invisibility of divine action and the secularity of empirical human existence, including that of the incarnate Son.

A meeting between two persons entails not only physical proximity but also communication. In this case, however, the reader knows that communication will be distorted; for the man comes to meet Jesus 'out of the tombs', he has been consorting with the dead rather than the living; further, it is said that he has an unclean spirit and actually *lives* among the tombs. A description is given of unsuccessful attempts to restrain him, and this indicates that his relationship to the living is a matter of fear on the one side and his own isolation in his superhuman strength on the other. His behaviour is inhuman: 'Night and day among the tombs and on the mountains he was always crying out, and bruising himself with stones' (v. 5). Possession by the unclean spirit has isolated him from human community and driven him instead to take refuge in the non-community of the dead. In his utter loss of human relatedness he has indeed come to resemble the dead, although he continues to live. Salvation would be for him a restoration to human community, a resurrection from the dead. Does he want this? On the one hand, he approaches Jesus: 'When he saw Jesus from afar, he ran and worshipped him' (v. 6). His running must be *towards* Jesus, and one might expect that his motive is to seek his help, as in the case of the woman with a haemorrhage who, later in this chapter, came up behind Jesus in the crowd in order to touch his garment (v. 27). In fact, the man desires to repulse Jesus, crying out: 'What have you to do with me, Jesus, Son of the Most High God? I adjure you by God, do not torment me' (v. 7). Unusually, the narrator first creates the impression that the man here *initiates* communication with Jesus, but subsequently indicates that this utterance is a response to Jesus' prior command, 'Come out of the man, you unclean spirit!' (v. 8). Thus the speaker who seeks to repulse Jesus is initially the man but subsequently the unclean spirit whom Jesus differentiates from the man; a confusion which is not to be ascribed to the supposed clumsiness of this particular evangelist but to the possessed man's impossible situation as both an agent capable of intentional action and speech and at the same time a mere vehicle for the action and speech of the satanic power that has driven him out of human community into superhuman isolation. Jesus' word of command initiates his cure by differentiating between the man and the unclean spirit, just as the divine creative word separated the light and the dry land from the dark, watery abyss (to which the demon will shortly return). It is therefore the demon to whom the question, 'What is your name?' is addressed; or rather, it is the man who is addressed but as mouthpiece of the demon – for the other man, distinguished from the demon, is not yet available to be spoken to.

The demon answers, 'My name is Legion, for we are many' (v. 9). Reference has previously been made to a single 'unclean spirit' (vv. 2, 8), and the sinister, threatening switch from singular to plural again indicates that we are dealing here with a chaotic world in which the man is both a free agent and occupied territory and in which the occupying force is at the same time single and multifarious. But the metaphor of occupied territory, overrun by a power which brutally plunders and oppresses the original inhabitants, fits the name 'Legion' so well that one must conclude that the explanation given – the sheer number of occupying spirits – is incomplete. If 'Legion' merely refers to the large number of the demons, why are they not named 'Herd' (*agelē*), thus providing a convenient link with the herd of pigs in v. 11? 'Legion' thus refers us to enemy occupation and associates Roman law and order with the power of Satan. Other possible connections follow (whether or not the evangelist 'intended' us to make them). Like his military counterpart, Legion possesses irresistible, superhuman strength; his terrible violence makes him an enemy of human community; and he is appropriately associated with death. The name introduces an allegorical dimension into the narrative.

Legion recognizes the superior power of Jesus and tries to agree terms of surrender. They – again the switch from singular to plural – will leave the man, but they like this country and plead to be allowed to take up new residences in it (vv. 10–12). Why does Jesus accede to their request that they should make the herd of pigs their new home? Why should one be so concerned about the comfort and convenience of demons? Will they not seize and occupy some other helpless human victim as soon as Jesus has left? But in suggesting this arrangement the demons have in fact signed their own death warrant, and their plunge to destruction along with their new hosts is a proof of the superior power and wisdom of Jesus, who clearly intended that in this way they would never again destroy human lives and human community. In the previous pericope, the miracle of the stilling of the storm ensured that Jesus and his disciples crossed the sea safely, whereas now the oppressors are drowned in it. The exodus typology suggests that Legion and the pigs correspond to the armies of Pharaoh, drowned in the sea which the people of Israel have safely crossed.[7]

The news of these dramatic events spread quickly, and the inhabitants of Gerasa and the surrounding region 'came to Jesus, and saw the demoniac sitting there, clothed and in his right mind, the man who had had the legion' (v. 15). The man whom Jesus initially distinguished from the demon ('Come out of the man, you unclean spirit') has now come into existence; he has been raised from the dead, and is now fit for restoration to human community, his time of superhuman isolation in the realm of the dead having been brought to an end. The reference to his being clothed suggests that he had previously been naked, and his clothing thus signifies his restored capacity for and acceptance of normal life within human community. The Gerasenes' reaction is, however, surprising. Far from being grateful to Jesus for solving a social problem which their fetters and chains had proved powerless to control, 'they were afraid... And they began to beg Jesus to depart from their neighbourhood' (vv. 15, 17). The more usual reaction to his mighty works is amazement, which, while an element of fear is not excluded, is more closely related to admiration. It brings people flocking to him from every quarter (1.45); he sometimes withdraws himself (6.31, 7.24), but no-one ever asks him to leave. Why is the Gerasene response different? The narrator does not tell us, but the explanation should be sought in the material which is unique to this particular story, and especially in the victory over the demonic 'Legion'. Pursuing the allegorical dimension this name has evoked beyond the letter of the text, the Gerasenes are afraid to be associated with one who has performed a symbolic act of resistance to, and indeed victory over, the institutionalized violence that imposes a law and order for the benefit of the powerful few at the expense of the powerless majority.[8] Powerful and powerless alike join in begging Jesus to leave, for even its victims prefer the predictability and stability of an unjust status quo to the uncertain, utopian prospect of a future in which, in the absence of Legion and everything this name represents, human beings are restored to their right minds so as to live in authentic community with one another.[9]

Allegorical reading of this kind must, however, be counter-balanced by an emphasis on the particularities of the text if the figure of Jesus is not to dwindle away into a mere symbol or cypher. Although the legendary character of this narrative in its present form seems clear enough, it remains rooted in material reality. It is located not in a mythical world but in the midst of real geographical co-ordinates: the eastern coast of the Sea of Galilee, the city of Gerasa and the rest of the Decapolis. The Gentile setting provides an apt location for a large herd of pigs. The story refers us to the disturbing social reality of the 'demonized' person incapable of normal social life and thus condemned to psychological and physical isolation within a chaotic private world. It also refers us to the socially-constructed role of the exorcist, a role in which Jesus (even 'the historical Jesus') achieved widespread recognition, and which he understood in the closest connection with his proclamation of the kingdom of God (cf. Matt. 12.28 = Luke 11.20). This is a story about Jesus – who, according to the Christian faith shared by implied author and implied reader, is far more than an itinerant exorcist – and it is therefore to be read within a theological framework inapplicable to other superficially similar stories from the ancient world. But if the quest for a more comprehensive import detaches the text from the particularities of person, time and place, then Jesus (the real Jesus) is lost and a docetic cypher bearing the same name takes his place.

Suspicion of allegorical reading, and a concern to assert the historicity and particularity of the biblical stories, are therefore not entirely without theological justification. The issue is not a new one, as the reference to Origen in chapter 13 has already indicated. In response to those who claim that 'the biblical writings do not preserve the narrative of actual events but point to something else, something profound which requires special understanding – something "spiritual", as they would like to say, which they have discovered because they are so spiritual themselves', Theodore of Mopsuestia may be right to warn that 'if they make history serve their own ends, they will have no history left'.[10] The loss of history would mean the loss of Christian faith; for history is, as it were, the world within which human beings live, and if history remains untouched by salvation then there is no salvation worth speaking of. What is unassumed remains unhealed, and this includes existence within history. But if an over-reliance on allegorizing interpretation leads towards docetism, then an over-emphasis on historical particularity results in ebionite impoverishment. If historical particularity must not be sacrificed for the sake of a comprehensive, universal meaning, neither must universal scope be lost in the anxious demonstration that, for example, the historical Gerasene swine really did plunge over a cliff into the sea.

The doctrine of the incarnation provides the necessary hermeneutical rule here. If the word (who in the beginning was with God and was God) became flesh, then the universal is to be found only in the particular, and the particular is significant only in its irreplaceable witness to the universal. Theological exegesis of the gospel stories must therefore find in them the mediation of the particular by the universal and the universal by the particular, in accordance with the enfleshed word who is always at their centre. But universality remains an empty, abstract category unless a comprehensive theological framework gives it content. We may therefore recall the christological thesis discussed in the previous section: that the doctrine of the person of Christ cannot be adequately developed without consideration of his transformation of human relations and of the eschatological goal of perfected community towards which this is oriented. In the light of this, the Marcan story must be read (1) as a believing testimony to the fact that Jesus transformed concrete, particular human relations; (2) as a testimony to the significance of this fact, which is that the universal, eschatological transformation and perfection of human relations is the goal towards which Jesus' activity is oriented; and (3) as a testimony to the identity of Jesus as the enfleshment of the divine *philanthrōpia*, which explains and grounds the move from the particular to the universal in the first two assertions. This theological framework cannot be extracted from this story considered in isolation; but I shall try to show that, even in Marcan terms, it is the proper context within which it is to be understood.

(1) According to Mark, Jesus' healing of the Gerasene demoniac restored a pathologically isolated, enclosed individual to human community. The demoniac ceased to live among the dead and was restored to the living. Refusing his request that he might accompany him, Jesus 'said to him, "Go home to your friends, and tell them how much the Lord has done for you, and how he has had mercy on you." And he went away and began to proclaim in the Decapolis how much Jesus had done for him, and everyone marvelled' (5.19–20). The incoherent, non-communicative cries of the demoniac who wandered through the mountains, bruising himself with stones, have given way to rational, communicative speech which restores community and whose content is the proclamation and celebration of that restored communicative ability. God – the Lord whose action is identical to Jesus' – is disclosed and praised in and through the transformation of human relations.

(2) Mark also represents Jesus as setting his activity as an exorcist within a much broader framework. In response to the claim of an investigating commission from Jerusalem that 'he is possessed by Beelzebul, and by the prince of demons he casts out the demons', Jesus uttered a series of parabolic sayings (Mark 3.22–27). The first four simply expose the oddity of the accusation: 'How can Satan cast out Satan? If a kingdom is divided against itself, that kingdom cannot stand. And if a house is divided against itself, that house will not be able to stand. And if Satan has risen up against himself and is divided, he cannot stand, but is coming to an end.' It is impossible to distinguish Beelzebul from the demons in the way that the accusation

implies, for their interests are one; and what strange death-wish could motivate Satan to operate through Jesus to liberate people from the power of his own agents? The anti-human power that divides kingdoms and houses through wars and hatred is not itself divided, for a single inhumanity runs through all its multifarious operations. The scribes' accusation was presumably a politically-motivated attempt to undermine Jesus' popularity and credibility.[11] According to Mark, Jesus disclosed the true meaning of his exorcistic activity in the saying that followed: 'No-one can enter a strong man's house and plunder his goods, unless he first binds the strong man; then indeed he may plunder his house' (3.27). Although Jesus' activity has been prominent enough to create concern in Jerusalem, its scope in time and space might appear to be fairly limited. However, his saying here denies that any such limitation exists. The strong man is Satan, Beelzebul, the prince of demons; his goods are those who are 'possessed' by him, reduced to the status of mere objects by the destruction of the ties that bind them to human community; the plundering of his goods is the liberation of his victims, their restoration to community. This plunder or liberation is impossible unless Satan is first 'bound' and rendered powerless. If, as Jesus implies, liberation is already taking place in his exorcisms, then the dark power that destroys human community has already been bound and nothing can hinder the final, universal liberation that will issue in the eschatological perfection of human community. This is, admittedly, a confession of faith rather than a statement based on incontrovertible empirical evidence, and it proceeds from Jesus' proclamation that 'the time is fulfilled, and the kingdom of God is at hand' (1.15). If the reign of God is at hand, then the inhuman reign of Satan is indeed 'coming to an end' (3.26), and the acts in which Jesus restored pathologically isolated, excluded individuals to human community are to be understood theologically as signs of the coming kingdom in which human community will be perfected. And if it is Jesus himself who has 'bound the strong man' through the power of the Spirit, then Jesus is not only the proclaimer but also the agent of the coming kingdom. He is the Danielic Son of man, the divine–human being who will establish humanity in place of bestial violence (cf.Dan. 7.13; Mark 8.38; 14.62). The identification of the accusation, 'he has an unclean spirit', with blasphemy against the Holy Spirit (3.28–30) indicates that it is the divine Spirit who empowers Jesus' acts, in accordance with the Spirit's role in establishing *koinōnia* or community (cf. 2 Cor. 13.14). One blasphemes against the Spirit when, desiring like the scribes from Jerusalem to preserve the established order, one speaks against those who work to establish the Spirit's new and authentic *koinōnia*.

(3) The startling movement from the particularity of Jesus' actions in and around Galilee to a universal role as agent of the coming kingdom of God indicates that he is not to be regarded simply as an itinerant Jewish exorcist and preacher; nor is he to be placed in any other merely relative category, such as 'prophet' (cf. Mark 6.14–16; 8.27–28). Yet from a perspective of faith rather than historical knowledge this movement is not really so surprising, for Mark has set the entire ministry of Jesus against the background of the divine acknowledgement, 'You are my beloved Son, in you I am well pleased' (1.11). This fundamental acknowledgment was repeated by the divine voice at the transfiguration (9.7), echoed in human confession (15.39; cf. 8.29) and, unwillingly, by the demons (3.11; 5.7), and accepted by Jesus himself at his trial (14.61–62), although in conjunction with his role as the coming Son of man. In Mark's presentation, Jesus' acceptance of the title 'Son of God' (or 'Son of the Blessed') was the blasphemy that led directly to his crucifixion (14.63–64). The Johannine view of blasphemy is apparently presupposed here too. In Mark as in John, Jesus must be put to death as a blasphemer 'because you, being a man, make yourself God' (John 10.33).[12] It follows that the Father's acknowledgement at the baptism was addressed to the divine–human Son – not to a purely human figure to whom a special role was being assigned, but to the eternal, divine Son who has, from the moment of conception, identified and united himself so completely with the human existence of Jesus of Nazareth that 'when Jesus came from Nazareth of Galilee to be baptized by John in the Jordan' it was he who could be addressed as the beloved Son (1.9, 11).

Using Johannine conceptuality to complete the Marcan picture, the Father's eternal love for the Son, which precedes 'the foundation of the world' (John 17.24), is here extended into the human sphere which the Son has now entered.[13] The human sphere, despite its fallenness, has never been alien to him, for the world was made through him and he therefore comes to his own home (John 1.10–11). But why does he enter the human sphere in this radical way, as a human? He does so because the eternal Father and Son do not will that their love should be an exclusive, self-contained, self-absorbed love. The Spirit, who is both one with the Father and Son and indwells the world, already represents the potential openness of the mutual divine love to include creaturely, human existence within itself; but this openness or opening is definitively effected by the Son's enfleshment or becoming-human. The divine *philanthrōpia* is not a generalized, benevolent providence; it takes the most concrete, costly form imaginable in the divine decision to exercise this *philanthrōpia* by entering the human sphere without reservation, as a human, so that the divine love for humankind is also a costly human love. 'God so loved the world that he gave his only Son...' (John 3.16); that is, God loved the world *in this way* (*houtōs*) and in no other, that he gave his Son to participate as a human in human life, so that humans should be brought by a fellow-human into the mutual love of the Father and the Son and thus into authentic community with one another. Jesus therefore prayed that those who believe in him 'may all be one, just as you, Father, are in me and I in you, that they too may be in us, so that the world may believe that you have sent me' (John 17.21). This divine–human *koinōnia* takes particular, ambiguous form in the community that Jesus and his disciples founded, but its horizons are universal; for if, seeing the community, the world believes 'that thou hast sent me', then the world shares in the *koinōnia* and divine–human community is perfected. The world's present hatred towards the *koinōnia* stems from 'the evil one', the enemy of divine–human oneness, into whose grip it has fallen (cf. John 17.14–15). But this fallenness is not the ultimate truth about the world, which is that it is created by the Father, through the Son, in the Spirit *for* communion with the Father, through the divine–human Son, in the Spirit; a communion which perfects human community.

All this establishes a theological-hermeneutical framework within which the individual gospel stories may be understood. In liberating the Gerasene demoniac from the inhuman state of isolation and exclusion to which he had fallen victim, and in restoring him to communal life, Jesus acted not simply as a well-disposed individual using his powers for the benefit of his fellow-humans, but as the enfleshed Son extending the divine love into the human sphere in such a way that it includes within itself a human love for other humans. The 'new commandment' that he brings and that he makes it possible to fulfil is therefore simply 'that you love one another; even as I have loved you, that you also love one another' (John 13.34). The manner of Jesus' exercise of this love, which took shape in an utterly concrete historical praxis, should exclude the suspicion that what is spoken of here is a kind of sentimental mythology, incapable of recognizing and addressing real human need. Lack of realism is more characteristic of those who, like the scribes from Jerusalem and the citizens of Gerasa, are broadly contented with the way things are, and who therefore manifest in their different ways the world's hatred towards the new *koinōnia*.

3. Insofar as this trinitarian hermeneutic presents itself as a framework within which the exegesis of texts will at the same time be an exegesis of reality, it must show itself to be capable of responding to objections proceeding from a different understanding of reality.

I have in mind here especially the antipathy towards the doctrines of the trinity and the incarnation which the historical-critical tradition has inherited from its Socinian roots.[14] According to Albert Schweitzer, the nineteenth-century quest of the historical Jesus 'loosed the bands by which he had been riveted for centuries to the stony rocks of ecclesiastical doctrine, and rejoiced to see life and movement coming into the figure once more' (*The Quest of the Historical Jesus* (1906), 397). The immobility and unreality of a Jesus interpreted in the light of the church doctrines of trinity and incarnation dissolves away as a living, moving historical figure appears on the scene. As is well known, Schweitzer claimed that much of this life and movement had in fact been breathed into Jesus by the nineteenth century, and that a truly living and moving Jesus only comes to light when he is allowed to return to his own time, where his true greatness, as an apocalyptic prophet who struggled against history and lost, is revealed. It is apparent, however, that the greatness of this Jesus too has been breathed into him from the modern age – in this case, from the late-romantic, post-Nietzschean but still idealist ethos that Schweitzer himself inhabited.[15] In contrast, the more circumspect scholarship of the late twentieth century has taken the way of scepticism that Schweitzer associated especially with Wrede.[16] Every saying or incident that might be ascribed to Jesus must be wrested out of the hands of the early church, and one can never escape from great uncertainty; and when, after much labour, a 'historical Jesus' emerges, he often proves to be a relatively uninteresting figure. Schweitzer speaks of his own generation as 'proud of our historical Jesus', and as ruled by the fixed idea 'that we could build up by the increase of historical knowledge a new and vigorous Christianity and set free new spiritual forces' (398). Such optimism is not much in evidence at the present stage of the 'quest'.[17] The quest continues out of its own self-generating momentum, but it has become entirely unclear why it might matter and what benefits are to be expected from it. Despite an awareness that theological or at least religious significance ought to be available somewhere in the vicinity of Jesus, there has been little serious attempt among biblical scholars to enquire whether the rejected 'ecclesiastical doctrine' might have something worthwhile to say on the subject. Perhaps Jesus has been riveted for centuries to the stony rocks of historical-critical scholarship, and perhaps ecclesial doctrine is needed to restore him to life and movement? No doubt some of this life and movement would proceed from ourselves, for theology cannot be a transcript of reality but only a response to it out of a given present. But perhaps, prior to this, life and movement might proceed in the opposite direction, from him to us, once one has seen that ecclesial formulations need not be the arid, harsh and immobile entities evoked by Schweitzer but may themselves be living and moving.

There are, however, a number of reasons why the interpretative community of biblical scholars is unlikely to look favourable upon such a proposal. At the heart of the problem is the dominance of a basically evolutionary scheme of christological development.[18] In the beginning, it is often said, Jesus was understood in purely human and functional terms which in no way compromised 'Jewish monotheism'. Here, 'Son of God' meant little more than 'messiah'. With the transition to a polytheistic Hellenistic environment, the title 'Lord' became prominent, especially in worship, and speculations about pre-existence began to develop, partially under the influence of Hellenistic Jewish wisdom traditions. But Paul remained reticent, and the incarnational model is virtually absent from the christology of the synoptic gospels. Only in the Gospel of John do we encounter an incarnational christology, and even here (it may be said) much if not all of the language about the oneness of Father and Son can be understood in functional rather than ontological terms. Crudely expressed, the further we move from the origin the higher christology becomes, a process which reaches its logical conclusion in the Councils of Nicaea and Chalcedon.

This position rests on four questionable assumptions. First, it is held that the original meaning of christological titles is controlled by their pre-Christian usage. Second, the historical evidence is thought to point to a single, linear process of christological development (even if there is also a certain emphasis on sheer christological variety). Third, it is assumed that the truth is to be found only at the moment of origin, and that it is corrupted by whatever is 'late'. Fourth, New Testament interpretation is here located within a unitary understanding of history as a single, all-embracing reality open to the historian's equally single and all-embracing interpretative approach. All four assumptions can be illustrated from the work of Reimarus, who since Schweitzer has been regarded as the founder of the modern 'scientific' study of the gospels. All are, in various ways, so deeply embedded in New Testament scholarship that only a preliminary and inadequate analysis and critique will be possible here.

(1) In the 'fragment' of Reimarus' *Apology* published by Lessing in 1778 under the title *Concerning the Intention of Jesus and his Teaching*, Reimarus turns in §10 to the issue of christological orthodoxy. 'Since nowadays the doctrine of the trinity of persons in God and the doctrine of the work of salvation through Jesus as the Son of God and God–man constitute the main articles and mysteries of the Christian faith, I shall specifically demonstrate that they are not to be found in Jesus' discourses' (*Fragments*, 76). Reimarus' main point about 'Son of God' is that 'the Hebrews understood something quite different by the term' (76–7). In scripture,

God calls those whom he loves his 'sons'. Israel is described as 'my first-born son' in Exod. 4.22–23, and the Davidic covenant established the king as God's son (2 Sam 7.14–15; Ps. 2.7). In these passages it is clear that it is 'mere men who are called sons of God' (78). Reimarus now seeks to demonstrate that this is so in the case of Jesus, and points in particular to the apparent identity of 'Son of God' in the gospels with 'Christ' or 'Messiah', which 'says nothing more of the redeemer of Israel than that he will be a great king' (83). The Messiah is the Son of God simply because he is beloved by God; 'Son of God' tells us no more about Jesus than that. Reimarus' deistic thesis – that Jesus introduced no new doctrines or practices – is thus confirmed, and the point is established that the meaning of New Testament christological titles is determined by their pre-Christian usage.

This position points backward toward English Deism and the Socinian tradition;[19] and, as Schweitzer rightly saw, it also points forward towards modern New Testament scholarship. Continuities between Old and New Testament usage obviously cannot – and, on theological grounds, should not – be denied: the gospel story is the culmination of the Old Testament history of God's covenant with Israel. Yet what is often overlooked is the extent to which the gospels themselves thematize the radical transformation of traditional concepts that occurs under the impact of Jesus and his story. Peter at Caesarea Philippi and the disciples on the road to Emmaus find it incomprehensible that the Christ should suffer (Mark 8.27–33; Luke 24.13–27). All four evangelists refer to the interpretative text placed above the crucified Jesus, describing him as 'the king of the Jews' (Matt 27.37; Mark 15.26; Luke 23.38; John 19.19–22), and, although they believe that this interpretation is in some sense true (contrary to authorial intention), its truth hardly lies in its 'literal' level. Much of the semantic content of traditional terminology has to be, as it were, poured out in order to be replaced by a new content deriving from the person and the life, death and resurrection of Jesus, and this fact testifies not only to the impact of Jesus but also to the relative flexibility and fluidity of language.[20] Thus, the commonplace observation that, for example, the divine acclamation 'You are my beloved son, with whom I am well–pleased' (Mark 1.11) is related to Ps. 2.7 ('You are my son, today I have begotten you') does not justify the assumption that the Old Testament passage must control the meaning of the passage from the gospels. The primary context within which to interpret the gospels' use of traditional language is the gospels themselves.

(2) Reimarus assumes that christological development in the early church was an essentially linear process. Under pressure of unexpected circum-

stances (the crucifixion), the disciples develop ways of thinking about Jesus that do not correspond to his own (purely Jewish) self-understanding. For Reimarus, this process is fraudulent: the disciples stol Jesus' body in order to make plausible their claim that he had been ıaised. Scarcely less fraudulent is the writer to the Hebrews' use of allegorical interpretation in explaining the meaning of Old Testament passages such as 'I will be to him a father and he shall be to me a son' as referring not to a human being but to one higher than the angels (Heb. 1.5). 'The writer of the epistle knew, of course, that the passages cited really speak of men, of David and Solomon'; but he nevertheless indulges in an irresponsible mode of interpretation 'by means of which one might make everything out of anything' (85). By such illegitimate means, conventional 'high' christology was born. While the fraud hypothesis already seemed dated by the time of D. F. Strauss,[21] modern New Testament scholarship shares with it not only the assumption of a linear christological development but also the belief that the history of this development seriously undermines 'orthodox' truth–claims.[22]

It would obviously be a mistake to deny all truth to the hypothesis of linear christological development. Johannine christology is not that of the earliest disciples (a point whose theological significance I shall explore below); and the sophistication of Nicaea or Chalcedon was unattainable in the second century. Yet the developmental model deserves a far closer and more critical scrutiny than it customarily receives. For example, it makes it impossible to recognize the extent to which a so-called 'high christology' is already to be found in the earliest New Testament texts, the Pauline letters. It leads scholars to play down the significance of the attribution to Jesus of the title *kurios*, and of the language of pre-existence and incarnation.[23] It creates the assumption of a qualitative difference between the Marcan presentation of Jesus as 'Son of God' and the ('late', incarnational) Johannine one, although this title is arguably as significant in Mark as in John.[24] It necessitates complex surgery on the synoptic tradition, allowing to Jesus only an 'implicit' christological claim and assigning more 'explicit' elements to the early church. That might be an acceptable procedure if room could be found for the possibility that the early church may on occasion have *rightly* understood Jesus, but in practice the early church is often regarded as a second source of the synoptic tradition, essentially independent of Jesus and at variance with him.[25] One of the primary goals of this enterprise is, as Reimarus again illustrates, a (relatively or absolutely) non-ecclesial Jesus, a Jesus prised from the grasp of the church in order to legitimate the self-understanding of an interpretative community which has long struggle to define and maintain its own (relative or absolute) autonomy in relation to the church. The point of the hypothesis of linear christological development in this context is that it enables one to postulate a starting–point which is essentially different from the end–product.

(3) This criticism of the linear model anticipates a further point, the privileging of the moment of origin as the locus at which the truth about Jesus is disclosed. Reimarus and his disciples argue that the continuities binding Jesus to his context within Jewish tradition are far stronger than the discontinuities, whereas their opponents highlight the originality said to differentiate Jesus both from contemporary Judaism and from the early church.[26] Underlying both positions is the protestant schema according to which truth in its purity is only to be found at the point of origin, whereas lateness corrupts it. Without denying the considerable theological and historical importance of this schema, one may perhaps question whether it offers an adequate hermeneutical framework for New Testament interpretation. For example, it leads to the claim that the Gospel of John, which is almost undeniably 'late', is more suitably regarded as a source for reconstructing the history of the Johannine community than as a possibly true witness to the incarnate Son. While it is clear that, in all four gospels, the representation of the life, death and resurrection of Jesus is communally mediated, it is equally important to emphasize that what is communally mediated is indeed thelife, death and resurrection of Jesus, and not something else. Otherwise, Jesus is supplanted by the community, which uses his name as a cypher for its own history or self-understanding.[27]

The Johannine theme of the Paraclete opposes the assumption that lateness disqualifies an attempt to bear witness to Jesus. According to John 16.12–13, Jesus said to his disciples on the night of his arrest: 'I have yet many things to say to you, but you cannot bear them now. When the Spirit of truth comes, he will guide you into all the truth.' If truth is disclosed only at the moment of origin, then the first disciples have an absolute advantage over all later Christians. Yet, according to Jesus, it is only in his own absence that the truth about him can come to light. 'I tell you the truth: it is to your advantage that I go away, for if I do not go away the Paraclete will not come to you' (16.7). The truth into which the Spirit leads the Christian community is still the truth about Jesus; for 'he will glorify me, for he will take what is mine and declare it to you' (16.14). The Spirit leads into all the truth by 'bringing to your remembrance all that I have said to you' (14.26), and this indicates that what the Spirit brings is not a new truth additional to or above the truth inherent in Jesus' incarnate existence.[28] It is, in fact, crucially important to achieve a correct balance between the assertion that the disclosure of truth lies in the future and the assertion that it lies in the past. What lies in the future is a true apprehension of what has already happened in the past; and revelation is thereby tied irrevocably to the historicity and particularity of human existence within the world and prevented from drifting away into gnostic fantasy. Conversely, however, the meaning of what happened in the past cannot simply be read out of that past, conveyed by means of an authoritative tradition. Revelation of the meaning of that past arrives, as it were, from the future. Among other things, this theology of the Paraclete serves to explain and to justify the Fourth Gospel's refusal either to present us with nothing but the plain historical facts, or to detach itself from its historical moorings in order to speak of something other than the enfleshed word. The 'conservative' desire to find in this Gospel the plain historical facts about what Jesus said and did is motivated by precisely the assumption – that at the moment of origin the truth about Jesus is disclosed in unmediated form – which it is the function of the doctrine of the Paraclete to reject. But the more 'radical' scholar is controlled by the same assumption, when it is implied, for example, that the presence in this text of a developed 'Johannine theology' makes it impossible to regard it as truthful testimony to Jesus.

To criticize the notion that the moment of origin gives access to unmediated truth is not to advocate uncritical acceptance of the products of later reflection. If a right 'remembrance' of what has been said in the past proceeds only from the future (cf. John 14.26; 16.13), then we cannot be exempted from the duty of critical assessment of the texts we inherit from the past.

(4) A final reason why the historical-critical tradition is so adamant that Jesus must be liberated from 'the stony rocks of ecclesiastical doctrine' is that it operates with a positivistic assumption of a unitary history. Reimarus's work again provides a convenient starting-point.

According to the Gospel of John, Joseph of Arimathea and Nicodemus provided spices for Jesus' body prior to the burial (John 19.38–40); Luke, on the other hand, says that the women bought spices immediately after returning from the tomb (Luke 23.56); and Mark has them buying spices after the sabbath (Mark 16.1). At this and at many other points, Reimarus notes that the gospel resurrection narratives diverge. Taken as a whole, the differences are not without weight, as Reimarus eloquently insists in a concluding apostrophe: 'Reader, you who are conscientious and honest, tell me before God whether you could accept as unanimous and sincere this testimony concerning such an important matter that contradicts itself so often and so obviously in respect to person, time, place, manner, intent, word, story?' (197). The law–court metaphor casts Reimarus in the role of counsel for the prosecution and his reader as a member of the jury.[29] But is it really the case that he and those who think like him are the only ones to display integrity in this matter? In failing to draw the conclusions that he draws, are Christian believers necessarily dishonest, negligent or blinded by prejudice? Or does the force of the prosecution's case derive not from the quasi–neutral 'evidence' it has mustered but from the interpretative framework within which that evidence is set? At issue here is not only the question of the resurrection of Jesus but also one's understanding of the nature of history.

It would be possible to apply Reimarus's forensic methods to the interpretation of the creation narratives in Gen. 1–2. We have, on the one hand, a traditional Christian belief (that the world was created by God, that God raised Jesus from the dead), and, on the other hand, a plurality of textual witnesses to these matters. Investigating the Genesis narratives with all due integrity and diligence, we discover that at point after point they are incompatible. In one, creation takes a week; in the other, a day. In one, human beings are created on the sixth day of creation, after all other living creatures; in the other, man is created at the beginning of the creative process and woman at the end. In one, humans are given the whole earth for their home; in the other, the first human pair is given a garden. Just such observations were leading, during Reimarus's lifetime, to a rudimentary awareness of the complexities of Pentateuchal prehistory. But what conclusion should be drawn from them? Do the differences between the creation narratives demonstrate that the belief that the world was created by God is untrue (possibly a priestly fraud)? Although Reimarus uses a precisely analogous argument about the resurrection, he will be unwilling to accept that the two cases are comparable; for as an orthodox Deist he is committed to the belief that the world was created by God, whatever his view of the Genesis narratives. He can justify the distinction he makes between the two cases by claiming that belief in creation belongs to the universal, rational religion of nature whereas belief in the resurrection is specific to a particular religious tradition. But this means that the rejection of the resurrection proceeds not simply from the 'evidence' but from the deistic belief that nature's revelation of the creator and his will is sufficient for us, and that anything added to this is evil, the product of malice or superstition.[30] Nature is unitary, operating by fixed laws which Newton and others have begun to uncover, and within this unitary nature there is also a unitary human history in which virtue and vice, truth and superstition, strive with one another.

All nature and all history lie open to the unifying gaze not only of the unitarian deistic God but also of the rational human observer. Because God is one and the world is one, positive religious traditions which speak of a revelation over and above that which nature makes universally available must be understood as purely human products. They may not be fraudulent; within a few decades of Reimarus's death it will become fashionable to regard them as imperishable monuments to the greatness of the human spirit. But they remained, as they still remain, purely *human* products, and when interpreted as such it becomes more and more difficult to retain the traditional language of divine action according to which God was in Christ reconciling the world to himself.[31] The notion of a unitary history within a unitary nature results in the insistence that the New Testament texts should be studied just like any other historical sources; for the claim to a qualitative uniqueness does not conform to the dogma of the oneness of the world and must therefore be disallowed in advance.[32] This dogma is not necessarily irreligious. Although it is compatible with secularism, it also permits the composition of variations on deistic, pantheistic or existentialist themes.

The dogma that nature and history constitute a single, seamless garment is a prime example of a modernist metanarrative of the kind that postmodernism now declares to be incredible. Whether this new incredulity helps to make room for the trinitarian Christian narrative is open to question; it is, as we saw in chapter 7, at least as likely to issue in a narrative theology according to which the Christian narrative is simply one communally–authoritative story among others. If it claims to be more than this, does it not set itself up as just another metatheory? Yet the Christian narrative does not claim that the unity of the world as God's creation and the object of his redemption is open and accessible to us. The God–forsaken death of the Son of God points to a present disharmony which is as far removed as possible from the optimistic religions of the Enlightenment. The unity of the world – a unity of community and therefore of reconciled diversity rather than a mere undifferentiated oneness – is therefore an eschatological concept and not something that is presently accessible to a detached observer. In addition, postmodern interest in communally–authoritative narratives will ultimately have to reckon with the fact that such narratives are authoritative not merely because they are traditional and formative of personal identity but also because they are believed to be true. An interpretation of a narrative from within its communal base can hardly be disqualified because it refuses to abstract itself from the question of truth. And a mode of interpretation which still operates with the hypothesis of a unitary history within a unitary nature, begins to look like one interpretative possibility among many – optional and no longer compulsory.

If the modernist metatheory of a unitary world accessible to the observing gaze has become unbelievable, so has the unitarian God who in various guises has continued to hover in the background of this failed project, especially in its theological manifestations. While this situation does not in itself point in the direction of a trinitarian hermeneutic, it does at least create a space within which to challenge 'the monocular anti-dogmatic and anti-trinitarian perspective of the practitioners of the historical-critical method' (Richard Roberts, *A Theology on its Way?*, (1991), 93).

This preliminary attempt at a critique of historical-critical antipathy to the doctrines of the trinity and of the incarnation is, obviously enough, 'inadequate'. Attacks on historical-critical 'presuppositions' often evade the legitimate and valid questions that have been raised, in their over-eagerness to achieve a rapid and a decisive refutation. In this area, however, no such easy refutation is possible. My intention has been the more modest one of trying to find ways of reformulating and reopening the *question* of the appropriateness of the early church's choice of trinitarian and incarnational conceptuality in its never–completed attempt to express the truth about Jesus in communally–normative fashion. We are of course free to dissent from the early church's choice, but it is not clear that we are obliged to do so.

Chapter 15

Praxis and Hope

In outlining a trinitarian hermeneutic and a corresponding exegetical practice, a further task is to reflect on the praxis that would follow from this understanding of the divine *philanthrōpia* manifested in Christ. Since a divine–human praxis already lies at the heart of this understanding, there can be no question here of the all-too-common tendency to isolate theology from ethics. The synoptic identification of love of God and of neighbour as the essential content of God's commandment and call to humankind (Matt 22.34–40; Mark 12.28–34; Luke 10.25–37) offers a focal point for the discussion.

1. There is no love of God which is not simultaneously love of neighbour.

This thesis need not imply a 'secularizing' of theology, the assertion that ethics or praxis is all–important and that theology's sole task is simply to maintain and elaborate that assertion.[1] The thesis that love of God occurs only by way of love of the neighbour must be elaborated not as an autonomous praxis but christologically.

In the Johannine epistles, the commandment to love one's neighbour as oneself is interpreted as 'the message [*aggelia*] which you have heard from the beginning, that we should love one another' (1 John 3.11). This *aggelia* is not a *didachē* or code of ethical teaching that can be separated from the *kerygma*, for the content of the *aggelia* proclaimed from the beginning may also be described as 'the eternal life which was with the Father and was made manifest to us' (1.2); the double use of the cognate verb *apaggellō* in connection with this message (1.2,3) confirms that the manifestation through Jesus Christ of eternal life and the command that we should love one another are, when correctly understood, the *same* message. There are not two divine words, one 'doctrinal' and the other 'ethical', but only the

265

single 'word of life' (1.1). However, while 1 John offers resources for a theological understanding of Christian praxis, two problems arise from its interpretation of love for the neighbour as love for the 'brother' (a term used thirteen times in this text).

The first problem is that a gender–neutral term is thereby replaced by one that is gender–specific: *adelphos* of course 'includes' *adelphē*, but at the price of rendering the women in the community invisible in contrast to its 'fathers' and 'young men' (2.13–14). The translation of *adelphos* as 'brother or sister' is semantically justifiable but often produces cumbersome results in practice ('If anyone... sees his or her brother or sister in need, yet closes his or her heart against him or her...' (3.17)). In interpreting this text it seems almost impossible to dispense with the increasingly anachronistic use of 'brother' and masculine pronouns as inclusive. Indeed, it may not always be desirable for translation to take on the role of censor in suppressing the fact that the biblical texts are written within the conventions of patriarchal language.[2]

The second problem is, in this context, more serious and more important. The 'brothers' who are to be loved are apparently to be identified as the members of the Christian community. The message heard from the beginning is that 'we should love *one another*' (3.11), and nothing is said of any such obligation towards non-members of the community.[3] Such people constitute 'the world' which lies 'in the power of the evil one' (5.19), and the community is not to be surprised by their hatred (3.13). This text does not teach the 'old commandment' that 'you shall love your neighbour and hate your enemy' (Matt. 5.43), even in the expanded sense of 'hatred' as including indifference (cf.1 John 3.15, 17); but it does not set as great a distance between the old commandment and the new as Jesus does when he commands his followers to love their enemies and to pray for those who persecute them (Matt. 5.44). When the author tells his readers that they must not 'love the world', and that 'if anyone loves the world, love for the Father is not in him' (1 John 2.15), there is a danger that hostility or indifference towards 'the things in the world' (2.15) will be extended to *persons* – a danger exacerbated by the ambiguity of the term 'world'. The commandment to love 'one another' at least makes it clear that a generalized *philanthrōpia* or love for humankind will be a disembodied abstraction unless it becomes concrete in particular relationships, as in the case of Jesus' own praxis. But, at least at first sight, this text does not appear to look beyond this concretion of love and seems to suggest a close-knit community sharply differentiated from society as a whole, where it perceives only darkness, evil and hatred. And so there arises the problem of the sectarian tendencies of the 'Johannine community', reinforced perhaps by its recent separation from fellow-Christians whom it now denounces as 'antichrists' (2.18–19).

In a canonical perspective, this text is not addressed primarily to a long-defunct 'Johannine community' but, as a 'catholic epistle', to the whole church, within which it functions as holy scripture.[4] But of course its language remains the same. One possibility would be to 'correct' it by means of Jesus' more inclusive vision of the heavenly Father who 'makes his sun rise on the evil and on the good, and sends rain on the just and on the unjust', and his incisive question, 'If you love those who love you… what more are you doing than others?' (Matt 5.45–47). If, however, one wishes to preserve the integrity of the Johannine text rather than subjecting it to interpretative violence, it would be more satisfactory to understand Jesus' critique of sectarianism as raising the question whether there are elements in the Johannine text itself which run counter to its undoubted sectarian tendencies and which might provide a more 'catholic' perspective within which to read it. The polyvalence of the term 'world' (*kosmos*) suggests that such a perspective is a possibility.[5]

In 1 John 5.4–5, it is said that our believing that Jesus is the Son of God is the victory that overcomes the world (*hē nikē hē nikēsasa ton kosmon*). The initial sense is that the world in its darkness poses an annihilating threat which faith nevertheless overcomes. In this sense Jesus Christ has overcome the world: 'The light shines in the darkness, and the darkness did not overcome it' (John 1.5). But Jesus Christ's victory over the world is not simply a victory *over* the world; it is a victory *for the sake of* the world. The whole world lies in the power of the evil one (1 John 5.19); but that is only the penultimate truth about the world, for the ultimate truth is that 'the Father has sent his Son as the Saviour *of the world*' (4.14). Jesus Christ is 'The sacrifice for our sins, and not for ours only but also for the sins of the whole world' (2.2), and an ontological dualism between those who walk in the light and those who walk in the darkness is thus both acknowledged as a theoretical possibility and simultaneously excluded: '*not* for our sins only…' When it is said that 'the love of God was made manifest among us' in that 'God sent his only Son into the world' (4.9), the world is seen not as a hostile or neutral environment within which the salvation of the elect must take place, but as itself the object of God's love and saving activity. The love of God is made manifest 'among us' (*en hēmin*), and this phrase must have the same meaning as in John 1.14 ('And the word became flesh and dwelt among us'), where it refers not to a secret revelation in the midst of the community but to a fully public life within and for the sake of the world of human society. At his hearing before the high priest, Jesus said: 'I have spoken openly to the world; I have always taught in synagogues and in the temple, where all Jews come together; I have said nothing secretly' (John 18.20).[6] This human and therefore public existence is the indispensable form which the mission of the Son must take if it is to express, as it must, God's love for the world (cf. John 3.16). This is one reason why the denial that Jesus Christ came in the flesh cannot be regarded as a difference of opinion to be tolerated and contained within a basically united community (cf. 1 John 4.2); for if, seeking to honour Jesus Christ, one distances him from too close an involvement in human reality, one thereby turns him into yet another arrogant, condescending and aloof deity who – in the light of the real, human Christ – can only be regarded as an anti-human antichrist.

Jesus Christ manifests the divine *philanthrōpia*, and not a pseudo-divine love for the elect only, and it is his divine–human praxis which, according to the author of 1 John, establishes the pattern of Christian praxis. 'In this is love, not that we loved God but that he loved us and sent his Son to be the sacrifice for our sins. Beloved, if God so [*houtōs*] loved us, we also ought to love one another' (4.10–11). God sent his Son for our sake, and an exclusive interpretation of this statement has already been ruled out: 'he is the sacrifice for our sins, and not for ours only but also for the sins of the whole world' (2.2). If human love is to follow the pattern of divine love, it must be directed not only towards 'one another' (other members of the Christian community) but towards every member of the human community for which Christ lived, died and rose again. If the addressees of this text confine their love to 'one another', then their human love does not adequately reflect the divine–human love for humankind. While a generalized praxis of universal love is in itself impossible, a particular, localized praxis may nevertheless concretize an orientation of love towards humankind as such, as in the case of Jesus' own praxis. 'He who says he abides in him ought to walk in the same way in which he walked' (2.6): only the analogy of praxis can justify and give substance to the claim to abide in him, which is otherwise wide open to illusion and fantasy.

To love is not to patronize. To patronize is to exert oneself for someone else's benefit within a hierarchical context which makes a truly reciprocal relationship impossible. The view that *agapē* entails the bestowal of divine or human favour upon an utterly unworthy, unlovable object overlooks the fact that love aims at reciprocity, the creation of community, and must therefore see a potential for reciprocity in its object. If one is enabled to concretize the commandment to love as God loved us, one is not 'doing good' in the sense of temporarily putting someone else's welfare above one's own, but attempting to establish a reciprocal relation in which to give is at the same time to receive; to open one's own existence to be affected and perhaps transformed by the existence of the other, so that one's own well-being is not sacrificed for the sake of the other but redefined as dependent on reciprocity with the other. If *agapē* is to be exercised outwards into the world as well as within the Christian community, and if it must aim at reciprocity and community, it follows that the practice of *agapē*, in analogy and conformity to Christ, is a possibility outside the Christian community.

The parable of the Good Samaritan illustrates this point. When, in response to the question 'Who is my neighbour?', Jesus tells of the man who was attacked and left half-dead by robbers (Luke 10.29–37), it appears at first that a very simple, straightforward answer is to be given: your neighbour is the needy person whom you encounter. The character in the story who loves his neighbour by giving the necessary aid will be a surrogate for the interlocutor, pointing him to a future praxis in which he acts likewise. Yet the one who sees in the figure at the roadside his neighbour who must be loved is, unexpectedly, a Samaritan, an outsider to the community. The love that he practises is an analogy of Jesus' own practice (as Augustine's much-maligned allegorical reading sees more clearly than its modern critics):[7] for Jesus fulfils in his praxis the scriptural promise that the lame will walk and the dead be raised up (cf. Luke 7.22), and the Samaritan's action in lifting the half-dead man onto his own beast and arranging for his care similarly has as its goal that he should walk and live again. The *agapē* of Jesus and of the Samaritan also have in common the capacity to subvert the social barriers that divide one human group from another. The Samaritan indicates that the human practice of the subversive *agapē* with which God loved the world in sending his Son may occur at any place and at any time, inside the Christian community or outside it. But there is a further destabilizing twist to this story. Jesus counters the initial question ('Who is my neighbour?') with a question of his own: 'Which of these three, do you think, proved neighbour to the man who fell among the robbers?' The interlocutor is not to identify himself with the Samaritan ('Go and do likewise') until he has first acknowledged that he himself is potentially the wounded man and that his neighbour, whom he wishes to recognize in order to fulfil the commandment, is the Samaritan: that is, not a passive object of charitable endeavour but an active subject who is himself familiar with the practice of *agapē* and who can therefore by 'my neighbour' only on the basis of reciprocity, however unequal the relationship may appear to be.[8]

A further dimension of the Johannine attack on docetism comes to light at this point. For docetism, the world is ultimately, ontologically evil; the elect derive their true being from elsewhere and have been plunged into an alien, material existence by a prehistoric cosmic accident. One is therefore saved by the only seemingly enfleshed Savour *out of* materiality, and to him material well-being or misfortune is entirely indifferent. But if in Jesus

Christ the Son of God is truly enfleshed, then material existence cannot be alien to him. The Samaritan's praxis is only analogous to his because he offers material assistance (in this case, bandages, medication, labour and money). The movement in Jesus Christ of the divine *philanthrōpia* into the realm of embodied, human existence is not a mere expedient, intended to facilitate a call to humans to turn away from the preoccupations that accompany their embodiment, in order to seek a disembodied truth in a higher sphere.[9] It is, instead, the clearest possible divine affirmation of embodiment and materiality; *agapē*, divine or human, is nothing unless it assumes embodied, material form. Thus, the Johannine author writes: 'If anyone has the world's goods and sees his brother in need, yet closes his heart against him, how does God's love abide in him?' (1 John 3.17). This point is made still more forcefully in the context of James's similar attack on the heresy (akin to docetism) of a purely verbal faith without a corresponding praxis: 'If a brother or sister [*adelphos ē adelphē*] is ill-clad and in lack of daily food, and one of you says to them, "Go in peace, be warmed and filled", without giving them the things needed for the body [*ta epitēdeia tou sōmatos*], what does it profit?' (Jas. 2.15–16). Love is not simply *expressed* in meeting the human need for warmth and food, as though it could formerly pre-exist in the privacy of the heart; it is *created* by such actions, indeed it is to be *identified with* such actions in their relational aspect.[10] 'Salvation' may be understood as the liberating divine action that creates the conditions within which this love can come into existence. 'The reason why the Son of God appeared was to destroy the works of the devil' (John 3.8); and, as we have seen, the devil is above all the adversary of human community. One of the chief works of the devil that the Son of God came to destroy is therefore the *closed heart*, which may take the form of good wishes and sympathy – 'Go in peace…' – unaccompanied by praxis.

Love of neighbour is the continuation and extension into the world of the divine *philanthrōpia* manifested in Christ, and therefore finds its source in God's grace and not in a Pelagian work-ethic. God's grace opens the closed heart and creates 'the *koinōnia* of the Holy Spirit' (2 Cor. 13.14). 'God is love' (1 John 4.8), and, since love wills reciprocity and thus creates love, the love of the Father, the Son and the Spirit flows into the human world, mediated by human love. 'If God so loved us, we also ought to love one another' (4.11). Yet this unilinear representation of love – constantly proceeding from God into the world – is puzzling. If love is relational, should there not be a reciprocal human movement of love back to its source? We are to love the Lord our God with all our heart, soul, mind and strength. But it is not said that if God so loved us we ought also to love God. It is said that 'if anyone says, "I love God", and hates his brother, he is a liar; for he who does not love his brother whom he has seen cannot love God whom he has not seen' (4.20). This raises the question whether love of God can be practised in any way except through love of neighbour. God's love is undoubtedly prior to our own: 'In this is love, not that we loved God but that he loved us...' (4.10). And, since its object is ourselves and our neighbours, then a response to it that neglects the neighbour cannot be genuine. But, assuming that love of neighbour is not entirely neglected, is there any other way in which the love of God can be reciprocated in our love for God? Worship is the obvious point at which one might identify a love of God distinct from, although not independent of, love of neighbour. If the priest or the Levite, returning from Jerusalem, had helped the wounded man, would their love of neighbour have proved the genuineness of the love of God they had practised through participation in the temple worship? That would suggest that love of God and love of neighbour are distinct although related realities: one practises the one in the temple and the other on the road from Jerusalem to Jericho, and the second is a necessary proof of the reality of the first.[11] The alternative would be to say that human responsive love for God occurs *exclusively* through the mediation of the neighbour.[12] The Samaritan has probably avoided the temple but loves God at the only point where he gives himself to be loved; that is, in the neighbour. One loves God by sharing in his work of extending human community. If this second view is correct (and something like it seems to be implied in the Johannine text), then an alternative account of the necessity of *faith* would be required.

In terms of his purely religious practice, the Samaritan falls within the scope of Jesus's dismissive remark about the Samaritan sanctuary at Mount Gerizim: 'You worship what you do not know' (John 4.22). Yet, though the religious traditions within which he is located are thus dismissed as heterodox and worthless (cf. 2 Kings 17.24–41), he participates in God's work of *agapē*, demonstrating in his action a tacit understanding that this work is a categorical imperative. In obeying the commandment of *agapē*, he loves God: 'This is the love of God, that we keep his commandments' (1 John 5.3). But the more it is emphasized that the Samaritan observes not just one but both of the two great commandments on which 'depend all the law and the prophets' (Matt 22.40), the greater the danger that faith may dwindle into insignificance. What place is there for the further commandment 'that we should believe in the name of his Son Jesus Christ' (1 John 3.23)? Since the God whom the Samaritan tacitly loves is the God whose *philanthrōpia* is manifested in Jesus Christ, and since the Samaritan's praxis is therefore analogous to Jesus', he may perhaps be said to possess a tacit or implicit faith in Jesus Christ. But the question of the value of an explicit faith remains to be answered.

According to the Johannine author, faith is a mode of knowledge.[13] The content of faith is mediated by communal testimony – 'That which we have seen and heard we proclaim also to you' (1 John 1.3) – and yet faith is ultimately not dependent on the reliability or otherwise of human witnesses, for it is confirmed by the Holy Spirit who indwells the community and works in and through its proclamation. Thus it c n be said that 'you have been anointed by the Holy One, and you all know' (2.20). The epistle concludes with a confident threefold declaration that 'we know', culminating in the claim that 'we know that the Son of God has come and has given us understanding, to know him who is true... This is the true God and eternal life' (5.20). The faith that Jesus is the Son of God (5.5) is *mediated* knowledge, in the sense that it can be attained only by way of the community's testimony. But it is also *knowledge*: not simply communal membership, or adherence to an inherited tradition, or the willingness to allow one's existence to be shaped by a particular narrative or language, although it is all of these things as well, but a knowledge of the way things are that does not permit one to peer behind or beyond the history of God's *philanthrōpia* into some ultimate and nameless abyss, because there *is* no 'wholly other' reality behind or beyond that history. 'God is light and in him is no darkness at all' (1.5): that is to say, there is no dark hinterland to God's self-manifestation as love, for that self-manifestation is the truth and not an ambiguous hint luring one towards deeper divine mysteries. The praxis of love is thus grounded in the knowledge that God is love. The Samaritan indicates that a purely tacit knowledge is a possibility, but an explicit, shared knowledge of the truth is a securer foundation for the praxis of love.

Faith, expressed and reinforced in a communal setting, is not in itself the love of God. Reciprocation of God's love occurs only through the mediation of the neighbour. Yet faith provides the context in which the praxis of love for the neighbour and of God in and through the neighbour can flourish.

2. Love of neighbour, as understood by Jesus, is a necessary hermeneutical criterion for a Christian interpretation of the Old Testament.

We have seen that the relationship between the two commandments enjoining love of God and of neighbour must be reinterpreted in the light of the praxis and teaching of Jesus Christ, in whom the divine *agapē* was made manifest. But in the synoptic gospels these commandments are initially identified as the sum of the law and the prophets, and this identification – and the reinterpretation that occurs in the course of it – will in turn shape the interpretation of the law and the prophets.

To refer to the law, the prophets and the writings as 'the Old Testament' is of course already to impose a Christian interpretation on this body of writings. Historical-critical reading of these texts took its starting-point in the acceptance by Christians of the Jewish claim that a direct relationship to Jesus cannot be established in them. (Christians had always associated 'literal' exegesis with Judaism, and the growing prestige of the literal-historical sense during the sixteenth and seventeenth centuries made the Jewish challenge to the Christian 'Old Testament' inescapable.)[44] It is therefore not surprising that there is currently a call to abandon the term 'Old Testament' altogether, replacing it with the more neutral 'Hebrew Bible'.[15] As defining a common ground within which Jewish and Christian interpreters can work together, this term is to be welcomed. At the same time, its current usage gives formal expression to a widespread unwillingness or inability to reflect upon the significance for interpretation of the status of these texts as *Christian* holy scripture. The historical-critical obsession with circumstances of origin makes it seem anachronistic and artificial to allow these texts to interact with another, much later body of texts (the so-called 'New Testament'); they must rather be understood 'on their own terms', and consideration of the relation between the testaments is thus relegated to marginal status, a fitting topic for a 'concluding unscientific postscript' rounding off a History of Israel or an Old Testament Theology.

Thus, according to John Bright, 'Old Testament history ultimately places one before a decisive question. And that question is: "Who do you say that I am?" It is a question that only faith's affirmation can answer' (*History of Israel* [1972²], 467). What is significant is that a question which is supposed to be 'decisive' can apparently only be raised in the final paragraph of the book, despite Bright's commitment to 'biblical theology'.[16] The strained reference to 'faith' implies a decision, to be made in the privacy of some inner sanctuary, which is too ineffable to enter into discourse. But that which cannot enter into discourse is, in practice, irrelevant. It is briefly evoked here in order to reassure Old Testament studies that it is still part of the enterprise of Christian theology, while relieving it of any obligation to reflect systematically on the implications of participation in such an enterprise. The vulnerability of this procedure makes it understandable that a more recent work in the genre of the 'History of Israel' abandons this residual desire for Christian theological legitimacy and concludes its narrative not with 'the fullness of time' (as Bright does) but with the defeat of the second Jewish revolt in 135 CE.[17] This strategy has its own integrity and logic; but an interpretative strategy which attempted – seriously, and not half-heartedly – to treat the Christian Bible as a single book might also have its own integrity and logic. It should not be presupposed that an explicitly Christian theological reflection on the holy scriptures of both testaments will necessarily be disingenuous or 'anti-Jewish'. The thesis stated at the outset of this section identifies one possible area within which such a reflection might take place.[18]

According to Mark, Jesus was asked by a scribe to identify a single commandment as 'first of all.' (Mark 12.28). The citation of the *Shema*^c – which enjoins love of God with heart, soul, mind and strength – follows as a matter of course, and the inclusion here of its opening words ('Hear, O Israel: the Lord our God, the Lord is one') underlines the fact that this commandment is integral to Israel's fundamental confession (12.29–30). Yet, although the questioner asks only about a single commandment and although the only possible response is duly given, there is more to be said. A second commandment is added, and takes its place alongside the first as of equal standing: 'The second is this, "You shall love your neighbour as yourself." There is no other commandment greater than these' (12.31). The emphasis thus falls on this unexpected supplement.[19] The scribe responds by endorsing Jesus' teaching, adding his own interpretative gloss by asserting that love of God and of neighbour is 'much more than all burnt offerings and sacrifices' (12.33). The setting of this debate within the temple (11.28; 12.35, 41–44), whose economic structure Jesus has just attacked (11.15–18) and whose destruction he will shortly foretell (13.1–2), lends particular force to this assertion. The scribe's endorsement confirms that Jesus does not here advocate any radical, controversial novelty in his reading of the law, but offers a hermeneutical key to the reading of the law from within the law itself – a reading which, while maintaining the obvious centrality of love of God, is at the same time oriented towards love of neighbour. The scribe's addition correctly understands Jesus' position as similar to the prophetic critique of a purely cultic interpretation of love for God. Jesus is thus another advocate of a prophetic rather than a priestly reading of the law, as Matthew indicates when he represents Jesus as responding to the Pharisaic version of the priestly purity code with the advice, 'Go and learn what this means, "I desire mercy and not sacrifice"' (Matt. 9.13, quoting Hos. 6.6; cf. Matt. 12.7). Although in his version of the Marcan pericope Matthew does not include the scribe's endorsement or the reference to sacrifices, the prophetic connection is underlined here too: for, although the initial question again concerns a single requirement of the law, the two commandments cited are said to be the foundation of 'all the law *and the prophets*' (Matt. 22.40). If the law and the prophets are to be reduced from a double to a single commandment, that single commandment is love of neighbour rather than love of God: 'Whatever you wish that people would do to you, do so to them, for this is the law and the prophets' (Matt. 7.12). Mark and Matthew both present Jesus as proposing (as well as embodying in his praxis) an ethical or prophetic hermeneutic in which love of neighbour is the indispensable criterion for establishing the right practice of the love of God inculcated by the *Shema*[c]. This hermeneutic is not imposed on the text by a dogmatic authority external to it, but represents a fundamental and defensible answer to questions concerning the practice of obedience to God which the text itself raises.

The Marcan pericope about the disciples' plucking grain on the sabbath points to further characteristics of this hermeneutic. According to Mark, the disciples' practice was challenged by 'the Pharisees' (a group which a theologically-oriented exegesis can hardly avoid seeing as representing an interpretation of holy scripture basically opposed to Jesus', although one should of course be wary of finding here the basis for a judgement on empirical Judaism). Jesus was asked: 'Why are they doing what is not lawful on the sabbath?' (Mark 2.24). The question derives from a reading of scripture in which human need must be subordinated to obedience to the divine command to desist from labour – except perhaps in life-and-death cases. (If the Lord commanded that a man found gathering sticks on the sabbath should be stoned (Num. 15.32–36), then a strict interpretation of the sabbath law can obviously be justified out of the literal sense of holy scripture.) Jesus' response takes a threefold form.

First, he points to a strand within holy scripture which favours his own more liberal interpretative principles. 'Have you never read what David did, when he was in need and was hungry, how he entered the house of God, when Abiathar was high priest, and ate the bread of the Presence, which it is not lawful for any but the priests to eat, and also gave it to those who were with him?' (2.25–26). The treatment of holy scripture as an unambiguous legal code is countered by an appeal not just to a single incident, used in proof-text fashion, but to a fundamental feature of the Old Testament's religious legislation: its embeddedness in narrative contexts. Legislation may represent itself as entirely independent of human need, a pure transcript of the divine commandment which must be obeyed simply because it is commanded. Narrative, however, reflects the exposure of legislation to the vicissitudes of human action and need within constantly shifting circumstances. Legislation attempts to represent the will of God from above; narrative, from below. The instance cited resembles the present occasion in that in both cases a tension between human need (hunger) and divine norms is resolved in favour of the former, despite the formidable textual support which might be mustered in favour of the opposite decision. Jesus does not answer the appeal to legality on its own terms, but suggests a more flexible hermeneutic in which narrative (where human action and need may be faithfully and sympathetically represented) serves to relativize the potentially anti-human dimensions of a legislation based on the premise of a distinct, self-contained religious sphere symbolized by the figure of the priest.

The flexibility attained by appealing to a narrative hermeneutic over against a legal one would no doubt be criticized by Pharisees and others as issuing in an *ad hoc*, random use of holy scripture. Yet this flexibility is motivated not by a doctrinaire hostility towards systematic thinking but by the systematic principle that there can be no legitimate service of God that impairs the service of the neighbour. To think otherwise is to serve a false god rather than the philanthropic God disclosed in Jesus, the end of whose ways is human well-being and community. The statement that follows – 'The sabbath was made for man, not man for the sabbath' – is thus a strictly theological one. If man was made for the sabbath, then the divine–human relation is a relation of exploitation and dominance of essentially the same kind as oppressive relations between humans. One serves various human masters for six days; and on the seventh day one serves a divine master who remains all too human in imposing the severest penalties for such offences as gathering sticks or plucking grain. At no point is one treated as a rational agent and dialogue-partner, for the relationship is in every case a monological one. The image of divine dominance here may serve to legitimate human dominance at the same time as appearing to limit it by reclaiming every seventh day from its grasp.

Jesus' saying identifies this image of divine dominance as an idol, exposed as such by the humanism of the true God who established the sabbath as a sacrament of the exodus or liberation from oppression which is at the heart of the scriptural narrative of salvation:

> Six days you shall labour and do all your work; but the seventh day is a sabbath to the Lord your God; in it you shall not do any work, you, or your son, or your daughter, or your manservant, or your maidservant, or your ox, or your ass, or any of your cattle, or the sojourner who is within your gates, that your manservant and your maidservant may rest as well as you. You shall remember that you were a servant in the land of Egypt, and the Lord your God brought you out thence with a mighty hand and an outstretched arm; therefore the Lord your God commanded you to keep the sabbath day. (Deut. 5.13–15)

The commandment to observe the sabbath day is here addressed not to all

Israelites without distinction, as are the other commandments, but to slave-owners or employers who as such are potential oppressors. Keeping the sabbath therefore means allowing slaves or employees to rest; the sabbath was made for men and women – and also for animals.[20] It is thus a sign of the divine resistance to oppression, as Amos recognized:

> Hear this, you who trample upon the needy, and bring the poor of the land to an end, saying 'When will the new moon be over, that we may sell grain? And the sabbath, that we may offer wheat for sale, that we may make the ephah small and the shekel great, and deal deceitfully with false balances, that we may buy the poor for silver and the needy for a pair of sandals, and sell the refuse of the wheat?' (Amos 8.4–6)

For one day in seven the work of oppression is thwarted, to the annoyance of the oppressors, and this antipathy between oppression and the sabbath commandment is a positive resource for the prophet in his denunciation of injustice. This is the true sense of the sabbath commandment, and not the persecution of the poor who, threatened by the prospect of cold or hunger, cannot afford the luxury of obedience to the letter of the law as defined by its self-appointed guardians and interpreters.[21]

The reference to David suggested a hermeneutic in which legal fixities may be relativized by their narrative context, since narrative is better able to represent the reality of concrete human needs. This choice for the human at the expense of the anti-human implies a strictly theological decision in favour of a humanized understanding of the divine over against an anti-human divinity. This decision underlies the dogmatic statement about the sabbath which aligns Jesus with the prophetic critique of a love of God abstracted from love of neighbour and with the corresponding prophetic hermeneutic of Israel's sacred traditions. This situation reveals the importance of regarding Jesus as a prophet, but also the inadequacy and insufficiency of this category; for the canon of holy scripture represents, among other things, a compromise between prophetic and priestly perspectives which allows space for both and so enables both Jesus and the Pharisees to appeal to scripture to justify their incompatible beliefs and practices. Jesus even concedes that the letter of scripture is on his opponents' side when, instead of rebutting the charge that his disciples' action was illegal, he justifies it by appealing to a similarly illegal act by David, who ate and distributed the bread of the Presence even though it was not lawful for any but the priest to eat it. The argument initially appears to rest on the more than doubtful premise that an act is justified if performed by David. The dogmatic statement about the purpose of the sabbath is perhaps a more effective answer to the pharisaic charge, but it is open to the criticism that it divides what scripture unites, that is, the priestly and the prophetic perspectives. If the pericope ended at this point, one would have to conclude that its representation of a 'prophetic' Jesus silencing the 'priestly' opposition is one-sided. Holy scripture does not permit closure at this point but merely generates an endlessly circulating argument in which two opposing perspectives (along with various attempts to mediate between them) revolve fruitlessly around a fundamentally ambiguous text.

In fact the pericope ends with a saying which, if true, resolves this dilemma: 'The Son of man is lord also of the sabbath' (Mark 2.28). Jesus' claim to a unique right to decide such matters enables him to transcend his equally indispensable role as reinterpreter of the tradition of prophetic critique. The prophet remains a relative figure; but the Son of man 'has authority on earth to forgive sins' (2.10), even though this claim entails an apparently blasphemous encroachment on a divine prerogative (2.7). It is initially unclear exactly what authority is claimed in the saying about the sabbath. If 'the sabbath was made for man' then 'man' is in some sense 'lord of the sabbath'. What then is added by the insertion of the phrase, 'Son of man', already identified as christological in content? On the one hand, it asserts the co-humanity of humankind generally and the enfleshed, human 'Son of God'. He and they are together beneficiaries of the divine *philanthrōpia* manifested in the sabbath command. On the other hand, it relates to his own uniquely sovereign action, for example in the sabbath healing recounted in the pericope that follows (Mark 3.1–6). His sovereignty 'also' (*kai*) over the sabbath is one expression of his sovereignty among the many that are narrated in the gospel accounts. He exercises this sovereignty as a human being, not as a god in human disguise, but he does so in a unique manner in accordance with the 'authority' given to him 'on earth'. In that he is lord over the sabbath, he is also lord over the scriptural text in which the observance of the sabbath is enjoined. The prophetic–humanistic hermeneutic that Jesus advocates is thus grounded not only in those strands of the scriptural witness that adopt a similar stance but also in his own unique sovereignty.

Admittedly there is no escape here from the constraints of textuality. From the standpoint of his pharisaic opponents, Jesus is merely compounding the arbitrariness of a prophetic perspective divorced from the priestly with the further and potentially blasphemous arbitrariness of a claim to an authority greater than that of holy scripture. So, for the contemporary hearer or reader, Jesus' claim is apprehended only in an irreducibly textual, written form which does not permit unmediated access to the pre-textual reality of divine authority of which it speaks. Indeed, the text thematizes this situation. When asked about the authority by which he acted, Jesus merely replied with a counter-question exposing his questioners' closedness to the possible reality of a divinely-given authority, to which they could only respond with an incurable agnosticism (Mark 11.27–33). However impressively what was said to the people of old is contrasted with what 'I say to you', the claim of a later sacred text to determine the sense and significance of an earlier one can never be established beyond question, since no non-textual, neutral ground is available upon which to test this claim.

The theological task is to explore, from within, the implications of this claim. Misapprehensions or one-sided views must be identified and corrected; for example, the belief that the relation between the Old Testament and the New stands or falls with the demonstration that a small number of traditional messianic proof-texts refer unambiguously and solely to Jesus. If Old Testament interpretation is to be undertaken on the presupposition of the Lucan Jesus 'that everything written about me in the law of Moses and the prophets and the psalms must be fulfilled' (Luke 24.44), then this statement must be understood in a sense broad enough to accommodate the Matthean assertion that the law and the prophets are fulfilled in the command, 'Whatever you wish that people would do to you, do so to them' (Matt. 7.12). To see Jesus Christ as the centre of a single Christian canon, comprising an Old and a New Testament, is not necessarily to impose an artificial unity on an irreducibly heterogeneous body of writings. It is to refuse the insidious Marcionite temptation to think of the law, the prophets and the writings as the holy scripture of the Jewish community alone.[22] It is to suggest that hermeneutical criteria might be found which would help to make some sense of the heterogeneity of these writings: criteria such as the privileging of the 'prophetic' over the 'priestly' perspective in the light of the praxis and teaching of Jesus.[23] Such criteria would have to be formulated, developed and corrected in the course of an interpretative practice in which one would again seek and expect to find substantive links between the writings of the two testaments.

3. Since it is grounded in the disclosure of the divine love in the divine–human praxis of Jesus Christ, love for the neighbour is also oriented towards the perfection of community which is the eschatological goal of that praxis.

This thesis paraphrases 1 Cor. 13.13: 'So faith, hope, love abide, these three; but the greatest of these is love.' Love is greater than faith and hope because the goal of God's act in Jesus Christ is community (*koinōnia*). Faith is the understanding and acknowledgement of this fact, while hope awaits its final eschatological confirmation; but it cannot be said that the goal of God's act in Jesus Christ is either faith or hope. The notion that God acted in Jesus Christ *so that* humans should come to believe that he did so and hope for a future fulfilment of that act risks emptying the divine act of all content. If that content is found in the restoration of the divine–human relationship in its purely vertical dimension, then the I–Thou relation to God is understood in a way that effectively excludes horizontal, human interrelatedness, and *koinōnia* is reduced to the gathering of like-minded individuals around a vertical axis. However, a trinitarian perspective makes it impossible to understand the divine–human relation in purely vertical terms. The incarnation represents the opening up of the *agapē* of Father and Son to human beings, and this takes place in the radical form of an *agapē* which is human as well as divine. There is no purely vertical relation with the exalted Christ, for he is the first-born among many brothers and sisters (Rom. 8.29). The extension of this a*gapē* in the world remains a divine–human task, for the author of human *koinōnia* is ultimately the Holy Spirit who frees human agents to enable them to bring it into being. Thus, it is not the case merely that a vertical divine–human relation is complemented by a human interrelatedness on the horizontal plane. Rather, the divine-human relation overflows from the vertical into the horizontal planes, comprehending within itself a new human interrelatedness, and abolishing the alienating dichotomy between vertical and horizontal dimensions which leads to a construal of love of God and of neighbour as separate claims upon us which may even be played off against each other.

A theological understanding of the present praxis of love of neighbour must emphasize not only the past in which it is grounded but also the future towards which it looks for the fulfilment of *koinōnia*, and thus for the full disclosure of the truth about past and present.[24] Except in the light of that future, this truth about past and present appears doubtful and ambiguous. If the past and the present are abstracted from this future, then empirical observation might suggest that the praxis of a subversive *agapē*, establishing *koinōnia* in place of division and oppression, is more likely to issue in crucifixion than in transformation. As one of the more extreme ways in which a hierarchical, divided society defends itself against a praxis whose goal is community, crucifixion discloses the apparently unbridgeable gulf between the overwhelming facticity of existing societal organization and the vulnerable, utopian vision of those who find themselves unable to accept the unacceptable. The Samaritan's conduct can be regarded as admirable only so long as it is safely confined within the limits of a vivid and pleasing story. But to fulfil the commandment to 'go and do likewise' would put one fundamentally at odds with a situation in which passing by on the other side, averting the eyes and refusing to see, counts as normality. Within this distorted but massively real normality, the Samaritan's action comes to seem only abstractly admirable. Factually, it is simply eccentric in the extravagance of its concern, which goes far beyond the duty to save life that in certain circumstances normality too will acknowledge.

In speaking of an unbridgeable gulf between the praxis of Jesus or the Samaritan and the normality represented by the priest and the Levite, it is important not to misrepresent the latter by depicting it as purely individualistic, the simple antithesis of authentic *koinōnia*. Normality is by no means the individualistic nightmare of Hobbes' state of nature, in which 'every man is enemy to every man... and the life of man, solitary, poor, nasty, brutish, and short' (*Leviathan* (1651), 186). The priest and the Levite have their own social contexts, and are in fact in transition from one (Jerusalem) to another (Jericho). They love those who love them and they greet their own brethren, just as the tax-collectors and Gentiles do (cf. Matt 5.46–47). Had the wounded man been identifiable as a fellow priest or Levite, the appropriate help would no doubt have been forthcoming. Yet the fact that they are unwilling or unable to transcend the limitations of an enclosed social world does not turn this world into a purely negative phenomenon. If tax-collectors and Gentiles know and practise a degree of solidarity with one another, then this must be seen as the gift of the Creator, like the sun that rises on the evil and on the good and the rain that falls on the just and on the unjust (cf. Matt. 5.45). The gift may be identified as an aspect of the divine image: it is the human being formed in and by social relations to others who is created in the image and likeness of God, as the reference in Gen. 1.27 to 'male and female' indicates. In the beginning, no limit is set to this human relatedness. Humankind as a whole is the recipient of the Creator's blessing, and there is no sense as yet that the fulfilment of the command to exercise dominion will occur only in a distorted form characterized by division, violence and exploitation. Yet, even though the fulfilment takes this distorted form, a limited but real human solidarity persists within this alienated state and is to be understood as a vestige of the divine image, marred by sin but not simply eradicated.

This vestige does not represent a point at which the human person is untouched by sin, for the solidarity of a particular group is inseparable from the injustice that divides one group from another. The point is that the *koinōnia* which is the beginning, the middle and the end of God's ways with humans is not something totally other and unheard of. Jesus does not bring some portentous revelation which simply negates existing reality, for existing reality itself proceeds from the creative act of God. He was in the world, and this world was not a wholly alien environment for him – for the world was made through him (cf. John 1.10). The divine–human praxis of *philanthrōpia*, which he exemplifies and which he frees his fellow-humans to participate in, represents the universalizing and perfecting of the limited, imperfect forms of community and solidarity without which human life is unimaginable. In Jesus Christ the divine image or likeness in humankind is restored. If we love only those who love us, we image the divine love only in fragmentary and distorted fashion; but if, liberated by Jesus' own praxis, we love even our enemies, our conduct will image that of 'the Most High', who 'is kind to the ungrateful and the selfish' (Luke 6.35). The *koinōnia* which is the goal of Jesus' praxis is, in one sense, a perfecting and a universalizing of an imperfect and limited possibility of community that is always and everywhere present. The Samaritan's action is, from the standpoint of 'normality', eccentric in its extravagance but not wholly unrelated to existing norms of human solidarity.

However, insofar as the limits of the existing norms are not accidental but essential to their proper functioning, a praxis which seeks to universalize them and which does not acknowledge their limits will inevitably be drawn into conflict with them. Thus, the necessity of the suffering of the Son of man (Mark 8.31, etc.) stems not from some arbitrary divine decree but at least in part from the inescapable conflict between a communal praxis stemming from the vision of the kingdom of God and the realities of power and domination.[25] In the end, the emphasis must fall on the *dis*continuities between the new community and the old, although this makes it impossible to evade the bitter dilemma that, under the conditions of a divided existence, the angelic gospel of peace on earth (Luke 2.14) will issue in renewed conflict: 'Do you think that I have to come to give peace on earth? No, I tell you, but rather division' (Luke 12.51).

If we abstract it from the eschatological future, the crucifixion represents not only the conflict between the new *koinōnia* and the old society, but also the defeat of the new at the hands of the old. The new wine cannot be contained within the old wineskins, and its novelty is its undoing: for 'no-one after drinking old wine desires new; for he says, "The old is good"' (Luke 5.39). New wine can be preserved only in new wineskins; but if these are unavailable, and if the new wine has to be poured into old wineskins, then it will be spilled upon the ground and go to waste when the wineskins burst. The old social structures are eventually unable to contain Jesus' praxis and teaching any longer, and, instead of the hoped-for transformation, the result is simply that his blood is spilled upon the ground. A comparable loss occurs when, after a time, the new wine 'matures' and becomes old, fit for the approval of the wealthy connoisseur. The new wine of Jesus' praxis was intended not for the pleasure of Dives or Herod but as good news for the poor (Luke 4.18), but it can be converted into its opposite with the ease and inevitability with which the new becomes old. The threat posed by Jesus can be overcome by the crude method of crucifixion but also by more subtle means of subversion, and the defeat of the utopian vision by those whose present is rooted in the past may seem to be a tragic law of human existence.

Considered empirically rather than eschatologically, the crucifixion thus represents the overtaking or overcoming of the new by the old in a circular movement which ensures that utopia is already subverted from the very moment of its proclamation. This circular movement is at the heart of the theological vision of Qoheleth, and if we are to set the new *agapē* in the context of hope, prior exposure to his rigorously hope-less vision is necessary.

Qoheleth proclaims a consoling gospel of resignation to the circular processes of fate and the world which expose every alleged newness as illusory. 'What has been is what will be, and what has been done is what will be done; and there is nothing new under the sun' (Eccles. 1.9). The implied author of this conservative tract is Solomon the king, the son of David (1.1), and among the various pleasures that his wealth opens up for him – wine, palaces, gardens, music, unlimited sex (cf. 2.1–10) – is the pleasure of calm, contemplative, philosophical despair in the face of the tragic ambiguities of human existence. 'I saw all the oppressions that are practised under the sun. And behold, the tears of the oppressed, and they had no-one to comfort them! On the side of their oppressors there was power, and there was no-one to comfort them' (4.1). Some such observation led Amos to denounce wealthy oppressors with all the rhetorical resources at his disposal, convinced as he was that their conduct was not an inevitable, quasi-natural state of affairs but an affront to Yahweh, the God of the covenant. The prophetic denunciations presuppose a belief that the continuation of the old is not inevitable and that the new is not an illusion, however far beyond present horizons it may lie.[26] Qoheleth, however, has already ruled out the possibility that the future will bring anything other than old injustice in new forms, and can only offer sensitive musings on the tragedy of it all. Faced with oppression, 'I thought the dead who are already dead more fortunate than the living who are still alive; but better than both is he who has not yet been, and has not seen the evil deeds that are done under the sun' (4.2–3). But despite Qoheleth's reputation for fearless integrity and realism,[27] this analysis of oppression as part of the tragedy of the human condition subtly evades and distorts the experience of oppression. The tears of the oppressed do not express a longing to escape from the troubles of existence by returning to the peace and rest of non-being. The oppressed desire not their own non-existence but the non-existence of oppression. It is the oppressors who consign the oppressed to non-existence if it suits them to do so, and Qoheleth's willingness to do the same places him in unsuspected proximity to the oppressors. For all his gentle compassion, he will not lift a finger to help the oppressed in their desperate plight, even if his own eyes are filled with tears as he passes by on the other side.[28]

Human suffering, removed from the prophetic hermeneutic of hope, is here naturalized and aestheticized – so effectively that it requires a conscious effort to resist the seductive vision of a world which is at the same time hopeless, pointless, tragic and beautiful. Even the tears of the oppressed do not fall outside the scope of this beauty, for there is 'a time for every matter under heaven... a time to weep and a time to laugh, a time to mourn and a time to dance' (3.1, 4). God 'has made everything very beautiful in its time; also he has put eternity into man's mind, yet so that he cannot find out what God has done from the beginning to the end' (3.11). 'God' is the mysterious power responsible for everything that happens, and this thought bestows a certain beauty on its otherwise banal pointlessness by enabling one to see it *sub specie aeternitatis*, in the light of an eternity which the human heart both knows and does not know. A great gulf is fixed between humans and the eternity they desire, and none may cross it. 'God is in heaven and you upon earth', and the verbosity of the religious should be regarded with suitably philosophical contempt (5.2). In place of the quest for God or for justice, this wise man recommends the pleasures of food and drink: 'Go, eat your bread with enjoyment, and drink your wine with a merry heart; for God has already approved what you do' (9.7). But greater still than the pleasure of food and wine (*old* wine?) is the pleasure of cool, sceptical contemplation and the rhetorical mastery with which it is put into words. If the rhetoric has its intended effect, then the reader should not only *believe* that there is nothing new under the sun but also *want to* believe it. The Preacher is an evangelist, a proclaimer of liberating good news (although not for the poor).

If one is able to remain detached from its own seductive pose of detachment, this wonderful book is of considerable hermeneutical and theological significance. Nowhere else in holy scripture is there so forth-rightly set out an *alternative* vision to that of the gospel, a rival version of the truth. Its basic dogma, that there is nothing new under the sun, conflicts fundamentally with the prophetic and early Christian orientation towards the future, which culminates in the vision of the one who is the Omega as well as the Alpha, the end as well as the beginning, who announces: 'Behold, I make all things new!' (Rev. 21.5–6; cf. 22.13). Whereas for Qoheleth the tears of the oppressed will not cease to flow, John the Seer envisages a consummation of the covenant relation between God and his people in which God 'will wipe away every tear from their eyes, and death shall be no more, neither shall there be mourning nor crying nor pain any more, for the former things have passed away' (21.4). It might be said that Qoheleth remains within the realm of this-worldly possibilities and that a transcendent eschatological future is simply beyond his chosen field of vision, rather than being definitely rejected. Yet that would be to subject him to an anachronistic distinction between 'revealed religion' and 'religion within the limits of reason alone.' In fact his assertion that 'what has been is what will be' allows no space at all for the possibility of 'new heavens and a new earth' in which 'the former things shall not be remembered or come into mind' (Isa. 65.17; cf. 66.22). The canonical significance of this book lies precisely in its challenge to the belief that underlies so much of the rest of holy scripture.[29]

Another way of expressing this challenge would be to say that Qoheleth rejects the scheme of promise (or prophecy) and fulfilment. On the road to Emmaus, the unknown stranger responds to his companions' sorrow and perplexity with the words, 'O foolish men, and slow of heart to believe all that the prophets have spoken! Was it not necessary that the Christ should suffer these things and enter into his glory?' The narrator adds: 'And beginning with Moses and all the prophets, he interpreted to them in all the scriptures the things concerning himself' (Luke 24.25–27). The Lucan view of the fulfilment of the law and the prophets is fundamentally opposed to Qoheleth, but there is in the Emmaus road narrative one possible point of contact with Qoheleth's vision. Asked about their conversation by the stranger who has joined them on the road, the two disciples 'stood still, looking sad' (Luke 24.17). They are sorrowful because the chief priests and rulers have crucified the prophet Jesus of Nazareth, whereas 'we had hoped that he was the one to redeem Israel' (24.21). The redemption of Israel has been a central theme of the Gospel of Luke from the beginning. On seeing the child Jesus, the prophetess Anna 'gave thanks to God, and spoke of him to all who were looking for the redemption of Jerusalem' (2.38). Simeon expressed the same hope in a more universal form: the child was to be 'a light for revelation to the Gentiles, and for glory to thy people Israel' (2.32). Zechariah likewise 'prophesied, saying, "Blessed be the Lord God of Israel, for he has visited and redeemed his people... as he spoke by the mouth of his holy prophets from of old, that we should be saved from our enemies and from the hand of all who hate us"' (1.67–70). The child's mother, Mary, rejoiced that God has 'put down the mighty from their thrones, and exalted those of low degree; he has filled the hungry with good things, and the rich he has sent empty away' (1.52–53). These hopes are, however, brought to an end by the crucifixion: '*we had hoped...*' – but we hope no longer. Utopian vision has again proved fragile in the face of the old world.

The situation is ripe, in other words, for the consoling gospel of Qoheleth. The two sorrowful disciples must learn to accept that what has been is what will be, and that there is nothing new under the sun. Their expectation of something new – the redemption of Israel – is the fundamental illusion which Qoheleth seeks to refute. Jesus, believing himself to be on the verge of the time of fulfilment, came to grief on the ever-rotating circle of time which ensures that whatever claims to be new is eventually disclosed as yet another repetition of what has always been. The mighty remain firmly upon their thrones, the lowly remain lowly, the rich are filled and the hungry are sent empty away – and that, for better or worse, is the way that the world is, has been and ever shall be. Yet (Qoheleth might continue) the abandonment of hope is not without its consolations. It enables one to seek enjoyment in the limited but real sphere in which enjoyment is to be found – in eating, drinking, dancing and embracing. It offers the satisfaction of an illusionless relation to reality. It finds a certain calm dignity in 'the still, sad music of humanity'. The world that actually exists, as opposed to the illusory world of the prophetic future, is a place of twilight and ambiguity in which Truth is inaccessible. But we are offered times of enjoyment as well as sorrow, and contemplation of the whole in the light of an unknown eternity discloses an austere, rarefied beauty to the sensitive onlooker.

This sentimental agnosticism is, of course, entirely alien to the Lucan narrative. The unknown stranger is not a disciple of Qoheleth and does not try to persuade the disciples to see anything beautiful in the brutal, unredeemed world in which the powerful and rich exploit and oppress the lowly and hungry. In the light of the gospel, nothing could be more illusory than the consolations of Qoheleth's celebrated 'realism'. The only possible consolation in the face of the tears of the oppressed is the gospel's promise that the conditions that produce those tears will be fundamentally changed: 'Blessed are you that weep now, for you shall laugh... Woe to you that laugh now, for you shall weep' (Luke 6.21, 25). In announcing that the law and the prophets bear witness to the death and resurrection of the Christ, the stranger asserts that this promise and this threat were not made in vain. Jesus' mission of preaching good news to the poor and setting at liberty those who are oppressed (4.18) has not come to an end, but, on the contrary, assumes in his death and resurrection its intended, definitive form. There are therefore grounds for hope that the future will not eternally repeat the past but will ultimately issue in an event in which all things are made new and in which human community (symbolized by the city descending from heaven) is perfected. Jesus departs, but his departure now issues not in the extinction but in the renewal of hope: for 'heaven must receive [him] until the time for the establishing of all [*apokatastaseōs pantōn*] that God spoke by the mouth of his holy prophets from of old' (Acts 3.21). In anticipation of that coming time, new forms of human community come into being here and now: 'All who believed were together and had all things in common; and they sold their possessions and goods and distributed them to all, as any had need' (Acts 2.44–45; cf. 4.32). Hope engenders *agapē*, and, conversely, the discovery of the power of the Spirit in the transformation of human community reinforces and gives shape to hope.

We here encounter the reality of the risen Christ and the *koinōnia* of the Holy Spirit in textual form. Can we be satisfied with a purely textual reality, or must we assert an intratextual *realism*, that is, the irreducibly textual mediation of realities that nevertheless precede and transcend their textual embodiment? In the former case, the text's promise of a perfecting of human community would be unrelated to reality outside the world of the text. The text would offer a temporary refuge from hopelessness, enabling us to *imagine* a hope, but no more than that. If, however, the text is speaking about *reality*, it offers grounds for the hope that in the praxis of love of neighbour the content of the eschatological, future kingdom of God is already disclosed and realized in anticipatory fashion.

Chapter 16

Resurrection, Text and Truth

In the preceding chapter, it emerged that the issue of hope is especially sharply focused in the events of Jesus' death and resurrection, which also form the immediate occasion for the coming into being of the new *koinōnia* at Pentecost. But, at least since the time of Reimarus, the gospel resurrection narratives have often seemed a thoroughly insecure foundation for any theological construction. It is one thing to assert the desirability of a theological hermeneutic of intratextual realism, but it is quite another to show that such a hermeneutic can issue in a persuasive interpretation of texts whose relation to reality is so deeply problematic. Where a theme such as 'love of neighbour' is under discussion, a certain relation to extra-textual reality is guaranteed; the 'neighbour' is, after all, not simply a textual construct. But what of those texts which speak of entities which seem to offer no obvious point of contact with known, extra-textual reality? One might interpret the gospel resurrection narratives from a historical-critical perspective, tracing the diachronic development of the tradition; or one might interpret them synchronically as self-contained narrative worlds. But how is it possible to understand them as interpretations of *reality*? Without the postulate of a relation to extra-textual reality, the trinitarian hermeneutic and interpretative practice I have sought to develop in earlier chapters becomes a futile playing with words. Whether one is merely indulging in word-play is not always within the interpreter's control, but the reading that follows of parts of Luke 24 tries to find further ways of incorporating the text/reality problematic more explicitly into interpretative practice.

What was it that turned disillusion and perplexity, which according to Luke persisted through most of Easter day, into hope-filled community? Luke's answer is not an idiosyncratic novelty but that of the New Testament as a whole: 'Whether it was I or they, so we preach...' (1 Cor.15.11).[1] In attempting to follow this answer, we are therefore not committing ourselves merely to a single text or author but exploring the logic of the general early Christian assumption that 'if Christ has not been raised then our preaching (*kerygma*) is vain and… your faith is futile (*mataia*)' (1 Cor. 15.14, 17). This hypothetical futility would lend further support to the rival *kerygma* which offers the consolation of a universal futility (*mataiotēs*) and hopelessness (Eccles. 1.2). But if the confession that 'in fact Christ has been raised from the dead' (1 Cor. 15.20) has any truth in it and does not deceive us, then the rival gospel is itself exposed as untruthful and deceiving. The early Christian confession of the risen Christ takes the form not of a generalized, agreed statement but of the particular testimonies of particular witnesses, so that here too we must seek the universal only in the particular.[2] How then does the Gospel according to Luke represent the genesis of faith in the risen Lord, and with it the renewal of hope and love?

As depicted in Luke's final chapter, the dawning of faith on Easter Day was anything but straightforward. A straightforward narrative would perhaps take its cue from Jesus' command to Simon Peter, 'When you have turned again, strengthen your brethren' (Luke 22.32). On Easter eve, in fulfilment of this command, Peter stands up in the midst of the sorrowing disciples and says: 'Remember how he told us, while he was still in Galilee, that the Son of man must be delivered into the hands of sinful men, and be crucified, *and on the third day rise*' (cf. Luke 24.6–7). The disciples agree, reluctantly perhaps, to his suggestion that they accompany him to the tomb in order to watch, for the third day is at hand. As dawn approaches, there is an earthquake, a great angel descends and rolls away the stone (cf. Matt. 28.2), and suddenly Jesus is before them in all his glory, his countenance altered and his raiment dazzling white (cf. Luke 9.29). Early Christian narrators had the resources at their disposal for telling such a story. But they did not tell it, for this story would not have been *true* story – in the empirical sense that the events it narrates did not happen, but above all in the profounder theological sense that it would untruthfully represent faith in the risen Christ as originating in an unmediated experience of the resurrection event itself. Faith is always a mediated knowledge. Even and especially on Easter Day, a particular way must be trodden before faith can come into being.

According to Luke, that way was shortest for the women, of whom Mary Magdalene, Joanna and Mary the mother of James are named (24.10). They did not behold the resurrection, despite visiting the tomb at early dawn, but they did experience a vision of angels who, rather than announcing Jesus' resurrection directly, asked why they were seeking the living among the dead and exhorted them to remember his earlier words about his dying and rising again (24.1–7). However, their report to the disciples met with disbelief. The account of the vision was dismissed as nonsense (*lēros*), a futile attempt to compel reality to conform to one's desires; and the emptiness of the tomb (which Peter was able to confirm) evoked only perplexity at the strange and distressing fact that Jesus' corpse had undoubtedly disappeared (24.10–12, cf.vv. 22–24). As yet, in other words, there was no framework available within which the message of Jesus' resurrection would make sense. It is for this reason that the two disciples on the way to Emmaus are represented as not recognizing the traveller who joined them on the road – not because he appeared to them 'in another form' (*en hetera morphē*), as the longer ending of Mark claims in an attempt to summarize the Lucan narrative (Mark 16.12), but because the conditions were not yet in place within which faith becomes a possibility. The statement that 'their eyes were kept from recognizing him' (Luke 24.16) stems ultimately not from the evangelist's narrative artistry (although that is certainly present) but from his understanding of faith. Faith in the risen Christ originated and originates not in unmediated experience but through the mediation of holy scripture.[3] According to the earliest Christian preaching accessible to us, Christ died for our sins in accordance with the scriptures, was buried, and was raised on the third day – again, *in accordance with the scriptures* (1 Cor. 15.3–5). Thus, in response to the two disciples' expression of sorrowful perplexity, the unrecognized Jesus did not simply make himself recognizable but engaged in scriptural interpretation, saying to them, '"O foolish people, slow of heart to believe all that the prophets have spoken! Was it not necessary that the Christ should suffer these things and enter into his glory?" And beginning with Moses and all the prophets, he interpreted to them in all the scriptures the things concerning himself' (24.25–26).

The disciples' earlier hope that the prophet Jesus 'was the one to redeem Israel' (24.21) was itself mediated by holy scripture and was not merely the product of unmediated experience of Jesus, his words and his deeds. Jesus became the bearer of their hope by way of the prophetic witness to the future redemption of Israel:

> On this mountain the Lord of Hosts will prepared a banquet of rich fare for all the peoples, a banquet of wines well-matured... On this mountain the Lord will swallow up the veil that covers all the peoples, the shroud that enwraps all the nations; he will swallow up death for ever. Then the Lord God will wipe away the tears from every face and remove the reproach of his people from the whole earth. (Isa. 25.6–8)

The two disciples' experience of the failure of the prophetic hope cast them back into the comfortless realization that Israel was still unredeemed and would remain so for the foreseeable future. It was therefore the role of the unrecognized interpreter of holy scripture to show them that they already possessed, in the experiences of today, yesterday and the day before, the key to the renewal of their scripturally-grounded hope which would set that hope for the first time on a firm, unshakeable foundation. They have already spoken of a case of unjust suffering and death, and of an alleged vision suggesting that this death and the accompanying injustice have been overcome (24.19–24). Is it not possible that precisely these events point to a divine act in which the linear movement of holy scripture towards a comprehensive, universal conclusion is resumed and given definitive shape? The movement of the beginning of the story, from the creation which the Creator pronounced very good to the entry of death and other evils into this good creation, would then be matched by a movement from a decisive, divine–human victory over death towards an ending in which 'the creation itself will be set free from its bondage to decay and obtain the glorious liberty of the children of God' (Rom.8.21). A possible symmetry begins to emerge: 'As by a man came death, by a man also has come the resurrection of the dead' (1 Cor.15.21). The resurrection of this man already signals in advance the ending of the story, for he is 'the first fruits of those who have fallen asleep' (15.20). The death and resurrection of Jesus Christ is thus one way in which the narrative thread running through the law and the prophets might reach a conclusion that corresponds to the universal horizons with which they open. Having momentarily glimpsed the risen Christ, the disciples recall how their hearts burned within them 'while he talked to us on the road, while he opened to us the scriptures' (Luke 24.32). The fire is the light and warmth of the dawning of faith in the resurrection, understood not as an isolated marvel but within the comprehensive context established by holy scripture.

The scriptural story *can* be completed in this way, but if it is, is it a true story? Or are we speaking purely about an enclosed textual world in which judgements about truth and falsehood are inadmissible? There are elements in the Lucan narrative which resist a restricted hermeneutic of enclosure. In representing the disciples' initial assessment of the women's report as 'nonsense' and as incredible (24.11), the narrative thematizes the issue of its own relation to the truth. If it does not bear witness to the truth, then it too is deluded nonsense. It is truthful, or it is deceitful; it testifies faithfully to the purpose and action of the one God, or it misrepresents God; it guides its readers into the truth, or it leads them astray. In other words, this narrative knows of no middle way between a purely negative and a purely positive judgement upon itself. To speak with sensitivity and insight about its literary artistry, but to refuse to go beyond that, is to evade the stark either–or that this narrative poses to all of its readers. If Christ has not been raised, then this story is worthless, and so too is a faith that corresponds to it (cf. 1 Cor. 15.14).

The emphasis here on the corporeality of the risen Lord can be interpreted in a similar manner. Jesus' mere presence was not in itself sufficient to create faith. When he appeared in the midst of his disciples, 'they were startled and frightened, and supposed that they saw a spirit' (Luke 24.37). The difference between Jesus and a spirit is that he has hands and feet, flesh and bones, and is capable – even in his risen form – of eating fish (24.39–43). But if this risen Jesus is *purely* the creation of the narrator, then he is a being not of flesh and bones but of words, incorporeal as a spirit. In other words, to read this narrative as self-enclosed is to fall prey to precisely the docetism that it so emphatically opposes. A docetic reading of an anti-docetic text can hardly be carried through without an overt or covert interpretative violence which the text will continue to resist. The corporeality of the risen Lord implies his refusal to be bound within the constraints of textuality. Indeed, holy scripture bears witness to him precisely as one who transcends it and lies beyond its limits. It is written that the Christ should suffer and on the third day rise from the dead (24.46), but this writing is empty and deceitful without persons and events, occupying a particular time and place, to fill it and to correspond to it. And if those persons and events and that time and space are again enclosed within the textuality of the written gospel, this new writing relates the corporeality and historicity of the risen Christ to the corporeal and historical existence of the church in its mission to the world: for repentance and forgiveness of sins are to be preached in Christ's name to all nations, beginning from Jerusalem (24.47). Participation in the church, within the world, is the context within which this text seeks to be read. Only here does it show itself to be truth rather than non-sense, truth not only in itself but also in its ability to make sense of that which is otherwise senseless. In speaking of the risen Christ's commission to the apostles and to the church to proclaim a message of repentance and forgiveness to all nations, the text refers us to the reality and the hope of new modes of human community, stemming from the life, death and resurrection of Jesus Christ and moving towards the eschatological perfecting of community.

An interpretative practice working within the world of the text may offer many insightful observations about the workings of that world. But it will tell us nothing at all about the one thing that actually matters, the relation of that imagined world to reality. If it wishes to engage responsibly in theological construction, biblical interpretation must therefore abandon the myth of the self-enclosed text and learn to correlate the text with the reality to which it bears witness, understanding the text as located primarily within the church which is itself located within the world. Interpretation must take the more demanding but also more rewarding way of *seeking to discern the truth* mediated in the texts of holy scripture. And it must not be deterred by the scepticism that such a project is sure to evoke.

Notes

Introduction

1. See S. Moore, *Literary Criticism and the Gospels*; A. Thiselton, *New Horizons in Hermeneutics*.

2. 'The *explanation* of a work is always sought in the man or woman who produced it, as if it were always in the end, through the more or less transparent allegory of the fiction, the voice of a single person' (R. Barthes, 'The Death of the Author', in *Image–Music–Text*, 142–8; 143). 'To give a text an Author is to impose a limit on that text, to furnish it with a final signified, to close the writing' (147). According to M. Foucault, 'The author is not an indefinite source of significations which fill a work; the author does not precede the works; he is a certain functional principle by which, in our culture, one limits, excludes, and chooses; in short, by which one impedes the free circulation, the free manipulation, the free composition, decomposition and recomposition of fiction. In fact, if we are accustomed to presenting the author as a genius, as a perpetual surging of invention, it is because, in reality, we make him function in precisely the opposite fashion... The author is therefore the ideological figure by which one marks the manner in which we fear the proliferation of meaning' ('What is an Author?', in *The Foucault Reader*, 101–20; 118–19).

3. 'What is fixed in writing has detached itself from the contingency of its origin and its author and made itself free for new relationships' (H.-G. Gadamer, *Truth and Method*, 357). 'Writing is not simply a matter of the material fixation of discourse; for fixation is the condition of a much more fundamental phenomenon, that of the autonomy of the text' (P. Ricoeur, *Hermeneutics and the Human Sciences*, 91).

4. In his *Treatise on the Free Investigation of the Canon* (1771–75, four volumes), J. S. Semler emphasized the public, ecclesial role of the canon in such a way as to deny its authority for the individual Christian reader. Since the fourth and fifth centuries, 'The Canon or list of public documents of the Christians has not been subjected to any further objection or doubt by Catholics. The primary reason for this, however, is the common agreement of the bishops who, especially in the Occident, fixed and ordered for all time, by express church laws, what books of the so-called Old and New Testament were to stand in the official list or canon and were now to be read in public. However..., all thoughtful readers are free to undertake the special investigation of these books, so far as their private use of them is concerned, and this right cannot be abrogated by a canon that was introduced for public use' (in W. G. Kümmel, *The New Testament: History of the Investigation of its Problems*, 165). Semler here assumes the priority of the individual reader over the ecclesial community. But insofar as the individual reader is Christian, he or she is formed *within* the ecclesial community, not in opposition to it.

5. The sufficiency of the reading of the biblical text is asserted by Richard Hooker on the basis of an objectivizing view of scriptural inspiration: 'Reading doth convey to the mind the

295

truth without addition or diminution, which Scripture hath derived from the Holy Ghost' (*Laws of Ecclesiastical Polity*, 5.22.6). Hooker is arguing against Puritans who, by 'overvaluing their sermons... make the price and estimation of Scripture otherwise notified to fall' (5.22.7), and who dislike 'the *bare* reading... even of Scriptures themselves' (5.21.1). Such people claim that salvation through the word of God ordinarily occurs 'as the same is *preached*, that is to say, *explained by lively voice*, and *applied* to the people's use *as the speaker in his wisdom* thinketh meet' (5.21.1). Hooker here relegates the doctrine of the Spirit to the margins where, in Anglican theology, it has tended to remain ever since.

6. This essential link between the ecclesial reading of scripture and its interpretation in preaching is already noted by Justin. The church being gathered, 'the memoirs of the apostles or the writings of the prophets are read, as long as time permits; then, when the reader has ceased, the president verbally instructs and exhorts to the imitation of these good things' (*First Apology*, 67).

7. Compare Frances Young's discussion of the hermeneutical significance of the 'rule of faith' in Irenaeus (*The Art of Performance*, 45–54).

8. Evans' statements are quoted here as illustrative of a particular ethos, and may not adequately represent his own views. In the introduction to his book he speaks of having learned from E. C. Hoskyns that, 'as an academic discipline in the universities, theology was in the last resort a function of the church' (*Explorations in Theology 2*, ix). But why only 'in the last resort'?

9. 'Either theology is an academic field or discipline essentially like every other and, therefore, bound by the same principles of academic freedom and institutional autonomy; or else, being an exception to these principles, theology has no moral right to be reckoned on a par with the other academic fields and disciplines and, therefore, is not an integral part of the university' (S. Ogden, 'Theology in the University: The Question of Integrity', 74).

10. Compare Christoph Schwöbel's understanding of systematic theology as the self-explication of Christian faith: 'The need for the self-explication of Christian faith arises out of the concrete experience of dissensus in the Christian community concerning the interpretation of the forms and contents of Christian faith... The task of systematic theology in this situation of dissensus is to propose a new consensus in the community of believers which reaffirms the foundation of that community in such a way that the difficulties which called the old consensus into question can be resolved' (*God: Action and Revelation*, 13).

11. If a reader of scripture 'sees only an empty spot at the place to which the biblical writers point', then 'there can be no question of a legitimate understanding of the Bible by this reader... There can be no question of his exegesis being equally justified with one which is based upon the real substance of the Bible, divine revelation' (K. Barth, *Church Dogmatics*, I, 2, 469).

12. 'In the incarnation of the Son the Trinity throws itself open, as it were. The Father of the Son becomes the Father of the new, free and united human race. Through the brotherhood of the Son God's children enter into the trinitarian relations of the Son, the Father and the Spirit. As people in the world, they simultaneously exist "in God" and "God in them"' (J. Moltmann, *The Trinity and the Kingdom of God*, 121–22; italics removed).

13. There is a related problem in the emphasis on personal 'appropriation' of the biblical texts as the goal of the reading or interpretative process. Here, the individual and the texts together constitute an enclosed, self-sufficient world, and the ecclesial and theological dimensions are neglected. This hermeneutic is closely related to Ricoeur's claim that 'the interpretation of a text culminates in the self-interpretation of a subject who henceforth understands himself better, understands himself differently, or simply begins to understand himself' (*Hermeneutics and the Human Sciences*, 158).

14. Compare G. Ebeling's well-known article on 'The Significance of the Critical Historical Method for Church and Theology in Protestantism' (*Word and Faith*, 17–61), in which biblical criticism's shattering of historical certainties is presented as the consistent outworking of the Reformation's antitheses of word rather than tradition, faith rather than good works (56–57). This use of Reformation categories to interpret the radical/conservative polarity derives, via Bultmann, from W. Herrmann, for whom a conservative Protestant view of the Bible is a 'sacrilege that makes a law out of this gift of God's grace' (*The Communion of the Christian with God*, 3).

Part One   The Autonomous Text

1. In distinguishing a theological interpretation from the canonical approach, I am in partial agreement with James Barr's claim that the latter is not yet properly 'theological', since it 'remains immanent within the contours of the text' and 'does not attempt to wrestle with the question of *truth*' (*Holy Scripture: Canon, Authority, Criticism*, 102).

1. Narrative and Reality

1. R. Morgan notes that 'histories of biblical scholarship are… sometimes presented as the progressive elimination of religious influence' (*Biblical Interpretation*, 27). See, for example, W. G. Kümmel, *The New Testament: The History of the Investigation of its Problems*, which begins as follows: 'It is impossible to speak of a scientific view of the New Testament until the New Testament became the object of investigation as an independent body of literature with historical interest, as a collection of writing that could be considered apart from the Old Testament and without dogmatic or creedal bias. Since such a view began to prevail only during the course of the eighteenth century, earlier discussion of the New Testament can only be referred to as the prehistory of New Testament scholarship' (13).

2. If we accept this idea of a linear movement from the old to the new, the moment of transition is illustrated by Spinoza's discussion of the scriptural miracles in his *Tractatus Theologico–Politicus* (1670). At certain points Spinoza uses the traditional notion of 'accommodation', according to which scriptural anthropomorphisms and other solecisms are employed out of consideration for the weakness of human faculties. Thus, 'Scripture does not explain things by their secondary causes, but only narrates them in the order and the style which has most power to move men, and especially uneducated men, to devotion; and therefore it speaks inaccurately of God and of events, seeing that its object is not to convince the reason, but to attract and lay hold of the imagination' (91). At other points, however, Spinoza begins to engage in historically-oriented criticism of the text itself. Thus, the alleged miracle in which 'the sun stayed in the midst of heaven, and did not hasten to go down for about a whole day' (Josh. 10.13) stems from the Hebrews' false opinion 'that the sun moves with a daily motion, and that the earth remains at rest' (93). The text is itself fully implicated in the error; it does not simply accommodate itself to that error.

3. 'We must diligently investigate what in the books of the New Testament was said as an accommodation to the ideas or the needs of the first Christians and what was said in reference to the unchanging idea of the doctrine of salvation' (J. P. Gabler, 'An Oration on the Proper Distinction between Biblical and Dogmatic Theology' (1787), 142–3). The Mosaic rituals and the Pauline injunctions about the veiling of women illustrate the fact that the significance of 'the great part of these books' is restricted 'to a particular time, place, and sort of man' (142).

4. For this view of Frei, see G. W. Stroup, *The Promise of Narrative Theology*, 142.

5. Frei is here (as elsewhere) developing Barthian themes, on which see D. H. Kelsey, *The Uses of Scripture in Modern Theology*, 39–50.

6. Frei's emphasis on the irreducibility of narrative is closely related to George Lindbeck's on the irreducibility of religious language. Lindbeck opposes what he calls the 'experiential–expressivist' view that 'experience of a certain kind... has a prior reality that necessarily expresses and fulfills itself in objective cultural and religious forms' (*The Nature of Doctrine*, 35), asserting to the contrary that 'human experience is shaped, molded, and in a sense constituted by cultural and linguistic forms' (34). The experiential–expressivist view leads to precisely the hermeneutic that Frei opposes, according to which one must penetrate the surface of the narrative to recover the experience that underlies it. Lindbeck's distinction between the 'cultural–linguistic' and the 'propositional' views may be compared to Frei's insistence that a 'realistic' or 'history-like' narrative does not necessarily correspond to empirical historical reality. When Lindbeck writes that 'intratextual theology redescribes reality within the scriptural framework rather than translating Scripture into extrascriptural categories' (118), the proximity to Frei is still more obvious. Conversely, in seeing church and faith as approximating to a culture or a linguistic system (*Types of Christian Theology*, 12–14), Frei comes close to Lindbeck. (On Lindbeck, see chapter 7.)

7. According to George Hunsinger, all this implies a relatively low christology, perhaps contrary to Frei's intentions: 'The union between God and Jesus as it emerges from the intention–action description is much more nearly moral than personal' ('Hans Frei as Theologian', 116).

8. Frei's position here is related to Barth's approach to the resurrection narratives, summarized as follows by George Hunsinger: 'Given this understanding of legendary text ("imaginative response"), referent ("real though incomprehensible, incomprehensible though real"), and their semantic relation ("analogy combining reticence and predication"), Barth felt justified in simply concentrating on the text itself' ('Beyond Literalism and Expressivism', 212). The incomprehensible reality of the referent throws one back upon the text, although conversely it is only the relation to an extra-textual referent that gives the text any significance.

9. In his posthumous *Types of Christian Theology*, Frei again insists that realistic or literal reading of the text is 'a logically different matter' to the question of its relation to extra-textual reality. We may wish to understand the text's referential dimension 'analogically rather than literally, or perhaps we may want to say its truth is something else yet, rather than a matter of its corresponding, either identically or analogically, with "reality"' (84). This might be seen as an example of the 'modesty' which, according to Paul Schwarzentruber, is a central characteristic of Frei's theological and hermeneutical position. 'Frei's modesty might be treated as a theological virtue, the postmodern theological virtue' ('The Modesty of Hermeneutics', 182). But perhaps this modesty is excessive?

10. This point led Frei to oppose David Tracy's claim, in *The Analogical Imagination*, 233–304 and elsewhere, that the biblical texts are to be understood with the aid of the general category of the 'classic'. According to K. Vanhoozer (summarizing Frei), 'Tracy's subsuming the Gospel narratives under the hermeneutic category "classic" has implications for theology as well as hermeneutics. If the Gospels disclose a universal truth about general human experience, what is the special significance of Jesus Christ?... "Jesus" functions no longer as the name for the principal character in a story about him, but rather as a label for a particular mode of consciousness, a possibility of self-understanding' (*Biblical Narrative in the Philosophy of Paul Ricoeur*, 159–60). Justified concern over this latter danger must, however, be accompanied by an awareness that 'the special significance of Jesus Christ' is also questionable if the gospels do *not* in some sense 'disclose a universal truth about general human experience'.

11. According to David Ford, Frei 'arrived eventually at the beginnings of a first-order *political* theology' ('Hans Frei and the Future of Theology', 208). But there seem few signs of this in his major published work.

12. Thus Stephen Prickett finds that Frei is unclear about 'the degree to which… prose realism is itself a highly problematic convention' (*Words and the Word*, 194).

13. As R. Scholes and R. Kellogg note, 'Auerbach's single-minded devotion to realistic principles leaves him unwilling or unable to come to terms with twentieth-century fiction, and especially with such writers as Virginia Woolf, Proust, and Joyce' (*The Nature of Narrative*, 5). For an influential attack on the privileging of realism, see W. C. Booth, *The Rhetoric of Fiction*, 23–64.

14. This analysis of Frei would be rejected by K. Vanhoozer, for whom he 'is not a narrativist if by this we mean someone who builds an epistemology or an ontology of human being on a narrative substructure', but a theologian 'who is seeking to understand the Christian faith, particularly its central narrative expression, on its own terms. That these terms happen to be narrative does not make Frei a narrative theologian…' (*Biblical Narrative in the Thought of Paul Ricoeur*, 178). Frei is indeed interested in the Gospels rather than the ontology of human being, but precisely this interest in the Gospels necessitates (rudimentary) ontological claims about narrative and identity.

2. Canon and Community

1. Compare E. D. Hirsch's claim that 'there can be only one sort of norm when interpretation is conceived of as a corporate enterprise', and that on purely practical grounds the author's meaning must be that norm (*Validity in Interpretation*, 25). Hirsch's distinction between a fixed 'meaning' and shifting assessments of 'significance' is closely related to Stendahl's 'what it meant' and 'what it means' (although in Hirsch's terminology 'meaning' is unchanging). Meaning and significance correspond to two modes of reading: 'Significance is the proper object of criticism, not of interpretation, whose exclusive object is verbal meaning' (57).

2. Stendahl's position echoes J. P. Gabler's plea for the separation of 'biblical theology' from 'dogmatic theology' ('On the Proper Distinction between Biblical and Dogmatic Theology' (1787)). W. Wrede similarly argued that New Testament theology ought to be indifferent to systematic theology and that it is not the role of the theologian to 'serve the church' ('The Task and Methods of "New Testament Theology" (1897), 69, 72–3).

3. Against this conventional view, R. Morgan rightly emphasizes that theological interpretation begins not where historical research ceases, but with the texts (*Biblical Interpretation*, 185). Morgan also notes that 'one effect of the new interest in theory across several disciplines has been to make nonsense of the old prejudice that such wider concerns are somehow "unscholarly"' (250).

4. Similar assertions in his *Old Testament Theology in Canonical Context* (1985) indicate the single-mindedness and consistency with which Childs has developed his hermeneutical programme and the corresponding critique of the historical–critical paradigm. Speaking of the importance of the discipline of Old Testament theology, Childs writes: 'Attention to the Old Testament within a theological discipline provides a major check against the widespread modern practice of treating it solely from a philological, historical or literary perspective. The inability of most systematic theologians to make much sense of the Old Testament stems in part from the failure of the biblical specialists to render it in a way which is not theologically mute' (17).

5. Compare Gadamer's understanding of the 'classical': 'The classical is what resists

historical criticism because its historical dominion, the binding power of its validity that is preserved and handed down, precedes all historical reflection and continues through it' (*Truth and Method*, 255). 'Historical objectivism, in appealing to its critical method, conceals the involvement of the historical consciousness itself in effective-history' (268).

6. Childs himself emphasizes this point: 'The approach which is being proposed is not to be confused with homiletics, but is descriptive in nature' (*Old Testament*, 14). With regard to the New Testament too, 'it belongs to the descriptive task to analyse the particular shape and function of this literature in relation to the community of faith which treasured and fashioned it' (*New Testament*, 37). James Barr's objection that canonical critics demand religious commitment, whereas in fact 'anyone, whether religious or not, can do canonical criticism' (*Holy Scripture*, 111) is thus beside the point, at least as regards Childs.

7. These insights also enable Childs to reformulate the concept of the 'literal' sense of scripture. Childs shares Frei's opposition to the view that critical exegesis operates in continuity with the Reformation in this respect, arguing that the literal sense loses all significance when its role is 'to provide a way behind the text to some historical reality' ('The Sensus Literalis of Scripture', 90). 'Whereas during the medieval period the crucial issue lay in the usage made of the multiple layers of meaning *above* the text, the issue now turns on the multiple layers *below* the text. The parallel consists in threats from both directions to undermine the literal sense of the biblical text' (92). The true literal sense is 'the plain sense witnessed to by the community of faith' (92).

8. 'The lure of the source…: to become again present to oneself, to come back to oneself, to find again, along with the pure limpidity of water, the always effective mirage of the point of emergence, the instant of welling up, the fountain or well surnamed Truth, which always speaks in order to say I' (J. Derrida, *Margins of Philosophy*, 277).

9. On a canonical approach to the gospels, see also R. W. Wall and E. E. Lemcio, *The New Testament as Canon*, 33–6.

10. This normative language (also freely employed by Childs) might be criticized on the grounds that, since 'the discipline encompasses different kinds of interpretative tasks', the canonical approach must be rescued from its own 'totalitarian tendency' through relocation in a pluralist context (M. Brett, *Biblical Criticism in Crisis?*, 6). But Brett also notes (at the end of his book) that 'pluralism is not an end in itself. A variety of interpretative interests may be intelligible and permissible, but not all will be edifying to the Christian community. We are in need of some attention to the ethics of interpretation' (167). These comments qualify Brett's advocacy of *laissez faire* pluralism, and re-open the possibility that the normative dimension in Childs' programme might be defensible after all.

11. John Barton criticizes the assumption, exemplified here, that critical study distances us from the biblical texts, arguing that 'the gap becomes a *problem* only if we start with an exaggerated view of biblical authority' (*People of the Book?*, 66). But, here and elsewhere, Childs' account is primarily descriptive and can thus be taken seriously even by those who question his view of biblical authority.

12. The generalized historicity of the biblical text (that is, their historic canonical role) would look somewhat different if the canon were understood as relativizing the barriers that separate one biblical text from another, thus making possible a network of intertextual relations. Northrop Frye is as concerned as Childs that the Bible should not be seen merely as 'a scrapbook of corruptions, glosses, redactions, insertions, conflations, misplacings and misunderstandings', but wishes to substitute for all this not a series of discrete canonical texts but 'the traditional typologies based on the assumption of its [the Bible's] figurative unity' (*Anatomy of Criticism* (1957), 315). 'A genuine higher criticism of the Bible, therefore, would be a synthetizing process which would start with the assumption that the Bible is a

definitive myth, a single archetypal structure extending from creation to apocalypse. Its heuristic principle would be St. Augustine's axiom that the Old Testament is revealed in the New and the New concealed in the Old' (315; cf. *The Great Code* (1982)). In maintaining the distinctness of the biblical books, Childs retains one of the crucial innovations of the historical–critical method, and this makes is difficult to speak of the shape of the canonical text as a whole.

13. So M. Brett, *Biblical Criticism in Crisis?*, 92.

14. James Barr argues that Childs' case is 'excessively dependent on one particular element, namely the contrast between the weaknesses and antinomies of historical criticism on the one hand and the virtues of the canonical reading on the other' (*Holy Scripture*, 160). 'Childs's valuation of traditional critical scholarship is almost exactly the same as the valuation attached to it by conservative/fundamentalist circles'; thus, 'the opening of this possibility is likely to have a strong pro-conservative effect' (148). The perceived political requirements of the conflict with fundamentalism lead Barr to claim dogmatically that 'new possibilities are likely to be fruitful only if they take up within themselves the fruits and the insights of the preceding period' (125). The careful, consistent working out of Childs' hermeneutical proposal over against certain of the assumptions and priorities of the historical–critical tradition is, in fact, precisely what makes it interesting.

15. Compare Mark Brett's suggestion that the canonical approach should be aligned with descriptive 'formalist literary approaches', and that 'there are good *theological* reasons for relieving the canonical approach of excessive theological claims' (*Biblical Theology in Crisis?*, 166). Formalist approaches, however, have little place for the communal dimension that is so important to Childs, as he himself notes (*Old Testament*, 74).

16. J. A. Sanders, referring to Childs' emphasis on the final canonical redaction, argues that 'to dissociate it [the text] from history altogether as though that final canonical redaction has a timeless theology in mind for all generations and centuries to come is unrealistic' (*From Sacred Story to Sacred Text*, 170). Against this emphasis on a final, frozen state, Sanders claims that 'the primary character of canon or authoritative tradition… is its adaptability' (83). Even after the text was stabilized, 'other types of hermeneutic arose to break it open for application to new circumstances to derive light from it and to find life in it' (170). Sanders fails to recognize that a description of the formal features of the canonical redaction can legitimately be undertaken in relative independence of the history of interpretation. Yet a problem does arise when Childs ascribes theological normativity and sufficiency to the canonical object so described.

17. This reading of Childs broadly accepts the descriptive level of his work but criticizes the theological claim that the text is fully adequate for the task of communal guidance, which ignores its actual historical functioning as an ideological battleground. It is possible, however, to locate the moment of concealment not in a particular protestant doctrine of scripture, as I have done, but in the canonical process itself. Thus, referring to Childs' claim that the canonical editors obscured their own identity, Norman Gottwald argues that 'one of the prime reasons for obscuring the identity of those who advocate authoritative decisions and interpretations is to make their judgments look unquestioned and ancient, even timeless, and certainly descended from divine authority. To overlook this psychosocial reality of ideology and mystification in religious assertions, canonical assertions included, is to deliver theology into an uncritical subjection to the unexamined self-interests of canonizers' ('Social Matrix and Canonical Shape', 321, cited by M. Brett, *Biblical Criticism in Crisis?*, 150–1). If one's interest lies, as Gottwald's does, in the social functions of the texts in their original historical contexts, then this criticism of Childs might be valid. If, however, one's interest lies in the social and theological functions of the texts in our own interpretative

traditions, then hypothetical ideological conflicts within ancient Israel will seem less significant.

3. Multiplicity and Coherence

1. The choice of a source-critical example reflects the fact that for many advocates of the narrative approach source analysis is the hermeneutical key to the entire historical–critical project. See for example Alan Culpepper's contrast between an emphasis on the integrity of the whole text and historical–critical 'dissection' (*Anatomy of the Fourth Gospel*, 3). Such 'dissection' is typically contrasted with the unity said to characterize the work of art: 'If our experience leads to the conclusion that we have found an organic whole which invites us to a positive opinion of its value, we can call the text a literary work of art' (J. P. Fokkelman, *Narrative Art in Genesis* (1991²), 5n). Mark Stibbe betrays similar assumptions when he offers an outline of 'some of the literary strategies which help to give the gospel [of John] its unity and which indicate a single, artistic imagination behind the narrative' (*John the Storyteller*, 16). Harold Bloom is unusual in his acceptance of the value of (pentateuchal) source criticism for contemporary literary criticism. According to Bloom, the value of the J Hypothesis is that it makes it possible to grasp 'the vast gulf between the Yahweh of the Book of J and the God of Judaism' (*The Book of J*, 229), and still more the God of Christians. Bloom is severely critical of E, D and P, who began the process of 'strong misreadings' or 'endless misprisions' which concealed the ironies of J's text (12, 13). J was probably a woman; if this is a fiction, so too are more scholarly imaginings (9).

2. Cf. A. Berlin, *Poetics and Interpretation of Biblical Narratives*, 147.

3. The latter possibility is accepted by S. R. Driver: 'V. 21 is tautologous beside v. 22a, but forms an excellent introduction to vv. 25–27' (*Introduction*, 18).

4. According to von Rad, the Genesis redactor combined J and E material to produce 'an organically constructed narrative, no single segment of which can have existed independently as a separate element of tradition' (*Genesis*, 347). H. N. Whybray's claim that there is an inconsistency here has been widely followed: 'We are forced to make a choice in our interpretation of the Joseph story between the documentary hypothesis on the one hand and the view that it is a "novel" of genius... on the other' ('The Joseph Story and Pentateuchal Criticism', 528). Westermann agrees: 'If Gen. 37–50 is "a short story through and through", then it cannot be a synthesis of pieces from several sources' (*Genesis 37–50*, 20).

5. It is also possible to argue the reverse: that, if the inconsistencies of the Joseph narrative do not require the documentary hypothesis, then the same may be true elsewhere – in which case the hypothesis is redundant (R. Rendtorff, *The Problem of the Process of Transmission in the Pentateuch*, 109–10). Rendtorff argues that the complexes of tradition that formed around the figures of the respective patriarchs were more independent of one another than has previously been thought (177). See also T. L. Thompson, *The Origin Tradition of Ancient Israel*.

6. So Thompson, *Origin Tradition*, 116; Hugh C. White, *Narration and Discourse in the Book of Genesis*, 240.

7. A comparable example of the retrospective detachment of an individual from a group occurs in John 20.24, where we read that Thomas 'was not with them when Jesus came', although the preceding paragraph has apparently referred to the total body of 'the disciples'.

8. Robert Alter acknowledges that in particular cases the composite nature of a text may make an integrated reading difficult or impossible. Thus, 'the perplexities raised by the intertwined stories of Korah and Dathan and Abiram [Num. 16] illustrate that there are aspects of the composite nature of biblical narrative texts that we cannot confidently encompass in our own explanatory systems' (*The Art of Biblical Narrative*, 136–7).

9. Edward L. Greenstein argues that equivocation over whether the Midianites or Joseph's brothers sold him is inherent in the narrative, and that the emphasis is on the divine providence that is secretly at work (cf. 45.8): 'By blurring the human factors leading to the enslavement of Joseph, the narrative sharpens our image of the divine factor in bringing it about... One sequence of human action rivals the other, leaving only the divine manipulation of events clear and intelligible' ('An Equivocal Reading of the Sale of Joseph', 123).

10. Thompson notes that in the variants Reuben and Judah fulfil parallel roles, whereas 'in the harmonization, Judah's plan serves as a plot motif, preventing Reuben's scheme of 37.19ff from succeeding' (*Origin Tradition*, 119–20; italics removed).

11. This also implies that 'an unacceptable proportion of criteria by which scholars have dated their material in literary, form, tradition, and redaction critical studies have proven to be either invalid or vastly inadequate for the task assigned to them' (R. Polzin, *Moses and the Deuteronomist*, 13). In contrast, John Barton argues that the 'new critical' premises on which most literary criticism of the Bible rests – texts as artefacts, the rejection of intentionality, canonical context – are flawed (*Reading the Old Testament*, 158–79) and that 'biblical scholars would do well to avoid putting much weight on them' (179).

12. As Gadamer puts it, we 'must destroy the illusion that there are problems as there are stars in the sky' (*Truth and Method*, 340).

4. The Rhetoric of Oppression

1. On the other hand, K. Stendahl argues that it is 'serious attention to original intentions of text' which the Bible's status as holy scripture requires, as opposed to the enjoyment of the Bible 'in a relaxed mood as a classic' which he oddly ascribes to literary perspectives ('The Bible as Classic', 9).

2. In opposition to 'the idea of a self-sufficient text' or 'a hermetic textual cosmos', Edward Said rightly asserts that 'texts have ways of existing that even in their most rarefied form are always enmeshed in circumstance, time, place, and society – in short, they are in the world, and hence worldly' (*The World, the Text, and the Critic*, 35).

3. This does not mean that we should accept Ricoeur's claim, made in opposition to Habermas, that 'nothing is more necessary today than to renounce the arrogance of critique and to carry on with patience the endless work of distancing and renewing our historical substance' (*Hermeneutics and the Human Sciences*, 246). See T. Eagleton, *Ideology*, 1–31 for a defence of the concept of ideology.

4. An entirely different explanation of Joseph's behaviour is suggested by Laurence A. Turner. Noting that Joseph's second dream predicts that not only his brothers but also his parents will bow down before him (37.9–10), Turner argues that Joseph's conduct is an attempt to bring about the fulfilment of this aspect of his dreams. The brothers' abject submission (42.6) fulfilled only the first dream. Joseph required that Benjamin be brought to Egypt because he expected that Jacob would come too (cf. 44.22), and the incident with the silver cup is another ploy to get Jacob to Egypt after the first had failed (*Announcements of Plot in Genesis*, 161–2). In fact the dream is never fulfilled: on the contrary, in 48.12 it is Joseph who bows down before Jacob (162–3). 'The reason why this dream as a whole fails is that Joseph tried to *make* it happen through his playing God with his family' (165). If the need for Jacob (and the long-dead Rachel (cf. 35.16–20; 48.7) to bow down before Joseph is so central to the narrative, it is surprising that this topic is never explicitly mentioned. The doubling of Joseph's dream could be better explained along the lines of Gen. 41.32 as a sign of the certainty of its fulfilment, and the narrator perhaps believes that the brothers in submitting to Joseph also represent their parents.

5. Compare Meir Sternberg's comments: 'If to a listener ignorant of the family situation and record, the brothers' attitude as expressed by their leader would appear admirable, then to one in the know it surely manifests nothing short of a transformation, from subnormal to abnormal solidarity. That the sons of the hated wife should have come to terms with the father's attachment to Rachel ("my wife") and her children is enough to promise an end to hostilities and a fresh start. That the second of these children should enjoy his brothers' affection is amazing. But that Judah should adduce the father's favoritism as the ground for self-sacrifice is such an irresistible proof of filial devotion that it breaks down Joseph's last defences and leads to a perfectly Aristotelian turning point, a discovery with peripety' (*The Poetics of Biblical Narrative*, 308).

6. White sees the origin of this deterministic strand in the Joseph story in the dream report, which is 'a predeterminating rhetorical force that operates without faith on the part of the characters, and mocks the free, conscious efforts of opponents to defeat its realization by turning those very efforts into its means of actualization' (*Narration and Discourse*, 244–5). This conflicts with the narrator's employment elsewhere of the divine Voice as a representation of the power of speech to create free, intersubjective relations. In this latter theme, 'what is conveyed… is "insight" or even "revelation" of the primacy of the Word as a force in the formation of human existence and the fundamental intersubjective character of human consciousness' (103). Abram's call into 'a primary intersubjective relation, the material consequences of which, though real, are very much secondary' (112) is contrasted with the first humans' quest for an autonomy which frees them from 'all dependency for self-knowledge upon other subjects (instances of speech)' (119).

7. I have in mind here the fundamental insight of liberation theology, that 'all theology is in part a reflection of this or that concrete social process' (G. Gutiérrez, *The Power of the Poor in History*, 90), and that even an apparently good and enlightened theology may serve the interests of oppression.

8. So Westermann: God's action is directed 'not only to the family of Jacob, but also to the Egyptians' (*Genesis 37–50*, 205). 'By means of the key sentence [50.20], the author validates a universal outlook… which served a critical function in a period of strong nationalistic aspirations: he points to the creator who is concerned for all his creatures' (251). Yet the speaker in 50.20 is not 'the author' but Joseph.

9. As White notes, 'In this statement he implicitly claims access to divine knowledge, while simultaneously effacing himself before the divine so that God, rather than himself, appears to be the source of the interpretation' (*Narration and Discourse*, 257).

10. Westermann brings out this reciprocity – 'Joseph points to God's action for good in Pharaoh's dream… and Pharaoh acknowledges God's power at work in Joseph's wisdom' (*Genesis 37–50*, 99).

11. Thompson notes that 'from the perspective of the final redaction of Genesis, we are not reading the story of Joseph, but the *Toledoth* of Jacob', and that the climax of the narrative is therefore the move to Egypt in chapters 46–47 (*Origin Tradition*, 121).

12. This locating of 47.13–26 within the narrative structure of the Joseph story resolves the difficulty that von Rad finds in this section: 'The reader now loses sight of everything that has previously occupied his attention: Joseph's relationship to his brothers, to Jacob, the question of their stay in Egypt, etc.' (*Genesis*, 408). These topics are now virtually concluded.

13. Calvin concedes that 'Joseph might be deemed cruel, because he does not give bread gratuitously to those who are poor and exhausted, but robs them of all their cattle, sheep, and asses' (*Genesis*, 2.408), and can only suggest in mitigation that Joseph was not acting as a free agent but in obedience to the will of Pharoah.

14. The link between 47.24 and 41.34 is noted by Westermann, who believes that 41.34b

is a gloss interrupting the continuity between v. 34a and v. 35, 'inserted here to give the later expansion (47:13–26) a base in the advice that Joseph gives to the Pharaoh'; the taking of one-fifth is not mentioned in 41.47–49 (*Genesis 37–50*, 92–3).

15. Compare Terry Eagleton's comments on criticism in general: 'In a spiral of mutual reinforcements, the literary text naturalises experience, critical practice naturalises the text, and the theories of that practice legitimate the "naturalness" of criticism. As a meta-literary practice, a *metaphor* of the text, criticism writes large the text's inability to think the condition of its own possibility, reproducing that capacity under the guise of knowledge. Under the form of an illumination, criticism renders natural the text's necessary self-blindness' (*Criticism and Ideology*, 18).

16. I. J. Mosala speaks of 'being galvanized by the configuration of historical and social forces today to identify the nature of and to take sides in the struggles that are signified by the text' (*Biblical Hermeneutics and Black Theology in South Africa*, 11). On this view, it is crucial 'to recognize the presence of the oppressor and oppression in the text itself' (26), and the movement is thus *from* present concerns and commitments *to* the ideological functioning of the biblical texts in their original contexts in the first-century Roman empire or ancient Israel. Thus, Gen. 4 is concerned with 'a ruling-class author's attempt to validate [the] landlessness of the village peasants on the grounds – hardly convincing – that their harvest was not an acceptable offering to the Lord' (34). Even if this highly speculative reading were convincing, it is not clear what it would mean to take sides, three thousand years too late, in the struggles of Judean peasants. Analysing the text in such a way as to shed light on the *current* workings of the rhetoric of oppression seems a preferable procedure. As Clodovis Boff argues, 'the entire work of exegesis can and should be conceived as a moment in a complex process bearing upon the hearer's or reader's present moment. Now word ceases to be simply text to be interpreted, and itself becomes interpretative code' (*Theology and Praxis*, 137).

17. Von Rad makes a similar point in conventional diachronic terms. The Joseph story is in itself completely detached from covenant theology, but 'the great collector and shaper of the whole patriarchal history has finally included even the Joseph story in the theme of the promise to the patriarchs', a connection achieved above all in 46.1–5 (*Genesis*, 439). In other words, a certain distance from Joseph's perspective has already been achieved in the final form of the text.

18. The possibility that Gen. 49 'is not an original part either of the patriarchal story of the Joseph narrative' (Westermann, *Genesis 37–50*, 221) does not justify the failure to interpret it within its present context.

19. In vol. 6 of the Loeb edition, from which the translation is taken. Elsewhere, Philo is generally critical of Joseph, who 'represents Opinion with its vast medley of ingredients. For there is manifest in him, on the one hand, the rational strain of self-control, fashioned after his father Jacob; manifest, again, is the irrational strain of sense-perception, assimilated to what he derives from his mother, the part of him that is of the Rachel type; manifest also is the breed of bodily pleasure, impressed on him by association with chief butlers and chief bakers and chief cooks; manifest too is the element of vainglory, onto which as onto a chariot his empty-headedness makes him mount up, when puffed with pride he lifts himself aloft to overthrow equality from its seat' (*On Dreams*, 2.15–16 (Loeb, vol. 5).

Part Two   Theology and Postmodernism

1. See especially chapters 7 and 8 of Moore's book.
2. On Jacques Derrida, briefly evoked here, see chapter 5.

3. K. Hart, *The Trespass of the Sign*, 323.

4. According to Hart, reading Pseudo-Dionysius from within a Derridean perspective, 'Negative theology plays a role within the phenomenon of positive theology but it also shows that positive theology is situated with regard to a radical negative theology which precedes it. In short, negative theology performs the deconstruction of positive theology' (*The Trespass of the Sign*, 201–2).

5. Mark Taylor's fragment on 'The Road to Emmaus' compactly illustrates the concerns of such a practice: 'When Jesus was present, he was absent, when absent, present. Why? Because he is Word. On the road to Emmaus, Jesus' presence is absence, and his absence is presence. They see, but do not see; they hear only the silence of an empty tomb.' Their eyes are opened only as Jesus vanishes. 'And what do they see? They see his presence in absence. But to do so, they must likewise see absence in their presence' (*Deconstructing Theology*, 124). Such observations could be expanded into a full-scale deconstructive exegesis of Luke 24.

6. On Lyotard, see chapter 7. An adequate 'map' of poststructuralist theory would have to account for many other theoretical practices (Foucault, 'new historicism', and so on) which do not fit within this distinction.

7. On the importance of the metaphors of 'depth' and 'surface' for postmodernism, see F. Jameson, *Postmodernism*, 12.

8. Paul Feyerabend gives characteristic expression to this postmodern ethic: 'People all over the world have developed ways of surviving in partly dangerous, partly agreeable surroundings. The stories they told and the activities they engaged in enriched their lives, protected them and gave them meaning. The "progress of knowledge and civilization" – as the process of pushing Western ways and values into all corners of the globe is being called – destroyed these wonderful products of human ingenuity and compassion without a single glance in their direction.' While a science adapted to human values is gradually developing, 'I am against ideologies that use the name of science for cultural murder' (*Against Method*, 3–4).

9. On the theological programme of George Lindbeck, see chapter 7 below.

10. 'The entities postulated by science… are *shaped* by special groups, cultures, civilizations; and they are shaped from a material which, depending on its treatment, provides us with gods, spirits, a nature that is a partner of humans rather than a laboratory for their experiments, or with quarks, fields, molecules, tectonic plates' (P. Feyerabend, *Against Method*, 260).

11. Deconstruction is also criticized on political grounds, with some justification. J. B. Metz claims that the postmodern celebration of a 'mythical polytheism', which 'is said to guarantee an innocent multiplicity of life', produces 'a voyeuristic attitude towards social and political crises' and therefore calls into question 'the substance of the Judeo–Christian religion' ('Theology in the Struggle for History and Society', 170). See also Terry Eagleton's study of 'Frère Jacques: The Politics of Deconstruction' in *Against the Grain*, 79–87, and his discussion of postmodernism in *The Ideology of the Aesthetic*, 373–415. David Jobling, who wishes to set the deconstruction of the biblical text in the context of liberation theologies and who believes in 'the political importance of what has been happening within literature departments', acknowledges the gulf between theoretical discourse and the concern with political praxis that he finds in the seminary ('Writing the Wrongs of the World', 92, 96). While Jobling is right to complain that 'complex debate on literary method has simply been outside the perspective of liberation biblical studies' (96), the solutions he offers are inadequate. He argues that those who work for political change need to learn from Foucault and Derrida that 'we are so much part of the system (or it of us) that we cannot determine in advance what it is we are after; any "program" we follow will simply encode the dominant

assumptions we are locked into' (103). A recipe, one would think, for helpless passivity. Deconstruction 'needs to recognize the urgency of immediate political struggles, and not to become wedded to indefinite deferral' (104). But would it still be 'deconstruction' if it followed these recommendations? 'Political interpretation needs to look at "carnivalizing" the biblical text, reading it against itself, "jokingly releasing its contradictions"' (108). Does the term 'political' retain any meaning in such a statement?

12. For Derrida's assertion about the ominipresence of textuality, see *Grammatology*, 158.

13. J.-F. Lyotard, *The Postmodern Condition*, xxiv. Jameson's *Postmodernism* understands literary theory as one manifestation of the postmodern condition among other; see too E. Ann Kaplan (ed.), *Postmodernism and its Discontents*.

5. The Musical Signifier

1. The contemporary practice of *glossolalia* of course represents itself as the revival and rediscovery of primitive Christian experience. But the cultural context in which *glossolalia* originally flourished (on which see the material cited in G. Kittel (ed.), *Theological Dictionary of the New Testament*, 1. 722–4) is quite different from the contemporary one, and to that extent it is appropriate to think of them as different phenomena.

2. So A. Loisy, *Les Actes des Apôtres* (1920), 723, cited in E. Haenchen, *The Acts of the Apostles*, 554.

3. The possibility is often noted that in reaffirming the resurrection of the dead in 1 Cor. 15 Paul 'misunderstood' his opponents (H. Conzelmann, *1 Corinthians*, 262, referring to R. Bultmann and W. Schmithals). The possibility of a comparable, although deliberate, 'misunderstanding' in 1 Cor. 14 has not been adequately noted. Corinthian enthusiasm for *glossolalia* is not addressed on its own terms where it is understood as a failure of communication.

4. With reference to Descartes' *cogito*: 'Its mad audacity would consist in the return to an original point which no longer belongs to either a *determined* reason or a *determined* unreason... Nothing is less reassuring than the Cogito in its proper and inaugural moment' (J. Derrida, *Writing and Difference*, 56).

5. With reference to Judaism: 'The breaking of the Tables articulates... a rupture within God as the origin of history' (*Writing and Difference*, 67). 'Writing is the moment of the desert as the moment of Separation' (68).

6. This last formulation recalls the persistent complaint that Derrida is philosophically 'unoriginal' (see J. Ellis, *Against Deconstruction*, 37–45).

7. Compare Roland Barthes: 'Modern literature is trying, by various experiments, to establish a new position for the agent of writing in writing itself. The meaning or the goal of this effort is to substitute the instance of discourse for the instance of reality (or of the referent), that mythic alibi which has dominated – still dominates – the idea of literature' ('To Write: An Intransitive Verb?' (1966), in *The Rustle of Language*, 20). The subject disappears along with the object: 'Writing is the destruction of every voice, of every point of origin. Writing is that neutral, composite, oblique space where our subject slips away, the negative where all identity is lost, starting with the very identity of the body writing' ('The Death of the Author' (1968), in *Image–Music–Text*, 142). Derrida's earlier and most influential work belongs within the structuralist milieu of 1960s Paris, before anyone had thought of adding the prefix 'post'. Jonathan Culler's *Structuralist Poetics* (1975), dating from before Derrida's large-scale North American reception, correctly integrates him into this milieu.

8. Derrida accomplishes here what he elsewhere describes as 'a kind of general strategy of deconstruction': 'On the one hand, we must traverse a phase of *overturning*. To do justice to this necessity is to recognize that in a classical philosophical opposition we are not dealing with the peaceful coexistence of a *vis-à-vis*, but rather with a violent hierarchy. One of the two terms governs the other (axiologically, logically, etc.), or has the upper hand. To deconstruct the opposition, first of all, is to overturn the hierarchy at a given moment' (*Positions*, 41). In the second phase, 'we must also mark the interval between inversion, which brings low what was high, and the irruptive emergence of a new "concept", a concept that can no longer be, and never could be, included in the previous regime.' The new concept of writing '*simultaneously* provokes the overturning of the hierarchy speech/writing, and the entire system attached to it, *and* releases the dissonance of a writing within speech, thereby disorganizing the entire inherited order and invading the whole field' (42). A mere inversion would preserve the hierarchical structure, whereas an inversion that simultaneously discloses the presence of the excluded member of a binary opposition in the midst of the privileged member undoes not only the particular opposition but also the hierarchical structure that holds it in place.

9. As J. Habermas notes, commenting on Derrida's statement that 'all graphemes are of a testamentary essence': 'This idea is merely a variation on the motif of the dependency of living speech upon self-sufficient structures of language' (*The Philosophical Discourse of Modernity*, 166).

10. 'A difference generally implies positive terms between which the difference is set up; but in language there are only differences *without positive terms*. Whether we take the signified or the signifier, language has neither ideas nor sounds that existed before the linguistic system, but only conceptual and phonic differences that have issued from the system' (F. de Saussure, *Course in General Linguistics*, 120).

11. Derrida's texts generally represent themselves as an activity of reading a prior text, and he and his expositors insist that this reading-activity is not to be regarded as a 'method'. That would be 'to set aside the detailed and specific *activity* of deconstructive reading in favour of a generalized *idea* of that activity, an idea assumed to comprehend all its differences of local application' (C. Norris, *Derrida*, 20). Yet Norris concedes that 'it is not too difficult to come up with a concise formula that would make it sound very much like a "method" and yet describe quite accurately some of Derrida's most typical deconstructive moves' (18–19). The repetition of certain 'moves' so that they become 'typical' does indeed sound very much like a method; but the main point here is that these moves are repeated because Derrida always wants to do essentially the same thing with the texts on which he writes: to invert their hierarchies and to show that the lower, excluded member is already inscribed within the higher. Since (as Norris rightly emphasizes) Derrida is a philosopher, a participant in a discipline which traditionally seeks to privilege truth and to exclude falsehood, his reading 'method' is oriented towards obtaining from a variety of texts confirmations of an ironized thesis about the impossibility of the philosophical quest.

12. As an example of the need to 'localize' Derrida, his obsession with the theme of the inaccessible 'origin' appears to be very closely related to Heidegger's ruminations on poetic language, although by way of a displacement rather than a repetition. For Heidegger, language may have a revelatory function. 'Only the word makes a thing appear as the thing it is, and thus lets it be present' (*On the Way to Language*, 65). 'The poet experiences his poetic calling as a call to the word as the source, the bourn of Being' (66). In the appearing of an entity through language, 'there shines forth its ancient origin out of the silent glow of the first dawn – the earliest dawn which, as the prior beginning, is coming toward everything that is becoming, and brings to it the advent, never to be overtaken, of its essential being'

(182). Saussurean structuralism gives Derrida the means of subverting this discourse by showing the idea of an originary, revelatory language of Being to be untenable, but the hold of the Heideggerian origin is still perceptible in the repeated renunciation of nostalgia for it. Derrida notes in Heidegger 'the dominance of an entire metaphorics of proximity, of simple and immediate presence', expressed by way of a massive privileging of spoken language and the voice (*Margins of Philosophy*, 130, 132), and these metaphors are located, in displaced form, somewhere near the 'origins' of his own thought too.

13. Here and elsewhere in my deconstructive reading of this passage, I am conscious of indebtedness to Stephen Moore, who does this kind of thing much better than I do: see his *Mark and Luke in Poststructuralist Perspectives*.

14. But see his essay, 'Des tours de Babel' (summarized by K. Hart, *The Trespass of the Sign*, 109–10).

15. Derrida's Nietzschean anti-humanism may be compared with Foucault's. 'Rather than the death of God – or, rather, in the wake of that death and in a profound correlation with it – what Nietzsche's thought heralds is the end of his murderer; it is the explosion of man's face in laughter, and the return of masks;... it is the identity of the Return of the Same with the absolute dispersion of man' (M. Foucault, *The Order of Things*, 385). It is language that occasions the laughter and the masks that accompany the human demise: 'Ought we not... to give up thinking of man, or, to be more strict, to think of this disappearance of man – and the ground of possibility of all the sciences of man [human sciences] – as closely as possibly in correlation with our concern with language? Ought we not to admit that, since language is here once more, man will return to that serene non-existence in which he was formerly maintained by the imperious unity of Discourse?' (386). As Terry Eagleton argues, when in *The Use of Pleasure* Foucault 'is finally able to fill one of the gaping voids in his work – the question of ethics – with an aesthetic alternative to humanist morality', the result is entirely inadequate: for, 'as with Nietzsche, Foucault's vigorously self-mastering individual remains wholly monadic. Society is just an assemblage of autonomous self-disciplining agents, with no sense that their self-realization might flourish within bonds of mutuality' (*The Ideology of the Aesthetic*, 391, 393). Mutuality is not a value highly esteemed by the *Übermensch*.

6. Persons in Dialogue

1. A certain tension appears here in the use of the term 'individual', which has a neutral or positive sense (the subtitle of McFadyen's book is 'A Christian Theory of the Individual in Social Relationships') but also a negative one ('isolated, individual entities'). The terminological problem is that the term 'individual' (unlike the term 'person') may already connote an isolated, non-relational entity. According to Colin Gunton, criticizing P. F. Strawson, 'to treat the person and the individual as the same thing – to define the person as an individual – is to lose both person and individual' (*The Promise of Trinitarian Theology*, 88). While a clear terminological distinction may often be desirable, the term 'individual' is still required to denote the singular instance of the person.

2. McFadyen sees the horizontal dimension of the image of God as grounded in the Trinity: 'A theory of human nature analogously informed by the nature of God as Trinity will lead to a specific understanding of individuality as a sedimentation of interpersonal relations which is intrinsically open to others as to God' (*The Call to Personhood*, 24). 'The individuality of the trinitarian Persons is not achieved through a private discreteness from relation, but through this trinitarian process of existing in and for the others' (29). For the trinitarian dimensions of Gen. 1, see chapter 8 below.

3. For an introduction to Habermas's critical social theory, see J. B. Thompson, *Critical Hermeneutics*, chapter 3.

4. McFadyen's theory is by no means apolitical, but there is perhaps a tendency to elide 'the social formation of persons', represented in neutral sociological terms, with 'the redemptive transformation of relation', a tendency reinforced theologically by the elision of creation and redemption. This makes it difficult to recognize the extent to which distortions are entailed in the 'normal' process of socialization.

5. Indeed, its strength lies precisely in its ability to mediate between the collective and the individual, or, better expressed, large-scale and small-scale relationships. It thus serves as a corrective to a praxis-oriented theology which rightly insists that 'a political option in favor of liberative change is an intrinsic element of faith' (J. L. Segundo, *The Liberation of Theology*, 97) but seems unable or unwilling to provide this claim with a theoretical basis. Clodovis Boff rightly asks 'whether the labor of assigning theology a better-defined and better-articulated theoretical structure is not perhaps more urgent than that of working with merely effusive, or even "revolutionary" theologies' (*Theology and Praxis*, 78).

6. For Saussure, *langue* is 'the social side of speech, outside the individual who can never create nor modify it by himself; it exists only by virtue of a sort of contract signed by the members of a community' (*Course in General Linguistics*, 15).

7. 'From first to last, and not merely in the epilogue, Christianity is eschatology, is hope, forward looking and forward moving, and therefore also revolutionizing and transforming the present. The eschatological is not one element *of* Christianity, but it is the medium of Christian faith as such, the key in which everything in it is set, the glow that suffuses everything here in the dawn of an expected new day. For Christian faith lives from the raising of the crucified Christ, and strains after the promises of the universal future of Christ' (J. Moltmann, *Theology of Hope*, 16).

8. As Gutiérrez argues, Christian eschatology stresses 'not only the provisional nature of historical accomplishments, but above all their openness towards the total communion of all human beings with God' (*A Theology of Liberation*, 75). This linear view is to be contrasted with the attempt to establish a *vertical* relation between inner-historical realities and the kingdom of God. According to Tillich, 'The ever present end of history elevates the positive content of history into eternity at the same time that it excludes the negative from participation in it. Therefore nothing which has been created in history is lost, but it is liberated from the negative element with which it is entangled within existence' (*Systematic Theology*, vol. 3, 397). This platonizing 'transcendental eschatology' leaves creation and history without hope.

9. On this view, any true perception of or encounter with the subject matter of Christian proclamation is dialogically mediated; the concern is primarily with the question of truth and its reception rather than of respect for the otherness of the other. This position may be clarified by comparison with Stephen Sykes' attempt to develop 'a conception of the identity of Christianity which is not committed to the attempt to resolve the problem of its unity and continuity by a methodological *tour de force*; but which is, rather, respectful in a more than theoretical manner of the multifaceted character of Christianity' (*The Identity of Christianity*, 265). The methodological *tour de force* is clearly a monological communication, but the dialogical alternative is not established merely by inculcating respect for otherness and difference. Would dialogue still be serious if the dialogue-partner's position can so readily be assigned to one or other of the many facets of Christianity, each of which deserves respect? Sykes also represents the identity of Christianity as an 'essentially contested concept', citing the philosopher W. B. Gallie (251), and an element of non-monological *contestation* would seem to be necessary to a serious understanding of dialogue.

10. The root of the problem may lie, as Moltmann argues, in a pervasive Christian monotheism which represents God as the almighty ruler of the universe: 'The doctrine of the Trinity which evolves out of the surmounting of monotheism for Christ's sake, must therefore also overcome this monarchism, which legitimates dependency, helplessness and servitude' (*The Trinity and the Kingdom of God*, 192).

11. For the exegetical arguments, see G. D. Fee, *The First Epistle to the Corinthians*, 699–705.

12. Karl Barth understands the silence required of speakers in tongues as a subordination in finite things which reflects 'the infinite subordination of man to God' which is ultimately the theme here (*The Resurrection of the Dead*, 98). The same is then true also of the silencing of women (99). On my own view, the silencing of the glossolalists is directed *against* any doctrine of the infinite subordination of humans to God.

13. It has recently been argued that this passage is non-Pauline (W. O. Walker, '1 Corinthians 2.6–16: A Non-Pauline Interpolation?'). Whatever the truth of the matter, such arguments may contribute to the formulation of a *Sachkritik* capable of a critical, theological sifting of the biblical material.

14. 'The others' probably refers to the whole congregation rather than to the other prophets (so C. K. Barrett, *The First Epistle to the Corinthians*, 328, against H. Conzelmann, *1 Corinthians*, 245). 1 Thess. 5.21 ascribes the function of judging prophecy to the whole congregation, and those with the gift of *diakriseis pneumatōn* are not necessarily those with the gift of *prophēteia* (1 Cor. 12.19).

15. According to Barth, the scriptural privileging of speech in the encounter between God and humans means that this encounter is to be understood as a rational communication between persons, over against, for example, Otto's category of 'the holy', which is to be understood as an irrational natural force (*Church Dogmatics*, I, 1, 135). But in this case the rational communication is limited to commanding on the one hand and hearing, understanding and obeying on the other, and it thus threatens to become monological or logocentric. 'The Word of God... is the Word which aims at us and smites us in our existence. No human word has the competence to aim at us in our existence...' (141). The human word which for Barth must always mediate the Word of God seems here to have become so translucent to its divine counterpart as almost to cease to exist. If the humanity of the Word in its threefold form (Jesus Christ, scripture, preaching) were taken more seriously, then the human speech which is the vehicle of the divine Word would have to be understood dialogically.

7. Narratives of Postmodernity

1. However, preoccupation with narrative does not necessarily signal characteristically postmodern concerns. As Kevin Vanhoozer notes, Paul Ricoeur's view of narrative rests on the assumption that 'narratives have an innate capacity to disclose the world as "graced"... This revelatory, world-displaying capacity is a *natural* prerogative of narratives and indeed, of all poetic language' (*Biblical Narrative in the Theology of Paul Ricoeur*, 180). This hermeneutic of narrative has its roots in Heidegger rather than postmodernism.

2. The significance of the category of 'narrative' for postmodernism is also explored by Christopher Norris, *The Contest of Faculties*, 19–46. Norris finds here 'the essential characteristics of all conservative ideology, from Burke to the current new Right', and especially 'the idea that *prejudice* is so deeply built into our traditions of thought that no amount of rational criticism can hope to dislodge it' (24).

3. Norris points out that, for Lyotard, modern technology is a hopeful sign in this respect:

'He predicts that the spread of information networks will break down monopolistic structures of authority and work to promote the free circulation of ideas. As the networks become more densely interactive, so society will learn to make do without absolute legitimating truth, and to live with its own kinds of "narrative" understanding' (*The Contest of Faculties*, 16).

4. When Frank Kermode states, with the gospels in mind, that 'interpretation… begins so early in the development of narrative texts that the recovery of the real right original thing is an illusory quest' (*The Genesis of Secrecy*, 125), interpretation-as-explanation is assimilated to interpretation-as-mere-interpretation. Thus one cannot raise the question whether one or other of the early interpretation of the original thing might be a true interpretation.

5. Here and elsewhere, postmodern theorizing faces acute problems in accounting for its own possibility. As Paul de Man puts it, 'The loftier the aims and the better the methods of literary theory, the less possible it becomes' (*The Resistance to Theory*, 19).

6. Richard Bernstein emphasizes that for Kuhn the choice of one paradigm rather than another remains a rational activity, 'although the reasons to which we appeal do not necessarily dictate a univocal choice' (*Beyond Objectivism and Relativism*, 54). Rorty's approach, however, rests upon a false dichotomy: 'either permanent standards of rationality (objectivism) *or* arbitrary acceptance of one set of standards or practices over against its rival (relativism)… In the course of the evolution of scientific developments we can come to see the force of the better practices and arguments and why certain historical practices and modes of argumentation are abandoned' (68).

7. Derrida too opposes the philosophical claim to jurisdiction over the various scientific fields, on the grounds that the philosophical text is simply one text among other: 'Beyond the philosophical text there is not a blank, virgin, empty margin, but another text, a weave of differences of forces without any present centre of reference (everything – "history", "politics", "economy", "sexuality", etc. – said not to be written in books…)' (*Margins of Philosophy*, xxiii).

8. Compare Terry Eagleton's account of Rorty's 'elitism': in Rorty's ideal society, 'the intellectuals will be "ironists", practising a suitably cavalier, laid-back attitude to their own beliefs, while the masses, for whom such self-ironizing might prove too subversive a weapon, will continue to salute the flag and take life seriously' (*Ideology: An Introduction*, 11).

9. 'For those attracted by the new varieties of relativism, the alleged incommensurability of language games, forms of life, traditions, paradigms, and theories has been taken to be the primary evidence for the new relativism' (R. Bernstein, *Beyond Objectivism and Relativism*, 79)

10. As Eagleton remarks, 'It is a sentimental illusion to believe that small is always beautiful. What small narratives does Lyotard have in mind? The current, gratifyingly minor tributary of British fascism?' For Lyotard as for poststructuralism in general, plurality 'is a good in itself, quite regardless of its ethical or political substance' (*The Ideology of the Aesthetic*, 399).

11. See Sabina Lovibond, 'Feminism and Pragmatism'.

12. In a more recent critique of Gutiérrez, Hauerwas argues that 'the kind of liberation that Christians experience and hopefully learn to live may not be easily translated into or identified with the liberation desired and sought in other contexts'. Why? Because 'too often the liberation is sought not as a means to serve, but as a means to dominate' ('Some Theological Reflections on Gutiérrez's Use of "Liberation" as a Theological Concept', 75). Christians' most important contribution to liberation struggles is 'to be a community of the liberated who can witness to paradigmatic forms of service' (75). As ever, the emphasis is on what *separates* Christians from others engaged in resistance to oppression. But Christian

distinctiveness need not be compromised by solidarity; and Christians could learn from this solidarity to recognize oppression, in all its complex material and ideological ramifications, as a genuinely theological problem. In Hauerwas's account, a purely ecclesial ethics leads to no such recognition.

8. Language, God and Creation

1. Although Wolfhart Pannenberg's attempt to base a christology on historical–critical reconstruction no longer looks convincing, some of his insights are transferable into a more narrative and text-centred context. Pannenberg understands Jesus' claim to authority (emphasized by Käsemann, Bornkamm and other practitioners of the 'new quest of the historical Jesus') as proleptic. His whole work is aimed at a future verification of his claim to authority through the arrival of the end-event (*Jesus God and Man*, 65). In his resurrection there occurs the divine legitimation of his ministry, and this event is itself proleptic of the final, universal eschatological event. 'Why the man Jesus can be the ultimate revelation of God, why in him and only in him God is supposed to have appeared, remains incomprehensible apart from the horizon of the apocalyptic expectation' (83). There is no reason why a theology of narrative should not work within a comparably broad framework.

2. G. von Rad and others find in the 'terminological unevenness' in Gen. 1.6–7 and throughout the chapter a trace of a diachronic process in which an older conception – God *makes* the world – was supplemented by a less anthropomorphic view of creation through *the word* (*Genesis*, 52). My own reading of this passage is a synchronic one; that is, while acknowledging that the textual phenomenon in question is open to diachronic explanation, it takes as its starting-point a text which lays these models of divine activity side by side without labelling one as 'old' and the other as 'new'. The text may therefore be said to conceal or erase the diachronic process that underlies it. This view would be compatible with the claim that the 'original' author(s) or editor(s) intended the original audience to perceive the combination of different traditions. It would still be true that, for whatever reason, the *text* does not signal any intention to harmonize divergent traditions, and it is therefore possible to appeal to the letter of the text over against the hypothetically-reconstructed authorial intention.

3. It is perhaps a prejudice against anthropomorphism that makes it seem that creation in Gen. 1 is accomplished solely through the word and that this displays 'the effortlessness of Yahweh's creative activity' (Paul Santmire, *The Travail of Nature*, 196). If it was effortless, why did he have to rest? The same one-sidedness is apparent when Walter Brueggemann states that 'it is by God's speech that the relation with his creation is determined' (*Genesis*, 24).

4. My reading is obviously and intentionally influenced by the canonical context of this passage as the opening of the Christian Bible, and also by its subsequent *Wirkungsgeschichte*, especially in the patristic period. It nevertheless remains a reading of the letter of *this* passage. The pluralism of contemporary hermeneutics makes it possible to reopen the question of the biblical origins of the trinitarian problem, in opposition to the anti-trinitarian consensus that has long held sway within both Old Testament and New Testament studies.

5. The triune God 'unremittingly breathes the Spirit into his creation. Everything that is, exists and lives in the unceasing flow of the energies and potentialities of the cosmic Spirit' (J. Moltmann, *God in Creation*, 9). In opposition to mechanistic views of the world, whether deistic, theistic or atheistic, and in quest of a view of the Creator sensitive to ecological issues, the relationship of Creator to creation must be seen 'as an intricate web of unilateral, reciprocal and many-sided relationships. In this network of relationships, "making",

"preserving", "maintaining" and "perfecting" are certainly the great *one-sided* relationships; but "indwelling", "sym-pathizing", "participating", "accompanying", "enduring", "delighting", and "glorifying" are relationships of *mutuality* which describe a cosmic community of living between God the Spirit and all his created beings' (14). 'The God who is transcendent in relation to the world, and the God who is immanent in that world are one and the same God' (15).

6. Although Moltmann claims to offer a *trinitarian* doctrine of creation, his use of the categories of transcendence and immanence can account only for the Father and the Spirit and not for the Son. Moltmann wishes to repeat the New Testament movement from 'the eschatological redemption of the whole creation through Christ' to 'the deduction that the protological creation had its foundation in Christ' (*God in Creation*, 94), but offers no basis for this in the creation narratives. My own emphasis on the threefoldness of the God of Gen. 1 attempts to meet this difficulty. While retaining the categories of transcendence and immanence, a mediating concept is interposed which speaks of a quasi-corporeal relationship between the maker and what is made. If the corporeality of the God who works with his hands is an indication of something analogous to humanity in God, connections might be made with the patristic ascription to the Son of Old Testament theophanies in which God appears in human or quasi-human form, and, ultimately, with the incarnation. The word who became flesh formed the heavens and the earth with his (quasi-fleshly) hands.

7. MT has here *lᵉśaḥēq bô*. RSV translates, 'which thou didst form to sport in it' (the sea); JB 'whom you made to amuse you', NEB 'whom thou hast made thy plaything'. Following the latter reading, A. Weiser notes that 'the poet here finds the religious meaning of creation in God's joy in his creature... a joy that is entirely detached from any thought of human calculation or expediency' (*Psalms*, 669).

8. In Gen. 1, God 'is seen as structuring the cosmos not just so that he may bless human creatures but also so that he might delight in his own works' (P. Santmire, *The Travail of Nature*, 198). Santmire is rightly critical of the view of G. von Rad, G. E. Wright, G. Lampe and others, that creation is a subordinate and secondary theme in Israel's faith.

9. The other side of dominion is the dependence of the apex on the base: 'As the last thing to be created the human being is also dependent on all the others... So while they are a preparation for him, he is dependent on them' (J. Moltmann, *God in Creation*, 187).

10. Walter Brueggemann notes both that 'the text wishes to focus on the creation of humankind', and also that vv. 3–25 oppose an exclusively anthropocentric view of the world: 'God has his own relation with the rest of creation' (*Genesis*, 31; italics removed).

11. Thus Gordon Wenham's description of the early chapters of Genesis as 'proto-historical' (*Genesis 1–15*, 54) arises out of the tension between the original readers' belief that these texts are factual reports and modern readers' belief that they were wrong. The value of the critical philosophy of science developed by Kuhn, Feyerabend, Lyotard and others is that it makes it possible to challenge the assumption of the superiority of the modern reader which even relatively conservative commentators tacitly concede.

12. Positivistic disparagement of this narrative evokes an apologetic defence which separates its 'basic theological affirmations' and the 'human experiences' that underlie it from its 'prescientific cosmology' (I. Barbour, *Religion in an Age of Science*, 133). If it is said that 'we can look on the Big Bang and subsequent evolution as God's way of creating' (133), then we understand the scientific narrative as a sacred text, supplanting an existing sacred text (Gen. 1) in the act of supplementing it. But the metaphor of the 'Big Bang' – the initial event, upon which all else is supposed to rest – connotes an apersonal, purposeless violence. The initial act of creation is understood in the light of the various explosions which human beings produce with the help of gunpowder, dynamite or atomic power, and the awe in the

presence of overwhelming, brute power that the metaphor expresses resembles that of the physicist, technician and general who have just successfully detonated their first nuclear device. How can 'Religion' or Christian faith acquiesce – even during a so-called 'Age of Science' – in the idea that the image and likeness of God the creator is fully realized only in the figure of the nuclear physicist?

13. An example of this would be Heidegger's notion of Dasein as 'thrown into existence' (*Being and Time*, 321). Immersion in the inauthentic world of the they–self enables Dasein to evade the fact of its thrownness, but in anxiety it is brought face to face with the strangeness of its fate as 'an entity which has to be as it is and as it can be'. Awareness of thrownness is awareness of not being at home in the world. The Cartesian gulf between the isolated, anxious ego and a mechanistic world is intensified here in a manner that recalls Gnosticism. In contrast, the world as creation is the world as home to humankind.

14. 'Only in community of humankind is God reflected. God is, according to this bold affirmation, not mirrored as an individual but as a community' (W. Brueggemann, *Genesis*, 34).

15. If we conceive God 'as three persons in communion, related but distinct', then 'we are in the image of God when, like God but in dependence on his giving, we find our reality in what we give to and receive from others in human community' (C. E. Gunton, *The Promise of Trinitarian Theology*, 113, 117).

16. 'The image of God (singular) is supposed to correspond to the "internal" plural of God, and yet be a *single* image. In the next verse the singular and plural are distributed in the opposite way: God (singular) created human being (singular), as man and women (plural) he created them (plural). Whereas the self-resolving God is a plural in the singular, his image on earth – the human being – is apparently supposed to be a singular in the plural. The one God, who is differentiated in himself and is at one with himself, then finds his correspondence in a community of human beings, female and male, who unite with one another and are one' (J. Moltmann, *God in Creation*, 218).

17. *Church Dogmatics*, III, 1, 182–205.

18. A. McFadyen criticizes the tendency to conceive the relation of Trinity and humanity as one of *analogans* and *analogatum*, which leaves us 'with an entirely static picture of a Platonist universe in which the Triune God's sociality and communication is restricted to the ideal world of pure forms' ('The Trinity and Human Individuality', 12). In fact, 'the dialogical openness within the trinitarian being of God overflows into all God's external relationships', calling created being 'to join in the fullness of divine life in a manner appropriate to its own creaturely existence' (15).

19. According to C. Westermann, the purpose of the reference to creation in the image and likeness of God is to indicate that here, uniquely, 'the creator created a creature that corresponds to him, to whom he can speak, and who listens to him' (*Genesis 1–11*, 157; Westermann might have added that the creature is intended to speak back). There is thus a parallel between Gen. 1.26 and Gen. 2, where the person is also created by God as his counterpart (157). As a reading grounded in what the text says, Westermann's interpretation should be distinguished from the hypothesis that *selem* and *dᵉmût* here democratize terms that elsewhere belong within kingship ideology. On the hermeneutical issues here, see M. Brett, 'Motives and Intentions in Genesis 1', 11–12.

20. According to Frank Kermode, 'Men in the middest make considerable imaginative investments in coherent patterns which, by the provision of an end, make possible a satisfying consonance with the origins and with the middle. That is why the image of the end can never be *permanently* falsified' (*The Sense of an Ending*, 17). This order is created by literature, and does not reflect an order inherent within reality: 'It is not that we are

connoisseurs of chaos, but that we are surrounded by it, and equipped for coexistence with it only by our fictive powers' (64). 'Novels have beginnings, ends, and potentiality, even if the world has not' (138). However, Terry Eagleton is rightly critical of the 'glib counterposing of coherent fiction to chaotic reality' which 'has become entrenched as the purest critical cliché' (*Against the Grain*, 51).

Part Three   Holy Scripture and Feminist Critique

1. 'If feminist criticism calls anything into question, it must be that dog-eared myth of intellectual neutrality' (A. Kolodny, 'Dancing through the Minefield', 163).

2. A feminist criticism oriented towards woman as reader (rather than as writer) is concerned with 'woman as the consumer of male-produced literature, and with the way in which the hypothesis of a female reader changes our apprehension of a given text, awakening us to the significance of its sexual codes' (E. Showalter, 'Toward a Feminist Poetics', 128).

3. 'It is striking that at mammoth meetings of the Society for New Testament Studies... there is barely a woman theologian to be seen. Even more shocking is the lack of much sense of incongruity about this' (R. Morgan, 'Feminist Theological Interpretation of the New Testament', 11).

4. In the 'General Introduction' to their *Literary Guide to the Bible*, Robert Alter and Frank Kermode understand the role of the literary critic as helping to 'make possible fuller readings of the text, with a particular emphasis on the complex integration of diverse means of communication encountered in most works of literature' (5). Yet they have to acknowledge that this orientation towards 'integration' or coherence has resulted in the exclusion from their project of 'certain varieties of contemporary criticism' which 'are not really concerned with reading in the sense we have proposed' (5): Marxist, psychoanalytic, feminist and deconstructionist criticisms, for example (6).

5. In her 1987 SBL Presidential Address, for example, Fiorenza is sharply critical of the ethos of modern biblical scholarship, with its 'rhetorical postures' of 'a-political detachment, objective literalism, and scientific value-neutrality' ('The Ethics of Biblical Interpretation', 11).

6. Fiorenza's position seems in practice to be close to that of Adela Yarbro Collins, who posits a two-sided relationship. On the one hand, 'Feminist biblical interpretation cannot do without historical-critical methods', which at least attempt a critical appraisal of the text. On the other hand, 'Feminists are challenging historical critics to be faithful to that tradition, to become aware of and to correct androcentric bias both in themselves as interpreters and in the texts' ('Introduction', 9).

9. Strategies of Containment

1. Margaret Macdonald concludes that 'the Colossian and Ephesian household codes appear to be employed primarily to manage internal communal relations, but possibly also to stabilize relations with outsiders' (*The Pauline Churches*, 121). No doubt this is correct. Yet the cautious language – 'appear', 'possibly also' – is symptomatic of an important aspect of the texts' self-presentation, the minimizing of the pragmatic dimension.

2. Markus Barth's comments on Eph. 5.33 are a good example of the kind of reading that such a text generates where there is a commitment to its theological normativity: 'She [the wife] can have many *good* reasons to fear her husband, and can fear him in a way that does not degrade her in her own or in his eyes. When a husband loves his wife with a love inspired by Christ's love and (however feebly) resembling it, she would be a fool to prefer or seek autonomy apart from him, sufficiency in herself, or a dominant position over him... Instead

of attempting to move him in the manner or by the tricks by which she may be able to move other men, she will be moved by him. Instead of shaping and changing him after her heart's desire, she will feel thoroughly changed by him. Instead of bringing him under control, she will be overwhelmed by his love… She will receive him as one who in his own imperfect way reminds her of the true head of all the world, the church, her lover and herself: Jesus Christ' (Ephesians 4–6, 649–50). It is important to recognize that these embarrassing remarks, dating from as recently as 1974, reflect not only the opinions of the commentator but also the ideology of the text.

3. In opposition to this tactic of using Judaism as a negative backdrop, see Fiorenza, *In Memory of Her*, 106–18, and Bernadette J. Brooten, 'Early Christian Women and their Cultural Context', 69–79. Brooten gives an example very similar to the one from Luke 10: 'A total prohibition of divorce in the context of patriarchal marriage cannot be seen as simply liberating for women… Could it be a recognition, perhaps unconscious, of this ambivalence that has led to wanting to see Jesus' prohibition of divorce against the backdrop of inegalitarian Jewish practice of divorce? Could it be that only against that backdrop it seems egalitarian?' (74). Brooten also cites here Judith Plaskow's complaint: 'Feminist research projects onto Judaism the failure of the Christian tradition unambiguously to renounce sexism… This is the real motive behind biased presentations of Jesus' Jewish background: to allow the feminist to present the "true" Christian tradition as uniquely free from sexism.'

4. Further research is needed into the presentation and the significance of the maleness of Jesus in the New Testament, in order to identify exactly where the problem lies – a problem felt by Christian as well as post-Christian feminism. According to Kathleen Fischer, 'One significant difference in the way women and men relate to Jesus is that women cannot experience same-sex identification with the male Jesus of Nazareth in the way men can' (*Women at the Well*, 77). But what is meant by such an 'identification', and is it really the purpose of the gospel narratives to promote it?

5. I owe the phrase 'textual harrassment' to Mary Ann Tolbert ('Protestant Feminists and the Bible', 12), who in turn derives it from Mary Jacobus. That this is more than a clever play on words is indicated by Dorothee Sölle's statement, 'I feel humiliated when I read what I Timothy says about women' (*Thinking about God*, 75).

6. Another way of defining the stance of conventional scholarship is to locate it at the mid-point between two extremes (traditionalism and feminism). Thus Ben Witherington differentiates his own work from 'books written by those who are so passionately tradition-alist or feminist in their approach that their personal interests and biases skew the interpretation of the data, or tend to lead the writer to highlight only that portion of the material which favors his or her own views on matters such as women's roles in the Church, and especially the question of women's ordination. Sadly, most of these last sort of books [*sic*] are forms of propaganda' (*Women and the Genesis of Christianity*, xii). This stance is very close to Heine's, and both reflect the conventional self-image of the academy.

7. S. DeVries notes that, according to this passage, 'it was their [his wives'] seduction of Solomon rather than Solomon's own waywardness that had led to this sad state of affairs' (*1 Kings*, 143).

8. Women's propensity to lead males out of a right relationship with Yahweh is merely a special case of the general deceitfulness which is 'a common characteristic of women in the Hebrew Bible' (Esther Fuchs, 'Who is Hiding the Truth?', 137). These female portraits are 'intended to validate the suspicion that women's apparent impotence is nothing but a deceptive disguise, that underneath their vulnerable coyness lurks a dangerously calculating mind… The repeated ascription of deceptiveness to them reveals not only a distrusting gynophobia but also a political statement that seeks to perpetuate the subordination of

women based on their alleged moral deficiency' (143).

9. Compare Jer. 44, where Israelite women's devotion to Ashtoreth is said to have led men astray and to have brought about destruction and exile (cf. vv. 9, 15, 19, 20, 24–25). The text's self-presentation is accurately reproduced when a modern commentator describes the prophet as confronted here with a 'fanatical chorus of shrieking women and womanish men' (quoted by J. Paterson, 'Jeremiah', 560).

10. The nature of this process is clarified when we can reconstruct the perspective that is excluded. In this respect, Carol Fontaine's discussion of the retention by royal wives of their native gods is illuminating, although not explicitly related to the Old Testament ('A Heifer from thy Stable', 77–92).

11. I am indebted for this imagery to Terry Eagleton, *Literary Theory*, 68.

10. Hebrew Narratives and Feminist Readers

1. See, for example, Alice Laffey's *Introduction to the Old Testament: A Feminist Perspective*, which lacks the hermeneutical sophistication of the work I shall discuss but sets out the sheer range of Old Testament material open to feminist analysis.

2. The representative character of *Texts of Terror* lies in the combination, shared with the other work discussed here, of a 'literary' concern with the final form of the text and a willingness to resist its dominant ideological perspective. (According to Judith Fetterly, the first act of a feminist critic is 'to become a resisting rather than an assenting reader and, by this refusal to assent, to begin the process of exorcizing the male mind that has been implanted in us' (quoted by J. Culler, *Deconstruction*, 53)). Trible's earlier *God and the Rhetoric of Sexuality* (1978) adopts a different strategy, seeking to recover positive elements in the texts overlooked or misunderstood by the interpretative tradition.

3. Although the text cannot acknowledge Hagar's perspective, Trible also demonstrates its inability finally to suppress it, by herself bringing it to the fore. Paul Joyce points out that, in this sense, Trible is able to use even 'negative' passages in a 'positive' manner ('Feminist Exegesis of the Old Testament', 4).

4. Translation taken from the Loeb edition of Josephus, vol. V.

5. J. A. Soggin draws attention to the parallel in 2 King. 3.26–27, where, after the king of Moab has sacrificed his eldest son upon the city wall, 'there came great wrath against Israel' (*Judges*, 216). Here too, causality is implied but not directly asserted.

6. According to Lilian Klein, 'Jephthah's law- and covenant-breaking piety, based on ignorance, is implicitly disclaimed by Yahweh, who becomes silent and inactive during the remainder of this narrative' (*The Triumph of Irony in the Book of Judges*, 95). But Yahweh is far from inactive: he bestows victory, in accordance with the vow.

7. Robert Alter rightly speaks of 'the anonymous authoritative author' as 'surrogate' to the omniscient God (*The Art of Biblical Narrative*, 184). This might also be reversed: Yahweh as a literary construct serves as surrogate to the omniscient author. 'The author is present in every speech given by any character who has had conferred upon him, in whatever manner, the badge of reliability' (Wayne Booth, *The Rhetoric of Fiction*, 18).

8. This characteristic technique of linking isolated scriptural women with each other can produce illuminating results. Thus Bal identifies three women victims in the book of Judges (Jephthah's daughter, the Levite's 'concubine' (ch.19) and Samson's bride (13.6) – all unnamed), and three murderesses (Delilah (ch.16), Yael (4.17–22; 5.24–27) and the woman who killed Abimelech with a millstone (9.53)). 'Three female killers, three female victims: a structure seems to emerge, a structure that accounts for the excessively violent impression the book makes, a structure which I will replace for the coherence of history and

theology that is usually the guideline for readings of the book as a whole' ('Dealing/With/ Women', 18). Bal points to the absence of the victims' mothers, and sees the murderesses as making the figure of the avenging mother present in displaced form; both Delilah and Yael 'have maternal features and their actions in the encounter with the men are colored by nursing and mothering' (36). Since the murderesses 'avenge the excessive violence done to the daughters, their role has to be, in turn, displaced. But where repression covers oppression, violence cannot but increase' (36). Further examples of the linking of female characters can be found in B. Meredith, 'Desire and Danger', *passim* (Delilah and Judith), R. Rasmussen, 'Deborah and the Woman Warrior', 91 (Jael and the women victims of Gen. 19 and Judg. 19, emphasizing the hospitality code), and F. van Dijk-Hemmes, *passim* (the two Tamars).

9. Robert Polzin argues that the question, 'Which of us shall go up first to battle against the Benjaminites?', addressed to 'God' (20.18), is deliberately contrasted with 1.1, where the people inquire of 'Yahweh', 'Who shall go up first for us against the Canaanites...?' (*Moses and the Deuteronomist*, 202). But in 20.18 as in 1.1, it is 'Yahweh' who responds to the people's query. Yahweh is equally closely involved in both situations.

10. This view seems to me more convincing than Alter's interpretation in terms of the author's reticence: 'In all this the writer is careful to conceal his own precise sympathies' (*The Art of Biblical Narrative*, 124).

11. On Michal, see also D. Clines and T. Eskenazi (eds.), *Telling Queen Michal's Story*.

12. In merging the presentations of Berlin and Bach, I am ignoring the fact that Bach also tries to maximize individual traits.

13. What status is claimed for such a reading? According to Bal, 'The alternative readings I will propose should not be considered as yet another, superior interpretation that overthrows all the others. My goal is rather to show, by the sheer possibility of a different reading, that "dominance" is, although present and in many ways obnoxious, not unproblematically established... For it is not the sexist interpretation of the bible as such that bothers me. It is the possibility of dominance itself, the attractiveness of coherence and authority in culture, that I see as the source, rather than the consequence, of sexism' (*Lethal Love*, 3).

14. Fuchs ('Literary Characterization', 117–18) rejects Trible's emphasis on the relative independence of the women's perspective in the story of Ruth (*God and the Rhetoric of Sexuality*, 166–99). These conflicting readings spring from two incompatible imperatives: the need to explore the positive possibilities which the tradition offers, and the need to expose patriarchal structures concealed even in apparently harmless or helpful texts. Texts are often open to both types of readings, and the choice between them is determined by one's general interpretative strategy.

11. The Limits of Patriarchy

1. Elisabeth Schüssler Fiorenza argues that 'the textual and historical marginalization of women is... a byproduct of the "patristic" selection and canonization process of Scripture' (*In Memory of Her*, 53). What is 'canonical' for feminist theology is therefore the struggles of women for liberation, to which the texts still occasionally bear witness, despite themselves.

2. Daphne Hampson's post-Christian position is occasioned in part by the representation of women in the biblical texts. According to Hampson, 'the fact that a negative view of women is conveyed at a level which must be largely subconscious makes these texts all the more dangerous. Biblical stories, and the narration of history in the bible, may be profoundly damaging to human relations' (*Theology and Feminism*, 86–87). Her claim that 'patriarchal presuppositions are woven into the writing in such a way that they cannot be

extricated' (86) is informed by the literary–feminist analysis discussed in the previous chapter.

3. 'Denied a language which seems appropriate to them, and which arises out of and gives expression to their perceptions of reality and of divine reality, some women want to overturn the Christian tradition *by means of* the tradition, and thus reshape it in possibly unforeseeable ways. They have scavenged for what there is to be found there, to reclaim it from assimilation to masculine understanding' (Ann Loades, *Searching for Lost Coins*, 90). The title of Loades' book (drawing of course on Luke 15.8–10) is a vivid metaphor for this theological programme.

4. Phyllis Trible's *God and the Rhetoric of Sexuality* is often cited as an example of the salvaging of non-patriarchal fragments from the Old Testament texts. (As Ann Loades puts it, this work 'has made the most of what is there to be found' (*Searching for Lost Coins*, 90)). But Trible also offers the beginnings of a more systematic approach by grounding her exploration of feminine imagery for the divine in the parallelism in Gen. 1.27 between the image of God and humankind in its male and female forms (17). Having noted examples of masculine and feminine imagery in language about God, Trible argues that 'the basic metaphor [that is, of the image of God] contrasts with the imbalance of these partial metaphors. It presents an equality in the image of God male *and* female, although the Bible overwhelmingly favors male metaphors for deity. In contrast to the dominant language of scripture, then, this equal stress upon the image of God male and female provides a hermeneutical impetus to investigate female metaphors for God' (22). Thus, Gen. 1.27 offers the basis for a critique of biblical patriarchy which is grounded in the text as well as in contemporary feminist sensibilities.

5. The Pauline identification of the problematic element in holy scripture as 'law' may be linked with the fact that, in Old Testament law, the woman was 'a legal non-person; where she does become visible it is as a dependent, and usually an inferior, in a male-centred and male-dominated society. The laws, by and large, do not address her; most do not even acknowledge her existence' (Phyllis Bird, 'Images of Women in the Old Testament', 56). Paul's assertion that in Christ there is neither male nor female (Gal.3.28) may be read as the abolition of this denial of woman's full personhood.

6. 'The historians of the Old Testament look behind the present state of division and alienation to an original and intended equality and harmony in creation, while the prophets focus upon the existing state of inequality and exploitation, addressing it with a concept of justice manifested in judgment - justice understood as a new act that God will perform to purge his creation, an act of retribution and rectification' (P. Bird, 'Images of Women', 76).

7. I have elsewhere argued that the Pauline/deutero-Pauline interpretation of Gen. 1–3 is exegetically possible, that is, an interpretation to which the text itself is open ('Strategies of Recovery and Resistance', 91–103). In what follows here, I am attempting to develop an inner-textual theological standpoint from which the Pauline interpretation might be resisted. The problem cannot be solved by exegesis alone.

8. The doctrinal structure that arises out of the conjunction of Gen.1.27 and 3.16 does not mean that, prior to 3.16, the texts show no evidence of patriarchal conditioning. The parallel between the fall of Adam and of Solomon, discussed in chapter 9, suggests that there is some basis in the text for the subsequent Judeo–Christian tendency to blame woman for the entry of sin into the world. An attempt to represent a non-patriarchal state will inevitably bear the marks of the patriarchal society from which it derives, but the fact that the attempt is made at all may still be significant.

9. This interpretation is rejected by C. Westermann on the grounds that the position of the woman as 'a helper fit for him' in Gen. 2.18 already implies an element of subordination:

'one could not say in 2:18 that man is created as a helper for the woman' (*Genesis 1–11*, 262). While Gen. 2 is in itself open to a non-egalitarian reading, my point here is that the hermeneutic established by the dogmatic statements in 1.26–27 and 3.16 makes the egalitarian reading exegetically possible as well as theologically necessary.

10. My reading of Exod. 1–2 is indebted to a dramatized rendering of this narrative by an Indian women's group, reprinted in R. S. Sugirtharajah (ed.), *Voices from the Margin*, 267–79; and to A. F. Anderson and G. da Silva Gorhulho, 'Miriam and her Companions'.

11. Augustine and many later Christian exegetes were scandalized by the suggestion in this passage that the midwives lied and were rewarded by God for it. In the following passage, Augustine has in mind Rahab of Jericho as well as the midwives: 'Whether it is ever right to tell a lie, even to save a person's life, is a question which even the most learned weary themselves in trying to resolve. This question was therefore far beyond the capacity of those poor women, set in the midst of those nations and accustomed to their manners. Thus God bore patiently with their ignorance in this as well as in other matters understood by the children who are not of this world but of that which is to come, and gave them an earthly reward (pointing towards a heavenly) because of the human kindness they showed to his servants' (*Against Lying*, 33; English translation in *The Nicene and post-Nicene Fathers*, first series, vol. 3 (American edition), which I have here adapted). Augustine's position appears to stem from an ethic of the spiritual progress of the individual towards the God who is Truth (cf. another discussion of the Hebrew midwives in *On Lying*, 7), by comparison with which even an ethic of solidarity in the preservation of life against the forces of death seemed inferior.

12. These women 'are the very instruments God chooses, according to the narrative, to build the people who become Israel. They are the people who save the child Moses who becomes Israel's deliverer' (A. Laffey, *Introduction to the Old Testament*, 48).

13. This identification is common in recent feminist theology (see, for example, R. Ruether, *Sexism and God-Talk*, 57–61), but there is also a background within early trinitarian thought. According to the apologist Theophilus of Antioch, 'God by his own Word and Wisdom made all things, for "by his Word were the heavens made, and all the host of them by the breath of his mouth [*tō pneumati tou stomatos autou*]"' (*To Autolycus*, 1.7, quoting Ps. 33(32).6 in such a way as to identify the divine wisdom with the divine spirit). This identification was adopted by Irenaeus, who, speaking of the Father, notes that 'with him were always present the Word and Wisdom, the Son and the Spirit, by whom and in whom, freely and spontaneously, he made all things, to whom also he speaks, saying, "Let us make man after our image and likeness"' (*Against Heresies*, 4.20.1). Scriptural evidence for the presence of the Spirit or Wisdom with the Father is found in Prov.3.19–20; 8.22–31 (4.20.3). Tertullian on the other hand understands the crucial passage from Prov. 8 as a reference to the Second Person: for God's Word 'is also set forth in Scripture under the name of *sophia*, Wisdom; for what can be better entitled to the name of Wisdom than the Reason or the Word of God?' (*Against Praxeas*, 6). Under pressure of christological controversies and a relative lack of interest in the Holy Spirit, it was this latter view that prevailed. (The patristic quotations are taken respectively from vols. 2, 1 and 3 of *The Ante-Nicene Fathers* (American edition).)

14. B. S. Childs finds links between this narrative and wisdom literature, for example in its positive presentation of Pharaoh's daughter (*Exodus*, 13), but is unable to exploit this finding in his 'theological reflection' on this passage (24–26), which is based instead on its use in Matt. 2 and the typological relation between Moses and Jesus that thus arises. The result is that the distinctiveness of the Old Testament narrative vanishes, including its remarkable representation of women. Paradoxically, a trinitarian approach, as outlined in

chapter 8 in connection with Gen. 1 and further developed here in the identification of the Holy Spirit with Wisdom, might have the effect of freeing Christian theological reflection on Old Testament narrative from christocentrism of this kind. If the second person in the triune God is the one who in creation works as a craftsman, corporeally with his hands (and who is therefore not characterized by the transcendent creative word or by an indwelling, dynamic creative presence), then a connection can be made with the patristic tradition that the theophanies of Genesis, Exodus and elsewhere are in fact appearances of the Son, for in these events God (or the angel of Yahweh) appears in the corporeal, creaturely form of one who eats and drinks (Gen. 18.8) or of fire in the midst of the bush (Exod. 3.2). Thus the Old Testament 'knows the one God a first time and then a second time in a very different way' (K. Barth, *Church Dogmatics*, I, 1, 317; for examples of the patristic interpretation of Exod. 3, see Justin, *Dialogue with Trypho* 59–60; Irenaeus, *Against Heresies*, 3.6.2.) If, however, the Old Testament also knows the one God a *third* time in a very different way, that is, in the person of the Spirit or Wisdom immanent within creation, then the significance of the theophanies as paradigmatic of the mode of the divine presence to the creature is relativized. In the present context, this trinitarian approach would serve to diminish the apparent contrast between the purely human action of Exod. 1–2 and the divine action of Exod. 3, which gives the impression that the actions of the women are mere prolegomena to a narrative which begins in earnest only with the call of Moses. The actions of the women have their own distinctive theological significance.

15. Thus G. von Rad, speaking of the prophetic call-story as exemplified by Exod. 3–4, states that in the divine call 'neither previous faith nor any other personal endowment had the slightest part to play in preparing a man who was called to stand before Jahweh for his vocation' (*Theology of the Old Testament*, 2.57). This statement, stemming from the insistence of dialectical theology on the occurrence of the divine word 'vertically from above', is exaggerated from an exegetical point of view and theologically misguided in its abandonment of the sphere of human capacities and acts to the inauthentic, secular world. From this theological perspective, one would first construe the action of the women as autonomous and then insist that it in no way contributes to the event of liberation, seen as originating in the call of Moses. For a critique of the tendency to make the prophetic call the sole paradigm of revelation, see P. Ricoeur, *Essays in Biblical Interpretation*, 73–104.

16. C. Westermann understands the command to 'remember not the former things' as an allusion to community laments which reproach God 'with the contrast between his present attitude towards his chosen people and the great thing he did for them in former days'; Isa. 63.11–14 is cited as an example (*Isaiah 40–66*, 128).

17. For Deutero-Isaiah, the agent of liberation is Cyrus (Isa. 44.28; 45.1), a highly 'secular' figure who may therefore serve as a corrective to the assumption that a theology openly related to secular realities has necessarily lost its true subject-matter (although, like any other theology, it may have done so). Thus Alexander McKelway argues that liberationist or feminist theologies 'impose upon the work of theology ideological commitments which are alien to its task and are the result of a failure to reflect upon the freedom of God' (*The Freedom of God and Human Liberation*, xiv). For McKelway, the freedom of God amounts to his non-commitment to human beings except on his own terms, terms that are wholly unrelated to anything that we could imagine or desire.

12. The Father of the Son

1. A similar ambivalence towards the father-image is expressed by Elisabeth Moltmann Wendel. While the application of 'Father' to God was 'useful for forming personality in a

patriarchal society', new images are now required (*A Land Flowing with Milk and Honey*, 92). Yet Jesus' use of *abba* is lacking in the respect for the father that patriarchy inculcates, and is to that extent anti-patriarchal (100).

2. The following attempt to exploit trinitarian language in an anti-patriarchal direction represents an alternative to the assumption that images may be abandoned and adopted at will. On this latter view, the problem of traditional male images such as father and son is their fixity. Gail Ramshaw writes: '"You shall not make yourself a graven image," it was said. Yet more solid than stone, more resistant to iconoclasm than bronze, are the images cast in theological language and so engraved on our minds and throughout our prayers' ('The Gender of God', 168). Janet Morley similarly points to the dangerous idolatry of 'familiar male language which *feels* transparent and literal. For religious language cannot but be metaphorical in character; that is, pointing in an imaginative way to a reality that is, in the end, unsayable.' Feminine terminology for God is illuminating 'precisely because it clearly draws attention to its own inadequacy' ('I Desire Her with my Whole Heart', 163). For a critique of this view of religious language, see Alvin F. Kimel, Jr. (ed.), *Speaking the Christian God: The Holy Trinity and the Challenge of Feminism*. Unfortunately some of the studies in this collection defend the traditional father–son language in a manner that is too dismissive of feminist concerns.

3. 'Monotheism was and is the religion of patriarchy, just as pantheism is probably the religion of earlier matriarchy. It is only the doctrine of the Trinity… which makes a first approach towards overcoming sexist language in the concept of God' (J. Moltmann, *The Trinity and the Kingdom of God*, 165). However, I do not here follow Moltmann in emphasizing supposedly 'motherly' aspects of the divine fatherhood (164–5).

4. I assume here that the parable is a story about God and that this fact should control its interpretation. John Dominic Crossan offers a Derridean reading according to which the paradoxical core of the story - the fêted prodigal, the unfêted dutiful son – makes it irreducibly polyvalent, an example of 'ludic allegory' which resists the violence of the official, final reading ('A Metamodel for Polyvalent Narration', 139). Thus, in a typical deconstructive inversion of reference into self-reference, Crossan sees the parable as 'a metaphor for the hermeneutical multiplicity it engenders' (140). Admittedly this reading is much more interesting than, for example, Jeremias's, according to which Jesus is here saying to the Pharisees, 'Behold the greatness of God's love for his lost children, and contrast it with your own joyless, loveless, thankless and self-righteous lives', etc. (*The Parables of Jesus*, 131). See S. Moore, *Literary Criticism and the Gospels*, 138–51, on Crossan and deconstruction.

5. According to Susan Durber, the parable is 'significant as a text that illustrates the absence of women; where is the mother (or mothers)? and where are the sisters? They are unimportant for the text because the story is structured around a patriarchal legal and inheritance system by which a father divides his property between his sons. This parable illustrates well the kind of texts that patriarchy produces, texts in which women are absent or present solely to satisfy male desire' ('The Female Reader of the Parables of the Lost', 70). The only women mentioned are the prostitutes in the far country, who are 'women regarded through male eyes; as low, sensual, shameful yet desirable, commodities to be bought, passive, to be looked at' (72).

6. C. H. Dodd overlooks the discrepancy between expectation and actuality when he says of the father in this parable that 'he is *any* father worth the name, as the hearers are expected to recognize' (*The Founder of Christianity*, 71–2). This interpretation stems in part from Dodd's commitment to narrative realism, and in part from the influence of this text on modern understanding of fatherhood, which in turn naturalizes the representation in the text.

7. In adopting and elaborating upon the parable's negative evaluation of the elder brother, I have tacitly decided against a deconstructive reading which questions and problematizes the evaluative system embedded in this text. Such a reading is offered by Jill Robbins, who shows how the parable shapes the narrative of Augustine's *Confessions* and how this self-interpretation is dependent on seeing the elder brother as a figure for the Jew in relation to the gospel. The elder brother remains outside, 'but this outside is a necessary outside. Just as Christian conversion depends on the death of an old self and the rebirth of the new, so too that conversion depends on an exegetical conversion, from a dead letter (old) to the living spirit (new)' (*Prodigal Son/Elder Brother*, 40). 'He has to be inside the parable, inscribed *as* its outside, as a trace of the rejected alternative – insensate, deaf, blind, unable to understand – yet he makes the spiritual understanding of the parable possible' (41). Following Geoffrey Hartman and others, Robbins is interested in the opposition between 'the Hebrew Bible, a scripture read without reference to the New Testament' (8) and its 'captive' existence in the form of the Christian Old Testament, subordinated to the New by way of figural reading. The real interest here lies not in the Hebrew Bible itself but in midrash, understood as 'a radically text-bound procedure that is not unlike what contemporary critics call reading', 'a commentary that does *not* seek to illuminate' (14, 15). Ironically, Robbins cannot escape the gesture of taking the old text captive that she seeks to undo: for just as in Augustine's hermeneutic 'the Old Testament is the *herald* of the New', so here midrash is 'seen to *herald* developments in poststructuralism' (4, 14, my italics).

8. Over against the conventional view that 'we must study the parable of the Prodigal Son apart from the interpretive introduction in 15:1–2' (J. D. Crossan, *In Parables*, 74), recent narrative criticism rightly argues that the parables in Luke 15 can only be properly understood in the context of the controversy mentioned at the outset (R. C. Tannehill, *The Narrative Unity of Luke–Acts*, 1.106; cf. D. A. Neale, *None but the Sinners*, 154–8). The tendency (ancient and modern) to isolate the parables from their narrative contexts is, arguably, gnostic: cf. *The Gospel of Thomas*, 9, 57, 63, 64, 76, 107, etc. (English translation in J. M. Robinson (ed.), *The Nag Hammadi Library*, 118–30). Here, parables are prefaced simply by the phrase 'Jesus said', without even a rudimentary narrative context.

9. Theological reading of the parable should highlight its political and eschatological dimensions, in opposition to the dominant pietistic-individualistic reading (for which see the quotation from Jeremias in n. 4 above). The latter is still perceptible, in secularized form, when Mary Ann Tolbert reads this text as a Freudian allegory in which the father represents the ego, the older son the superego, the younger son the id or pleasure principle, and the far country the unconscious. The parable 'speaks to the wish of every individual for harmony and unity within themselves' ('The Prodigal Son', 12).

10. I am indebted to Rosemary Ruether for the phrase 'the kenosis of the father' (see her *Sexism and God-Talk*, 1–11).

11. The presence of Wisdom or the Holy Spirit within the triune being of God, alongside the other two divine persons, counteracts Daphne Hampson's assertion that 'the trinity does not as a symbol embody equality between male and female' (*Theology and Feminism*, 154). Recast as a historical claim about the past functioning of this symbol this would be largely correct, but it may still offer possibilities which have so far been inadequately exploited.

12. 'Without the Spirit it is impossible to behold the Word of God... since the knowledge of the Father is the Son, and the knowledge of the Son of God can only be obtained through the Spirit' (Irenaeus, *Demonstration of the Apostolic Preaching*, 6, quoted by J. N. D. Kelly, *Early Christian Doctrines*, 107). For Irenaeus's identification of Spirit and Wisdom, see n. 13 on chapter 11, above.

13. The setting of this identification of Wisdom with the Holy Spirit within a trinitarian

context differentiates this approach from that of feminist theologians such as Fiorenza and Ruether. For Fiorenza, as we have seen, 'the Sophia-God of Jesus' virtually excludes all reference to the father or the son. Ruether believes that 'it is doubtful... that we should settle for a concept of the Trinity that consists of two male and one female "persons". Such a concept of God falls easily into an androcentric or male-dominant perspective. The female side of God then becomes a subordinate principle underneath the dominant image of male divine sovereignty' (*Sexism and God-Talk*, 60). Such a claim would only be justified if the notion of male divine sovereignty was inherent in the doctrine of the trinity. If, on the other hand, this doctrine can be interpreted as a critique of that notion, the situation would be very different.

14. Eugene E. Lemcio points out that 'although the "narrative art" of the Evangelists has been explored so far as story, plot, character, and tone are concerned, writers on these subjects have not addressed the "pastness of the past" in the gospels in a thoroughgoing way' (*The Past of Jesus in the Gospels*, 107–8). Working entirely from within the gospel narratives and without engaging in hypothetical reconstructions, Lemcio shows how the evangelists convey the pastness of the past by differentiating between the language appropriate to the pre-Easter and the post-Easter periods: 'They spoke to the present in the idioms of the past' (26).

15. D. Rhoads and D. Michie, *Mark as Story*, 3; it is stated here that all four gospels are 'autonomous stories about Jesus'.

Part Four   Theology, Hermeneutics, Exegesis

1. I use this concept here in a sense akin to Schleiermacher's, emphasizing the dialectical relation of part to whole at many levels in interpretation, rather than the relation between the text and the pre-understanding of the interpreter (as in the reformulation of this concept by Heidegger, Bultmann and Gadamer). According to Schleiermacher, 'Complete knowledge always involves an apparent circle, that each part can be understood only out of the whole to which it belongs, and vice versa' (*Hermeneutics*, 113).

13. Theological Hermeneutics

1. Symptomatic of this difficulty is Frei's use of the term 'realism' in a literary–formalist sense rather than a philosophical–theological one. Thus, while he cites passages from Barth's *Church Dogmatics* as exemplary narrative readings of biblical texts (*Eclipse*, viii), Frei is silent about the Barthian concern with the 'reality' to which the texts bear witness. On this latter topic, see George Hunsinger, 'Beyond Literalism and Expressivism: Karl Barth's Hermeneutical Realism': in a Barthian perspective, 'Intratextuality without extratextuality would merely aestheticize the subject matter' (221).

2. See *Eclipse*, 142–54, 202–24.

3. See the discussion in chapter 1 above, 24–5.

4. The two views referred to here are associated especially with H. E. Tödt, *The Son of Man in the Synoptic Tradition* (German original, 1959), 224–26, and G. Vermes, *Jesus the Jew* (1973), 160–91.

5. The examples are my own rather than Kähler's, and they represent positions too widely held to require extensive documentation. The first position (that Jesus was relatively unremarkable in his own context) is essentially that of J. Weiss's *Jesus' Proclamation of the Kingdom of God*. E. P. Sanders' *Jesus and Judaism* can be seen as a restatement of this position; here too Jewish eschatology is the linchpin of the argument. The second position (that Jesus differs at crucial points from the early church) is perceptible, for example, in E. Käsemann's

claim that Jesus' view of all life as lived before God is to be sharply differentiated from the eschatological message of the earliest Jewish Christian community (*New Testament Questions of Today*, 114). The closely-related third position (that originality guarantees value and truth) is the assumption that underlies and justifies concern with matters of authenticity. Thus, A. J. B. Higgins opens his book, *Jesus and the Son of Man* with the statement: 'If it is important to understand early Christian beliefs about Jesus as recorded in the New Testament, it is even more important to attempt to discover how far these beliefs may have been derived from Jesus' own teaching, *and consequently to what extent they were justified*' (9; my italics). The fourth position (that religious experience is more important than dogma) accounts for A. Harnack's claim that the gospel as preached by Jesus 'is in no wise a positive religion like the rest; that it contains no statutory or particularistic elements; *that it is, therefore, religion itself*' (*What is Christianity?*, 65; italics original). The point of citing such views is not to deny that each of them may contain an element of truth but to illustrate the prevalence of *comprehensive* hypotheses deriving from perhaps questionable dogmatic schemas.

6. For Barth's endorsement of Kähler's position on this issue, see *Church Dogmatics*, I, 2, 64–65.

7. See too the brief and lucid discussion of this point in Barth's *Evangelical Theology*, 29–30.

8. Werner Jeanrond rightly emphasizes that genre is in part a matter of reception: if there are 'theological text genres', there are also 'theological reading genres' (*Text and Interpretation as Categories of Theological Thinking*, 118).

9. At the end of his *Life of Jesus Critically Examined* (1835–36), D. F. Strauss reflects on the ministry of the historically-aware theologian within the church, and identifies four main possibilities: to attempt to raise the church to one's own level; to lower oneself to the church's level; to leave the ministerial office; or – the strategy that Strauss recommends – to emphasize the spiritual side of popular conceptions, for example at Easter (782–83). Underlying this is a notion of two levels of knowledge, the spiritual and the carnal (the elite and the popular), which may be found in Origen, in Gnosticism and, at one point, in Paul (1 Cor. 2.6–16). A theological critique of this conception might begin from the communal recitation of the creed, which indicates that, whatever the differences and gradations of knowledge, there can ultimately be no question of two distinct levels. There is rather a single knowledge of Christ in which individuals share unequally and differently (cf. Eph.4.4–16).

10. Strauss's critique of Schleiermacher (*The Christ of Faith and the Jesus of History* (1865)) is a particularly clear early manifestation of this ideology. Schleiermacher is depicted as drawn simultaneously in two opposite directions: towards the faith of the church, which leads him into an essentially docetic view of Jesus' sinlessness, among other errors, and towards criticism, in which dogma is subjected to properly scientific procedures. What really offends Strauss is Schleiermacher's insistence on locating critical questions within a framework that is ecclesial and theological from the outset. Strauss's construal of the situation is arguably still in place wherever there is talk of 'the Jesus of history', although the sharpness with which this figure is demarcated from 'the Christ of faith' varies and fluctuates.

11. I paraphrase here Schweitzer's well-known statement: the study of the life of Jesus 'loosed the bands by which he had been riveted for centuries to the stony rocks of ecclesiastical doctrine, and rejoiced to see life and movement coming into the figure once more...' (*The Quest of the Historical Jesus*, 397). On this statement, see further below, 255-6.

12. John Dominic Crossan's *The Historical Jesus: The Life of a Mediterranean Jewish Peasant* illustrates some of the points at which the distinction between the ecclesial and the

scholarly Jesus is currently drawn. Jesus 'must be understood within his contemporary Judaism' (417), that is, as 'a peasant Jewish Cynic' (421). It is not as such that he is significant for Christian faith, and Crossan addresses this problem by appealing, somewhat casually, to the New Testament's christological pluralism as an indication that 'there will always be divergent historical Jesuses' as well as 'divergent Christs built upon them' (423). 'Scholarly reconstruction' is also potentially at odds with 'ecclesiastical faith' when it engages in systematic dismantling of the gospel portrayal in order to present the world with a 'reconstructed historical Jesus' (424–25). The hermeneutic of the Jewish context, of christological pluralism and of scholarly reconstruction is anti-ecclesial not in an old-fashioned positivistic sense, but because it systematically marginalizes the communally normative christology that ecclesial faith presupposes.

13. Origen employs his discussion of historicity in the service of a spiritualizing hermeneutic propounding a dual knowledge of Christ for the educated and for the simple respectively (see n. 9, above). My reading removes it from this context, on the assumption that Origen here identifies an issue that remains important even after the demise of theological neo-Platonism.

14. The commentary, published in 1535, is based on a series of thirty-six lectures that Luther gave in Wittenberg between July 3 and Dec. 12, 1531. (The details are give in Karl Drescher's foreword to vol. 40 of the Weimar edition (*WA*), 2; Jaroslav Pelikan's summary of this in *Luther's Works* (*LW*) 26, ix, is not quite accurate.) The lectures were taken down in shorthand by Georg Rörer, whose transcription forms the basis of the printed commentary; both are included in *WA* 40/1, 2, where the transcription is printed in the upper part of each page and the published commentary beneath. Rörer also availed himself of the notes of Caspar Cruciger and Veit Dietrich, and it was he, not Luther, who was responsible for the publication of the commentary. According to Drescher, Rörer's expansions do not affect the content but only the expression (*WA* 40/1. 2). Luther himself acknowledged that 'all the thoughts which I find set down in this book with such diligence by the brethren are really mine, so that I am compelled to admit that all of them, or at least most of them, were spoken by me in my public presentation' (*WA* 40/1.33.4–6 (= *Luther's Works* (*LW*) 27.145)). A second edition of the commentary followed in 1538, a German translation in 1539, and English translations in 1575 and 1578. I have sometimes followed Jaroslav Pelikan's translation (*LW* 26–27), sometimes modified it, and sometimes made my own.

15. The difference between this and the Pauline view is rightly noted by G. Ebeling: 'When we turn from the Reformers' doctrine of law and Gospel to Paul, the most striking difference is that the successive elements in a unique transition which can never again be reversed are turned by the Reformers' schema into a peculiarly simultaneous conjunction, so to speak a permanently occurring transition...' (*Word and Faith*, 260).

16. According to B. Lohse, 'Luther's distinction between law and gospel... referred to something other than the division of biblical statements into the two parts of the biblical canon. This distinction rather describes the fact that *God* both judges and is merciful' (*Martin Luther*, 157). The distinction 'can only be understood on the basis of Luther's doctrine of God' (171). But insofar as this God is known only through the biblical text, the text itself evokes the dual response of repulsion and attraction. This hermeneutical dimension to Luther's theology is frequently overlooked, partly because of a tendency to separate his experience of the law from the biblical text.

17. For this reason, according to Karin Bornkamm, 'die formale Berufung auf die Schrift hat keine letzte Beweiskraft – die Annahme eines Teufels, der sich Worte der Schrift aneignet, macht das unmöglich... Deshalb dienen Luther die theologischen Erkenntnisse und Begriffe, die er aus der Schrift gewonnen hat, nun umgekehrt dazu, im Gespräch mit

der Schrift die rechte definitio der Gestalt Christi herauszuarbeiten' (*Luthers Auslegungen der Galaterbriefes*, 191).

18. The significance of such passages is noted by O. Hof, who argues that for Luther exegesis is a means of resisting *Anfechtung*: 'Die Schriftauslegung im Sinne der Rechtfertigungslehre ist der Existentialakt, in dem der in der Anfechtung stehende Christ durch die Gnade des Heiligen Geistes um die Erhaltung des vom Gesetz unterschiedenen und mit ihm unvermischten Evangeliums von Christus ringt' (*Schriftauslegung und Rechtfertigungslehre*, 14). 'Es handelt sich nicht um das mechanische Funktionieren einer von bestimmten Prinzipien geleiteten Auslegungsapparatur, sondern um eine Kampfhandlung' (25). Hof has in mind especially those biblical passages which appear to teach salvation by works.

19. Owen's theology derives from the Puritan tradition; but, as Basil Hall has shown, the term 'Puritan' fell increasingly into disuse from around 1640 onwards (*Humanists and Protestants*, 245–52).

20. The argument of H. Graf Reventlow's *The Authority of the Bible and the Rise of the Modern World* involves the claim that 'the Puritans were just as much heirs of Humanism as they were of the Reformation' (166). This argument, which oddly assumes that in the beginning Reformation and Humanism were quite distinct, locates Puritanism within a straight line which leads from Erasmus to Deism, and would lead one to deny the seriousness of Owen's opposition to the liberal Anglicanism of the post-Restoration period. This strange presentation, which evidently has the function of absolving Luther and Calvin from blame for the rise of the historical-critical method, detracts considerably from the value of Reventlow's important book.

21. According to Owen, it is not only Quakers who dismiss the doctrine of the Trinity: 'There are others, and those not a few, who either reject the doctrine of it as false, or despise it as unintelligible, or neglect it as useless, or of no great importance' (*Pneumatologia*, 66).

14. Christology and Community

1. According to M. Dibelius and H. Conzelmann, the claim that the epiphany has taken place in the past is a sign that 'the church has obviously adjusted to the thought of the world's duration and has learned to become at home in it' (*The Pastoral Epistles*, 10). The emphasis would perhaps be better placed on the world not as 'home' but as 'workplace': the site, in other words, of the church's task or mission of extending the divine *philanthrōpia* manifested in Christ.

2. Barth refers to Tit. 3.4 in this connection in *Church Dogmatics*, IV, 1, 35 and IV, 3, 667.

3. Some comments on Rom. 8.3 illustrate the christological dimension of Barth's earlier theology. God sent his Son in the likeness of sin-controlled flesh, and in Jesus Christ 'sin-controlled flesh becomes a parable or *likeness*. What is human and worldly and historical and "natural" is shown to be what it veritably is in its relation to God the Creator – only a transparent thing, only an image, only a sign, only something relative' (*The Epistle to the Romans*, 280–81). Thus, in Gethsemane and finally on Golgotha, 'it is imperative that the incognito of the Son of God should increase and gain the upper hand, that it should move on to final self-surrender and self-abandonment' (281). In him we must see 'our flesh dissolved and our sin condemned' (282). Jesus Christ, and especially the crucified Jesus Christ, is therefore a parable of the merely relative value of everything human and finite in the face of the divine infinity.

4. This does not mean, however, that Barth 'denies the historical nature of revelation', or that his christology 'is constructed with only the most superficial contacts with human

history', in that historical revelation 'merely recapitulates its eternal antecedents' in the pre-temporal divine decision (A. E. McGrath, *Modern German Christology*, 110).

5. Symptomatic of this situation is the fact that a major collection of essays on *Jesus and the Politics of his Day* (ed. E. Bammel and C. F. D. Moule) construes the political issue almost exclusively in terms of Jesus' relation to the Zealots. If Jesus was not a Zealot, then his ministry was essentially religious and apolitical: 'Jesus revolted against the Torah of his fathers, nay he wrestled with God, but it is not likely that he descended to ordinary revolutionary activity or allowed himself to be used by the mouthpieces of the different activisms of his day' (E. Bammel, 'The revolution theory from Reimarus to Brandon', 56).

6. The orientation would have to be towards a future that is communal as well as eschatological, an emphasis that is missing in Pannenberg's christologically-shaped view of the future. According to Pannenberg, the question of a fulfilment of human destiny beyond death arises from the fact that individuals cannot ultimately be absorbed into society (*Jesus – God and Man*, 84–85). Salvation is that wholeness of life for which one longs but which one does not attain in earthly existence, and Jesus calls us to be open to this universal destiny (192–94). Social or communal existence seems here to be a threat to individual destiny rather than its fulfilment.

7. 'Enemy soldiers being swallowed by hostile waters of course brings to mind the narrative of Israel's liberation from Egypt' (C. Myers, *Binding the Strong Man: A Political Reading of Mark's Story of Jesus*, 191).

8. On this point see E. Cardenal, *The Gospel in Solentiname*, 2.195–97.

9. A more prosaic explanation for the Gerasenes' desire to be rid of Jesus is the disastrous economic loss entailed by the destruction of the herd of pigs (so H. C. Waetjen, *A Reordering of Power: A Socio-Political Reading of Mark's Gospel*, 118).

10. The quotations are from Theodore's commentary on Galatians (4.22–31), excerpted in K. Froehlich (ed.), *Biblical Interpretation in the Early Church*, 95–103; 97.

11. 'When the ruling class feels its hegemony threatened, it tries to neutralize challengers by identifying them with the mythic cultural arch-demon. The logic of the scribes was simple: because they believed themselves to be God's representatives, Jesus' "secession" necessarily put him in allegiance to Satan' (C. Myers, *Binding the Strong Man*, 165).

12. V. Taylor finds the blasphemy primarily in the reference to the Son of man sitting at the right hand of Power (*Mark*, 569–70); cf. C. E. B. Cranfield, *Mark*, 445. Both commentators are influenced by the consideration that in a Jewish context the claim to messiahship was not blasphemous. But if Mark understands the term 'Christ' in the light of 'Son of God' (or 'Son of the Blessed'), then the Johannine view becomes a possibility (cf. John 5.17–18; 8.58–59; 10.30–36). If this is not the case, the high priest's question and Jesus' initial reply ('I am') become redundant. It is the entirety of Jesus' reply – the acceptance of the titles 'Christ' and 'Son of the Blessed', and the statement about the enthronement of the Son of man – that constitute the blasphemy for which he is crucified.

13. In reading Mark in the light of John I also have in mind B. S. Childs' suggestion that in a canonical perspective the gospels are to be read alongside one another and not played off against each other. The interpretative task is to perceive the unity of the one gospel in its fourfold form (*The New Testament as Canon*, 197–98). On this see chapter 2 above, 36–37.

14. For discussion of the importance of the Socinian tradition in this context, see K. Scholder, *The Birth of Modern Critical Theology: Origins and Problems of Biblical Criticism in the Seventeenth Century*, 26–45. John Locke's *The Reasonableness of Christianity* (1695) is a good example of a text that mediates between the Socinian tradition and modern historical awareness. This work is based upon the claim that the earliest Christian confession, that Jesus is the Messiah, does not necessitate belief in the incarnation or the trinity. A similar position is later to be found in Reimarus.

15. For example, the opposition between world-denial and world-affirmation, fundamental in Schweitzer's final chapter, is characteristically Nietzschean, as is the sense that
world-affirmation only attains its true being, as something deeper than thoughtless
complacency, through victorious struggle with world-denial (400); compare *Also sprach
Zarathustra.*

16. Schweitzer's book reaches its climax not so much with Wrede (as the German title,
Von Reimarus zu Wrede would suggest) as with the choice between Wrede's 'thoroughgoing
scepticism' and his own 'thoroughgoing eschatology' (328–95). Bultmann is largely
responsible for the twentieth century preference for the sceptical alternative.

17. However, the importance of 'the historical Jesus' in Latin American liberation
theology should be noted. Jon Sobrino's statement is typical: 'There can be no Christology
of Christ apart from the history of Jesus of Nazareth' (*Christology at the Crossroads*, xxii).
Other relatively recent works that remain optimistic about the theological significance of the
quest include E. Schillebeeckx's *Jesus* and J. Mackey's *Jesus the Man and the Myth.*

18. The summary that follows does not exactly represent the view of any individual
scholar. For differing but related examples of the general approach, see J. D. G. Dunn,
Christology in the Making, and Maurice Casey, *From Jewish Prophet to Gentile God.* In both
of these works, the evolution is in some sense a decline, a gradual drift away from the concrete
historical–theological reality experienced so vividly in the beginning. In particular, the
Gospel of John (perhaps the fundamental biblical text for later trinitarian reflection) is
criticized for tending to stretch Jewish monotheism into an unacceptable ditheism –
however understandable this move was within a particular cultural milieu (cf. Dunn,
Christology, 264).

19. See C. H. Talbert's remarks on the intellectual background of Reimarus' work in his
'Introduction' to the *Fragments*, 4–18.

20. Cf. U. Luz, 'The Son of Man in Matthew: Heavenly Judge or Human Christ?', where
it is argued that the meaning of 'Son of man' in Matthew must be derived from within
Matthew itself.

21. See D. F. Strauss, 'Hermann Samuel Reimarus and his Apology'.

22. W. Wrede's *The Messianic Secret in the Gospels* has been especially influential in its
postulation of a linear movement *backwards*: Jesus' Sonship or Messiahship, initially
bestowed on him at his resurrection is later traced backwards into his earthly life and
ultimately to a pre-existent, heavenly state.

23. Thus, J. D. G. Dunn presents Paul's christology against the primary background of
pre-Christian Jewish wisdom speculation, rather than seeking its own inner logic (*Christology
in the Making*, 163–96). The purpose is to legitimize a supposedly more flexible (and
ultimately unitarian) christological language in which Jesus is 'the exhaustive embodiment
of divine wisdom' (195), in opposition to notions of deity, pre-existence, incarnation and
trinity. In fact, Paul speaks explicitly of Jesus as 'the wisdom of God' in only one passage (1
Cor. 1.24, 30), where a background in Jewish usage is anyway doubtful: *sophia* is associated
rather with 'Greeks' (1 Cor. 1.22).

24. Thus H. C. Kee distinguishes between 'Hellenistic usage, where the phrase [Son of
God] has mythological or metaphysical connotations', and Mark's more Jewish use of this
phrase to designate Jesus as 'the redemptive figure of the end-time' (*Community of the New
Age*, 121, 122).

25. To take a typical example, Bultmann asserts that 'the "I-sayings" were predominantly
the work of the Hellenistic church'. They bear no relation to the earthly Jesus, for they are
uttered 'in the name of the ascended Lord' (*History of the Synoptic Tradition*, 163). There is
sometimes an acknowledgement that a saying created by the church might perhaps be 'an

answer to Jesus' whole person and mission' rather than 'the mere product of imagination' (G. Bornkamm, *Jesus of Nazareth*, 21), but there is little attempt to make this important insight exegetically fruitful.

26. J. Weiss's *Jesus' Proclamation of the Kingdom of God* is an obvious example of the first procedure; compare Bultmann's treatment of 'the eschatological preaching of Jesus' under the heading of 'Judaism' rather than of 'Primitive Christianity' (*Primitive Christianity in its Contemporary Setting*, 86–93). For a defence of the second procedure against the first, see A. Harnack, *What is Christianity?*, 54–58.

27. Thus, according to R. E. Brown, John 4 attests a group of Jewish Johannine Christians 'of peculiar anti-Temple views who converted Samaritans and picked up some elements of Samaritan thought, including a christology that was not centered on a Davidic Messiah' (*The Community of the Beloved Disciple*, 38); this event proved to be 'a catalyst toward a higher christology' (43; emphasis removed). But if the Gospel is *about* the gradual heightening of christology, what has happened to the figure who is supposed to be the object of christology?

28. The Spirit will guide 'not into further new truth, but into the whole truth concerning that which was concretely and concisely set forth by the Son of God... Inspiration does not detach men from the Truth which is in Jesus, and set them free to wander into new realms of truth apart from the sanctuary of God' (E. C. Hoskyns, *The Fourth Gospel*, 574; the concluding phrase is derived from Ignatius of Antioch). 'If we are to interpret the Fourth Gospel, we must take our stand where the Evangelist stood and endeavour to follow him and to hear what he is saying... And we must take him at his word when he says that the Spirit does bring to light the meaning that lies in the History of Jesus of Nazareth...' (124).

29. For the theoretical background to this empiricist concern with 'evidence', see John Locke's *Essay concerning Human Understanding*, 4.15–16.

30. Matthew Tindal's *Christianity as Old as the Creation: Or, The Gospel the Republication of the Religion of Nature* (1730) is the classic deist statement of this position.

31. Compare the critique of the quest of the historical Jesus in C. E. Gunton, *Yesterday and Today*, 56–63.

32. Thus D. E. Nineham dismisses the objection that, in regarding Jesus as an ordinary man and the gospels as ordinary books, the 'quest' merely begs the question: the accessibility of a unitary perspective on a unitary world is, and is likely to remain, 'a cardinal presupposition of the historical method' (*Explorations in Theology 1*, 115). It is consistent with this unitary perspective when, in his 'Epilogue' to *The Myth of God Incarnate*, Nineham rejects the suggestion that a qualitative uniqueness might be ascribed to Jesus on historical if not on metaphysical grounds. The dogma that there can be no qualitative uniqueness naturally obliges one to reject any counter-claim, whether 'metaphysical', 'historical', or both.

15. Praxis and Hope

1. This appears to be the position of J. L. Segundo, according to whom 'not one single dogma can be studied with any other final criterion than its impact on praxis' ('Capitalism vs. Socialism', 250).

2. On this see Roland M. Frye, 'Language for God and Feminist Language', 21–26.

3. See, however, David Rensberger's positive evaluation of Johannine 'sectarianism' (*Overcoming the World*, 135–154): it is the sect rather than the established religion 'that is able to present a fundamental challenge to the world's oppressive orders' (142).

4. See B. S. Childs, *The New Testament as Canon*, 487.

5. It seems more apt to speak of the 'polyvalence' of the Johannine term *kosmos* than to find here a conflict between 'positive' and 'negative' uses (R. E. Brown, *The Epistles of John*, 222–24).

6. As R. Schnackenburg points out, John 18.20 recalls Jesus' public ministry as presented in the first main section of this gospel (*The Gospel according to St. John*, 3.237).

7. See, for example, C. H. Dodd's dismissive remarks in *Parables of the Kingdom*, 13–14.

8. This interpretation suggests that the problematic relation of story to setting should not be ascribed to 'Luke's capacity for combining fine writing with confusion in presentation', as C. F. Evans suggests (*Saint Luke*, 468).

9. As in the christology of Origen, on which see C. E. Gunton, *Yesterday and Today*, 36–39.

10. The close relationship between Jas. 2.15–16 and 1 John 3.17 suggests a way of responding to Luther's claim that the Epistle of James fails to 'preach and inculcate Christ' (*LW* 35.396): the explicitly christological orientation of 1 John may be said to bring to light an implicit christology in James.

11. '"Jesus might have given the example of a priest who is going to the temple to fulfill all his duties in the worship of God, and on the way he helps the wounded man"' (E. Cardenal, *The Gospel in Solentiname*, 3.100).

12. See G. Gutiérrez, *A Theology of Liberation*, 106–16.

13. This follows from the fact that 'the truth-claims implied in Christian faith are ontological in character, they concern the constitution and structure of reality' (C. Schwöbel, *God: Action and Revelation*, 11). The relation between faith and knowledge in Johannine theology is outlined by R. Bultmann, *New Testament Theology*, 2.73–74.

14. See the attack on the notion of 'fulfilment' in Anthony Collins, *Discourse of the Grounds and Reasons of the Christian Religion* (1724); excerpts in J. Drury, *Critics of the Bible 1724–1873*, 21–45.

15. See J. Sawyer, 'Combating Prejudices about the Bible and Judaism', and the reply by W. Moberly, '"Old Testament" and "New Testament": The Propriety of the Terms for Christian Theology'.

16. Von Rad's *Old Testament Theology* might serve as a counter-example, for the discussion of 'the Old Testament and the New' occupies about a quarter of volume two. But what is at issue is not the commitment of individual Old Testament scholars to maintain some form of contact with the New Testament but the limitations which the discipline imposes on the thorough investigation of this relationship.

17. J. Alberto Soggin, *A History of Israel: From the Beginnings to the Bar Kochba Revolt, AD 135*. Jesus receives here only a paragraph, for 'he belongs more to the history of the church than to that of Israel' (326).

18. A currently-popular view of the relation between the Jewish and the Christian scriptures is stated by Gabriel Josipovici, who asserts a contrast between the open-endedness of the Hebrew Bible and the closure of the Christian version. 'The Christian order is one we find perfectly natural and easy to understand, partly because we ourselves, whatever our beliefs, have been conditioned by Christian culture, and partly because it corresponds to a profound need in each of us for closure and for a universe shaped according to a clearly comprehensible story... But just because the Christian pattern is so simple to grasp, it is easy to overlook the extraordinary nature of the Hebrew Bible's *refusal* of such a pattern' (*Book of God*, 47). We know that 'we will always be enmeshed in uncertainty. What is extraordinary is that a sacred book should dramatize this, rather than be the one place where we are given what we desire' (87). 'Christianity expresses profound desires and suggests that these can eventually be fulfilled. The Hebrew Bible refuses that consolation. The deep argument

between the two may then rest upon the question of whether that fulfilment is bound to be a fake, a denial of reality, or is the expression of a reality which we persist in refusing to see' (89). Thus the Hebrew Bible subverts its Christian counterpart, and the Bible in its twofold form dramatizes the modern literary critical preference for indeterminacy, plurality and openness over logocentrism and closure. (See also D. Boyarin, 'The Song of Songs: Lock or Key? Intertextuality, Allegory and Midrash'.)

19. So C. Myers, *Binding the Strong Man*, 317–18.

20. Against Childs, who, ignoring the broader canonical context, claims that 'the Deuteronomist's concern is not primarily humanitarian, but theological' (*Exodus*, 417). Why is it assumed that the adjectives 'humanitarian' and 'theological' are mutually exclusive?

21. The sabbath is also traced back to the creation of the world (Gen. 2.2–3, Exod. 20.11; 31.17). When linked with Deut. 5.15, these passages 'draw into a single perspective the exodus experience and belief in creation, making it clear that the God of the exodus is the Creator of the world, and that God the Creator is also the God of the exodus' (J. Moltmann, *God in Creation*, 285).

22. This Marcionite perspective is evident when, for example, Burton Mack speaks of the early Christians' 'aggressive requisition' of the Hebrew scriptures (*A Myth of Innocence*, 359). But this denial of the legitimacy of a distinctively Christian perspective on these texts is a simple mirror-image of the Christian attitude towards Judaism that Mack deplores.

23. This privileging of the prophetic over the priestly perspective has been deeply embedded in Old Testament studies since Wellhausen; see John Barton's defence of Wellhausen's achievement in this area in R. Morgan with J. Barton, *Biblical Interpretation*, 76–88. Fear of the charge of 'anti-Judaism' should not make it impossible to express a theologically-grounded preference for (say) Amos over Ezra.

24. Compare W. Pannenberg's argument that Jesus' ministry is divinely authorized only by the Easter event, which casts a retroactive light back upon it (*Jesus – God and Man*, 135–36). 'Only the future decides what something is' (136).

25. So C. Myers, *Binding the Strong Man*, 244.

26. In addition to the canonical ending (Amos 9.11–15), Amos's exhortations to 'seek Yahweh and live', etc. (5.6; cf. vv. 4, 14, 15), to 'take away from me the noise of your songs' (5.23), and to 'let justice roll down like waters' (5.24) presuppose the possibility of a future that is different from the present.

27. 'Within the Old Testament or Old Testament "wisdom", Koheleth is the first… to have discovered and treated thematically the historicity of existence – *in tormentis*' (K. Galling, *ZTK* 58 (1961), 1, cited by M. Hengel, *Judaism and Hellenism*, 1.116). The popularity of Ecclesiastes during the era of theological existentialism may be contrasted with the late Victorian strictures of S. R. Driver: 'Of course, Qoheleth takes a false view of life… A life not circumscribed by merely personal ends, but quickened and sustained by devotion to the interests of humanity, is not "vanity", or the pursuit of wind' (*Introduction to the Literature of the Old Testament*, 472).

28. A connection might be made between Qoheleth's scepticism and the atheism of Ivan Karamazov, which rests in large part on the stories of the sufferings of children that he recounts to his brother Alyosha in *The Brothers Karamazov*, 2.5.4 (immediately before 'The Grand Inquisitor'). Dostoyevsky's 'answer' is, in part, to represent Alyosha as not answering Ivan verbally but as engaging in a praxis which aims at alleviating a particular child's mental and physical suffering by restoring him to authentic communal existence (4.10) – a praxis which exposes the hollowness of a protest-atheism which remains at a purely theoretical level.

29. Childs claims that, canonically, 'Koheleth's sayings do not have an independent status, but function as a critical corrective, much as the book of James serves in the New

Testament as an essential corrective to misunderstanding the Pauline letters' (*Introduction to the Old Testament as Scripture*, 588). But it is hard to read the dogmatic denial of the new in Eccles. 1 as a mere corrective.

16. Resurrection, Text and Truth

1. According to Barth, Paul's intention in 1 Cor. 15.1–11 is to deflect attention away from his own person and the idiosyncracies of his preaching towards the gospel that he shares with the whole primitive church (*The Resurrection of the Dead*, 139). This important point should be applied generally to every individual New Testament testimony to the resurrection, so as to emphasize that, in all their differences, they are still testifying together to the same thing.

2. Taking Luke 24 as an exemplary statement of the resurrection faith necessitates dissent from the evolutionary view that attempts to reconstruct the process by which 'late' appearance stories eventually came into being (see, for example, R. H. Fuller, *The Formation of the Resurrection Narratives*, W. Marxsen, *The Resurrection of Jesus of Nazareth*, E. Schillebeeckx, *Jesus: An Experiment in Christology*, 320–97). This procedure privileges hypothetical reconstructions of the original events at the expense of the gospel narratives.

3. To say that 'Luke has his own way of reading the OT and here puts it on the lips of Christ himself' (J. A. Fitzmyer, *The Gospel according to St. Luke X–XXIV*, 1558) is to turn this theme into a personal idiosyncracy that requires no further interpretative attention.

Bibliography

Alter, Robert. *The Art of Biblical Narrative*. London: George Allen & Unwin, 1981
   'Introduction' (The Old Testament). In Alter and Kermode (eds.), *Guide*, 11–
   35
Alter, Robert, and Kermode, Frank. *The Literary Guide to the Bible*. London:
   Collins, 1987
   'General Introduction'. In Alter and Kermode (eds.), *Guide*, 1–8
Anderson, Ana Flora, and da Silva Gorgulho, Gilberto, OP. 'Miriam and her
   Companions'. In Ellis and Maduro (eds.), *The Future of Liberation Theology*,
   205–19
Auerbach, Erich. *Mimesis: The Representation of Reality in Western Literature*. ET
   Princeton University Press, 1953
Bach, Alice (ed.). *The Pleasure of Her Text: Feminist Readings of Biblical and
   Historical Texts*. Philadelphia: Trinity Press International, 1990
   'The Pleasure of Her Text'. In Bach (ed.), *Pleasure*, 25–44
Bal, Mieke. *Lethal Love: Feminist Literary Readings of Biblical Love Stories*.
   Bloomington and Indianapolis: Indiana University Press, 1987
   (ed.) *Anti-Covenant: Counter-Reading Women's Lives in the Hebrew Bible*.
   Sheffield: The Almond Press, 1989
   'Dealing/With/Women: Daughters in the Book of Judges.' In Schwartz (ed.),
   The Book and the Text, 16–39
Bammel, Ernst and Moule, C. F. D. (eds.). *Jesus and the Politics of his Day*.
   Cambridge University Press, 1984
   'The revolution theory from Reimarus to Brandon'. In Bammel and Moule
   (eds.), *Jesus*
Barbour, Ian G. *Religion in an Age of Science: The Gifford Lectures 1989–91, Volume
   1*. London: SCM Press, 1990
Barrett, C. K. *A Commentary on the First Epistle to the Corinthians*. Black's New
   Testament Commentaries. London: A. & C. Black, 1971[2]
Barr, James. *Holy Scripture: Canon, Authority, Criticism*. Oxford: Clarendon Press,
   1983
Barth, Karl. *The Epistle to the Romans*. ET Oxford University Press, 1933
   The Resurrection of the Dead. ET London: Hodder & Stoughton, 1933
   Church Dogmatics. ET Edinburgh: T. & T. Clark, 1956–69
   Evangelical Theology: An Introduction. ET Edinburgh: T. & T. Clark, 1979

Barth, Markus. *Ephesians 4–6.* New York: Doubleday, 1974

Barthes, Roland. *Image–Music–Text.* Ed. Stephen Heath. London: Fontana, 1977
   The Rustle of Language. ET Oxford: Basil Blackwell, 1986. Ed. François Wahl

Barton, John. *Reading the Old Testament: Method in Biblical Study.* London:
   Darton, Longman & Todd; Philadelphia: Westminster, 1984
   People of the Book? The Authority of the Bible in Christianity. London: SPCK, 1988

Bartsch, Hans Werner (ed.). *Kerygma and Myth.* London: SPCK, 1954

Berlin, Adele. *Poetics and Interpretation of Biblical Narrative.* Sheffield: The
   Almond Press, 1983

Bernstein, Richard J. *Beyond Objectivism and Relativism: Science, Hermeneutics and
   Praxis.* Oxford: Basil Blackwell, 1983

Bird, Phyllis. 'Images of Women in the Old Testament'. In R. R. Ruether (ed.),
   Religion and Sexism: Images of Women in the Jewish and Christian Traditions.
   New York: Simon and Schuster, 1974, 41–88

Bloom, Harold, and Rosenberg, David. *The Book of J.* New York: Grove
   Weidenfeld, 1990

Boff, Clodovis. *Theology and Praxis: Epistemological Foundations.* Maryknoll, NY:
   Orbis Books, 1987

Booth, Wayne C. *The Rhetoric of Fiction.* Harmondsworth: Penguin Books, 1987[2]

Bornkamm, Günther. *Jesus of Nazareth.* ET London: Hodder & Stoughton, 1963

Bornkamm, Karin. *Luthers Auslegungen des Galaterbriefs von 1519 und 1531. Ein
   Vergleich.* Berlin: de Gruyter, 1963

Boyarin, Daniel. 'The Song of Songs: Lock or Key? Intertextuality, Allegory and
   Midrash'. In Schwartz (ed.), *The Book and the Text,* 214–30

Brett, Mark C. *Biblical Criticism in Crisis? The impact of the canonical approach on
   Old Testament studies.* Cambridge University Press, 1991
   'Motives and Intentions in Genesis 1', *JTS* 42 n.s. (1991), 1–16

Bright, John. *A History of Israel.* London: SCM Press, 1972[2]

Brooten, Bernadette J. 'Early Christian Women and their Cultural Context: Issues
   of Method in Historical Reconstruction'. In Collins (ed.), *Perspectives,* 65–
   91

Brown, Raymond E. *The Epistles of John: A New Translation with Introduction and
   Commentary.* Anchor Bible. New York: Doubleday, 1982; London: Geoffrey
   Chapman, 1983
   The Community of the Beloved Disciple. London: Geoffrey Chapman, 1979

Brueggemann, Walter. *Genesis.* Interpretation. Atlanta: John Knox Press, 1982

Bultmann, Rudolf. *Theology of the New Testament, Volume 2.* ET London: SCM
   Press, 1955
   Primitive Christianity in its Contemporary Setting. ET London: Thames and
   Hudson, 1956
   History of the Synoptic Tradition. ET Oxford: Basil Blackwell, 1963
   The Johannine Epistles. Hermeneia. ET Philadelphia: Fortress, 1973

Calvin, John. *Genesis.* Edinburgh: Banner of Truth Trust, 1965

Cardenal, Ernesto. *The Gospel in Solentiname* (four vols.). ET Maryknoll: Orbis,

1976–82

Casey, Maurice. *From Jewish Prophet to Gentile God: the origins and development of New Testament Christology.* Cambridge and London: James Clark and Co., 1991

Childs, Brevard S. 'Interpretation in Faith', *Interpretation* 18 (1964), 259–71
Exodus. Old Testament Library. London: SCM Press, 1974
Introduction to the Old Testament as Scripture. London: SCM Press, 1979
The New Testament as Canon: An Introduction. London: SCM Press, 1984
Old Testament Theology in Canonical Context. London: SCM Press, 1985
'The Sensus Literalis of Scripture: An Ancient and Modern Problem'. In H. Donner et al. (eds.) *Beiträge zur Alttestamentlichen Theologie: Festschrift Zimmerli.* Göttingen: Vandenhoeck & Ruprecht, 1977.

Clines, David J. A., and Eskenazi, Tamara C. (eds.). *Telling Queen Michal's Story: An Experiment in Comparative Interpretation.* Sheffield: JSOT Press, 1991

Collins, Adela Yarbro. (ed.) *Feminist Perspectives on Biblical Scholarship.* Chico, California: Scholars Press, 1985
'Introduction.' In Collins (ed.), *Perspectives*, 1–9

Collins, Anthony. *A Discourse of the Grounds and Reasons of the Christian Religion* (1724). Repr. New York and London: Garland, 1976

Conzelmann, Hans. *A Commentary on the First Epistle to the Corinthians.* Hermeneia. Philadelphia: Fortress Press, 1975

Cranfield, C. E. B. *The Gospel according to St. Mark.* The Cambridge Greek Testament Commentary. Cambridge University Press, 1959

Crossan, John Dominic. *In Parables: The Challenge of the Historical Jesus.* New York: Harper & Row, 1973
The Historical Jesus: The Life of a Mediterranean Jewish Peasant. Edinburgh: T. & T. Clark, 1991
'A Metamodel for Polyvalent Interpretation', *Semeia* 9 (1977), 105–47

Culler, Jonathan. *Structuralist Poetics: Structuralism, Linguistics and the Study of Literature.* London: Routledge, 1975
On Deconstruction: Theory and Criticism after Structuralism. London: Routledge, 1983

Culpepper, R. Alan. *Anatomy of the Fourth Gospel: A Study in Literary Design.* Philadelphia, Fortress Press, 1983

Cupitt, Don. *Creation out of Nothing.* London: SCM Press, 1990

Daly, Mary. *Beyond God the Father: Toward a Philosophy of Women's Liberation.* Boston: Beacon's Press, 1973; London: The Women's Press, 1986[2]

De Man, Paul. *Blindness and Insight: Essays in the Rhetoric of Contemporary Criticism.* Minneapolis: University of Minnesota Press; London: Methuen, 1983[2]
The Resistance to Theory. Manchester University Press, 1986

Derrida, Jacques. *Speech and Phenomena and Other Essays on Husserl's Theory of Signs.* ET Evanston, Ill.: Northwestern University Press, 1973
Of Grammatology. ET Baltimore: Johns Hopkins University Press, 1976
Writing and Difference. ET University of Chicago Press, 1978

Dissemination. ET University of Chicago Press, 1981

Positions. ET University of Chicago Press, 1981

Margins of Philosophy. ET Chicago University Press; Brighton: Harvester Press, 1982

'Des Tours de Babel'. In Joseph F. Graham (ed.), *Difference in Translation*, Ithaca, NY: Cornell University Press, 1986, 165–207

DeVries, Simon J. *1 Kings*. Word Biblical Commentary. Waco, Texas: Word Books, 1985

Dibelius, Martin and Conzelmann, Hans. *The Pastoral Epistles*. Hermeneia. Philadelphia: Fortress, 1972

Dodd, C. H. *Parables of the Kingdom*. Glasgow: Collins Fount, 1978

The Founder of Christianity. London: Collins Fontana, 1973

Driver, S. R. *An Introduction to the Literature of the Old Testament*. Edinburgh: T. & T. Clark, 1913[9]

Drury, John. *Critics of the Bible, 1724-1873*. Cambridge University Press, 1989

Dunn, J. D. G. *Christology in the Making: An Inquiry into the Origins of the Doctrine of the Incarnation*. London: SCM Press, 1980

Durber, Susan. 'The Female Reader of the Parables of the Lost.' *JSNT* 45 (1992), 59–78

Eagleton, Terry. *Criticism and Ideology: A Study in Marxist Literary Theory*. London: NLB, 1976; Verso, 1978

Literary Theory: An Introduction. Oxford: Basil Blackwell, 1983

Against the Grain: Selected Essays. London: Verso, 1986

The Ideology of the Aesthetic. Oxford: Basil Blackwell, 1990

Ideology: An Introduction. London: Verso, 1991

Ebeling, Gerhard. *Word and Faith*. ET London: SCM Press, 1963

Edwards, Ruth. *The Case for Women's Ministry*. London: SPCK, 1989

Ellis, John M. *Against Deconstruction*. Princeton University Press, 1989

Ellis, Marc H., and Maduro, Otto (eds.). *The Future of Liberation Theology. Essays in Honor of Gustavo Gutiérrez*. Maryknoll: Orbis Books, 1989

Evans, C. F. *Explorations in Theology 2*. London: SCM Press, 1977

Saint Luke. TPI New Testament Commentaries. London: SCM Press, 1990

Exum, J. Cheryl. 'Murder They Wrote: Ideology and the Manipulation of Female Presence in Biblical Narrative'. In Bach (ed.), *Pleasure*, 45–67

Fee, Gordon D. *The First Epistle to the Corinthians*. New International Commentary on the New Testament. Grand Rapids: Eerdmans, 1987

Feyerabend, Paul. *Against Method*. London and New York: Verso, 1988[2]

Fiorenza, Elisabeth Schüssler. *In Memory of Her: A Feminist Theological Reconstruction of Christian Origins*. London: SCM Press, 1983

Bread not Stone: The Challenge of Feminist Biblical Interpretation. Edinburgh: T. & T. Clark, 1984

'The Ethics of Biblical Interpretation: Decentering Biblical Scholarship'. *JBL* 107 (1988), 3–17

Fischer, Kathleen. *Women at the Well: Feminist Perspectives on Spiritual Direction*. London: SPCK, 1989

Fish, Stanley E. *Is There a Text in this Class? The Authority of Interpretive Communities*. Cambridge, Mass.: Harvard University Press, 1980.

Fitzmyer, Joseph A. *The Gospel according to Luke X–XXIV*. The Anchor Bible. New York: Doubleday, 1985

Fokkelman, J. P. *Narrative Art in Genesis: Specimens of Stylistic and Structural Analysis*. Sheffield: JSOT Press, 1991²

Fontaine, Carole R. 'A Heifer from Thy Stable: On Goddesses and the Status of Women in the Ancient Near East'. In Bach (ed.), *Pleasure*, 69–95

Ford, David. 'Hans Frei and the Future of Theology', *Modern Theology* 8 (1992), 203–14

Foucault, Michel. *The Order of Things: An Archaeology of the Human Sciences*. ET London: Tavistock, 1970

The Use of Pleasure: The History of Sexuality, Volume 2. ET Harmondsworth: Penguin Books, 1987

The Foucault Reader. Ed. Paul Rabinow. Harmondsworth: Peregrine Books, 1986

Frei, Hans W. *The Eclipse of Biblical Narrative: A Study in Eighteenth and Nineteenth Century Hermeneutics*. New Haven and Yale: Yale University Press, 1974

The Identity of Jesus Christ. Philadelphia: Fortress Press, 1975

Types of Christian Theology. Ed. George W. Hunsinger and William C. Placher. New York and London: Yale University Press, 1992

Froehlich, Karlfried (ed.). *Biblical Interpretation in the Early Church*. Philadelphia: Fortress, 1984

Frye, Northrop. *Anatomy of Criticism*. Princeton University Press, 1957

The Great Code: The Bible and Literature. London: Routledge & Kegan Paul, 1982

Frye, Roland M. 'Language for God and Feminist Language: Problems and Principles'. In Kimel (ed.), *Speaking the Christian God*, 81–94

Fuchs, Esther. 'The Literary Characterization of Mothers and Sexual Politics in the Hebrew Bible'. In Collins (ed.), *Perspectives*, 117–36

'Who is Hiding the Truth? Deceptive Women and Biblical Androcentrism'. In Collins (ed.), *Perspectives*, 137–44

Fuller, Reginald H. *The Formation of the Resurrection Narratives*. London: SPCK, 1980²

Gabler, Johann Philipp. 'An Oration of the Proper Distinction between Biblical and Dogmatic Theology and the Specific Objectives of Each' (1787). Ed. John Sandys-Wunsch and Laurence Eldredge, *SJT* 33 (1980), 133–58

Gadamer, Hans-Georg. *Truth and Method*. ET London: Sheed and Ward, 1975

Gottwald, N. K. 'Social Matrix and Canonical Shape'. *Theology Today*, 42 (1986), 307–21

Greenstein, Edward L. 'An Equivocal Reading of the Sale of Joseph'. In Kenneth Gros Louis and James Ackerman (eds.), *Literary Interpretations of Biblical Narratives, Volume II*. Nashville: Abingdon, 1982, 114–25

Gunton, Colin E. *Yesterday and Today: A Study of Continuities in Christology.* London: Darton, Longman & Todd, 1983

The Promise of Trinitarian Theology. Edinburgh: T. & T. Clark, 1991

Gutiérrez, Gustavo. *A Theology of Liberation.* ET Maryknoll: Orbis, 1973; London: SCM Press, 1974

The Power of the Poor in History: Selected Writings Maryknoll: Orbis; London: SCM Press, 1983

Habermas, Jürgen. *The Philosophical Discourse of Modernity.* ET Cambridge: Polity Press, 1987

Haenchen, Ernst. *The Acts of the Apostles.* ET Oxford: Basil Blackwell, 1971

Hall, Basil. *Humanists and Protestants 1500–1900.* Edinburgh: T. & T. Clark, 1990

Hampson, Daphne. *Theology and Feminism.* Oxford: Basil Blackwell, 1990

Harnack, Adolf. *What is Christianity?* ET London: Williams and Norgate, 1904[3]

Hart, Kevin. *The Trespass of the Sign: Deconstruction, theology and philosophy.* Cambridge University Press, 1989

Hauerwas, Stanley. *Vision and Virtue: Essays in Christian Ethical Reflection.* Notre Dame and London: University of Notre Dame Press, 1981

A Community of Character. Toward a Constructive Christian Social Ethic. Notre Dame and London: Notre Dame University Press, 1981

'Some Theological Reflections on Gutiérrez's Use of "Liberation" as a Theological Concept', *Modern Theology* 3 (1987), 67–76

Hauerwas, Stanley, with Bondi, Richard and Burrell, David B. *Truthfulness and Tragedy: Further Investigations into Christian Ethics.* Notre Dame and London: Notre Dame University Press, 1977

Hayter, Mary. *The New Eve in Christ: The Use and Abuse of the Bible in the Debate about Women in the Church.* London: SPCK, 1987

Heidegger, Martin. *Being and Time.* ET Oxford: Basil Blackwell, 1962

On the Way to Language. ET New York: Harper & Row, 1971

Heine, Susanne. *Women and Early Christianity.* ET London: SCM Press, 1987

Hengel, Martin. *Judaism and Hellenism* (two vols.). ET London: SCM Press, 1974

Herrmann, Wilhelm. *The Communion of the Christian with God.* ET Philadelphia: Fortress, 1971; London: SCM Press, 1972

Hick, John (ed.). *The Myth of God Incarnate.* London: SCM Press, 1977

Higgins, A. J. B. *Jesus and the Son of Man.* Philadelphia: Fortress, 1964

Hirsch, E. D. *Validity in Interpretation.* New Haven and London: Yale University Press, 1967

Hobbes, Thomas. *Leviathan.* Ed. C. B. Macpherson. Harmondsworth: Penguin Books, 1981

Hof, Otto. *Schriftauslegung und Rechtfertigungslehre: Aufsätze zur Theologie Luthers.* Karlsruhe: Evangelischer Presseverband für Baden, 1982

Hooker, Richard. *Of the Laws of Ecclesiastical Polity* (two vols.). London: J. M. Dent; New York: E. P. Dutton, 1907

Hoskyns, E.C. *The Fourth Gospel* (two vols.). Ed. F. N. Davey. London: Faber & Faber, 1940

Hunsinger, George. 'Beyond Literalism and Expressivism: Karl Barth's Hermeneutical Realism'. *Modern Theology* 3 (1987), 209–23
'Hans Frei as Theologian: The Quest for Generous Orthodoxy', *Modern Theology* 8 (1992), 103–28

Jameson, Fredric. *The Political Unconscious: Narrative as a Socially Symbolic Act.* London: Methuen, 1981
Postmodernism: Or, The Cultural Logic of Late Capitalism. London and New York: Verso, 1991

Jeanrond, Werner G. *Text and Interpretation as Categories of Theological Thinking.* ET Dublin: Gill and Macmillan, 1988

Jeremias, Joachim. *The Parables of Jesus.* ET London: SCM Press, 1972[3]

Jobling, David. 'Writing the Wrongs of the World: The Deconstruction of the Biblical Text in the Context of Liberation Theologies', *Semeia* 51 (1990), 81–118

Josipovici, Gabriel. *The Book of God: A Response to the Bible.* New Haven and London: Yale University Press, 1988

Joyce, Paul. 'Feminist Exegesis of the Old Testament: Some Critical Reflections'. In Soskice (ed.), *Eve*, 1–9

Kähler, Martin. *The So-Called Historical Jesus and the Historic, Biblical Christ.* Ed. Carl E. Braaten. ET Philadelphia: Fortress, 1964

Kaplan, E. Ann. *Postmodernism and its Discontents: Theories, Practices.* London and New York: Verso, 1988

Käsemann, Ernst. *New Testament Questions of Today.* ET London: SCM Press, 1969

Kee, Howard C. *Community of the New Age.* London: SCM Press, 1977

Kelly, J. N. D. *Early Christian Doctrines.* London: A. &. C. Black, 1965[3]

Kelsey, David H. *The Uses of Scripture in Modern Theology.* Philadelphia: Fortress Press; London: SCM Press, 1975

Kermode, Frank. *The Sense of an Ending: Studies in the Theory of Fiction.* Oxford University Press, 1967
The Genesis of Secrecy: On the Interpretation of Narrative. Cambridge, Mass.: Harvard University Press, 1979

Kimel, Alvin F. *Speaking the Christian God: The Holy Trinity and the Challenge of Feminism.* Grand Rapids: Eerdmans; Leominster: Gracewing, 1992

Kittel, G. (ed.) *Theological Dictionary of the New Testament.* ET Grand Rapids: Eerdmans, 1964-74

Klein, Lilian R. *The Triumph of Irony in the Book of Judges.* Sheffield: Almond Press, 1988

Kolodny, Annette. 'Dancing through the Minefield: Some Observations on the Theory, Practice, and Politics of a Feminist Literary Criticism'. In Showalter (ed.), *Criticism*, 144–167

Kuhn, Thomas. *The Structure of Scientific Revolutions.* University of Chicago Press, 1970[2]

Kümmel, W. G. *The New Testament: The History of the Investigation of its Problems.* ET London: SCM Press, 1973

Laffey, Alice L. *An Introduction to the Old Testament: A Feminist Perspective.*
    Philadelphia: Fortress, 1988; London: SPCK, 1990 (British title: *Wives,
    Harlots and Concubines: The Old Testament in Feminist Perspective*)
Lemcio, Eugene E. *The past of Jesus in the Gospels.* Cambridge University Press,
    1991
Lindbeck, George A. *The Nature of Doctrine: Religion and Theology in a Postliberal
    Age.* London: SPCK, 1984
Loades, Ann. *Searching for Lost Coins: Explorations in Christianity and Feminism.*
    London: SPCK, 1987
    (ed.) *Feminist Theology: A Reader.* London: SPCK, Louisville: Westminster/
    John Knox Press, 1990
Locke, John. *An Essay concerning Human Understanding* (two vols.). Ed. John W.
    Yolton. London: Dent; New York: Dutton, 1961
    The Reasonableness of Christianity as delivered in the Scriptures. Ed. I. T. Ramsey.
    Stanford University Press, 1980
Lohse, Bernhard. *Martin Luther: An Introduction to his Life and Work.* ET
    Philadelphia: Fortress, 1986
Lovibond, Sabina. 'Feminism and Pragmatism: A Reply to Richard Rorty', in *New
    Left Review* 193 (May/June 1992), 56–74
Luther, Martin. *D. Martin Luthers Werke.* Kritische Gesamtausgabe, Weimar,
    1883–
    Luther's Works. Philadelphia: Fortress; St. Louis: Concordia, 1955–
Luz, Ulrich. 'The Son of Man in Matthew: Heavenly Judge or Human Christ?'.
    JSNT 48 (1992), 3–21.
Lyotard, Jean-François. *The Postmodern Condition: A Report on Knowledge.* ET
    Manchester University Press, 1984
Macdonald, Margaret Y. *The Pauline Churches: A socio-historical study of insti-
    tutionalization in the Pauline and Deutero-Pauline writings.* Cambridge
    University Press, 1988
Mack, Burton L. *A Myth of Innocence: Mark and Christian Origins.* Philadelphia:
    Fortress, 1988
Mackey, James P. *Jesus the Man and the Myth: A Contemporary Christology.* London:
    SCM Press, 1979
Marxsen, Willi. *The Resurrection of Jesus of Nazareth.* ET London: SCM Press, 1970
McGrath, Alister E. *The Making of Modern German Christology.* Oxford: Basil
    Blackwell, 1986
McFadyen, Alistair I. *The Call to Personhood: A Christian Theory of the Individual
    in Social Relationships.* Cambridge University Press, 1990
    'The Trinity and Human Individuality: The Conditions for Relevance', *Theol-
    ogy* 95 (1992), 10–18
McKelway, Alexander J. *The Freedom of God and Human Liberation.* London:
    SCM Press, 1990
Meredith, Betsy. 'Desire and Danger: The Drama of Betrayal in Judges and Judith.'
    In Bal (ed.), *Anti-Covenant*, 63–78.

Metz, Johann Baptist. 'Theology in the Struggle for History and Society'. In Ellis and Maduro (eds.), *The Future of Liberation Theology*, 165–71

Moberly, Walter. '"Old Testament" and "New Testament": The Propriety of the Terms for Christian Theology', *Theology* 95 (1992), 26–32

Moltmann, Jürgen. *Theology of Hope*. ET London: SCM Press, 1967
   The Trinity and the Kingdom of God: The Doctrine of God. ET London: SCM Press, 1981
   God in Creation: An Ecological Doctrine of Creation. ET London: SCM Press, 1985

Moltmann-Wendel, Elisabeth. *A Land Flowing with Milk and Honey*. ET London: SCM Press, 1986

Moore, Stephen D. *Literary Criticism and the Gospels: The Theoretical Challenge*. New Haven and London: Yale University Press, 1989
   Mark and Luke in Poststructuralist Perspectives: Jesus Begins to Write. New Haven and London: Yale University Press, 1992

Morgan, Robert. 'Feminist Theological Interpretation of the New Testament', in J. Martin Soskice (ed.), *After Eve*, 10–37

Morgan, Robert, with Barton, John. *Biblical Interpretation*. Oxford University Press, 1988.

Morley, Janet. 'I Desire Her with my Whole Heart'. In Loades (ed.), *Feminist Reader*, 158–65

Mosala, Itumeleng J. *Biblical Hermeneutics and Black Theology in South Africa*. Grand Rapids: Eerdmans, 1989

Myers, Ched. *Binding the Strong Man: A Political Reading of Mark's Story of Jesus*. Maryknoll: Orbis, 1988

Neale, David A. *None but the Sinners: Religious Categories in the Gospel of Luke*. Sheffield: JSOT Press, 1991

Nietzsche, Friedrich. *The Gay Science*. ET New York: Random House, 1974
   Thus Spoke Zarathustra. ET Harmondsworth: Penguin Books, 1969

Nineham, Dennis E. *Explorations in Theology 1*. London: SCM Press, 1977
   Epilogue.' In Hick (ed.), *Myth*, 186–204

Norris, Christopher. *The Contest of Faculties: philosophy and theory after-deconstruction*. London and New York: Methuen, 1985
   Derrida. London: Fontana, 1987

Oesterley, W. O. E., and Robinson, T. H. *An Introduction to the Books of the Old Testament*. London: SPCK, 1934

Ogden, Schubert. 'Theology in the University: The Question of Integrity'. In David Ray Griffin and Joseph C. Hough (eds.), *Theology and the University: Essays in Honor of John B. Cobb, Jr*. Albany: State University of New York Press, 1991

Origen. *De Principiis* and *Against Celsus*. The Ante-Nicene Fathers, Volume IV (American edition). Ed. Alexander Roberts and James Donaldson. Repr. Grand Rapids, Michigan: Eerdmans, 1976

Owen, John. *Pneumatologia: Or, A Discourse concerning the Holy Spirit. Works*, Vol. 3, repr. Edinburgh: Banner of Truth Trust, 1965

Pannenberg, Wolfhart. *Jesus – God and Man.* ET London: SCM Press, 1968
Paterson, John. 'Jeremiah.' In Matthew Black and H. H. Rowley (eds.), *Peake's Commentary on the Bible.* Sunbury-on-Thames: Nelson, 1962, 537–62
Plato, *Phaedrus & Letters VII and VIII.* Ed. Walter Hamilton. Harmondsworth: Penguin Books, 1973
Polzin, Robert. *Moses and the Deuteronomist: A Literary Study of the Deuteronomic History.* New York: Seabury Press, 1980
Powell, Mark Allan. *What is Narrative Criticism?* Minneapolis: Fortress Press, 1990
Prickett, Stephen. *Words and The Word: Language, poetics and biblical interpretation.* Cambridge University Press, 1986
Räisänen, Heikki. *Beyond New Testament Theology: A story and a programme.* London: SCM Press, 1990
Ramshaw, Gail. 'The Gender of God'. In Loades (ed.), *Reader,* 168–80
Rasmussen, Rachel C. 'Deborah the Woman Warrior'. In Bal (ed.), *Anti-Covenant,* 79–93
Reimarus, H. S. *Fragments.* Ed. Charles H. Talbert. Philadelphia: Fortress, 1970; London: SCM Press, 1971
Rendtorff, Rolf. *The Problem of the Process of Transmission in the Pentateuch.* ET Sheffield: JSOT Press, 1990
Rensberger, David. *Overcoming the World: Politics and Community in the Gospel of John.* London: SPCK; Philadelphia: Westminster Press, 1988 (as *Johannine Faith and Liberating Community*)
Reventlow, Henning Graf. *The Authority of the Bible and the Rise of the Modern World.* ET London: SCM Press, 1984
Rhoads, David, and Michie, Donald. *Mark as Story: An Introduction to the Narrative of a Gospel.* Philadelphia: Fortress Press, 1982
Ricoeur, Paul. *Essays on Biblical Interpretation* (ed. Lewis S. Mudge). Philadelphia: Fortress Press, 1980
Hermeneutics and the Human Sciences (ed. John B. Thompson). Cambridge University Press, 1981
Robbins, Jill. *Prodigal Son/Eldest Brother: Interpretation and Alterity in Augustine, Petrarch, Kafka, Levinas.* University of Chicago Press, 1991
Roberts, Richard H. *A Theology on its Way? Essays on Karl Barth.* Edinburgh: T. & T. Clark, 1991
Robinson, James M. (ed.) *The Nag Hammadi Library in English.* Leiden: E. J. Brill, 1984[2]
Rorty, Richard. *Philosophy and the Mirror of Nature.* Oxford: Basil Blackwell, 1980
Ruether, Rosemary Radford. *Sexism and God-Talk: Towards a Feminist Theology.* London: SCM Press, 1983.
Ruthven, K. K. *Feminist Literary Studies: An Introduction.* Cambridge University Press, 1984
Said, Edward W. *The World, the Text, and the Critic.* Harvard University Press, 1983; London: Faber and Faber, 1984
Sanders, E. P. *Jesus and Judaism.* London: SCM Press, 1985
Sanders, James A. *From Sacred Text to Sacred Story.* Philadelphia: Fortress Press,

1987

Santmire, H. Paul. *The Travail of Nature: The Ambiguous Ecological Promise of Christian Theology.* Philadelphia: Fortress Press, 1985

Saussure, Ferdinand de. *Course in General Linguistics.* ET New York: McGraw-Hill, 1966

Sawyer, John. 'Combating Prejudices about the Bible and Judaism', *Theology* 94 (1991), 269–78

Schleiermacher, F. D. E. *Hermeneutics: The Handwritten Manuscripts.* Ed. Heinz Kimmerle. ET Missoula, Mont.: Scholars Press, 1977

Schillebeeckx, Edward. *Jesus: An Experiment in Christology.* ET London: Collins, 1979

Schnackenburg, Rudolf. *The Gospel according to St. John* (three vols.). ET Tunbridge Wells: Burns and Oates, 1968-82

Scholder, Klaus. *The Birth of Modern Critical Theology: Origins and problems of biblical criticism in the seventeenth century.* ET London: SCM Press, 1990

Scholes, Robert, and Kellogg, Robert. *The Nature of Narrative.* Oxford University Press, 1966

Schwartz, Regina (ed.). *The Book and the Text: The Bible and Literary Theory.* Oxford: Basil Blackwell, 1990

Schwartzentruber, Paul. 'The Modesty of Hermeneutics: The Theological Reserve of Hans Frei', *Modern Theology* 8 (1992), 181-95

Schweitzer, Albert. *The Quest of the Historical Jesus: A Critical Study of its Progress from Reimarus to Wrede.* ET London: A. and C. Black, 1954[3]

Schwöbel, Christoph. *God: Action and Revelation.* Kampen: Pharos, 1992

Segundo, Juan Luis. *The Liberation of Theology.* ET Maryknoll: Orbis Books, 1976

'Capitalism vs. Socialism: Crux Theologica.' In Rosino Gibellini (ed.), *Frontiers of Theology in Latin America.* ET Maryknoll: Orbis, 1979; London: SCM Press, 1980, 240-59

Showalter, Elaine (ed.). *The New Feminist Criticism: Essays on Women, Literature, and Theory.* New York: Pantheon, 1985; London: Virago, 1986

'Toward a Feminist Poetics.' In Showalter (ed.), *Criticism*, 125-43

Sobrino, Jon. *Christology at the Crossroads: A Latin American View.* ET London: SCM Press, 1978

Soggin, J. Alberto. *Judges: A Commentary.* Old Testament Library. ET London: SCM Press, 1981

A History of Israel: From the Beginnings to the Bar Kochba Revolt, AD 135. ET London: SCM Press, 1985

Sölle, Dorothee. *Thinking about God: An Introduction to Theology.* ET London: SCM Press, Philadelphia: Trinity Press International, 1990

Soskice, Janet Martin (ed.). *After Eve: Women, Theology and the Christian Tradition.* London: Collins/Marshall Pickering, 1990

Spinoza, Benedict de. *A Theologico-Political Treatise* (1670). Ed. R. H. M. Elwes. New York: Dover Publications, 1951

Stendahl, Krister. 'Biblical Theology, Contemporary'. *Interpreter's Dictionary of the Bible,* New York: Abingdon Press, 1962, Vol.1, 418-31

'The Bible as a Classic and the Bible as Holy Scripture.' *JBL* 103 (1984), 3–10

Sternberg, Meir. *The Poetics of Biblical Narrative: Ideological Literature and the Drama of Reading*. Bloomington: Indiana University Press, 1985

Stibbe, Mark W. G. *John the Storyteller: Narrative criticism and the fourth gospel*. SNTS Monograph Series, 73. Cambridge University Press, 1992

Strauss, D. F. *The Life of Jesus Critically Examined*. Ed. Peter C. Hodgson. ET Philadelphia: Fortress Press, 1972; London: SCM Press, 1973

The Christ of Faith and the Jesus of History: A Critique of Schleiermacher's Life of Jesus. Ed. L. E. Keck. ET Philadelphia: Fortress Press, 1977

Hermann Samuel Reimarus and his Apology. Excerpts in *Reimarus: Fragments*, ed. Talbert, 44–57

Stroup, George W. *The Promise of Narrative Theology*. London: SCM Press, 1984

Sugirtharajah, R.S. (ed.) *Voices from the Margin: Interpreting the Bible in the Third World*. London: SPCK, 1991

Sykes, Stephen. *The Identity of Christianity: Theologians and the Essence of Christianity from Schleiermacher to Barth*. London: SPCK, 1984

Tannehill, Robert C. *The Narrative Unity of Luke–Acts: A Literary Interpretation* (two vols.). Philadelphia and Minneapolis: Fortress Press, 1986 and 1990.

Tapp, Anne Michele. 'An Ideology of Expendability: Virgin Daughter Sacrifice'. In Bal (ed.), *Anti-Covenant*, 157–74

Taylor, Mark C. *Deconstructing Theology*. New York: Crossroad Publishing, 1982

Taylor, Vincent. *The Gospel according to St. Mark*. London: Macmillan, 1952

Thielicke, Helmut. 'The Restatement of New Testament Mythology'. In Bartsch (ed.), *Kerygma and Myth*, 138-74

Thiselton, Anthony C. *New Horizons in Hermeneutics: The Theory and Practice of Transforming Biblical Reading*, London: Harper Collins, 1992

Thompson, John B. *Critical Hermeneutics: A study in the thought of Paul Ricoeur and Jürgen Habermas*. Cambridge University Press, 1981

Thompson, Thomas L. *The Origin Tradition of Ancient Israel: I. The Literary Formation of Genesis and Exodus 1–23*. Sheffield: JSOT Press, 1987

Tillich, Paul. *Systematic Theology 3: Life and the Spirit; History and the Kingdom of God*. London: SCM Press, 1978

Tindal, Matthew. *Christianity as Old as the Creation: Or, The Gospel a Republication of the Religion of Nature* (1730). Repr. New York and London: Garland, 1978

Tödt, H. E. *The Son of Man in the Synoptic Tradition*. ET London: SCM Press, 1965

Tolbert, Mary Ann. 'The Prodigal Son: An Essay in Literary Criticism from a Psychoanalytic Perspective', *Semeia* 9 (1977), 1–20

'Protestant Feminists and the Bible: On the Horns of a Dilemma'. In Bach (ed.), *Pleasure*, 5–24

Tracy, David. *The Analogical Imagination: Christian Theology and the Culture of Pluralism*. London: SCM Press, 1981

Plurality and Ambiguity: Hermeneutics, Religion, Hope. London: SCM Press, 1988

Trible, Phyllis. *God and the Rhetoric of Sexuality*. Philadelphia: Fortress Press, 1978
    Texts of Terror: Literary–Feminist Readings of Biblical Narratives. Philadelphia: Fortress Press, 1984
Turner, Laurence A. *Announcements of Plot in Genesis*. Sheffield: JSOT Press, 1990
Van Dijk-Hemmes, Fokkelien. 'Tamar and the Limits of Patriarchy: Between Seduction and Rape'. In Bal (ed.), *Anti-Covenant*, 135–56
Vanhoozer, Kevin J. *Biblical Narrative in the Philosophy of Paul Ricoeur: A study in hermeneutics and theology*. Cambridge University Press, 1990
Vermes, Geza. *Jesus the Jew: A Historian's Reading of the Gospels*. London: Collins, 1973
Von Rad, Gerhard. *Old Testament Theology, Volume 2*. ET London: SCM Press, 1965
    Genesis: A Commentary. Old Testament Library. ET London: SCM Press, 1972[9]
Waetjen, Herman C. *A Reordering of Power: A Socio-Political Reading of Mark's Gospel*. Minneapolis: Fortress Press, 1989
Walker, William O. '1 Corinthians 2.6–16: A Non-Pauline Interpolation?', *JSNT* 47 (1992), 75–94
Wall, Robert W., and Lemcio, Eugene E. *The New Testament as Canon: A Reader in Canonical Criticism*. Sheffield: JSOT, 1992
Watson, Francis. 'Strategies of Recovery and Resistance: Hermeneutical Reflections on Gen. 1–3 and its Pauline Reception'. *JSNT* 45 (1992), 79–103
Weiser, Artur. *The Psalms*. Old Testament Library. ET London: SCM Press, 1962
Weiss, Johannes. *Jesus' Proclamation of the Kingdom of God*. Ed. Richard H. Hiers and David L. Holland. ET Philadelphia: Fortress Press; London: SCM Press, 1971
Wenham, Gordon. *Genesis 1–15*. Word Biblical Commentary. Waco, Texas: Word Books, 1987
Westermann, Claus. *Isaiah 40–66: A Commentary*. Old Testament Library. London: SCM Press, 1969
    Genesis 1–11: A Commentary. ET Minneapolis: Augsburg, 1984
    Genesis 37–50: A Commentary. ET Minneapolis: Augsburg, 1986
White, Hugh C. *Narration and Discourse in the Book of Genesis*. Cambridge University Press, 1991
Whybray, R. N. 'The Joseph Story and Pentateuchal Criticism'. *Vetus Testamentum* 18 (1968), 522–28
Witherington III, Ben. *Women and the Genesis of Christianity*. Cambridge University Press, 1990
Wrede, William. *The Messianic Secret*. ET Cambridge and London: James Clarke and Co., 1971
    The Task and Methods of 'New Testament Theology' (1897). In Robert Morgan (ed.), *The Nature of New Testament Theology*. London: SCM Press, 1973, 68–116

Yoder, John Howard. *The Politics of Jesus.* Grand Rapids: Eerdmans, 1972
Young, Frances. *The Art of Performance: Towards a Theology of Holy Scripture.*
    London: DLT, 1990

Index of Biblical Passages

Index of Subjects

Index of Authors